POWER TRIP

POWER TRIP

A Decade of Policy, Plots and Spin

DAMIAN McBRIDE

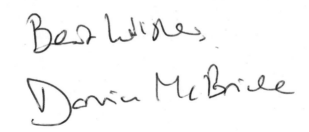

Biteback Publishing

First published in Great Britain in 2013 by
Biteback Publishing Ltd
Westminster Tower
3 Albert Embankment
London SE1 7SP
Copyright © Damian McBride 2013

ISBN 978-1-84954-596-9

10 9 8 7 6 5 4 3 2

A CIP catalogue record for this book is available from the British Library.

Set in Sabon

Printed and bound in Great Britain by
CPI Group (UK) Ltd, Croydon CR0 4YY

To my beloved Mum, the best person
in this best of all possible worlds.

To my late, much-loved Dad, who taught me
the joy of writing, among other things.

To my three brilliant big brothers, Chris, Nick and
Ben, who had the right idea sticking to law.

To Penny and Balshen, who put up with me for ten
years of this story, and deserved much better.

To my closest pals, Steve, Anthony and Damien,
who were there through thick and thin.

To Mr and Mrs Bradley, without whom this
book would not exist. So blame them.

And to Gordon, the greatest man I ever met:
thanks for all you did.

CONTENTS

PREFACE

I've spent many years writing things for other people: heartfelt letters, influential speeches, front-page stories, but all in other people's names.

Even the emails that got me sacked in 2009 were written for someone else in the voice of someone who doesn't exist.

This is my chance to write in my own name, and tell my own story, from the point of view of someone who had an extended chance to see behind the scenes, for the benefit of all those who'd like to do so.

This is not a day-to-day memoir. I have taken issues, people and events in the order that I encountered them over the years, and tried to tell a full and rounded story about each of them, from the decadence of party conferences to the dark arts of political spin.

It's also the account of my dealings with, among others, Gordon Brown, Ed Balls and Ed Miliband, and the impressions I gained of them. Whatever the flaws that I describe about each man, if my story helps people to understand and admire them the way I do, then I believe that can only be a good thing.

In particular, I was never blind to Gordon's shortcomings, and I acknowledge them in this book, but I also try to explain why he inspired such fierce loyalty from me and others throughout his career.

I started working in government aged twenty-two and was sacked from No. 10 shortly before I turned thirty-five. I gave my best years to that life and, ultimately, all I had to show for it were a lot of stories, experiences and lessons learned.

That's why I've decided to write them down.

SLOW ASCENT INTO HELL

1

EASTER MONDAY, 2009

You know you're in trouble when you have to introduce yourself to two complete strangers and ask to climb out of their kitchen window.

The young couple in the ground-floor flat were obliging enough, if slightly baffled. As I began my manoeuvre, climbing up onto the window-sill, the bloke's mum arrived.

'What's happened? Why are there cameras outside?'

I got back down again, shook her hand, and said: 'I'm really sorry, I was staying upstairs, and I'm afraid they're looking for me, so I'm just making a bit of an escape.'

For all they knew I could have been a mass murderer on the run; nevertheless, they cheerily wished me good luck as I jumped down from the window into the row of garages at the back of the flats, where my girlfriend Balshen had parked the car.

I climbed into the boot and, with a sympathetic smile, she gently closed it on me.

It was only a short drive, past the camera crew and up the road to the local pub, but time tends to lag when you're locked in the boot of a car.

I lay there curled up in the pitch black, turning over every question in my mind. How had that camera crew found me? Where was I going to hide now? When was life going to go back to normal? What on earth was my 'normal life' even going to be now?

And most of all, again and again: why had I been so bloody stupid?

I had everything: a great education; a fantastic, high-flying career; as much money as I'd ever needed. I'd visited places, met people and had experiences that were beyond any of my dreams, and I'd enjoyed power and influence beyond anything I ever deserved.

And now I was locked in a car boot wondering where I was going to stay that night, with no one to blame for the whole bloody mess but myself.

Alone with my thoughts in the darkness, one word came to my mind: 'Twat.'

2

WARNING SIGNS

I wasn't always a nasty bastard, but you could argue the signs were there.

For the most part, my years at Cambridge University from 1992 to 1996 were the happiest of my life. As well as enjoying every minute of my degree and Master's in history, I spent four years managing the bar at my college, Peterhouse, made dozens of fast friends, fell madly in love with at least six girls (even managing to speak to some of them) and – when I wasn't drinking, quizzing or watching *Home and Away* – I filled every spare minute of time with some kind of sporting activity.

But throughout that time there were signs of trouble to come, most particularly in my attitude to student politics and football.

I was captain of the Peterhouse First XI, coach of the ladies' team, played for our Seconds, and – when no formal match was available – I'd go round the college rounding people up for a kickabout in the park. But it didn't matter what level the game was at; if I was involved, it would at some point descend into a punch-up.

Years hence, when I met people of my age who'd been to Cambridge and compared notes on our sporting experiences, there would be a terrible moment of recognition which would end up with them saying: 'Oh God, it's you – you were an absolute wanker.'

One of those contemporaries was Tony Blair's future top aide, Philip Collins, now a columnist on *The Times*. He was one of Cambridge's elite sportsmen, captain of the University Blues football team and of the top football college, St John's.

When tiny Peterhouse drew St John's in the cup competition, I was never so fired up. We led 1–0 at half-time, at which point

Philip put on his fellow Blues players from the subs' bench. I waited until we went 5–1 down in the second half before loudly instructing my players that it was time to 'put these fuckers out of the Oxford game'.

The next ten minutes saw a horrible set of ugly challenges and confrontations, before the referee called a halt, told me I was an absolute disgrace and said he'd be reporting our behaviour. Philip himself wrote to the University Football Association asking for me to be disciplined and for Peterhouse to be banned from the cup the following year. Those Blair–Brown feuds started early.

If some part of me had got kicks from rampaging round like a lunatic, you could perhaps understand it psychologically, but I never did. I just could not stand losing and, much as I loved taking a bag of footballs to a pitch and practising shots for pleasure, I played in matches with no sense of fun at all, just a dread of defeat.

The poor Peterhouse girls' team who I coached probably had any burgeoning love of football destroyed for life by my cynical approach, instructing them to boot the ball out of play at the byline, then surround the box and wait for the opposition keeper to fluff a goal kick.

When it came to fighting, the odds never mattered to me.

Steve, a school friend from Finchley, came to visit one May and we went to the notorious Wiley's party, several hours of drunken debauchery in a cow field. Steve and I concentrated on the drunken end of the equation and soon got into a fight with some other blokes. We were out-numbered about fifteen to two and all our opponents seemed enormous, but we kept hammering away, eventually limping off with a few bruises and several million brain cells lighter.

The next day it was reported in the student paper that there were renewed calls for the party to be banned after a 'shocking pitched battle between two townies and the Cambridge Rugby Blues XV'.

But if I was bad when it came to football and fighting, it was as nothing to my approach to student politics. I never got involved in either the Labour or Conservative clubs, or the Cambridge Union. My obsession was running the student side of Peterhouse and ensuring that it was my mates who got plum jobs on the student committee and therefore the best rooms in college. That also meant we could rig the voting on how to spend the student budget, and I could make sure as much as possible went on the sports clubs and on the college bar.

I once succeeded in getting our star footballer elected to a junior position on the committee, even though he had no idea he'd applied for the role. At the hustings I explained that he'd had to run down to London at the last minute because of a family illness, but had asked me to deliver his speech for him. When I told him the next day he'd been elected after a rave reaction to the speech and his manifesto, he couldn't have looked more baffled. 'What do I have to do?' 'Nothing,' I said. 'I'll do it all for you. Just turn up at the meetings and vote the way I tell you.'

In my final year, my best female friend was standing for student president, but another friend, Nick Perry, later a Liberal Democrat candidate for Parliament, had been urged to stand against her. I leant on him to pull out and told him that if he didn't we would be finished – and I'd make sure he didn't win. He refused and I tried my best to follow through on the threat. But it was a failing cause, not least because as a postgraduate I didn't command the voting bloc I once did.

My last throw of the dice, at the hustings, was to challenge Nick on his views on homosexuality, which I wrongly thought at the time were closer to Leviticus than Liberace. He gave a perfectly tolerant answer, the crowd cheered and he won handsomely.

A short while later, as I got off a bus taking students home from the funeral of a popular college steward, Nick was waiting with a large crowd around him, and – given the nature of the day – asked me to shake hands and make peace. 'Fuck you,' I told him, 'you fucking hypocrite,' and walked on. What a twat, the crowd said.

The bitterness of that election and my behaviour in the aftermath destroyed my friendships with about two dozen individuals across the college and killed what remained of my reputation.

Fortunately, the one person who didn't even notice – she was too busy reading Henry James to bother with student politics – was a brilliant and beautiful Shropshire lass named Penny Tallents, with Huguenot blood and a regal air. I was madly in love with her throughout my twenties and ended up going out with her for the latter half of them.

Penny notwithstanding, most fellow students were glad to see the back of me when I left Peterhouse, and the college authorities were pretty glad too.

I was frequently in trouble with them for all the fighting and such, but no more so than when the student common room in one of the thirteenth-century buildings was hit by a fire in 1995. It was a total accident and I wasn't the culprit, but a guest of mine from London was, and – given I'd been seen with him in the room before the alarms went off – I was immediately the prime suspect.

I know I should have owned up to the accident immediately and faced the music, but given I was in my final exam year and everyone expected the guilty party to be dismissed from the university, my survival instincts kicked in and I determined to tough it out, even when the college announced that all student facilities would be closed until the culprit came forward.

When the college authorities finally summoned me for a grilling, I walked in and, almost without waiting for a question, launched into a long and impassioned argument that, as long as they kept the college bar closed, it was going to be impossible for me to gather intelligence on possible suspects, and, while I wanted the individual caught as much as anyone, I wasn't sure these punitive measures on the rest of the student body were the right way to go about it.

I also told them the rumour was that two lads from a neighbouring college had been boasting about their act of arson, but frankly I didn't believe it – I knew one of them and he didn't have it in him.

Avoidance, obfuscation, diversion, but no actual lies, and I came out of the interrogation unscathed. An interesting lesson to learn, and when – nine years later – I was grilled for ten hours over three gruelling sessions as part of a leak enquiry by retired Special Branch officers, I remembered that Peterhouse experience and followed exactly the same method of lying-without-lying.

To understand that concept, it's always worth remembering the earliest recorded lie, which came just after the earliest recorded murder. In the Book of Genesis, Cain initially answered God's question 'Where is Abel?' with an outright lie: 'I don't know', but quickly followed it up with a spin-doctor's classic: 'Am I my brother's keeper?'

Incidentally, while I was learning all these dubious skills, I also managed to get a good 2:1 in my history degree. One of my tutors, the Balkans expert Dr Brendan Simms, wrote a reference for me afterwards saying that if I'd concentrated on revising rather than playing so much football I would have got a First. He had a point.

I then did a Master's dissertation on the policy impact of black urban rioting in the United States from 1964 to 1968. Listening to and reading the interviews with President Lyndon Johnson's inner circle describing the policy-making process and the pressures they faced, and explaining how the application of any principles came and went according to the mood of the media and the state of the opinion polls, I was totally fascinated.

So it was that, just turned twenty-two, I left university hooked on the intricacies of power and policy-making, with a talent for avoiding the truth without actually lying, a win-or-die competitive streak, a penchant for negative, thuggish tactics, and a reckless disregard for the consequences of my actions.

There was only one possible career choice.

3

THE FAST STREAM

The civil service is the last great closed shop in all the British professions.

While almost every other bit of industry and public service has been forced to break down any restrictive recruitment practices over the last forty years, the civil service is allowed to plough on – recruiting new members to its own fixed standards and in its own image.

To get on the Fast Stream Civil Service scheme, an accelerated career development programme in either the 'Central Departments' or the 'Diplomatic Service', you must first of all be a graduate with at least a second-class degree. So even before one application form is filled in, millions of young people have been ruled out by the criteria, and a numbers bias has been built in towards those from better schools and more affluent parts of the country.

As for the recruitment process itself, while all the material says the civil service is looking for a diverse range of people, what they're actually looking for is good members of a pub quiz team. That means someone who'll get on with everyone, with good ability across a range of subjects and a bit of specialism in one key area. If they're good at working out anagrams, that's a bonus.

Of course, this is simply an extension of what already happens during the university application process, where a good personal statement about a student's wider qualities, accomplishments and interests will give them the edge over a more introverted person with the same academic record.

To use a cricketing analogy, it's like picking a team full of players who are not only good at batting, bowling and fielding, but the first to lead the songs at the bar afterwards.

But that search for all-rounders necessarily leads to the exclusion of the specialists, the eccentrics, the quiet types and those lacking in confidence or experience. I used to look at Penny and think she wouldn't stand a chance in the civil service recruitment process – she'd just be too thoughtful and analytical for it – and yet she could wipe the floor with anyone in terms of intellect and common sense.

By contrast, I was made to be a civil servant – I was a card-carrying member of the closed shop. I came from a good school in an affluent area, I got on with people easily when not playing football against them, and – when it came to proving I was a confident, rounded personality and good at most academic disciplines – I'd just had four years of intense training at Cambridge.

These days, the entrance tests for Fast Stream applications are all completed online, but back in 1996, aspiring civil servants at Cambridge had to troop to a large community centre on an estate miles outside the city to take the tests exam-hall style.

My good friend Chris Spink, doing a Master's on the social history of golf, drove us out to the community centre. After I failed even to complete the numerical reasoning test in the morning, I'd pretty much given up. So while Chris and the other students sat studying the sample questions for the afternoon tests, I went to the pub on the estate and had a pint.

If I'd had more cash on me, I probably would have stayed, but faced with the prospect of nursing one more pint for two hours while I waited for my lift back from Chris, I decided to go back to the exam hall. Perhaps liberated by the drink, I did far better in the afternoon tests and, a few weeks later, I was invited to London for the Civil Service Selection Board (CSSB), a day of individual tests and group exercises with fellow candidates.

Frankly, CSSB was a piece of cake. There was an interview, an in-tray exercise, a written exercise and a group exercise, where five of us played at being a town hall committee deciding how best to invest money in a local park.

There are only two rules in a civil service role-play group exercise. First, get stuck in; some people feel so embarrassed at the artificiality of it that they just freeze. Second, be the anti-dick. There's always one dick and, once they identify themselves, you just need to say and do the exact opposite of everything the dick says and does. He says: 'I'm not sure that idea really works, Caroline'; you say: 'Actually, I really wanted to hear more about it, Caroline.'

The final test was an interview with a psychiatrist, designed to test whether I was an egomaniac, liar or potential security risk. All I know is I passed. I went to the Lord Moon pub on Whitehall at the end, absolutely confident that I was through to the next round, and now beginning to accept the reality that – if I didn't get funding to continue my PhD on rioting – this might be the best option for me.

That next round, a few weeks on, was called the Final Selection Board, and we were told in advance that no preparation would be either necessary or helpful, except for keeping abreast of current affairs.

I was escorted into a large wood-panelled room in Whitehall, where fifteen po-faced, middle-aged senior civil servants – mostly men, all but one white – were sat in a horseshoe around a single chair. I took that seat and, with no welcomes or niceties, the chairman launched in: 'What considerations do you think the government makes when formulating its policies on shipping?'

'Shipping,' I began emphatically. 'Well let's first um ... think about what um ... policy areas we'd be talking about ... and then we can think about um ... the considerations.' Fifteen pairs of eyes were boring into me. 'Um ... well there's shipping safety ... the ship-building industry of course. Um ... then shipping ports and their economies... Um ... military ships... Um, shipping waters, including um ... erm ... issues around shipping lanes.'

It was like an episode of *Family Fortunes* scripted by Harold Pinter. 'Are those the kind of policy areas you had in mind?' I asked. The chairman replied icily: 'Some of the things you have mentioned are some of the aspects of policy on shipping. Please go on.'

I continued waffling in a hesitant and deeply unimpressive way, even more so at all the follow-up questions from those sitting round the room. The reason I know I was deeply unimpressive was that I happened across my personnel file later in my career, and the verdict from the board was: 'We found this candidate deeply unimpressive.'

They went on to say that – given my very high rating from the CSSB panel – they could only assume I'd been affected by nerves, but 'that does not entirely explain his total lack of understanding of basic concepts and issues'. They concluded that they did not wish to overturn the CSSB verdict entirely, but I should be considered a very low-ranked entrant to the Fast Stream scheme.

So, there it was. At no point in that whole Fast Stream recruitment process were my violent competitive streak, excess drinking, duplicitous instincts, preference for football over work, fervent Irish nationalism or even my rampant homogeneity with every other person on the scheme exposed as potentially good reasons not to appoint me. But, by God, they nearly found me out for my ignorance on shipping.

Given my low ranking from the Final Selection Board, it was no surprise to get a letter telling me that I'd been appointed to HM Customs & Excise, which usually only had two Fast Stream recruits per year and was considered – rather unfairly – a bit of a backwater when it came to the importance and influence of different civil service departments.

The good thing was that any Fast Streamer who ended up there had a good chance to make their mark, and some of the best civil servants I worked alongside in my entire career – Paul Gerrard, Heidi Popperwell, Andy Leggett, Sue Connaughton and Rebecca Hall to name a few – all came in through that route.

Perhaps the pick of the bunch was a young economist named Rita Patel, who went on to be a high flier in the Treasury and the Department of Culture, and became a Whitehall legend on her first day working in Gordon Brown's private office.

In front of a large gathering of external businesspeople, he introduced her as 'Ruth'. She'd been warned he was bad with names and had to be corrected early, so shouted at him: 'It's Rita,

Chancellor, RITA!' I'd like to say that he coolly replied: 'OK, Rita, but it's not Chancellor, it's Gordon', but I think he was too taken aback. He never got her name wrong again though.

I always blamed Gordon's religious upbringing. He was fine with any names that were in the Bible, but if he was told any that weren't, he would immediately resort to the closest Biblical equivalent. This came to a head in 2006 when he was introduced to his new private secretary, Jean-Christophe Gray. There was no way Gordon could manage that, so he became the Biblical abbreviation J-C instead, and is still known by that name in his current role as David Cameron's official spokesman.

Anyway, back in 1996, I was told to report to Ms Diana Barrett at Customs HQ in Blackfriars on 30 September. I spent that summer working in the stock room at Argos in Hendon, all the while thinking: 'How on earth have I ended up a civil servant?' In retrospect, it was stamped on my forehead from the moment I presented my first pub quiz at Cambridge.

Is there any way this closed shop on Fast Stream recruitment could be changed? There are some simple things that could be done immediately. For example, it should not be existing civil servants assessing future civil servants; that just reinforces the tendency for the organisation to recruit in its own image.

However, to really break open the system, I would – even just for one experimental year – do something entirely different.

Instead of all the criteria, numeracy tests, group role-play and psychological profiling, I would open the competition to any young person in the country who wants to join the Fast Stream scheme, regardless of their qualifications. I'd invite them – whether in writing, by film or down a phone line – to submit an idea, in as much detail as they can, for one practical thing they would do to change the country or their community for the better.

Of course there would be thousands of crazy, uncosted, undeliverable ideas, doubtless many of them from students with good degrees, and lots of submissions revealing political bias, prejudice or psychosis. But there would also be hundreds of sensible, imaginative and transformative proposals, and the young people who'd submitted them could then be invited to come and present their ideas to each other, and have genuine discussions about which would work best.

The civil service could then simply choose those individuals who came across on the day as the most intelligent, thoughtful, nice and genuine people.

It would put creativity, thoughtfulness and common sense at the heart of Fast Stream recruitment for at least one year.

4

CUSTOMS AS I AM

'I want to work in an office with my own desk.'

When I was nine years old, at St Theresa's primary school in Finchley, our teacher Sister Eucharia – a fearsome nun who had given me and my friend Tim a memorable thrashing for crying about the death of John Lennon three years previously – went round the class asking us what we wanted to do when we grew up.

For all the firemen, astronauts, nurses and soldiers in the room, I was clear: I wanted to be an office worker. And not any old office. I wanted to work in the gigantic IPC Magazines building in Southwark where, that past summer, our 'Uncle' Tom had taken me, my dad and my brothers round the offices where he worked as an advertising draughtsman.

He took us to the floor where *Roy of the Rovers* was created, showed us the amazing view and invited us to choose a photo from their collection. I broke my dad's heart by choosing Arsenal's young midfield maestro Paul Davis ahead of Celtic's Paul McStay.

That aside, it was the happiest day of my young life: free hot chocolate; whatever we wanted for lunch from the canteen; men in swishy suits laughing with women in shiny blouses; and everywhere you looked, people drawing and writing at their desks, just like I did in my tiny room at home.

I'd forgotten most of that day until I turned up for work at Customs fourteen years later, walked across Blackfriars Bridge, and realised that New Kings Beam House – where I was going to be based – backed onto the IPC building. I took this as a tremendous omen, and from the moment I was taken round the building and saw the giant glass corner offices overlooking the river where the directors and chairwoman sat, I knew this was where I wanted to spend the rest of my working life.

The wind was rather taken out of my sails when I sat down with my new boss and was told what to expect in terms of career progression. Diana was the tough and experienced head of the Customs anti-smuggling division, responsible for policy on the illegal trade in drugs, pornography, alcohol, tobacco, fuel and endangered species, and helping to coordinate major operations across the different Customs regions, as well as joint operations with the police or our international colleagues.

She explained that I'd work about four or five years in different Fast Stream posts, with modest annual increases in my starting salary (£16k). Then, if I was ready, I'd go to an assessment centre to be considered for promotion to a Grade 7 manager's position (£40k), do seven or eight years at that level, and then start applying for jobs at a senior civil service role at Grade 5 (£60k), but without expecting to get one in a hurry.

After that... well, Diana herself was still waiting for promotion beyond that level, so she wasn't going to hold out the prospect for me. But those glass corner offices overlooking the river for the Grade 3 directors suddenly looked very far away. As it was, and entirely because of my eventual wheeze of twice zigging over sideways to the Treasury, then zagging back to Customs on promotion, I ended up becoming the youngest ever Customs senior civil servant just over six years later, at the age of twenty-eight.

But I packed more experiences and education into that first year, working across the full range of anti-smuggling policies and operations, than I did in any other civil service post. Less than a year out of university, without any formal training or indeed rigorous background security checks, I was helping Dutch customs staff in Rotterdam search banana boats from Colombia for shipments of cocaine, and sitting in on planning sessions with the RUC and the security services for a major crackdown on IRA smuggling operations.

With a colleague named Bob Pennington, I was sent round Britain's container ports to investigate a rash of large seizures of cigarettes, as a result of which we wrote the first official report revealing that tobacco-smuggling was no longer about blokes in overloaded white vans at Dover, or teenagers with bulging suitcases on flights back from Tenerife; it was a massive organised crime operation with millions of tax-free 'exported' cigarettes returning to Britain every day by the ship-load.

It was like a giant great adventure holiday. And, as with any holiday, there were fascinating discoveries too. Go round the back of the luggage carousels at airports and you'd find anti-smuggling staff ... ahem ... taking a peek (and breaking the odd padlock to do so) inside the bags of passengers who'd been identified as suspect to see whether there was indeed a good reason to stop them.

What made someone suspect? One more bag than they went out with; an almost empty bag when they went out which was now full; or travelling back with different people than they'd travelled out with. All things that could simply be told by comparing the passport and check-in information at either end.

But most of all, we'd receive intelligence on likely suspects: informants within gangs; people we'd nicked, trying to get an easy ride by giving up their fellow smugglers on other flights; handlers who'd already been identified and picked up in the arrivals area doing likewise.

Now, if an informant has identified a suspect, and their bag has been checked behind the carousel, how do you arrest them without giving both games away? No experienced smuggler will believe they were pulled over at random. Simple: smear the bag with some invisible canine catnip, put one of the 'drug dogs' in the exit hall and let them go nuts when they smell it. The smuggler thinks he got unlucky with Britain's best bloodhound and the informant can continue his or her work.

Another fascinating – or disturbing – discovery came at the unit at the Mount Pleasant sorting office responsible for checking parcels. Mainly they were looking for drugs, but in the days before the explosion of internet porn they were also looking for video cassettes and magazines containing indecent or obscene material.

Finding anything like that was very, very rare, but nevertheless, if you discovered a home-made or imported pornographic video in a parcel, you had to watch or slow-wind through the whole tape to check that – at some stage – it didn't turn into something illegal. 'Better pause it, Bob, that Alsatian's looking frisky.' The same was true with magazines and collections of photos on discs.

So it was that a couple of Customs officers had to spend all day watching entirely legal pornographic films and slideshows, looking for a needle in a haystack, so to speak. It was felt that work was best done in pairs, for what I hope are obvious reasons; and usually not by a mixed couple, ditto.

It was also felt that you couldn't expect someone to do that work every day for too long without becoming a bit jaded, so anti-smuggling staff from around the country were invited to apply for rotations in the Mount Pleasant porn section just to maintain a healthy level of turnover. This did of course bring its own problems, when one or two people started requesting a rotation rather more often and enthusiastically than appropriate.

But if there were one or two bad apples and dodgy practices in the Customs world, as in any walk of life, the vast majority of people I worked with in my first job were entirely good eggs, committed to their work until Friday lunchtime, when the office would empty into one of the nearby pubs and rub shoulders with the swishy suits and shiny blouses from the IPC building.

As well as the week ending at midday on Friday, I also got Wednesday afternoons off to represent Customs HQ at football against the other big Customs bases, playing matches on freezing hilltops in Dover or plush pitches near Heathrow. Despite playing with the torn cruciate ligaments I'd been nursing since my last year at Peterhouse, it was the best standard and most enjoyable football of my life. I also learned you don't rampage around starting fights with sixteen-stone Customs officers.

I never talked politics with my colleagues or teammates, and I didn't discover any of their affiliations until the day after the 1997 election, when I limped across Blackfriars Bridge around 11 a.m., hugely hungover after a night of celebrating Labour's victory and staying up to watch Tony Blair's majority mount up. I was astonished to see the entire riverside area outside the Doggett's Coat and Badge pub brimming with people from the Customs office, including all of my team.

I thought they were all out celebrating and went down the steps to join them, but – while there was plenty of drinking going on – the atmosphere was sour.

'What's going on?' I asked one of the Grade 7s in the team: 'We've walked out.' He gestured angrily down the river towards Westminster. 'We're not working for that bloody woman', by whom he meant Dawn Primarolo, the incoming Customs minister, who'd made herself unpopular with the hard-bitten Customs lads, largely on account of being a woman.

Despite the odd political and attitudinal difference, I felt thoroughly sad when I was transferred from the anti-smuggling team to work on a new review into the taxation of charities, set up by Gordon Brown in his July 1997 Budget speech. It was led by the Inland Revenue, but our little Customs project team was supposed to mop up any issues raised about VAT or other indirect taxes. We sat for months just compiling and analysing responses from charities all over the country.

It was an education in how best to perform political lobbying. We'd receive thirty- or forty-page submissions from major charity associations or accountancy firms detailing incredibly complex or impossibly expensive proposed changes to tax law, which had no chance of going through. And we'd receive hundreds or thousands of identikit postcards, petitions or emails, which – while impressive in terms of sheer numbers – didn't have any emotional punch.

Much more effective were the sheer numbers of elderly people persuaded by religious charities to write by shaking hand to campaign for VAT relief on repairs to their local churches. Never the same letter twice; most of them tear-jerking. They might have wondered if it was a waste of a stamp, given they were just compiled and processed by some kid like me, but when I got the chance to push through a special VAT refund scheme for church repairs in 2001, those letters were what was in my mind.

I was less keen on the campaign to solve the VAT problems of the national museums and galleries, largely because it was driven by elderly millionaires saying that if we didn't change the VAT rules they would sell their art collections for profit rather than bequeath them to the nation when they died; they weren't the most tear-jerking letters to read.

At that time, museums and galleries which allowed free admission were not considered to be conducting a business, and could not therefore reclaim the VAT they spent in running their buildings – heat, lighting, cleaning services and so on – in the way other businesses can. For the same reason, churches couldn't reclaim VAT on their repair bills.

The museums proposed various wheezes to get around this problem, all totally illegal under UK or European VAT law, but ultimately they kept coming back to the obvious solution: they wanted to charge for entry and run themselves as businesses. And why not, when they could charge a fiver a head and still see tourists pouring through their doors each year?

We held firm during the charity tax review and it was only in 2001, when the situation with the art patrons became critical, that Tony Blair insisted on something being done. This message was conveyed through David Miliband, then Blair's special adviser, to Ed Miliband, then Gordon Brown's, in a one-line email saying: 'VAT and museums: Get this sorted.'

As I was an old veteran of this debate from the charity tax review, I was called in by Ed Miliband, and – despite telling him the dozen different reasons we couldn't legally do what was being proposed – he kept smiling out of one corner of his mouth and said: 'You've got to find a way... I know you'll find a way.'

Working with two other great Customs veterans of the charity tax review, Judith Warner and David Ogilvie, we eventually worked out a convoluted mechanism for refunding a prescribed group of museums and galleries their VAT bills, without breaching EU law.

When I told Ed Miliband we'd cracked it, I had my first taste of his Disraeli-style approach to management. He told his entire office that I was a genius, and kept shouting the phrase 'You're a genius! You're a genius!' at me as I walked away down the corridor. I hope his brother said the same when he told him the good news.

So, in their different ways, the heart-rending letters written by those hundreds of church-going pensioners and the blackmailing letters sent by a few millionaire art patrons turned out to be by far the most effective representations we received to the charity taxation review.

When the art of a well-crafted or even painfully written letter dies out in modern life, our politics will be much the poorer for it, while – conversely – we will never lose the art of political speeches, well written or not, because politicians will never stop making them.

Back in November 1997, long before I was a twinkle in Ed Miliband's eye, Dawn Primarolo appeared at a charity conference to encourage further submissions to the review, and I was asked to write some suggested text for the speech. I can't remember what rubbish I wrote, but the feeling of sitting in an audience and hearing my words read out on stage will never leave me.

To me, way beyond being told I was a genius, someone being prepared to read out or sign off my words in their own name remained one of my single greatest thrills in the job.

5

THE TREASURY TYPE

In 1997, if you walked towards what used to be the Treasury's main entrance, you could look up and see the balcony from which Winston Churchill hailed the crowds in Whitehall and Parliament Square on VE Day. As you entered, stretching up in front of you was an enormous marble staircase to the Treasury's second floor – plush-carpeted corridors and thick wood-panelled doors, behind which the Chancellor, his junior ministers, advisers and key aides had their offices and meeting rooms.

If you could experience all that for the first time and not feel over-awed, almost intimidated, you have the advantage on me. Frankly, I felt terrified. I'd been summoned across by the Treasury official responsible for charity taxation, Tabitha Jay, a scion of the great Jay political dynasty, not much older than me but a world apart in terms of her authority and confidence.

As she explained to me over a hurried coffee, she was also responsible for about thirty other bits of tax policy and couldn't afford to spend her time re-writing all of the draft material emerging from officials working on the charity tax review. She'd read the speech Dawn had given that month at the Charities Aid Foundation, said: 'It looks like you can write', and was going to propose that I take over from our Inland Revenue colleagues as the main author of submissions and documents for the rest of the review.

Ten minutes and the meeting was over. Tabitha whizzed off to do one of her other thirty jobs and I, having booked the whole afternoon out, went to the pub. And not for the first or last time in my life, my seventh pint brought on some soul-searching. I was torn between wanting Tabitha's level of responsibility and authority, and not feeling up to it. I wanted to walk up that marble staircase and feel my shoes sink into those second-floor carpets every day, but the idea of having to brief Dawn personally – let alone big, scary Gordon – made my knees shake.

The more I got to know Treasury people, including some ex-Customs Fast Streamers who'd made the jump across, I realised I wasn't the only one who found the new Brown regime simultaneously exciting and daunting. In pre-Gordon days, even under the avuncular Ken Clarke, there was a strict process and hierarchy by which the Treasury operated. Junior officials briefed their line managers, who briefed their branch heads, who briefed their team leaders, who briefed their directors, who briefed the responsible minister, who made recommendations to the Chancellor.

If the Chancellor wanted to meet to discuss a recommendation, his office would summon the minister and the director, and occasionally the team leader. The official responsible for an area like charity taxation would never get in the room, let alone the poor mugs from the Inland Revenue and Customs actually doing the work. When, in pre-Gordon days, the Chancellor took all the directors and ministers away to his country retreat at Dorneywood to make all his Budget decisions, it physically precluded the possibility of the 'lead official' having any input.

Even if they got their name on a submission that went to a minister, there was a mandatory section saying 'Approved by…' where the management chain above them would be listed in order of seniority, just to reinforce the hierarchical structure.

Imagine what a culture shock it was for the Treasury when Gordon, Ed Balls and Ed Miliband came in, and tore down that structure. It didn't happen overnight, but the more meetings that the Eds had where they appeared to understand the issues and policies better than the directors who were briefing them, the more they insisted on drilling down into teams and talking to the experts. That's why when Ed Miliband wanted the museums' VAT problem solved I got dragged in, not my boss.

And by extension, whenever Gordon wanted to talk about a particular subject, the Eds didn't automatically tell his office to summon the relevant director, but whatever official they thought would be able to answer his questions.

And no matter how junior you were, if Gordon thought you knew your stuff, you'd become his go-to 'guy' or 'girl'. You knew you'd made it when he'd shout out to his office: 'We need the Surestart Girl' or 'Get me the OPEC Guy'. And if he passed you in the corridor, usually without wanting or waiting for an answer, he'd give you a cheery 'How's Surestart?' or 'What are OPEC up to?'

The Eds were better with names, and with small talk. While they worked hand-in-glove in their adjoining offices, with a shared group of support staff, you would – depending on the issue you were responsible for – usually be dealing with one or the other, and young Treasury officials were forever comparing notes on whom they preferred. But they were both well liked and admired, except of course by those directors who missed their weekends at Dorneywood.

While the machinery of the Treasury was not massively altered in those early days, the cogs began to work more effectively, each individual knowing their function and how they were contributing to the central goals, even the unstated ones like keeping Britain out of the euro, redistributing income to poor working families and – through his 'spending teams' – helping Gordon stretch his right of initiative and veto into every aspect of government policy.

A Treasury that had been humiliated during the early 1990s with the shabby exit from the European Exchange Rate Mechanism, the recession that followed and the House of Commons' defeat of the 1993 Budget began again to feel – under Gordon and the Eds – back to its most powerful and authoritative, with a clear sense of purpose and mission.

And imagine what it was like for the young Treasury Fast Streamers meeting their contemporaries from other departments in Westminster pubs after work, and comparing notes on what kind of day they'd had. Civil servants from the Foreign Office or Home Office who were still anxiously awaiting their first audience with Robin Cook or Jack Straw would be told casually: 'Oh yeah, Gordon passed me in the corridor today and asked me what OPEC were up to. Just a quick chat.'

Gordon himself was looked on like a stern father figure, despite his insistence on being called 'Gordon' to his face. Like any stern father, officials knew he was tough to please, but that tended to act as a motivation. When he was just a distant figure to me, I always imagined him a bit like Charles Dickens's Mr Dombey, and when he lost a child, that comparison hit me again. That terrible night in 2002, I was far from alone among Treasury officials, many of us who barely knew him or Sarah on a personal level, in weeping for their loss as though we did.

When Gordon returned to the Treasury after the election in 2005 and then left for the last time in 2007, there was an element of my orchestration in ensuring that officials from every team were in the right place for the cameras to see them cheering him in and applauding him out, but there was no shortage of enthusiasm and affection among the staff who did so.

One of those officials was the long-standing head of the Treasury's Parliamentary Unit, the wonderful David Martin, who had worked for Chancellors stretching back to Nigel Lawson in the 1980s, and has now sadly passed on. When he was asked at his retirement party in 2009 who was his favourite Chancellor, he replied without hesitation: 'Gordon'. Why? 'Well... I mean, for once, we knew what we were doing.'

He recounted that, on the day of Gordon's departure in 2007, another long-standing and senior civil servant approached him and said: 'Right, now we can go back to the way things used to be', to which David said he replied: 'Why on earth would we want to do that?'

For me, ten years before that day, reflecting on my meeting with Tabitha, I decided that – even if I wasn't sure I was up to it – I at least had to try my luck in the Treasury. Once the charity tax review was finished in 1998, I started looking for secondment opportunities.

After a failed bid to get a job in Dawn Primarolo's private

office, I tried for a secondment in Tabitha's old tax policy team. The job would be specialising in transport and road taxes within the indirect tax branch. As long as they didn't ask me about shipping, I reasoned, I might have a chance. I went for my interview on 10 March 1999, the day after Gordon's third Budget.

I knew I'd got the job when I bonded with my interviewer, a cerebral middle-aged Scotsman named John Pavel, over the fact that neither of us drove a car, which he said would make us the perfect team. In retrospect, I was very lucky to be interviewed by John, someone who actively liked the idea of working with a rough-and-ready bloke who'd only recently been working on anti-smuggling. He said to me: 'You're not exactly the Treasury type', but he seemed to think that was a good thing.

And he had a point – I wasn't. I may have been able to get onto the Fast Stream, but becoming a Treasury Fast Streamer is far tougher and requires an even greater level of self-assuredness and natural authority – which was why so many young graduates were able to thrive in the atmosphere created in Gordon's Treasury. It was egalitarian, yes, but only if you'd got through the door in the first place. And that remains a problem to this day.

Now, as then, the Treasury's recruitment process for Fast Streamers specifies the minimum requirement of a 2:1 degree. Their current recruitment literature says: 'We want to do everything we can to ensure that we reflect the society we serve', but while the recruitment forms, tests and interviews will be daunting to many candidates, they would be routine to many others who made entrance applications to grammar school, private school or Oxbridge.

The Treasury's standard application form for more senior jobs contains a sequence of three sections for 'Higher Education', 'Subject of Postgraduate Research' and 'Professional Qualifications'. These are not mandatory fields but it would surely take a particularly confident soul to leave them blank and carry on in good heart with the rest of their application, hoping that their prospective Treasury manager would carry on reading it with an open mind.

That matters if, like me, you have friends or colleagues who are naturally intelligent, hugely creative and politically astute, but could never even get their foot in the Treasury's door – let alone have the chance to rise to the most senior positions – because they did not go to university, or because they would be unable to present themselves as a 'Treasury type' at interview, even though, having worked in the Treasury and seen many of its failings first-hand, I could guarantee some of the individuals I know who fit that bill could do a far better job.

It may be extremely difficult to broaden the base from which we select our politicians because of all the financial and practical barriers that lie in the way of people becoming MPs, but for the Treasury and the rest of the civil service, widening the field of civil servants they recruit should be relatively easy, simply by removing some of the unnecessary restrictions on who is able to apply and reviewing the type of tests they must take to prove their calibre.

Nevertheless, on that spring day in 1999 when John told me I'd got the job, I didn't care who else could get into the Treasury and – for the time being – I didn't care whether I was up to doing the job or not. I was just delighted that I had the chance to try, and I practically danced down the marble staircase on the way out.

6

A TRUCKING MESS

'Right, now you're here, let me tell you what's really going on.'

That Gordon's Treasury was a well-drilled machine is illustrated by the fact that, on each of the three occasions I was appointed to jobs there, my predecessor or manager sat me down on my first day and said: 'Right, this is what we're actually doing', with 'we' used interchangeably and indistinguishably to mean the team, the Treasury and Gordon's staff.

In the case of the transport tax job, John Pavel explained that we were trying to switch the burden of taxation from income to consumption in order to reward work; that motoring was historically under-taxed and annual above-inflation increases in fuel duty were the best means of addressing that; but that we didn't want to look anti-motorist or anti-haulier so we were using road tax (aka vehicle excise duty or VED) to direct tax cuts in their direction, all targeted at 'greener' cars and lorries, but in no expectation of any serious environmental impact, and never to give away any big money.

John then told me about trucking. He said the British haulage industry was massively inefficient, with just too many small, old haulage firms for the amount of work to go around. In that kind of market, haulage contracts would always go to the lowest bidder and the small hauliers were finding themselves increasingly under-cut by competitors from the continent. Ultimately, the continental hauliers were just more efficient operators, but the small hauliers blamed their loss of business on high rates of diesel duty and VED in Britain, compared to the rest of Europe.

I was in charge of the VED end of things, and I loved the role. Within a week or two of starting, I was summoned to Economic

Secretary Patricia Hewitt's office. She was due a visit from junior Transport minister John Reid ahead of the first meeting of the 'Road Haulage Forum', a sop to the two main hauliers' trade bodies, the Freight Transport Association (FTA) and the Road Haulage Association (RHA).

Reid came in, leant back on his chair, put his feet up on Patricia's meeting table, and went through a succession of Bourbon biscuits with one hand and cigarettes with the other, a nod to his later outspoken opposition to the ban on smoking in public places. Not only that, but – between bites of Bourbon and drags of fag – he harangued my minister, in a way that made me feel rather aggressively defensive on her behalf: 'You've got to give me something, Patricia. These hauliers are killing me. They're going to walk out of this meeting if we're not careful.'

Reid was promoted to the Cabinet shortly after that, but whenever I saw him over the next decade, I always looked back to his slightly bullying attitude in the meeting, right down to putting his feet up on Patricia's desk and smoking without permission. I didn't even know I had a 'list' at that stage in my career, but he went on it from that moment.

At that first Road Haulage Forum meeting, the FTA and RHA demanded a study of comparative fuel duty and VED rates across Europe, and John Reid agreed wholeheartedly. Patricia nodded sagely and said we'd be happy to consider a study of comparative costs, but that we would need to look at the total tax burden on haulage firms, including income and corporation taxes (lower in the UK), and a comparison of overall efficiency.

The Treasury would never agree to commission the fuel duty and VED comparison the hauliers wanted, because it would support their argument, and the hauliers wouldn't agree to support our total tax burden and efficiency comparison because it would support ours.

For a year, under successive ministers, that was the impasse. In the meantime, Gordon decided to scrap the fuel duty escalator, but pressed ahead with the annual inflation duty rise in Budget 2000, getting an unpleasant shock when *The Sun*'s front-page splash the next day said that – as a result – it would now cost £50 to fill a Mondeo.

Nevertheless, there was not much hint of the trouble to come and, indeed, when John left the tax policy team and I became head of the indirect tax branch, we congratulated ourselves on a job well done. We'd taken the fuel duty rises as far as they'd go, we'd pushed through our reforms of VED and we'd held the line against the hauliers to the point where we barely needed to go through the motions at the Road Haulage Forum meetings.

I was looking forward to getting stuck into the other aspects of the job – tobacco, booze, betting and VAT – if I got the job permanently, so I was gutted when it was awarded instead to a very bright girl named Katy Peters. Looking back, I can see the rationale: she was a highly regarded and experienced Treasury official, albeit with no tax background, rather than a Customs secondee in his first Treasury job; and whereas one senior manager used to tell me that my submissions to ministers were 'economically obtuse', Katy was a fully trained economist.

I'd also offended some civil service sensibilities before the 2000 Budget by taking action that was deemed 'political'. One morning, I put in my submission to the Financial Secretary Stephen Timms, known as 'Ten-Foot' for his legendary height, proposing the VED rates for new cars, set in bands according to their level of carbon emissions.

That lunchtime, Ten-Foot's office received a letter from the Ford motor company warning him that if one of the bands was set at a certain level, then production of a new car due to take place in the UK would be scrapped, with the loss of hundreds of jobs. Inevitably, that was exactly the level I'd just proposed.

Rather than leave Ten-Foot – the nicest and most morally upstanding MP and minister I've ever encountered – to take a difficult decision, I simply went to his office, said I'd made a mistake in my proposals, and re-submitted them with the bands at the level that suited Ford. Even in Gordon's Treasury, it was frowned on for a civil servant to engage in that kind of chicanery.

Whether that cost me the indirect tax job, I don't know, but my handover with Katy wasn't the friendliest. Nevertheless, I did take her through the drill on the Road Haulage Forum, and we agreed she would shadow me at the next meeting in the early summer of 2000 to see how it all worked. It was the most desultory meeting we'd had up to that point, to the extent that I was representing Ten-Foot and my opposite number at Transport was representing his minister.

As always, towards the end of the meeting, we went through the ritual of the FTA and RHA saying we needed a comparison of motoring taxes, the Transport official agreeing, and me nodding along but saying it was all very difficult because we needed to compare all operating costs and take a look at comparative efficiency. And that – for the umpteenth time – would have been that.

Except it wasn't. There was an interjection from behind my shoulder.

'What we could agree', said Katy, as though she'd just come up with a new map of Israel, 'is to *start* with the comparison on motoring taxes, provided that we *agree* the next stage is to consider the wider comparative context.'

If the room had been hit by an earthquake, more people couldn't have fallen off their chairs. The RHA and FTA practically rushed for the door to release the news that we had finally conceded the study they wanted, each claiming credit for the breakthrough. Katy looked at me blankly, wondering what the problem was. Back at the Treasury, the firm view from ministers and the Eds was that this was a catastrophe, and the least bad option was to stick to our original position and accept the fallout that would result.

Whether that was the right call or not, there was – in retrospect – a sickening inevitability about what happened next. The impasse had only lasted because neither side had ever blinked; there was no going back to it now. When Ten-Foot returned to the forum, and reverted to the normal script, the RHA walked out, said that there was no point continuing in discussions and that they would not blame any member associations if they now took direct action against the government.

As the Tories, *The Sun* and the *Daily Mail* got behind the calls for a boycott of petrol stations in July 2000, the volatile atmosphere grew, and the militant local haulage associations who'd previously been kept in check by the RHA literally became a law unto themselves, blockading oil refineries in early September and causing panic-buying at petrol stations across the country.

Back in Customs by now, working on VAT policy, I watched the evening news and saw the same hauliers that I knew by name and had kept reasonably onside for a year now acting and sounding like French farmers, demanding that Gordon cut diesel duty immediately or see the country shut down. I felt a bit of despair at all my good work gone to ruin, but also a bit of vainglorious *schadenfreude* that this was a consequence of that work going unrecognised.

It's a popular myth that the crisis ended when the newspapers that had helped to stoke it became fearful of the impact on the NHS and food stocks. But that was only once they'd also had clear guarantees from Gordon that – while he couldn't be seen to give an emergency cut in fuel duty – he would definitely take action in a more orderly way in the Pre-Budget Report.

That's where I came in again. In October I was asked to come over to the Treasury for a meeting with Ed Balls. I'd hardly dealt with him while I was working on transport tax, which was never his brief, and our only proper encounter to that date was memorable for all the wrong reasons.

He was working the room at the Budget party in 2000 and found his way to our small tax policy gaggle. He explained how he had to leave soon to get back to his young baby, and how difficult it was when he was working late nights on the PBR and Yvette had a late vote in Parliament. For some reason, I said: 'You must need round-the-clock nannies.' He gave me a filthy look: 'Nannies? Nannies? They're called our parents.' He stalked off to the next group, and my colleagues winced.

I was hoping he wouldn't remember that when I walked into his office, but he barely looked up from his sheaf of papers. 'What's this one?' he asked his private office official, and was told: 'Fuel Duty – Damian from Customs'. 'Ah right, welcome. How's Customs? Now what we need for the day before the PBR is a twenty-page report, full of charts, making the principled scientific, environmental and economic case for cutting 3p off low-sulphur petrol and diesel, and explaining how everyone will benefit. I'm told you can do that for us.'

'Erm, yep, sure, I think so.' He looked at me. It was the 'This is what we're actually doing' moment. 'This is very, very important. We're not going to let people say we're cutting duty because *The Sun* told us to or some truckers blocked the roads. Otherwise they'll just do it again. We're doing it because it's the right thing to do and it's good for the environment. And I'm asking you to write the report because I'm told you know all this stuff. Are you with me?'

'Yes,' I said, much more robustly. 'Right, you haven't got long to do it, so sorry about that. But at least it means you'll get an invite to the party.' He gave a menacing chuckle. I left the office unsure whether that was a reference to what my old colleagues still called Nannygate, but after delivering the report exactly as required four weeks later, he shook my hand briefly at the post-PBR drinks and said sardonically: 'I liked all your charts. Very, very good charts.'

That PBR may have resolved the problem, and Gordon was always highly cautious with fuel duty after that, but the legacy remains from that period. Even taking into account the 3p reductions, duty on the main types of petrol and diesel was left at 45.82p per litre on the eve of the 2001 election, compared to 36.86p when Labour took office in 1997: an increase of more than a quarter. Forget that the last Tory administration raised it at a far faster rate from 1993 onwards; what matters is the comparison with George Osborne's decisions from 2010 onwards.

Through his forgoing of the normal inflationary duty rises, a one-off 1p reduction in 2011, and some marvellous sleight of hand in terms of the timing of his duty decisions, George Osborne is able to go into the 2015 election having never once increased fuel duty, and indeed having cut it by one penny. Obviously it makes a mockery of his insistence on deficit reduction at all costs and the comparison ignores the 2010 VAT rise, which has arguably cost motorists far more over the years. Nevertheless, it makes for a potent contrast with Labour's first term in office.

If you're standing by an election billboard, watch that space.

7

VAT MAN AGAIN, AND AGAIN

If you'd told me the day I first picked up a VAT guide that the knowledge I gained would involve me in three of the most crucial decisions of Labour's time in office, in 2002, 2008 and indeed – a year after my sacking – in 2010, I'd have yawned and said: 'Sorry, what did you say? I lost you at VAT.'

And that's the reality: most people's eyes glaze over when you start talking about VAT, so when I found myself in a senior position under Gordon, my colleagues and bosses were more than happy with me acting the resident expert, which was their flattering way of saying: 'You get this stuff; just tell us what to do.' And I always retained that status, hence being consulted even after my sacking.

It didn't come easy though. The great mystery of VAT is that, despite being all about everyday things – what we eat, drink and wear – the laws and language that surround their taxation are utterly impenetrable. Being a new boy in the Customs VAT team was like travelling to a distant country where every so often you'd hear an English phrase inserted into the otherwise indecipherable local dialect – 'Spongy Texture', 'Stretchy Fabric' and often an anguished cry of 'Loophole' – and wonder what on earth the rest of the conversation could be about.

That was partly because I sat near one of the greatest of all civil service teams – the VAT Reliefs Unit. Every week, this team is sent a steady succession of new clothing, food and other products which businesses accept are on the borderline between what qualifies for zero or 5 per cent VAT on one hand and the standard rate on the other, then 17.5 per cent, now 20 per cent. Rather than wrongly start selling them at the lower rate and face a retrospective tax bill down the line, the manufacturers or retailers are looking for a favourable ruling up front.

So it is that a group of VAT experts will spend a good part of their working week eating small foodstuffs and discussing among themselves whether the texture is more that of a cake or a biscuit, or pulling out the bust on a tiny T-shirt to decide if it should qualify as children's clothing or is in fact designed for young women headed to Ayia Napa. And when not doing that, they are fighting case after case at tribunals, the High Court, the Court of Appeal and the European Court of Justice, often with hundreds of millions of pounds at stake, trying to close the loopholes and defend the borderlines.

For that reason, the VAT establishment in general hate loopholes and hate the borderlines that create them even more. That is why, for years, they urged Gordon Brown, Alistair Darling and George Osborne in succession to start taxing Cornish pasties, sausage rolls and other zero-rated food sold hot over the counter in order to equalise their VAT treatment with takeaway pizzas, curries and so on. They finally got their way, albeit temporarily, in Osborne's 2012 Budget.

One example of this hatred of loopholes came early in Labour's first term when Dawn Primarolo asked for advice on whether she could reduce the VAT rate on tampons, on the grounds that they were clearly essential for women and VAT should – where possible – not apply to essentials.

She received an impossibly patronising reply explaining that it was a great myth that VAT did not apply to essentials. Try living life without toilet paper, toothpaste and soap, she was told, all of which carry VAT.

Nevertheless, Dawn patiently explained in response that she was aware of all that, but had looked at the list of items to which EU member states were entitled to apply reduced rates of VAT and, while toilet paper wasn't on there, sanitary protection clearly was, and given it was legal and affordable to do so, she would like to recommend it to the Chancellor for the Budget. The VAT bosses in Customs were enraged: 'This bloody woman wants to create a new borderline – a new one!'

Their next tactic was to argue that, since this would be the only VAT relief specific to one sex, it would introduce gender discrimination into a VAT system, which – unlike its direct tax cousins – had always been pleasingly androgynous. Dawn would have been forgiven for losing her patience at this point, but instead suggested that if the team could identify one item which was equally as essential but exclusive to men as tampons were to women, then she'd happily consider their argument.

The subsequent, intensive brain-storming exercise at Customs HQ came up with two answers, presented almost with defiance in an email reply to Dawn's office: beard-trimmers and Jewish circumcision knives. Needless to say, the measure eventually went ahead in 2000, although it remains that rare item, a tax cut not actually announced in the Budget, due to Gordon's reluctance to refer to tampons at the despatch box. The same was true when he cut VAT on condoms in 2006, another initiative of Dawn's.

My grounding in this area and the work I'd done on the fuel crisis got me an invitation in late 2000 to a private meeting with the two Eds and Katy, who had found her feet after the screw-up at the Road Haulage Forum. Ed Balls began, ominously, by saying: 'We are not having this meeting and we are not asking you to do any of the work you'll be undertaking – anything you do will be your own research and thinking.'

With that understood, they explained that they wanted some-one to develop radical options for the 'structural reform of VAT', which boiled down to creating a new tier of reduced rates on certain goods and services, paid for by raising the standard rate to 20 per cent. They described this in shorthand as 0–5–10–20. They said they wanted two options at either end which would give away or raise in the region of £10 billion, and a mix of options in between.

They continually repeated the importance of getting robust analyses of the distributional impact on pensioner households, low-income families and so on. When I tentatively asked what all this was geared towards, they just waved away the question, saying we were coming up to a new parliament and it was impor-tant to look at everything fresh.

I worked on what was termed the 'special VAT project' for several months, and had a number of further meetings with the Eds. They were constantly hankering after new reduced rates which could make the system less regressive: 'What would you cut VAT on if you wanted to target support to lower-income households?' 'Cigarettes and alcohol,' I said. 'But we can't under EU law.' 'We can't full stop,' Ed Miliband replied, as if I was an idiot.

'Alright,' Balls said impatiently, rolling his pen in his hand, which is his equivalent of rolling his eyes: 'What VAT cut *can* we do under EU law that will make the biggest difference to lower-income households?' 'The best option?' I said. 'Hands down the most progressive tax cut we could make? That would be 5 per cent VAT on pet food.' 'Pet food?!' they both said. 'Yep, compared to other options, there's a hugely disproportionate benefit for pensioners and low-income families with kids. The distributional charts are fantastic.' Now they were both looking at me as if I was an idiot.

As time went on, they became less interested in the options for VAT cuts, and more in Option 4(iii) – the one which raised the maximum £10 billion, with minimal additions of new reduced rates, the standard rate raised to 20 per cent, and new housing taxed for the first time at 10 per cent. They pored over the distributional charts, and seemed remarkably phlegmatic about how terrible the figures looked for low-income families and pensioners.

My work was done and I was still none the wiser as to what it was all about, until the 2002 Budget when rates of national insurance contributions were raised to pay for a £10 billion increase in NHS spending. Some counterpart of mine in the Inland Revenue had clearly been doing a parallel 'secret project' on NICs, and – from what I could see – their proposals had beaten mine.

But Ed Balls told me years later: 'You will never know how important your work was. Blair was absolutely insistent we had to raise the money through VAT not NICs, but we saw him off, and it was all your distributional analysis that did it.' So my special project had been a straw man all along: the worse the figures looked the better; and the less credible the potential ameliorative reduced rates were, the more that clinched the argument. Imagine how they enjoyed telling Blair about pet food.

However, the work I'd done and the reputation I'd earned as a VAT expert would come back to the fore during the financial crisis after 2008.

As many people lost their jobs and others started counting their pennies, and as companies went bust or retrenched, billions of pounds of potential spending was being lost to the economy, hence the steady slide into recession. At the same time, the surviving high street banks were all going through their own retrenchment and refusing to lend any more money.

If the government had started cutting its own spending or increasing taxes at the same time, a bad situation would have become catastrophic. Instead, we tried to fill some of that void by increasing short-term government spending – albeit through increased borrowing – and the Bank of England did what it could through so-called quantitative easing to encourage the banks to lend.

However, it's also vital to try to arrest the slide in spending by households and businesses, and keep the real economy going. After all, the government and the Bank of England couldn't save Woolworths; only actual people buying actual products there could do that. In that situation, a VAT cut is by far the most effective mechanism to give that 'fiscal stimulus' and I was one of those who argued most strongly for it.

The reason why, not that we ever said it publicly, is that it actually didn't matter if businesses kept the VAT cut or passed it on. As long as the savings were spent by someone, whether it was a business keeping someone in a job or a household increasing their weekly shop, then the amount of cash going round the economy would be increased and the fiscal stimulus would be achieved.

Conversely, the great danger of a large, one-off income tax cut or rebate is that many people will do what comes naturally in a recession – keep the extra money for a rainier day rather than spend it – thus defeating the object of the stimulus. It's precisely because the savings from a VAT cut are small and cumulative that people or businesses automatically recycle them through their spending and therefore keep the cash in the economy.

That was why Gordon and Alistair Darling decided VAT should be reduced to 15 per cent for a year in 2009. However, Alistair was urged by the Treasury to recommend a quid pro quo, whereby – when the temporary cut came to an end – the standard rate would go to 20 per cent, not back to 17.5 per cent. Senior Treasury officials had long hankered for such a move, seeing it as a simple means of banking extra billions in the Exchequer's plus column for the years to come, and arguing that the standard rate of 17.5 per cent that had been in place since 1991 had – over time – fallen way behind the European average.

Gordon dismissed the idea out of hand, not least because of the analysis I'd done back in 2001, but even though he won that argument, Alistair kept coming back to the issue, as if going to 20 per cent was simply a question of 'when', whatever the economic and distributional impact.

Gordon became increasingly angry about what he saw as the Treasury civil service working to a political agenda, trying to force Labour to make unpopular tax decisions to make life easier for an incoming Tory government, and could not understand why Alistair was going along with it. 'These Treasury guys are already working for Osborne,' he said, 'and Alistair doesn't see it.'

The truth is that Gordon would never have allowed VAT to rise – it was total anathema to him, and always had been. We couldn't even get him to consider marginal extensions of VAT to junk mail or pornographic magazines (more borderlines!), let alone an increase in the standard rate. And – based on the 'special project' work I'd done – Ed Balls and Ed Miliband felt exactly the same. How could they ever go along with a move that they'd ruled out in 2002 precisely because it was so regressive?

The issue came to a head again before the election in 2010 when several of Gordon's advisers urged him to rule out a VAT increase in Labour's manifesto, the idea being that – if the Tories refused to follow suit – this could become one of the defining issues of the campaign. It made perfect sense. Given that Gordon would never countenance an increase in VAT, then even if further tax rises were needed after the election to tackle the deficit, you could guarantee VAT wouldn't be one of them.

Even though I was long gone by that stage, I was always listened to when it came to VAT, and I used various back channels to supply the figures that would be needed on the doorstep about what a rise to 20 per cent would mean for different household types.

But given the strength of Treasury feeling on the issue, Alistair refused point blank to sign up to any commitment on VAT, leaving Gordon's advisers fearing he would resign on the eve of the election campaign if they tried to force it. Looking at things from the outside, I was tearing my hair out. As far as I was concerned, the Labour Party was being held to ransom by a Chancellor who was more concerned about his internal reputation with Treasury civil servants than about winning the election.

By the time the third leaders' debate came around, Gordon was being urged from many quarters to call Alistair's bluff and put Cameron on the spot, by saying: 'I can make a solemn promise that – as long as I am Prime Minister – VAT will not rise, and I will resign if I ever break that promise. Now, let's see if David Cameron will say the same.' But then the Mrs Duffy incident happened, and all thoughts of throwing down game-changing gauntlets went out of the window; it would have looked like desperation rather than tactical genius.

I remain convinced it was a massive mistake for Labour not to rule out a VAT rise in 2010, and for that reason – whatever the other arguments in favour – I am always slightly baffled when I see calls in the media for Alistair Darling to be restored as shadow Chancellor before the 2015 election. Why on earth would Labour put up against George Osborne the only opposition figure who agreed with him in 2010 on raising VAT, in place of Ed Balls, who has been fighting against 20 per cent VAT for thirteen years?

8

SPORT OF QUEENS

Depending on your point of view, it is either a great constitutional tradition or a ridiculous anachronism that, the night before the Budget, the first person outside the Treasury made privy to its full contents is Her Majesty the Queen.

On those hectic evenings, when documents and press notices are still being finalised and printed, and the speech is receiving the famous 'finishing touches' – or in Gordon's case, great big black lines put through whole pages with accompanying shouts of 'Who writes this bloody stuff?' – the Chancellor must visit Buckingham Palace for an hour, present the key measures and figures in the Budget, and answer the Queen's questions about them.

The next morning, in theory, the Prime Minister and the Cabinet are given a similar briefing, although Gordon took his constitutional duty to inform the Queen rather more seriously than he did the need to take questions from Alan Milburn or Charles Clarke. Indeed, for a man who usually complained about having to do almost anything in his diary, he was never anything but diligent and obliging when it came to his audiences with the Queen.

And usually nervous too, especially in 2001, when newspaper speculation about our planned Budget reforms to betting duty caused a last-minute panic in Gordon's office in case the Queen wanted to grill him about the impact on her beloved horse-racing.

By that point, betting duty was one of my areas. Once the 'special VAT project' was complete and Katy Peters had moved on in early 2001, I'd finally been appointed head of the Treasury's indirect tax branch by a new head of the tax policy team, a titan of an official named Alex Gibbs.

Gibbsy had the unenviable but essential task of going before the Treasury select committee each year after the Budget, and refusing to admit that the tax burden was rising. John Pavel used to tell me that any civil servant who answered that question wrongly would find themselves 'counting puffins on the Orkney Islands' the following week.

So the committee would ask Gibbsy thirty different times in thirty different ways to read out the set of Red Book figures for the proportion of national income taken in tax, and say whether the last number was higher than the first.

And thirty different times, Gibbsy would answer the question in exactly the same way as Gordon always did, explaining that tax revenues tended to rise during prolonged periods of growth, but referring them to the 1996 Red Book under the Tories which projected higher totals for the tax burden than those currently seen. It takes an iron will to tough it out like that.

His successor folded under the pressure of being asked whether one number was higher than another number the very first time he was up before the committee, leading to a *Daily Mail* splash and banner headlines in every other paper. He wasn't quite sent to the Orkney Islands, but did choose to move to Newcastle Council not long afterwards.

Gibbsy was also a betting man, once recounting an agonising journey stuck in motorway queues unable to explain to his wife why he was getting so agitated by the huge second innings total that India were accumulating at Lord's. They finally made it to a Little Chef where he could sprint to get online and stop his mounting losses on the spread betting market. But that was a rare setback.

Helped by Gibbsy's expertise and impeccable contacts within the industry, my first job as head of indirect tax was working out how to deal with offshore bookies offering online tax-free betting to punters. Unable to beat them, the big UK bookmakers were all threatening to close their high-street outlets and join them, representing a massive risk to tax revenues and jobs.

Our plan was to abolish betting tax on punters to remove the online advantage, and replace it with a tax on bookmakers' profits, a high-risk strategy given this would also remove the advantage that British racecourses then enjoyed offering a tax-free day out. The hope was that the resulting tide of tax-free betting would raise all ships and soaring bookies' profits would plug the revenue gap.

It was a major reform but in the broader context of a pre-election Budget, Gordon hadn't paid it much attention, leaving Ed Miliband and Ten-Foot Timms to get on with it, who in turn trusted me and Gibbsy to get it right.

So Gordon faced the prospect of having to brief the Queen on an issue which he knew little about, but where she was potentially an expert with very strong views. What happened if she disagreed with the planned reforms? What if she told him he was going to destroy her days out at the races?

I was instructed to write Gordon an urgent briefing note: everything he needed to know about the issue on one page and a script for presenting it to the Queen on another. I threw in some extra material about the state of the racing industry and how Her Majesty's horses had been doing over the past year, and whizzed it to his office.

I was immediately summoned for my first ever one-to-one meeting with Gordon, where he grilled me the way he was worried the Queen would grill him and scribbled wild notes. When he returned from his audience, I received an unusually effusive note from his office saying how grateful he was for the briefing and how useful he'd found it.

Not, incidentally, that it had any effect on Gordon, as he maintained his Presbyterian horror of gambling. When we managed to deliver the abolition of betting duty earlier than planned, I gave the Treasury communications team a draft press notice, which included the top ten bets that punters would be able to have tax free between October and January as a result: Sol Campbell to score for Arsenal on his November return to Spurs, Robbie Williams to get the Christmas No. 1 and so on.

Ian Austin, Gordon's political press adviser, loved it and it was all set to go, but when Gordon was asked to sign off his quote he was furious at the idea of us suggesting bets: 'What are you doing? This is the Treasury, not bloody Las Vegas!' The original press notice was scrapped and something that would have been a very popular announcement with punters was reduced to a bland technical note – although that didn't stop Ian supplying the list of bets to *The Sun* so they could do it themselves.

Despite Gordon's disapproval, from the night of my pre-Palace briefing, I acquired my first ever sobriquet from him: 'Betting Guy', and even my own special corridor greeting: 'How are the horses?' When I was his political adviser six years later, one of my pre-Budget duties was still providing Gordon with a briefing note about betting, racing and the Queen's horses, in case the subject ever came up again.

By that stage, I'd devolved production of the note to a true racing expert, the Treasury press office administrator Robbie Browse, who'd enjoyed a past career looking after the royal family and other VIPs on their days out racing. In January 2006, Robbie found himself in huge trouble after inadvertently emailing a daft joke about the Chinese to the entire copy list for Treasury press notices.

I went into overdrive with the media trying to kill the story and save Robbie's job, including threatening the *Evening Standard* that if they didn't get a reporter and camera away from his flat, then I wouldn't give them any help with the Budget that year. But the real job was persuading Gordon that he should look the other way, rather than leaning on the Treasury hierarchy to give Robbie the sack.

For the sake of relations with the Chinese – not least Rupert Murdoch's then wife Wendi Deng – Gordon's instinct was that the Treasury should show no mercy, but after I explained that Robbie was the person who wrote his annual note on the racing industry for his audience with the Queen, his position shifted and Robbie survived: definitive proof that Gordon considered the Queen more important than Murdoch.

Indeed, I don't think any of her prime ministers can have respected and admired her more. He and Sarah were genuinely thrilled about their first visit to Balmoral and determined to show due decorum, in contrast to Tony and Cherie's first stay, when they not only conceived their youngest child, but told the world that they'd done so. Gordon was particularly tickled to be driven round the country estate in a Range Rover by the Queen herself, and to see her getting out to grapple with collapsed fence posts.

And because of that admiration and respect he had for the Queen, I was constantly on the look-out for stories where Gordon could display his monarchist tendencies. One of my proudest splashes was in the *Daily Mail* on Budget Day 2005, when I trailed Gordon's announcement that we would fund a statue to the Queen Mother overlooking The Mall next to that of her husband, George VI. I'd rarely seen Gordon as happy on a Budget morning as when I showed him the front page.

Of course the even bigger prize for me was any story which simultaneously made Gordon look like Charlotte Corday and Tony Blair look like Jean Marat. I hit the jackpot not long before the election in 2005, when relations between the two men were at possibly their lowest ebb, with a *Mail on Sunday* splash saying that Gordon had thwarted Tony's plans to scrap the 'Royal Flight' and instead planned to provide the Queen with a new luxury fleet. Gordon called when he saw the paper, said: 'I hope you had nothing to do with this', but I could hear the lilt in his voice.

By contrast, some of the few times I felt in real trouble with him were when I'd done anything that he thought might damage his relationship with the Palace.

One of his lesser-known responsibilities as Chancellor was 'Master of the Mint', in which capacity he submitted to the Queen – in his own name, but usually without any input – the recommendations of the Royal Mint Advisory Committee for new coin designs. When, in 2005, I saw their proposals for a 50p coin marking the anniversary of the Victoria Cross, which portrayed a soldier in the sights of a sniper rifle, I drafted a letter for Gordon's office to send back to the mint saying:

Before he writes to HM The Queen to request approval he would like further thought to be given to the design. He appreciates the designer's attempt to portray the courage and selflessness of the British soldier carrying a wounded comrade while under fire. But he feels that the particular image of a British soldier apparently about to be shot in the back will not seem appropriate to many people.

I leaked the letter and the 50p design to *The Sun*, who splashed them in their Saturday edition with suitable outrage and rare praise for Gordon on an issue relating to 'Our Boys'.

As my mobile rang at five o'clock that morning, I knew without looking that it was Gordon and I was in trouble. 'How can you do this to me?' he screamed. 'This is the Queen! THE QUEEN!' It offended Gordon's sense of constitutional propriety to leak any details of his dealings with the Queen, even about recommendations he wasn't prepared to send her.

If there's a lasting legacy from Gordon's loyalty to the Crown, it is that despite the republican streak that historically runs through the Labour Party the two Eds who lead it are firmly in the opposite camp, and both fervent admirers of Prince Charles. If they are in Numbers 10 and 11 Downing Street when Charles ascends the throne, those people who fear and resent his influence over government policy may have good reason to worry.

I can imagine Balls's first pre-Budget audience with the new king: 'Now, Sir, I understand you're interested in my plans for VAT relief on pot plants.'

9

MY DEMON BOOZE

Putting me in charge of alcohol taxes was like putting Ian Paisley on the papal conclave.

I had an almost worrying lack of experience when it came to my other lead tax areas: I'd never smoked a cigarette or driven a car; and I usually only bet on the Grand National. But I made up for it when it came to my excess of experience in alcohol consumption.

I'd started drinking lager alongside my dad when I was very young: watching the Gaelic football or a Bob Hope film on TV together meant five cans from the six-pack for him, one for me, and don't tell your mother.

When I was fourteen, after my first day's shift on a building site, tearing up cracked paving stones and hauling around new ones, the foreman took me to the pub and it was the first time in my life that I equated the exhaustion of a hard day's work with the need for a pint of lager.

Four years working behind the college bar at Cambridge saw my tolerance and waist size soar, not least because of the bottles I'd take back to my room every night of the week to help me work.

By the time I was earning a Grade 7 salary at Customs aged twenty-five, and spending three-quarters of it in the pub either on myself, mates or colleagues, I was by any measure an alcoholic, albeit probably the dictionary definition of a functioning one. I used to walk past Smithfield Market on my way to Blackfriars at 7 a.m., and – if I had lots of paperwork in my bag to get through that morning – I'd conclude it made perfect sense for me to do it in one of the 24-hour bars rather than at my desk.

In the Treasury tax team, it was more complicated. I had to be

on call for ministers at any time, and the day was usually so busy
with meetings and submissions that I couldn't just slope off to the
pub. So my daily routine became a quick two pints while going
out 'to get a sandwich' at lunchtime, two hours in the pub with
colleagues straight after work, then back to the Treasury with a
six-pack to do another three hours' work before the last Tube
home, a can on the Tube (pre the Boris ban), and another four
at home before falling asleep on the sofa. And repeat.

Occasionally, I'd arrive at the Treasury in the morning knowing
I'd done three hours' work the previous night, but not remembering what I'd done. Sometimes I was pleasantly surprised; other
times I'd go through my sent mail wincing as I read some excoriating rejection of a planned submission from one of the Customs'
teams, explaining in sarcastic detail exactly how shit it was, and
then attaching an admittedly perfect re-drafted version that they
should send instead.

I didn't have to send too many of those emails until I became as
unpopular in parts of Customs as Katy Peters and John Pavel had
been before me, even more so because I was seen as a turncoat.
I was particularly despised by the Manchester-based team which
administered alcohol duties, and – almost to spite them one year
– I started asking questions about one of the perennial proposals
that ministers were lobbied on before each Budget: small brewers' relief.

The proposal, which was to halve the duty rate on beer produced
by the smallest breweries, had been around for more than two
decades, in which time dozens of them had gone out of business
and the monopoly of the major regional and national breweries
over what was sold in pubs had increased. It had always been
resisted by Customs and the Treasury because it was literally such
small beer: why introduce complexity into the system just to hold
back inevitable market forces?

It didn't help that the lead campaigners for the proposal, the
Small Independent Brewers Association (SIBA), were a lovely
bunch but so used to having the proposal rejected that they
barely put up a fight any more, and could not hope to compete

with the slick lobbyists representing the big companies within the industry, who were dead set against it.

This became, without doubt, my finest hour as a civil servant. Working with SIBA and advising them on their campaigning tactics, I personally drove the measure through, encouraging Ten-Foot Timms to get behind it and persuading Ed Miliband, who referred to it as small brewers' droop, at least to look the other way. Customs fought me at every stage, but come Budget Day 2002, Gordon was able to announce cheerily that the new relief would come in by the time of the World Cup.

There was a bit of a backlash, rather proving the need for the reforms, as the papers searched Westminster for a single pub where punters could find a qualifying beer, but we rode that out and now the tide has turned. The number of breweries in the UK has risen from 400 to more than 1,000 and craft beer is thriving in every region of the country.

Not that I ever sampled any myself. My choice of alcohol went largely unchanged as time went on – lager and white wine, usually at the same time – but my levels of consumption got ever worse, especially after I realised that my role as Gordon's press adviser only really required me to be at the end of a phone to him and to the media, and that I was practically encouraged to take thirsty journos for the boozy lunches, long afternoons in the pub and late-night karaoke sessions that led to stronger relationships and the open sharing of intelligence.

Gordon didn't care if I wasn't to be seen on Thursday or Friday afternoons as long as I could tell him what was going to lead the Sunday papers, and guarantee that it wouldn't be him in the firing line. Similarly, he didn't care if I spent foreign trips sampling the local *cerveza* with the travelling press entourage if it kept them happy and ensured they didn't screw us over on the trip.

The occasions when I couldn't remember the previous night's events became more frequent and more worrying. Even when I could remember what I'd done it was with a fair degree of embarrassment; I once tried to obtain entry to the Treasury at 2 a.m. and had a rambling row with the custodian who wouldn't let me in, only for his supervisor to come down and tell me I was outside the Foreign Office.

It took an almighty toll on my health and my personal life. I would almost certainly have lost Penny and Balshen – my only long-term girlfriends – anyway in the end, but spending most of my time in the pub certainly didn't help. And yet, I can barely remember anyone in my entire time in the civil service or politics taking me to one side and telling me to take it easy.

At the end of a September 2003 trip to the G7 meetings in Dubai, one of my first overseas trips as the Treasury's head of communications, we all gathered at the end of the day in the recreation room at the British embassy to watch Arsenal's Sunday visit to Old Trafford. The embassy can't technically sell alcohol, so we had to buy tokens and then exchange them for cans of beer. Not having my spectacles, and not wanting to go back and forth to the counter all evening, I exchanged all my tokens for fifteen cans and sat on the floor in front of the big screen.

I was absorbed in the game in my usual terrified way, drinking at a ridiculous pace and oblivious to what a big crowd had gathered behind me, including Gordon, the Eds and Treasury Permanent Secretary Gus O'Donnell, a Man United fanatic. When United were awarded a last-minute penalty and a chance to win the game, I sat in silence, necking the last of my cans as Gus shouted happily: 'That's justice! That's justice!'

I pictured in my mind that as soon as Ruud Van Nistelrooy scored the penalty, I would walk out calmly, go some distance, find a palm tree and beat the shit out of it. Except he missed. To which my reaction was to jump up and yell at the screen: 'Have that you fucking arsehole! You cheating wanker!' Then, turning to the bar: 'There's your fucking justice, Gus, there's your fucking justice!' It was only at that point I realised quite how many children were in the room, as well as the ambassador and his family. Gordon and Gus looked horrified; Ed Balls rather amused.

Even when – as a special adviser – I had a one-sided physical altercation with a civil servant in front of half the Treasury staff at a quiz night, and Gordon was told to speak to me about it, he addressed it bashfully in terms of me having a bad temper, not being a bad drunk.

That was at least in part because alcohol is so much an aspect of the culture of Westminster and Whitehall that – while I was seen as a big drinker – I wasn't seen as totally beyond the norm. When Freddie Flintoff famously pissed in the flowerbeds at the No. 10 reception for the 2005 Ashes victors, the reaction of many hardened Westminster drinkers was: 'Sounds a bit tame.' And there were lots of journalists, politicians and civil servants who were seen as infinitely worse than me.

The glass windows in the Treasury's atrium still carry the facial imprint of a journalist who tried to walk through one after a particularly heavy night at the Exchequer's expense; the same journalist who I rang one day to ask why he hadn't printed the fantastic scoop – now too late – that I'd given him at lunch two days previously. He had absolutely no memory of it.

When, in 2009, I got a job in my old school, where spending long afternoons in the pub and drifting in at lunchtime was simply impossible, my own behaviour had to change and part of getting a grip of my life after leaving Downing Street was doing that: I gave up drinking at home, never drank during the working day, cut it out entirely at least a couple of nights a week and almost never – I stress almost – got so drunk I didn't know what I was doing. I even managed to give up booze entirely for forty-six days during Lent 2012.

It's no exaggeration to say that making those changes would have been impossible – certainly for someone with my lack of resistance – if I'd still been trapped in that Westminster culture: lunch – booze; afternoon reception – booze; meeting a journalist – booze; 5 p.m. – traditional post-work booze even though it wasn't post-work; late night in the office or the House of Commons – booze; and always a nightcap or two at home.

And that was in a normal week. The summer and Christmas party season was on a different level entirely, with journalists staggering between one party and another, and the politicians, government departments or media outlets hosting each party buying far more booze than was necessary and feeling obliged to finish it all off themselves.

When it came to chucking-out time at Downing Street parties, it was my job to make sure all the guests actually left. It didn't matter how many glasses of wine they'd had, no journalist could walk past a desk covered in confidential papers and not get tempted to take a look. On occasion though, I had the opposite role, standing at the exit holding back furious mobs of civil servants and journalists trying to make last orders at the Red Lion on the grounds that *Newsnight* were still broadcasting live outside and half of them couldn't stand up.

The Westminster I experienced was truly the binge-drinking capital of Britain and they still had the cheek to chastise others. But if there's one man who always resisted, one politician who exemplified dipso-discipline, it was Gordon. He was quite capable of nursing the same glass of wine for two hours at a Downing Street reception. For him, those occasions were work, and he never touched a drop when there was still work to do in the day.

Despite his own discipline, Gordon showed tremendous tolerance of me missing morning meetings or flights to Brussels; falling over or dropping glasses at receptions; and even the odd occasion when he'd come into my office late at night and ignore the eight empty cans of lager on the desk. But that was always because I retained the ability to talk to him coherently and authoritatively about what was in tomorrow's papers and what our line should be, no matter how pissed I was.

Except once. I'd just returned from a rare long weekend away in Riga in September 2006 for my friend Anthony Glackin's stag do. We drank for about thirty-six hours straight through the Saturday, the plane home and then through Arsenal's 1–0 away win on Sunday at Old Trafford. Gordon called at the end and said through his usual gritted teeth whenever Arsenal won, especially against Manchester United: 'Well done to your team.'

He then asked me what was going to be in the papers. I barely even knew what day it was. I rambled incoherently, staggering around the beer garden of the Orange Tree pub in Southgate, eventually becoming absorbed with how newspapers were printed and shouting: 'It's words. It's words. Just words. Written in ink. It's just ink, Gordon.' My friends from the stag do were sitting on the wall of the pub listening and killing themselves laughing.

'Mm-hmm, I see,' he said, then gently: 'And, erm, what will be in the *Telegraph*?' At this point, I think he put me on speaker-phone, and – for the benefit of whoever was listening – kept up the conversation for a full ten minutes, working his way through every paper, letting me dig myself ever deeper into the hole. He concluded: 'Well, thank you, Damian. Get back to your … ah … celebrations.' When I'd recovered slightly that evening, I had Ed Balls on the phone, not to chastise me, but just to say: 'Are you mad? Why did you answer the phone?'

The next time I was in the Orange Tree beer garden on the phone to Gordon I was stone-cold sober, on the day I resigned, two-and-a-half years later. And I only wish I had drink as an excuse.

10

MEETING THE MOTHER

The only downside of driving through your own relatively obscure Budget measures, is that you then have to drive your own, relatively obscure legislation through Parliament.

I always tell people that – if they want to get a real flavour of parliamentary business – they should go to hearings of the Finance Bill committee, where the legislation which enacts the Budget measures is debated and voted on. The rooms where committee business is held are like a flatter, miniaturised version of the House of Commons.

The government and opposition sit ranged against each other, ministers and shadow ministers on their respective front benches. The chair of the committee sits – like the Speaker – in the neutral centre in front of them. The civil servants and special advisers sit to the right of the chair. The public and other interested parties sit at the back. And the press lurk around, often just sitting outside.

What separates it from the House of Commons is that you're close enough to see the sausages being made: ministers desperately filling time while they wait for a note to be passed down telling them what to say next; MPs listening to a frontbench colleague and exchanging little smirks and remarks wondering how the dimwit got promoted above them; and civil servants bearing the unmistakeable expression of 'Bollocks, we were hoping no one would ask that' on their faces.

Of course there is all the same formality and procedure that takes place in the main chamber, but done with a bit more good humour. On a particularly hot July day, sun beating in through the lead-latticed windows, one of the committee chairs said he would allow the members present to remove their top garments, greeted with a collective removal of suit jackets by the mostly male MPs but a gale of laughter from the largely female group of Treasury ministers, all wearing dresses.

The informality in those committees could go too far on occasion. I'll always admire the current Speaker, John Bercow – the most feared and forensic legislative scrutineer – for the look of utter outrage on his face when his fellow Tory MP, Nicholas St Aubyn, replied to Dawn Primarolo's introduction of legislation enacting some European directive by complaining about the lack of resistance to such measures, saying that – on the contrary – 'the Honourable Lady seems just to lie back and think of Brussels'. The glare from Bercow made him apologise.

Each minister is responsible for different Finance Bill clauses, and for responding to any proposed amendments to those clauses. They come to the committee room armed with a huge file containing introductory speeches for each clause, a large file of Q&A material and – hopefully in their head – a wealth of background knowledge from all the submissions and briefings they've had.

The minister introduces the clause, explains why it is vital for Britain's good; a host of opposition MPs stand up and explain why it is total tosh and threatens our very future; a few government MPs say what they were told to say beforehand; then the minister replies to all their points and asks for a vote. Naturally, the committee's membership is weighted to ensure the government gets every clause through, although more troublesome are the votes on small amendments proposed by MPs which the government feels obliged to oppose, no matter how reasonable they are.

If the civil servant responsible for the clause has done their advance preparation well, their role in the committee room is simply to dig out from the file the prepared answers to each question or counter-argument they've anticipated and quickly scribble answers to those they haven't, then pass these forward to the minister via one of the backbench MPs, all in the correct order, so he or she can respond to each point that has been made in turn.

Of course it isn't always that simple, largely depending on

which ministers you have in front of you. Take Paul Boateng. He was a great Treasury minister to work for: he'd invariably accept his officials' advice as long as he thought they knew their stuff; and the cocktail parties he threw in his office were legendary, Paul mixing the margaritas himself, which usually ended up all fourteen parts tequila.

He also had a great knack for making every trade association that visited him in the Treasury feel as though he was their champion: 'I TOO enjoy a pint of scrumpy as my first of the day' to the National Association of Cider Makers; 'There is NOTHING I enjoy more than a game of Housey-Housey' to the Bingo Association, all such proclamations made in his magnificent stentorian voice. But he did have a habit of becoming distracted from his task.

When Paul was appointed the first black Cabinet minister in 2002, Ian Austin explained to him that the key to his success as Chief Secretary to the Treasury was to disappear for a month, get his head in the books, and then defy his flamboyant reputation in his first media appearance by doing a serious and heavyweight interview with the *Financial Times*. Two weeks later, Ian was sitting in his office when he saw Paul pop up live on Sky News being presented with a birthday cake on the House of Commons terrace by Uri Geller and Michael Jackson. It wasn't exactly what Ian had in mind.

The expectation was that all Treasury ministers – Gordon excluded – would be on the front bench of the committee, or at least nearby, every session, in case one of their clauses came up sooner than expected. One morning, I found myself supporting Dawn in the civil servants' chairs on a host of VAT measures, when – whether because the opposition were all hungover or they were up to some mischief – several clauses we expected would take hours to get through passed without debate, and we were rapidly approaching some of Paul's clauses on environmental taxes.

'Where is Paul?' mouthed Dawn to me. I shrugged my shoulders. She thought I meant what did you say, so opened her mouth slightly wider: 'Where. The. Fuck. Is. Paul?' I was having my own kittens about where the officials responsible for the clauses were and before either of us could find out, the chair of the committee announced that we had now come to whatever nonsense subsidy for sandals had been introduced by our environmental tax team that year. We traditional tax policy team types didn't always get on with our green brethren in the neighbouring office.

Dawn and I had to wing it, by which I mean that I tore out the legalistic 'Explanatory Note' from the Finance Bill and handed that down so Dawn had something – anything – to read out in order to introduce the clause.

Having no detailed Q&A to draw on and knowing nothing about the subject, I did my best to scribble suitably bland, vaguely coherent answers to the dozens of questions from MPs and kept handing them down to Dawn to read out. By the end, she was reading them out as fast as I could write them, with anguished glances to her left for each next one and elongated pauses between every word. From the Tory benches John Bercow was killing himself laughing at the spectacle. I have never worked harder in my life, and I wrung my right hand afterwards as exhausted as the Fisher King's fluffer.

When Paul Boateng finally came rushing onto the bench and the Treasury's Swampy Brigade rushed in to the civil service chairs to relieve me, Dawn and I simultaneously mouthed to them both: 'Where the fuck have you been?' and Bercow laughed even harder. But look at the Hansard record, and you'd never know the chaos.

But for all the drama, late nights and forests of wasted paper that went into the Finance Bill, I did love the whole thing, and there was honestly nothing like getting to the end of a long day and having Dawn or Ten-Foot Timms come over and give a genuinely profuse thanks for getting them through it, not least because I had the most enormous crush on Dawn, and my girlfriend Penny thought Ten-Foot looked like Christopher Lambert and liked hearing about his handshake.

When my parliamentary experiences switched to the big league, being Gordon's eyes, ears and mouthpiece in the press

gallery sitting above the House of Commons chamber, there
were moments both of mind-fizzing joy and of stomach-splitting
anguish, but – compared to the Finance Bill – there was also a
sense of detachment and helplessness. He was down there on the
pitch; I was just up in the stands silently willing him on, and every
time he appeared, it felt like kick-off in the North London or Old
Firm Derby, with the only sensation – as ever with me – the abject
terror of defeat.

I never loved the experience of working in Parliament the same
way I did the Treasury, No. 10 or Customs. Everything about it
is hierarchical, from who gets a seat as an MP in the first place
to who gets a seat in the chamber on a big occasion; from the
distribution of offices to the silencing of civil servants who dare
to speak above a whisper when waiting in the corridors to go and
do their jobs.

Even my favourite area of the estate – the sprawling warren
of little offices in the shadow of Big Ben which houses the
Parliamentary Lobby – is itself a manifestation of that hierarchy:
a way – in my time – of saying to *The Sun*'s Trevor Kavanagh
that he may call himself 'the most powerful man in politics' in
the most widely read daily newspaper, and he may be given the
privilege of a pass to come and go from the House as he pleases,
but he'd still have to do his work up in the attic.

And that was Trevor, let alone his country cousins from the
regional papers or newswire services sat cheek-by-jowl in tiny
offices or impromptu open-plan areas, and not even mentioning the poor sods at the windows who didn't even qualify for a
Lobby pass.

Yet, for all its obvious flaws – including the sense of assumed
entitlement that drove the abuse of MPs' expenses – I wouldn't
swap our Parliament for any other in the world: not the wedding
speech atmosphere of the Scottish or Australian chambers, or the
bureaucratic processes and stalemate of the US Congressional
system.

And if I ever lost faith in the British system, I'd just go back
into a Finance Bill committee debate, and see the ministers being

put under real pressure and scrutiny; the stressed-out civil servants fighting to explain the legislation they've introduced; and
today's backbench equivalents of John Bercow sitting enthralled,
engaged and amused by every second of the thing.

As Sam Cooke said, that's where it's at.

11

THE ART OF THE BUDGET

Working on the Budget scorecard is the Holy Grail for a Treasury official. When Gibbsy asked me to take it over in 2002, I gushed my thank-yous like Sally Field at the Oscars.

The scorecard was only an Excel spreadsheet, but no ordinary spreadsheet. It contained every single potential Budget measure: its description and the details of what it would cost or raise over the next five years, before and after inflation, all updated on a weekly basis for a Friday meeting chaired by the Eds.

Well, not every potential Budget measure. There were some ideas – like the 20 per cent VAT or national insurance options in 2002 – that were so explosive or newsworthy that they would never be put on the scorecard for fear of leaking: the Eds would just keep the figures in their heads, and add or subtract them when they saw the official bottom line.

And there were other ideas – like small brewers' relief or VAT refunds for church repairs – that never made it onto a scorecard until some Treasury official like me got excited about them. Every year, hundreds of proposals would be submitted by members of the public, charities and businesses, and other government departments, and would usually be dismissed by arrogant or over-worked junior civil servants before they ever got near ministers or the Eds.

By contrast, if there were ideas from officials in the Inland Revenue or Customs, from Treasury civil servants, from special advisers and ministers, or from Gordon himself (and whoever he'd been speaking to lately), they would automatically be put on the scorecard for consideration, and worked up as formal proposals.

Each of them was called a 'starter' – as opposed, in racing, to a non-runner – and, like horses, each was given a number, corresponding to the chapter of the Budget Red Book in which they would appear if successful. If Chapter 5 of the Red Book was about 'Fairness to Working Families', each relevant idea would be numbered Starter 501, 502 and so on, and where there were lots of different options for a particular proposal – such as increases in child tax credit – they would be listed as 503a, 503b and so on, each with their different revenue costs.

Each starter was then given a snappy five- to six-word description to go in the Excel spreadsheet – 'Replace Betting Duty with Profits Tax', for example, a useful discipline to check whether it could be explained simply. Then one official, one Ed and one minister were assigned to lead on it.

All the starters – perhaps a maximum of 200 – were then placed on different sheets within the scorecard. Continuing the racing theme, Sheet 1 would contain the clear favourites, including the lead options on changes in duty rates and tax thresholds. Sheet 2 would contain strongly fancied contenders, Sheet 3 some long-odds possibilities, Sheet 4 rank outsiders and Sheet 5 those poor nags which had fallen at the first, or been got at by the handicappers.

Over the course of a few months, successful proposals would gradually be promoted to Sheet 1, and at the bottom of that sheet – constantly evolving – would be the Budget arithmetic, which said how much the entire package cost or raised. While this would change over time, the Eds and Gordon would go into each Budget with a clear sense of how much money they needed to raise in any one of the next three years, or alternatively how much they could afford to spend. Many starters which had sat on Sheet 1 from the very first scorecard meeting would find themselves jettisoned at the last minute in favour of some arriviste from Sheet 3, just in order to make the overall package tally up.

The reason that no starter ever went to the glue factory, but was kept on Sheet 5 even with both legs broken, was that you never knew if you might need one measure at the last minute to raise a certain amount of money or target support at some particular segment of society, if the final Budget arithmetic or the distributional analysis required it.

When the time came, Sheet 1 would literally be copied and pasted as a table into Chapter A of the Red Book, entitled 'The Budget Decisions', which is what politicians and journalists generally turn to first to see what the Chancellor has actually announced after he's announced it.

Every Friday, Ed Balls and Ed Miliband would go through the scorecard, sheet by sheet, line by line, with a core group consisting of me, Gibbsy, James Bowler (then an adviser to the Eds – later Gordon's Principal Private Secretary in No. 10) and Michael Ellam (my predecessor as the Treasury's Head of Communications, and later Gordon's official spokesman in No. 10).

Over and over again, that group would examine the same starters and the two Eds would ask a dozen questions about each one: Why are we doing this again? Who benefits? Who loses? Why does it cost so much? Does it affect pensioners? What does Dawn think?

In general, Gibbsy and I were expected to explain every measure and answer every question, but at times – on a particularly sensitive issue – the lead officials for individual starters would be summoned for a grilling, or we'd take the meeting to Dawn or Ten-Foot's office to go through all their starters. Not Paul Boateng – that would have just been one long evening of 'I TOO agree with this starter' or 'I TOO share your concerns'.

In a separate weekly meeting, the two Eds and the ministers would then sit down with Gordon and repeat the process, officials would occasionally be summoned for detailed discussion, additional analysis would be commissioned and digested, and from those intense sessions, emails would eventually emerge from his Principal Private Secretary, Mark Bowman, in the week or so before the Budget saying: 'The Chancellor has taken the following decisions...'

Treasury officials would wait every night for the Bowman email like passengers at the Gatwick baggage carousel, hoping that theirs would be the next to come through unscathed, and dreading that it had somehow been diverted to Sheet 5 by mistake. And I'd wait too, slowly finalising Sheet 1, updating the arithmetic, getting ever closer to the bottom line that had been planned all along.

It was a meticulous process – and aside from all the benefits in terms of getting the measures and the numbers right – it meant that on each of the twenty occasions Gordon Brown stood up to announce his Budgets and Pre-Budget Reports (PBRs), he did so as confident as he could be that every decision had been comprehensively analysed and thought through, if not by him, by his most trusted aides.

Sometimes that confidence was misplaced, usually when it came to the uprating or freezing of rates: what the 75p pension rise in the 1999 PBR and the '£50 to fill your Mondeo' outcome of the 2000 fuel duty increase had in common was a failure to look past the simple decision about whether to go ahead with an inflation rise, and what it would actually mean in the pension packet or at the pumps.

I found out to my cost how those decisions could escape attention when, not the night before, not even on the morning of the speech, but less than an hour before the 2002 PBR, Gibbsy came into my office with an intensity only usually reserved for a late tip on the 3:30 at Chepstow.

'Erm, you need to look at this.' He showed me the Budget Measures Table in the Red Book, and then the booklet of press notices which explained all the measures. Thousands of each were about to be trucked out and deposited at Parliament and at media outlets across London.

The Red Book said we were uprating one of the national insurance thresholds; the press notices said we were freezing it. There wasn't a huge revenue difference between the two, but nevertheless, I'd got the Red Book wrong. Dawn's decision, confirmed in the Bowman email, had been a freeze.

Not wanting to bother Gordon while he was getting ready for the speech, we rushed to see Ed Balls and told him we couldn't re-print the Red Book so we would have to stick an addendum in it. He narrowed his eyes. 'An addendum in the Red Book? We've never done that. You can't do that. Look, the scorecard is sacrosanct. Whatever the scorecard says is true. You'll have to change the press notices. I'll tell Dawn that's what we've had to do.'

So it was that half the Treasury – many of them about to troop off to the pub to watch the speech – were told instead to work on printing and stapling together fresh copies of the press notices, and the other half were told to report to the large circular car park to stack and load the new booklets into the trucks and get the old ones out. I was part of the production line, of course, but felt about as popular as the Pudding Lane baker during the Great Fire of London.

But for all the very occasional mishaps, and the one catastrophic misjudgement Gordon made over income tax and inheritance tax in his last Budget, the scorecard process allowed him to dodge hundreds of bullets over those twenty major speeches – starters which officials and sometimes even ministers had recommended rightly failed to make the final cut because of the intense scrutiny they were put under in the preceding weeks.

Whether it was a deliberate move against Gordon's way of doing things, or simply a loss of calibre among those doing the scrutiny, there has been a notable increase in the number of basic mistakes made in post-2007 Budgets, under both Alistair Darling and George Osborne.

What most clearly marks this out is the adoption by both Chancellors of long-standing proposals which barely ever made it onto the scorecard under Gordon and the Eds, or – if they did – found themselves speedily exiled to Sheet 5, never to return. Officials who had seen those starters rejected in the past, usually by tax administration teams in what is now HM Revenue and Customs, clearly thought they would give them another whirl with a new Chancellor in charge.

In Alistair's very first Budget, he adopted a proposal which Gordon had rejected for the past five Budgets in a row – not least at my prompting – to raise the road tax rate for older, high-emission cars to the much higher rate charged on their brand new equivalents.

The disparity between the two was something that was always going to happen after we decided to reform the road tax system so that more polluting cars would pay more, but chose not to do so retrospectively. Gordon knew that – whatever the administrative or environmental arguments in years to come – he was never going to punish millions of families for a choice of car they'd made under the old flat-rate system.

Inevitably, Alistair had to reverse his announcement in the face of a media and public outcry, but what was telling was that none of the people who worked closely with him even seemed to realise that it might be a difficult or controversial measure. Either they weren't doing their jobs or the scorecard process was no longer functioning.

The same was true of George Osborne, who – after two very simple and straightforward Budgets, only concentrating on big-ticket measures, including some so unpopular that he didn't need a scorecard process to ring alarm bells – came into his 2012 Budget with an obvious emphasis on scraping the revenue barrel to try and keep his deficit reduction plan on track. That is a very dangerous message to give to officials. There are many unsavoury items at the bottom of that barrel that they have been trying to entice Chancellors with for years.

As I listened to Osborne say the words in his speech: 'We will address some of the loopholes and anomalies in our VAT system', my ears pricked up. Worst of the lot – and notorious as it turned out – was his vow to tackle the loophole on hot takeaway food, aka the 'pasty tax'. I'd lost count of the number of times the scorecard process had blocked that proposal, so often that Dawn had stopped letting the VAT team in Customs even put a submission in.

And of course, those relatively small errors were indicative of a lack of scrutiny – a lack of care even – that then showed itself in much bigger measures such as the 'granny tax', the announcement of which more than anything else determined in the mind of the media that it was an 'Omnishambles' Budget, and brought Osborne next-day headlines the like of which Gordon never had to endure.

And similar to Alistair with the road tax hike, one of the great indicators that the process had totally broken down was the fact that the officials and advisers to George Osborne who were on the spot taking questions immediately afterwards appeared absolutely unaware that any of these measures might be a problem, let alone how to respond to journalists' questions about them.

Contrast that with Gordon's 2001 Budget, when in response Leader of the Opposition William Hague stood up with a flourish – clutching a single A4 page – and revealed, like an am-dram Sherlock Holmes, that what Gordon hadn't mentioned in his speech was that Customs were now about to start putting 17.5 per cent VAT on the sale of spectacles.

Sitting in my office, I spat out whatever I was drinking at the time, and simultaneously phoned, emailed and texted every person in Customs who could conceivably know what this was about, while seventeen different Treasury people – including half of Gordon's private office – took turns running into mine to say: 'Are you listening to Hague? What's this all about?'

It took me five minutes to get to the bottom of the story, find out it was rubbish and get a message through to the House of Commons for the Treasury officials to pass to Gordon for his rebuttal and to Ed Balls for his post-Budget briefing to the Lobby. I thought I'd done a great job, but I got the message back that – when Ed was told – he'd simply said: 'Yeah, don't worry, I know.'

When I saw Ed at the Budget party that night, I asked him: 'How did you know the spectacles thing today was OK?' Recognising my interest in VAT from my work on the secret project, he just said: 'Well, you understand how this works: if it's not in the scorecard, it's not in the Budget; and if it's not in the Budget, then it's bollocks.'

When I came to the end of the Budget and Finance Bill in 2003, having done indirect tax to death and managed the scorecard, there was nothing more to do, and I reckoned I'd reached the realistic pinnacle for a Customs secondee to the Treasury.

I was offered a promotion to a Grade 5 senior civil service job back at New Kings Beam House to work alongside a highly rated young economist, Sue Roper. Even Customs knew I needed some help with the economics. Sue and I were invited to put together the pick of all the best Fast Streamers, writers and policy analysts in Customs and build a VAT policy team that wouldn't require my successor in the Treasury to re-write all our submissions.

I liked the challenge, the money and the new team, and I knew at the age of twenty-eight, it put me one promotion away from the glass corner office overlooking the river and the job I'd always dreamed about. So I left the Treasury for what I thought would be the last time. They gave me a big baseball bat as my leaving present, and told me to go and bash some heads.

12

RISING TO THE TOP

Over the next few months, when I looked wistfully out of the window at Customs HQ over the river towards Westminster, one of the fondest memories that came to mind was attending the UK Corporate Games in Aberdeen in 2000 – before the height of the fuel crisis – as a ringer for the Treasury's official mixed netball team.

The team gathered at King's Cross station for the long journey north, each of the men – and some of the women – having had the same bright idea to bring a large case of lager or Smirnoff Ice for the journey. By Doncaster, we were hammered, and by the time we got to Pittodrie stadium for the opening ceremony, we were dangerous.

After being booed as we paraded round the pitch, we returned fire vigorously at the various banks and oil companies who came round after us, kept up a barrage of obscene chanting throughout the ceremony, and – having re-arranged the magnetic letters spelling 'HM TREASURY' on our banner – paraded out under the legend 'HURT MY ARSE'. The hours in the nightclub that followed were mayhem.

I was woken in the morning by my fellow Customs secondee and long-time drinking partner, Aakash Patel: 'Mate, you gotta get up, I'm not kidding. Don't freak out but this girl from reception just came up and said the Treasury press office is on the phone for you.' 'Fucking hell,' I said. 'What about?!' 'I dunno, mate, something about the *Daily Mail*.' Aakash waited until I was running down the corridor before saying: 'Aaaaah, got ya, dickhead.'

Saying the Treasury press office was on the phone became something of a running joke after that. So when I returned to Customs from a long lunch one sunny day in July 2003, a colleague said with a laugh: 'I'm really not kidding, but the Treasury press office has been on the phone. Michael Ellam's left his number for you to call back.' I couldn't think for the life of me why he'd want to speak to me, and sat planning excuses and lies-that-aren't-lies for every terrible thing I'd done that month.

'Ah, thanks for calling back,' said Michael, who'd been in the Head of Communications post for three years by that stage. 'Now, I'm moving jobs shortly so we need to fill my post. There's been a bit of discussion here about who should do the job and we think you'd be very good at it, so we'd like you to come across for a chat with me and Ed Balls.'

I felt hugely daunted, knowing it was too good an opportunity to turn down, but that I might be humiliatingly rubbish at it. I was also enjoying working with Sue building the new team in Customs and seeing the individuals we'd picked all thriving on the responsibility.

The chats with Michael and Ed just increased the fear factor. Michael warned that one misplaced word or nuance from the Treasury spokesman could send the financial markets haywire or cause a political shit-storm. When I explained to Ed that I found the potential responsibility intimidating, he said blithely: 'Well, everyone screws up once or twice; it's only if you keep screwing up we'd have to get rid of you.'

I spoke to Penny and asked what she thought. At that stage, she was working in Great Ormond Street Hospital in a patient liaison role, supporting families whose babies required high-risk brain surgery. Doing that job, she didn't have much time for me finding things daunting, but she was quite intrigued at the prospect of me working directly for Gordon and said I should go for it. She hadn't been intrigued about much where I was concerned for a while, least of all VAT policy, so that made my mind up.

So I applied, and had a decent interview with Gus O'Donnell, then the Treasury's top official, and Ivan Rogers, then Director of Budget and Tax Policy. Of all places, I was on a Customs media skills training course a couple of days later, when Gus called to tell me I'd got the job, subject to having an informal chat with Gordon to check that we would get on.

Having looked over my CV again, Gus said Gordon would almost certainly spend the time grilling me about my Master's degree on Lyndon Johnson.

While everyone reassured me this would be straightforward, interviews never were with Gordon. He once interviewed two young Treasury officials for a role in his private office, having been told in advance he had to choose between them. He liked them both, told them both that they'd got the job, and his office ended up having to create two roles. From that point on, Gordon's office only let him interview the final candidate for each job.

I was escorted into his meeting room, arranged with two chairs sat opposite each other, and a sofa to one side crammed with observers – both Eds, Michael, Gus, Ivan and Gordon's Principal Private Secretary, Mark Bowman. It felt like speed-dating in front of six chaperones. Gordon looked down my CV silently, occasionally muttering a word from it, as if trying to work up some enthusiasm either for me or the process: 'Customs'; 'V-A-T' (each letter spat out with contempt); 'Riots?'; and then finally, as he read my 'personal interests', he came alive:

'Celtic? You support Celtic? How can you support Celtic?' He seemed genuinely affronted. 'Where were you in '94, eh? I bet you didn't do any singing that day,' alluding to Raith Rovers' famous League Cup final victory over my dad's team. 'Yeah,' I said, 'but it was at Ibrox,' the home ground of Glasgow Rangers, 'and they did deliberately flood the pitch so we couldn't play our football.'

'That's a bloody lie!' he yelled at me, then – turning to the sofa of rather confused Englishmen – 'These bloody Celtic fans; they can't take losing. Always the same. You got beaten fair and square. Fair and square!' My CV was now scrunched in his hand. At this point, I was more worried about escaping alive than getting the job, but we ended up going back and forth for half an hour swapping stories and jokes about Scottish football. 'When can you start?' he concluded, with a beaming smile.

His only comment about the press role was to tell me I was

going to be having lots of lunches with journalists, so I'd have to learn to order salad if I didn't want to get 'too fat'. I went out of the room with a new corridor sobriquet, 'Bloody Celtic', and a new job. Ed Balls shook my hand and said: 'An entire interview talking about football. You jammy sod.'

The buoyant feeling didn't last long. Word got around the Treasury about the appointment and when I went to the nearby Westminster Arms that afternoon, there was a large group of officials standing outside who ushered me over for a congratulatory pint. Or so I thought. What they actually wanted – with the benefit of a few drinks in them – was to take a pickaxe to my bubble.

'We were just talking about you,' said one, 'and we were saying that – while we can imagine you speaking to the political editor of *The Sun*, and you'll probably be quite good at that – we were thinking that the economics editor of the *FT* might be more of a challenge.'

I wish I'd thought of something clever to say in response, but I didn't, and the conversation continued in similar vein, my new colleagues barely disguising their contempt that some oik from Customs had landed one of the plum Treasury senior civil service posts.

It was easy to develop an arrogant streak working for the Treasury. In those days, before they introduced their own graduate recruitment scheme, they had their choice of the best new Fast Streamers, so were taking the pick of an already highly refined crop. And the reason that my appointment seemed to cause resentment – even bafflement – was that I was going to spend at least two years blocking one of the real crème de la crème jobs for that group.

Crucially, it was one of the jobs which were regarded as gateways for ex-Fast Streamers into top jobs in 10 Downing Street, the ultimate fast track into roles as directors and permanent secretaries, within touching distance of the Cabinet Secretary's job, the pinnacle of the civil service profession.

The current Principal Private Secretary (PPS) to David Cameron

– effectively the top official in No. 10 – is Chris Martin, a former Treasury Head of Communications. Bar one short-term stint by ex-Palace spokesman Simon Lewis, the last three prime ministers' official spokesmen have all been former Treasury Heads of Communication. And of course, Gus O'Donnell – doyen of all Treasury civil servants – took that same route to become Cabinet Secretary.

Being a top civil service aide to the Chancellor has almost become the pre-requisite of getting a senior post in Downing Street. Prior to Chris Martin, the role of PPS had been held by four Fast Stream graduates of Ken Clarke's or Gordon Brown's Treasury private office, and one who was Gordon's key adviser on public spending.

It could be argued that, since the Treasury gets the best Fast Stream recruits to the Home Civil Service and the best of those will usually end up in the most important Treasury positions, then their further ascendance to the top jobs in No. 10 is simply a case of natural selection doing its work.

It could also be argued that there is no better training for those No. 10 jobs than their equivalent posts in the Treasury, and that the preference for Treasury types reflects the centrality of the economy to No. 10's work, at least since 2008.

Before then, it tended to be a case of Tony Blair poaching the best of Gordon Brown's talent, or Gordon putting his best spies in place, depending where your paranoia lay. Now it's more simply a case of No. 10's chief political strategist, George Osborne, recommending people who have worked for him who he thinks are up to the job.

However, if every time there is a vacancy in a senior post in No. 10 it is filled from the same narrow gene pool of top Treasury candidates, all with similar outlooks and experiences, there is a clear risk of exacerbating the homogeneity which already exists in the civil service Fast Stream, leading to a loss of fresh, or even just different, ways of thinking about and doing the job.

The longer that same cycle of recruitment is unbroken, the more the effects are multiplied. Given that interviewers tend to select the candidate who most resembles themselves, the fact that almost all of those PPSs and prime ministers' spokesmen recruited each other at various points continually reinforces the trend, as does the fact that they all came at the top of the selection process to get on the Fast Stream originally.

Again, given that these individuals are generally the best and brightest Whitehall has to offer, this could be viewed as no bad thing, and some will say I'm not in a position to criticise it, being one of the beneficiaries. And yes, like all the others, I'm white, male and heterosexual, with a degree from Oxbridge. Most of those involved in the process of appointing me as Head of Communications – either as interviewers or chaperones – were the same.

But – while I may have looked the same as everyone else, and enjoyed the same educational background – the reality was, as my 'colleagues' at the Westminster Arms that day were only too keen to point out, I didn't quite belong there. It was a curiosity that I'd got so far, and nobody in their right mind would have had me marked out as a future Cabinet Secretary.

In that moment outside the pub, I had the same feeling I'd experienced just once before when an extremely posh history fellow at Peterhouse put my weekly essay to one side after praising it fulsomely, and asked me: 'Why are you good?' I told him I didn't understand.

'What does your father do?' I said he taught kids who'd been excluded from school. 'Mmm, what did his father do?' I said that he'd done the bins in Glasgow and dug peat in Donegal. 'I mean,' he went on, rolling his eyes, 'with that kind of background, the school you went to, all this hanging around in the college bar and playing soccer, you really shouldn't be any good. So I'm asking: what makes you good?'

Even redder in the face than normal, I again couldn't think of anything clever or articulate to say in response, even – God forgive me – to speak up for my dad, who'd taught me every inch of history I knew up to that point, after teaching himself most of it from scratch.

He continued: 'The reason I say this is that you have to realise that you're good, that you're better than you have a right to be, and that you have to set your aspirations high, otherwise you'll waste your talent, you'll revert to type and you'll end up amounting to nothing.'

As I left his college room that day, I had the same response I did when I walked away from the Westminster Arms that night in 2003: 'I'll fucking show you.' And, after a fashion, I guess I did.

GOING TO THE DARK SIDE

13

WHAT MAKES THE TWO EDS TICK?

Given that they feature heavily in my story from this point on, it's worth pausing to give some reflections on Ed Miliband and Ed Balls: who they are in reality and how they worked together.

Besides having my own formative early encounters with them – being called a genius by one, being made to feel like I'd gravely insulted the other – I attended two meetings long before I became the Treasury's Head of Communications which I thought told me everything I needed to know about the two men. And I was dead wrong.

Before the Budget in 2001, Ed Miliband was chairing a meeting about funding for museums, which was joined late by Ollie Robbins, a studious and loveable official who went on to be Tony Blair's last Principal Private Secretary. Ed started reeling off a set of questions he'd been saving for Ollie, who became visibly distressed.

He explained that he'd just been working out the costs of the ongoing cull of thousands of cattle affected by the foot-and-mouth outbreak, and was feeling upset by the whole thing. Rather than be embarrassed or dismissive, Ed said he totally sympathised, was very sorry, and would understand if Ollie would rather take a break and do the meeting later. What a lovely bloke, I thought.

Some time later, in a scorecard meeting very close to Budget Day with a large number of officials present, a senior Treasury tax adviser who'd been working on an anti-avoidance measure – raising huge sums of money – suddenly announced that he was worried he may have misjudged the impact it would have on the financial sector, and it might be better to withdraw it.

Confronted with the prospect of the entire Budget arithmetic being thrown into disarray at the last minute, Ed Balls was less than sympathetic or understanding. He eviscerated the guy, suggesting he was just covering his own arse when he already knew it was too late and implying that he'd been got at by his friends in the City. It was vicious, so much so Ed Miliband needed to intervene and tell Balls to go easy. What a scary bloke, I thought.

Yet, over the years, I came to realise that Ed Balls's tough exterior and bullish style belied real warmth and sensitivity, as well as some level of insecurity, while Ed Miliband's friendly demeanour and natural good humour obscured a steely ruthlessness about his ambitions and a single-minded sense of mission.

I always believe that there is one key to every politician's personality: one thing that explains so much else about them. With Gordon, I think it was almost certainly the several weeks he had to spend after a rugby accident at the age of sixteen just lying on his back in total darkness in a hospital bed hoping that at least one of his eyes would heal and he wouldn't be left blind.

For Ed Balls, I think it is his stammer. I worked with Ed for years before I even knew about his condition, and that tells its own tale. Throughout his time as a special adviser, he favoured informal situations with small groups of people, where the stammer tended not to surface. Before 2004, the closest I ever saw him come to speaking in public were his briefings for journalists after the Budget, themselves quite informal and spontaneous occasions.

The problem came – and often still does – when there was some formality to proceedings or a set script to be delivered – a TV interview or an actual speech – where the pressure of the situation and the fear of making a mistake compounds the ever-present dread simply of being unable to get the words out. That would have put many people off a career in front-line politics altogether, and it says a lot about Ed that he hasn't let it do so to him.

In those early days when he hadn't yet gone public about his stammer, watching him do interviews or make appearances in the House of Commons was almost as much of an ordeal for us as his friends and colleagues as it was for him. We'd see his throat tighten and his fist clench – the telltale signs that he was fighting to get through a 'block', in the days before he realised that was exactly the wrong thing to do.

And strange as it might sound to people – given Ed's robust reputation – but, whether it is the stammer or the very introspective treatment required to deal with it, he has an awareness of his own weaknesses and a vulnerability that is all too often missing in politicians. That comes across most clearly in his desire to reach out to journalists and fellow politicians who've been critical of him in a way Gordon would never have done. When told by others how much David Cameron hates him, he doesn't revel in it; he seems genuinely baffled.

For Ed Miliband, I think the key to his personality is his father. There's a whole book to be written about British politicians and their paternal relationships: Gordon, Tony Blair, Ed Balls, David Cameron, George Osborne and Boris Johnson have all been hugely influenced by the character and drive of their fathers. How often do you hear of a successful modern British politician who lost their father early, or regards them as a philanderer, chancer or drunk? In America, Presidents Clinton and Obama – who barely knew their fathers – have shown the reverse can be true.

But few fathers have influenced their politician sons as much as Ralph Miliband, the refugee from Nazi-occupied Belgium who rose to become one of the top academic analysts on modern socialism. He died just a few days after John Smith in 1994, and Ed started working for Gordon Brown two months later. The domestic triangulation and aggressive foreign policy of New Labour would probably have appalled Ralph, and his younger son would doubtless have sympathised but equally felt he wasn't in a position to effect wholesale change in that approach. Now of course he is.

It's hard to listen to any of Ed Miliband's occasionally tortured, over-academic speeches about New Labour's record and his own political vision without hearing his father's voice, especially when he talks about recasting the capitalist model, and re-shaping society through the empowerment of ordinary people in the decisions affecting their communities and workplaces.

And that's not just about Ed's politics; it's also undoubtedly central to how he explains to himself and to the rest of his family why he felt it essential to challenge his older brother for the Labour leadership. What better reason than needing to achieve his father's vision and ensure that David Miliband did not traduce it? An act of supposed disloyalty to his brother becomes transformed in his mind into the ultimate act of tribute to his father.

As well as there being one key to every politician's personality, I believe each of them has one – often related – driving ambition. It's easy to say they all want to be Prime Minister, but if that was true, they'd all work as hard at it as Gordon. There's usually more to it than that.

For Ed Balls, I'd say his driving ambition has always been to deliver a Budget. Not just that, but to take all his years of experience and observation, and deliver the perfect Budget. Perfectly calibrated with no screw-ups; cheered by the punters, applauded by the *FT*; loved by his own side, grudgingly admired by the opposition; one to go down in recent history alongside Geoffrey Howe's in 1981 and Gordon Brown's in 2002.

And, perhaps most of all, it would be an opportunity to stand and speak to a packed House of Commons and a watching TV audience of millions for an hour: the ultimate test, and potentially the ultimate triumph, for a man who has refused to let his stammer hold him back.

Ed would feel that he was thrice denied that chance: first when Gordon played safe on his choice of Chancellor in June 2007; second when he cancelled the election later that year which would have allowed him to recast his Cabinet; and third when he bottled his planned reshuffle after the local elections in 2009. Ed might have thought the chance had gone forever when Ed Miliband chose Alan Johnson as his shadow Chancellor in 2010, but now it is there again in touching distance.

For Ed Miliband, I think his driving ambition, in terms of fulfilling his father's legacy, would be to win a second term in office as Prime Minister, having proved he was up to the job and earned the right – with the public and within his own party – to set out a more radical plan to change Britain's society and economy for good. It's what Tony Blair wanted to do but couldn't achieve after 2001. It's what every American President dreams of doing but rarely delivers in their second term. Ed has the innate self-confidence and sense of destiny to think he would be different.

The way I see it, each man is to some extent reliant on the other to achieve his ambition: Ed Balls needs Ed Miliband to keep him in post for starters, and Miliband needs Balls to deliver an election-winning formula and message on the economy, both in 2015 and again, if successful, in 2020. If they can keep their personal relationship on the rails, there is no reason both things can't happen.

When working together in the Treasury, Ed Balls was clearly always the senior partner in terms of his set of responsibilities compared to Ed Miliband's, but it was a genuine partnership. Back in 2003, in my first month in the job, I was hanging around their office on a Friday afternoon, and Ed Balls invited me to come and join them for their usual end-of-week drink at Rebato's, a tapas restaurant on the South Lambeth Road, now sadly closed.

They held court there all evening, enjoying telling their old stories to a newcomer: Balls all anecdotes and impressions; Miliband more of the straight man, but with a sharp line in sardonic asides. They were a proper double act. The idea that Miliband was ever made to feel subordinate to Balls is just baloney, along with the myth of him bringing Balls his morning coffee.

However, the reality is that Miliband often found himself acting as confidant for some of the more sensitive members of the Treasury special adviser or ministerial teams who occasionally felt ignored or dismissed by Balls, and – besides reassuring them that they were geniuses – it was natural for Miliband to sympathise and say he knew what they were going through; it was the same for him. That's how such myths grow.

Whether that was just good management, or artful bolstering of his clique, it worked. When the two stood against each other for the Labour Party leadership in 2010, it was interesting to watch how many of those former Treasury advisers and ministers

who had cried on Ed Miliband's shoulder in the Treasury years
joined his camp, while the more robust types who never sought
or required his sympathy – Ian Austin or John Healey for example – were firmly with Balls.

But if Ed Miliband did snipe about Ed Balls behind closed
doors with some of my former colleagues, it was never recip-
rocated. The first time I ever heard Balls say anything remotely
negative about Miliband was at the end of 2008, when the latter
had effectively threatened to resign from the Cabinet if a decision
was made to build a third runway at Heathrow.

Balls was genuinely outraged that Miliband could ignore the
need to expand airport capacity just for the sake of his reputation
with the green lobby and his own political positioning. He was
also angry that Gordon had been made to look weak in front
of his Cabinet at a time when he was already so vulnerable, by
having to kow-tow to a supposed ally.

A clear subtext to Ed Balls's irritation that day was seeing his
former junior partner so brazenly betraying his political ambitions. Doubtless David Miliband felt the same way, and you could
see that same irritation again and again during the leadership
hustings in 2010, Balls and David regularly exchanging looks of
incredulity when they'd hear Ed Miliband distance himself from
New Labour.

If David could never reconcile himself to his brother's leadership, Ed Balls clearly has. While there will be inevitable
disagreements between them over policy issues and rivalries
between their respective staff members and allies, they have
inherited from Tony Blair and Gordon Brown the ability to sort
those things out between them, but crucially without the unresolved tension of who is really in charge which made Blair and
Brown's disputes so toxic.

People say Labour needs more hardened, experienced grey-
beards in its shadow Cabinet. They are wrong, chiefly because
the longest-standing veterans are already running the show.

By the time of the next election, whatever posts they've held
or brief sabbaticals they've enjoyed along the way, Ed Miliband

and Ed Balls will have been working at the heart of the Labour Party – central to its strategising, decision-making and election-planning – for twenty-one years.

None of the other truly integral characters of that period have lasted as long. Tony Blair and Gordon Brown only notched up fifteen and eighteen years respectively from the time they assumed true central status under John Smith in 1992. And Alastair Campbell, David Miliband and Peter Mandelson have all left the stage, even if they can occasionally be heard whispering advice from the wings.

Compared to David Cameron and George Osborne, who will only have enjoyed a decade of true central influence by 2015, the two Eds will go into that next election with more experience of how to frame debates, win arguments and demolish opponents than anyone else currently at the top of British politics. If they can't do it for Labour, no one can.

14

BREAKING BAD NEWS

The first time I got front-page newspaper coverage was a total accident.

Well, for me it was. The journalist – the *Telegraph*'s then economics editor, George Trefgarne – knew exactly what he was doing. It was late on a Friday, always a dangerous time for phone calls. George started out discussing with me the upcoming meeting of OPEC, when the world's major oil producers would decide whether to increase production levels, something which in theory would cut oil prices and eventually mean cheaper petrol at the pumps.

In the course of that chat, George pointed out that Gordon had deferred the Budget inflation increase in fuel duty to the autumn because of the high level of world oil prices. He then asked: 'Is it unreasonable to assume that he'll maintain the freeze if oil prices are no lower?'

My rather mannered answer was: 'It's not an unreasonable assumption that the Chancellor will take the oil price into account – along with other factors – when making his decision.' Goodnight Vienna. The resulting front-page splash said Gordon was due to cancel the duty increase, quoting the Treasury's spokesman saying it was not an unreasonable assumption.

I'd committed the first sin of spin-doctoring: echoing the question. There's a reason journalists phrase their questions in a certain way; so if you say 'Yes' or echo the question in your answer or even refuse to respond, they've got enough of a basis to write the story. Always take the question they've asked and re-phrase it into one you're prepared to answer.

If a journalist puts a series of allegations to you, especially if they're true but can't be proved, all you can say is that you find the very question extraordinary and will not dignify it with a response, or that you'll be consulting your lawyers. You say that again and again no matter how often they ask the question, and usually the story will evaporate. If, on the other hand, you repeat the allegations back at them or actively deny them, they have something they can write.

If – worst of all – a journalist asks why these allegations are knocking around and whether someone may be trying to smear you, and you agree that it's all very unfair and upsetting, then a story that otherwise wouldn't work can be written up as your fury or anguish about anonymous, unproven smears, which enables the paper to allude to their substance and the internet to do the rest.

When the *Telegraph* appeared with the fuel duty splash, I was advised by Michael Ellam to go and speak to Ed Balls for advice on how to handle it. Balls rolled his pen in his hand when I told him, said 'Oh dear', then told me to come with him and learn how to break bad news to Gordon.

'You know that bloody Tory at the *Telegraph*, Trefgarne...' Ed began. Even before hearing the rest of the sentence, Gordon knew who to blame: the bloody Tory rather than me. 'He's totally screwed us over,' the use of 'us' reinforcing a sense of collective responsibility. 'He's taken some throwaway line from Damian and turned it into a splash about us scrapping the fuel duty rise. Total tosser.'

It was a magnificent performance, and left Gordon fuming about bloody Tory journalists rather than his incompetent new spokesman. As Ed and I walked out, he said: 'Right, next time, you have to do that yourself, but try and make sure there's no next time.'

Ed wasn't always so collegiate. A few weeks later, Penny and I made our first journey back to Cambridge together as a couple, but in desperately sad circumstances, attending the funeral of a close and very young friend of my family. On the train journey up from London, my phone exploded with calls and urgent text messages from Ed Balls, Ian Austin and Michael Ellam.

Penny asked me to turn off the phone for the day and focus on what mattered, but I didn't ignore Ed Balls's phone calls at the best of times, let alone a month into the job. That time, I wish I had. He was in a highly animated state. I'd given a set of quotes to Reuters that morning in his name, gently putting pressure on the Monetary Policy Committee over interest rates, which Reuters had – with our agreement – presented as though it was an interview.

The trouble was that the reporter who'd filed the 'interview' – Ashley Seager – had followed it up five minutes later with a near-unprecedented and highly market-sensitive leak of the upcoming monthly retail sales figures. People naturally assumed Ed Balls was the source of the leak and would have to resign, while Ed himself knew I was the only person in the Treasury to speak to Ashley that morning and assumed it was me.

And this was the dilemma. For Ed's name to be cleared, either he needed to admit we'd falsified the Reuters interview, which he wasn't prepared to do, or I needed to admit responsibility for the leak, which I was even less prepared to do. There was huge tension in the phone calls between us, given he was suspicious of me, I was wary of him, and it was assumed one of us was going down over this.

Eventually the truth started to emerge from Reuters – that the 'source' was a junior Treasury official stupidly boasting to his Reuters flatmate about the secrets in his briefcase – and Ed and I were reconciled. But it did occur to me afterwards that at no stage did Ed or anyone else apologise for intruding on the funeral that day, and nor did I protest at them doing so. I'm not sure which appalled Penny more, but her early taste of politics was a total turn-off.

I had my first experience of breaking bad news to Gordon as a follow-on from the Trefgarne fuel story, when the OPEC meeting that was supposed to increase oil production – and therefore lower prices enough for Gordon to go ahead with the duty rise – instead announced a surprise cut in production, leaving prices even higher.

I went into Gordon's private office with a print-out of the
Reuters story on OPEC's decision. The poker-faced Mark
Bowman said: 'You'd better go and tell him then,' ushering me
into Gordon's office, and shutting the door behind me, leaving us
on our own. 'What is it?' Gordon said with alarm. I told him the
news. It was the first time I ever saw him really lose his temper.

He got up from his chair and came storming across the room
to read the Reuters story, shouting: 'How has this happened?'
The way he approached – fists balled and a face like thunder – I
genuinely thought he was coming at me. I took up a defensive
stance with my own fists balled. Not that I planned to hit him.
I mean, you don't 'plan' to hit your boss at the best of times, let
alone when you're brand new to the job and he's the Chancellor.
But I thought I might need to defend myself.

Then I thought of a different approach; I just went berserk –
kicking a chair over and screaming about the fucking idiots in
the DTI who'd given us bad advice on OPEC's intentions. It had
an instant effect, Gordon looking at me with alarm, telling me to
calm down, and picking up the chair with a disapproving glare.

I went out having learned another lesson about working for
Gordon: always to be angrier than him about bad news, even if
that was sometimes near-impossible. The patrician figure in him
didn't like to see his staff ranting and swearing.

I once had to turn that act on to protect Sue Nye, Gordon's
indispensable adviser on all things political and personal. After one
comically irrational outburst from Gordon about some screw-up,
Sue followed me back to my office and we were laughing about it,
doing impressions of his reaction, when in he walked behind us.
Sue was in mid-flow and had her back to him, and would have
been rumbled for sure, but I went into full-scale rant mode, kicking
my bin over and shouting that the whole thing was a shambles.

He cut me off: 'What's wrong?' 'I'm sorry, Gordon,' I said holding
my head as if I was suffering real anguish, 'but we're just letting off
a bit of steam – you know, so many of these fuckers keep letting you
down.' Sue's face had gone white, but Gordon bought it and gently
chided us that, as the experienced people in the office, we couldn't

let the pressure get to us. If he was wondering why Sue apparently lapsed into a bad Scottish accent when angry, he didn't say so.

Screw-ups are an inevitable fact of life in any press office, especially in government, although it helped that as well as having the best events-planners, the Treasury also had the best press officers in Whitehall – long-serving class acts like Charles Keseru, Malcolm Graves, Steve Field, Simon Moyes, Shazia Ejaz, Paul Kissack, John Battersby and Alex Dawtrey. But they couldn't all be as good as that lot, and every so often, I'd discover there'd been a screw-up in someone's handling of a press call.

The worst of those was when – of all the terrible places to put out a terrible quote – the Press Association quoted a 'Treasury spokesman' in 2003 explaining that tax credits for middle-income families had been frozen because 'they don't need the money'. I got the quote withdrawn, but the *Standard* still splashed it the next morning as: 'Brown: Middle Classes "don't need the money".'

Ian Austin came into our open-plan office, face puce with rage, staring at the paper and shaking with incredulity. He looked up and said to us all: 'Why? Why? I put all this effort into persuading people that Gordon's not anti-Middle England, and then you do this!' He hurled the paper with huge force against the far wall and shouted at me: 'You're telling Gordon!'

I had many such occasions to break bad news to Gordon over the years, and I'd like to think I became about as good at it as Ed Balls, relying less on my own Incredible Hulk routine, and more on getting the timing and wording right, and – most importantly – knowing what he'd want done about it and ensuring that was already happening.

There is a Westminster myth that you'd deliver bad news to Gordon in what's described as a 'news sandwich', where you'd give him one bit of good news to improve his mood, slip in the bad news and then give him a second bit of good news to cheer him up again. This is utter bollocks. Anyone who worked for Gordon would know that would be a total waste of two pieces of good news, which he would ignore to focus only on the bad thing you'd told him.

Individual newspaper stories aside, the worst bit of news I had to break to him was that Robin Cook had died in August 2005. I'd been called by George Pascoe-Watson at *The Sun* asking if we'd heard anything, long before the news broke officially. I phoned Gordon in Scotland, told him that I had some very sad news and he should brace himself, then said: 'Robin Cook seems to have been taken ill while he was out hill-walking, and there's a strong rumour that he's died. I've got the office on the phone checking and I'm drafting a statement for you in case it is true.'

Gordon was so upset he could barely speak. He and Robin had only recently resolved their long-standing feud and become firm friends again, talking almost every day. It was central to Gordon's plans for his premiership that Robin would become his Deputy Leader or Chancellor, or be restored as Foreign Secretary, symbolising a break from the Blair years more than any other appointment could, following Robin's resignation over the Iraq War.

As the silence continued on the other end of the phone, a text came through from George saying: 'Definitely true.' I told Gordon, and said I was very sorry. It was strange to hear him use one of his catchphrases – 'How has this happened?' – not with the usual roar of anger, but with a quiet, breaking voice. He called out for Sarah and hung up the phone.

The only time that Gordon didn't get upset or angry about bad news was when he'd been the one responsible for the screw-up and couldn't find anyone to blame but himself. In those circumstances, he became reflective, sheepish and almost apologetic, as though he'd let everyone down. People who assumed he would have had several staff members summarily executed after the Mrs Duffy incident at the 2010 election don't know him at all.

On one occasion, Jon Snow trailed his *Channel 4 News* bulletin saying he'd be reporting the astounding view of a senior Treasury figure that, in a matter of years, Britain would no longer be making any cars. I went rampaging round the corridors, vowing to eviscerate the culprit with a corkscrew, before Sue Nye – hearing the commotion – drew me to one side and said: 'I think you might find Gordon sat next to Jon Snow on the plane this morning.' While he wouldn't admit his guilt, Gordon was unusually shifty about the story and said we shouldn't respond.

Much more seriously, on the eve of the 2005 Budget, Gordon screwed up in a way that almost cost him his job. Around 6 p.m., with everything quiet and settled, my phone rang and my email pinged simultaneously. Uh oh. A reporter at one of the broadsheets said he'd just emailed me a photo which had been sent in to their picture desk. It was a close-up of a sheaf of papers Gordon was carrying out of Downing Street, with a large set of numbers scrawled in black marker pen.

'We're just wondering if the numbers are Budget-related. Someone on the news desk thought the row in the middle with years next to them looked like they might be the borrowing figures for tomorrow.'

With false bravado, I told him I sincerely doubted it, but I'd ring him back once I'd looked, then waited with a knot in my stomach at the printer for the photo to emerge. I could have been sick when I saw it. There were the borrowing figures, the growth forecasts, net debt, unemployment, the bottom line of the scorecard. Every key, market-sensitive number in the Budget. Everything.

I walked down the corridor to Gordon's office thousands of times over the years, but never so slowly. When I walked in, he was doing a read-through of the speech in his meeting room with the Eds and a handful of others. He didn't stop but Ed Balls looked up at me and, seeing the expression on my face, said: 'Hold on, something's wrong.'

When I told them all and passed round the photo, the only sound in the room was gulping. Gordon looked up and said quietly: 'I'm going to have to resign. Hugh Dalton did nothing compared to this', a reference to the Labour Chancellor who'd been forced to quit for telling a journalist a minor but market-sensitive secret on his way to deliver the 1947 Budget.

'I'm serious, I'm going to have to resign,' Gordon said, with genuine shock and distress, before coming back to his normal self and remembering there might be someone else to blame. 'Blair!' he roared. 'Blair made me give him the figures. Why did I ever agree? Why has he done this to me?'

Ed Balls was sardonic as ever. 'I don't think you can really blame Tony Blair for this. But look, let's think this through. The paper asked, are those the borrowing numbers? And when was the meeting, this morning? Well, get Graham Parker round and check the figures are still right.'

Graham, the head of forecasting – currently one of the big wigs at George Osborne's independent Office of Budget Responsibility – came round, looked at the figures, rocked back and forth on his heels, gave a little wince, and said: 'If the question is: are those the exact borrowing figures in the Red Book, no they're not. But they're pretty bloody close.'

Balls told me: 'Well, it's your call.' There was no instruction to mislead the paper; I'd been given the facts, now it was up to me how to use them. I called the reporter back and did my finest ever lying-without-lying, the key being to come up with a plausible explanation for what the figures were if they weren't the borrowing numbers, and get off the phone quickly before he thought to ask about the other figures in the photo.

'Hi there,' I said. 'Sorry, it's manic here tonight, you know what it's like. I've checked the Red Book and no, those aren't tomorrow's borrowing numbers. I'm not totally sure what they are, but Gordon was at a political meeting in Downing Street, so they might well be the latest calculations of what the Tory black hole on public spending will be in the next parliament. So you could do a story speculating about that, if you still want to use the picture? No? Ah OK, well, I thought it was worth a try. OK, cheers then, talk soon.'

I knew that mentioning the mythical Tory black hole was the single easiest way to make a journalist's heart sink, but it was entirely plausible that Gordon would have obsessively worked it out while sat in a meeting. Plus the fact that I was actively encouraging him to use the photo would have allayed any suspicion that it was a problem for us.

I went back to the office and told everyone the good news. The paper wasn't going to run the photo. I got thumbs-ups and cheers from everyone except Gordon, who just looked back down at his speech and said gruffly: 'Where were we?' He'd gone from having to resign thirty minutes previously to acting as though I'd caused an unnecessary interruption.

By then, I'd got used to the fact that Gordon greeted good news with barely a smidgeon of the emotion with which he received bad news. But, even so, I didn't half walk out of the room thinking: 'Miserable git.'

Whenever I think about that evening, I feel a pang of sadness because, all alone back at my desk with no one to share the story with, I instinctively went to call Penny. She'd broken up with me the previous year but I was in denial about it, and still rang her often enough that she'd started gently hinting that I shouldn't.

I told myself: well, surely she'll want to hear this story, it's a belter. But I then had a moment of realisation that she didn't really want to hear any of these stories any more – she wasn't that interested in whether I got the splash or the page 2 lead in the *Telegraph*, and the fact that was the only thing I seemed to care about any more was the last nail in my coffin with her.

She was still at Great Ormond Street on 7 July 2005 when two of the 7/7 bombs went off nearby. I called her office non-stop in panic for what seemed like hours, until a nice, young Australian guy named Richard answered, and very kindly and gently told me that he knew how worried I must be, but everything was fine, Penny had been at work early before the bombs went off, and was now busy performing heroics in the emergency triage tent.

Penny and that lovely guy became a couple not long after that, and they now live together in Australia with their beautiful son, Dylan.

15

THE ART OF BUDGET BRIEFING

Aside from those occasional nights when the Chancellor almost had to resign and I realised I would never get back together with my ex, working on the Treasury's media in the run-up to the Budget was the best job in government.

So here's how it all worked.

The first story we always did was the date of the Budget, which was usually announced to Parliament, although on one of Gordon's trips to China we were short of a story for the final day, so did the date with the travelling press entourage, accompanied by some words from Gordon about the need for the Budget to show that Britain could respond to the global challenge. It worked a treat, although some constitutional sticklers weren't too pleased.

Next we did a scene-setter, usually a briefing to the economics editors and columnists about our priorities for the Budget and the economic and fiscal backdrop. While this was often fairly bland, it was crucial to get expectations in the right place on some of the key growth or borrowing figures, just so there were no nasty surprises on the day for the markets and no shocked headlines in the post-Budget papers. We'd brief nothing remotely specific, but we might take the most accurate of the external forecasts that were out there and gently nudge the journalist to describe that as the 'emerging market consensus'.

If that sounds a bit dodgy, the next stage of briefing the Budget was downright skulduggery. In the fortnight before the speech, you want as little speculation about the Budget as possible, to keep your powder dry for the crucial few days beforehand.

So I'd tend to leak a few stories or planned announcements from other government departments that could be guaranteed to cause a bit of distraction and keep the journalists busy for a day or two. That obviously wasn't very helpful to my Whitehall colleagues, but it's a time-honoured trick to help the successful presentation of the Budget, which was to my mind the biggest priority.

If all that activity worked successfully, it meant we would get to the weekend before the Budget without a single good story from the package having leaked and with any bad news on the fiscal side already reported and discounted ahead of the day.

That's when it became fun. From the forty to fifty ready-made stories in the Budget, we would generally decide two to three that had to be held back until the day at all costs, and a few dozen that were too complicated, boring or unpopular to do in advance. That left us with about fifteen that could be released before the day, equating to one each for the main Sunday and daily papers, if the Sundays couldn't be persuaded to go for some skulduggery instead.

There is a certain etiquette to these Budget stories. Journalists tend not to write definitively days in advance that a particular measure will happen, both because – from the Treasury's point of view – it looks a bit too 'leaky' and because – from the journalist's – it's always wise to have a get-out clause in case the scorecard changes at the last minute. So the usual form is to say, for example, that the Budget is 'expected to freeze fuel duty' or that the Chancellor is 'considering announcing a boost for first-time buyers', and so on.

Now, what do you do if some enterprising journalist calls up, either because they've had a genuine tip from elsewhere or – more likely – because they're just having a punt, and says: 'I'm thinking of writing that you're going to scrap TV licences for pensioners' and that is exactly the big headline measure that the Chancellor wants to announce with a fanfare at the end of the speech, not see wasted on one newspaper a few days out?

Well, frankly, you're back to lying-without-lying: 'Hmm, I've seen some external representations on that, so I know where this is coming from, but I would be very, very cautious if I were you.

The costs and the admin are very difficult, and frankly if it came out in advance and it looks like someone's trying to bounce us, it almost certainly won't even be floated, so you'd end up looking a bit silly. I'll keep you posted if anything changes, but if I was you, I'd steer clear of that one for now.'

Obviously that particular journalist risks ending up a bit miffed when they hear the announcement on Budget Day, so you need immediately to follow up by offering them the best of your fifteen stories as an alternative, or even a couple if you're really worried.

Before Alistair Darling's 2008 Pre-Budget Report, *The Times* thought they'd ask whether there were any plans for a temporary VAT cut and, rather than urge caution and offer an alternative as I would have done, Alistair's people stood up the story, thus pissing away the centrepiece of the whole statement, and the only good news in it, several days in advance, leading to predictably disastrous headlines on the day after the PBR.

The day before the Budget, we would do the first of our two photo-calls. This involved a snapper and a TV cameraman being invited into the Chancellor's office to get stills and film of him sitting around flicking through a copy of the final Red Book – fresh from the printers – and chatting casually with his staff, projecting an image of relaxed bonhomie for the evening news and the next day's papers.

Everything about this photo-call was a lie. The Red Book was not the Red Book, because that tends not to be printed until the early hours of Budget morning once all the last-minute score-card shenanigans are complete. What Gordon would be flicking through was last year's Red Book with the new front cover stuck on it. The people with whom Gordon would be chatting casually were often not his staff – they were usually a sample of the most attractive, diverse, smartly dressed and smiley Treasury officials that could be rounded up at the time. And the relaxed bonhomie? Well, this was Gordon the day before a Budget; anguished hostility was more like it.

I never slept the night before the Budget. There were too many press notices and web pages to read through and sign off, and a number of other overnight rituals to complete: providing a generic briefing to all the broadcasters about the main Budget themes and providing a quote along the same lines to the *Evening Standard*, which they were always able to present as their exclusive from Gordon on Budget morning.

For me personally, the other ritual for the night before was briefing Gloria De Piero – then the political editor for *GMTV*, now the Labour MP for Ashfield – with one of the big stories we'd be holding back for the day of the Budget.

I did this for several reasons: first, Gloria always said that the generic briefing I'd given to all the other broadcasters was bullshit and demanded to know how the Budget was going to affect the lives of her millions of viewers; second, I'd rapidly become great mates with Gloria and her colleagues, Clare Nasir and Katie Myler; and third, despite Gloria always having fantastic scoops on the morning of every Budget and PBR, no one ever noticed. They were all too busy watching Nick Robinson and Adam Boulton fishing in the dark on the BBC and Sky.

While the timings have changed since I was doing the job, every Budget morning started with 'sorting out the *Standard*'. They are usually in the hideous position of needing to produce an edition which will go to print while the Chancellor's making his speech, but hit the streets after he's sat down, in which they're expected to have full coverage of what he's said.

So at 6 a.m., I'd have a strictly confidential discussion with the *Evening Standard* political editor, the great Joe Murphy, to ensure he could get his pages and themes right for the first edition, and then be able quickly to update them later. I'd tell him: 'Big boost for primary schools'; 'Small boost for apprenticeships'; 'Massive Whitehall efficiency package – that's the biggest revenue-raiser'; 'Nice surprise on gambling taxes'; 'No big surprises on the other duties'; and 'Nice measure for pensioners at the end – that's the biggest expenditure'.

That conversation was also a chance for Joe to check the reliability of any other stories that had been around the previous week, to which my responses varied from 'That's fairly safe' to

'I'd be very cautious with that' to 'They're in the right territory but they've got the wrong rate'. Again, that would help Joe plan his pages, and – where I'd indicated a story was reliable – he could write it hard in his first edition and save himself a job later.

I'd also point Joe towards one phrase in the exclusive quote we'd given him from Gordon, for example 'further help for those who need it most', which – put together with the broader briefing – would allow him to write a splash headline for the first edition saying something like: 'Brown's Bonanza for OAPs'.

Having sorted the *Standard*, we'd then tackle the broadcasters. This consisted of Ed Balls in his capacity as Chief Economic Adviser (and later his successor Michael Ellam) having a similar planning conversation with Nick Robinson, Adam Boulton and anyone else who'd be doing live coverage or putting together evening bulletins, although with a little more emphasis on timing: 'He'll do about a minute on tax avoidance, and announce a few measures, then a whistle-stop through all the duties – no big surprises there.'

The final bit of legitimised leaking before the speech was called 'giving the snaps' to Reuters. Whenever Gordon was giving a speech containing important messages on the economy, I'd pull out about a dozen extracts – single lines from the speech – and give them in advance to Sumeet Desai, the suave and canny Reuters economics editor, with strict instructions that he had to wait until they were delivered before publishing them on the wire. This was vital in the good old days when the closest equivalent to Twitter was the Reuters terminal every journalist in the country had on their desks pumping out breaking news as it happened.

There was a practical reason for this: if Gordon misspoke or missed a crucial word out of a sentence, you risked the markets going haywire – even just temporarily. Similarly, if a stressed Reuters journalist was listening and typing at the same time, they could be the ones to make the mistake. There was also a presentational reason in that other journalists would often look at Reuters to see what was perceived as important in the speech, and the snaps allowed us to highlight the lines where we wanted the attention focused.

After that, it was time for the second photo-call – the departure from Downing Street with the famous red Budget box or from the Treasury on PBR days. There was rarely anything different or difficult about this, aside from telling Ten-Foot Timms to crouch a bit so he didn't tower above Gordon too much. My main function was texting or calling the dozen or so Treasury press officers and other staff at No. 11 to facilitate the departure, and telling them alternately, repeatedly: 'Stop opening the fucking door' or 'Get out of the fucking shot'.

Once Gordon was over in the House of Commons, I'd run into his office, wish him good luck, and show him the splash in the first edition of the *Standard* with a large thumbs-up and a 'Wahey!' just to boost his confidence and let him know everything was on track.

I'd then run up to the parliamentary press gallery and have the second crucial conversation with Joe Murphy, usually a frantic two-minute whisper just after Gordon had got up to speak, going through all the themes discussed previously and filling in the gaps with detailed facts. Joe would run off and make the necessary additions to his stories, fire them off to the *Standard* news desk and their presses would begin to roll.

People might wonder why we had to be so coy and secretive with the *Standard*, the broadcasters and others, but the reality is there are vast amounts of money to be made – not least in the betting markets – from any advance information on the detail of Budget announcements, and I knew it would be career death for me, if not Gordon, for any market-sensitive numbers to leak in advance.

That was brought home to me the one time we cocked things up, when – after I'd given him the facts and figures far too late – Joe hurriedly inserted them into sentences like: 'Gordon Brown is expected to ease the burden on motorists', but forgot to change the tense, so it read as though he was still speculating but knew the exact detail of what Gordon would announce. Questions were asked in the House of Commons with angry Tory MPs waving that edition of the *Standard*, demanding an explanation. They didn't get one.

After the *Standard* really cocked up at the 2013 Budget, and posted their Budget front page before George Osborne had started speaking, there was an inquiry by the Treasury into whether these pre-briefing arrangements should continue. When I read their final report, I was genuinely astonished at how lax things had become since 2007, both in terms of how early Joe and others were being given full details of the Budget, but also that my successors were now briefing the fiscal data in advance and even showing the broadcast political editors the full scorecard on Budget morning!

Anyway, once Joe was sorted, I'd go and take my appointed seat in the parliamentary press gallery. There was a genuine satisfaction in looking around the gallery as each of the fifteen pre-briefed stories were announced and getting a grateful nod from the journalist who'd written them as their Budget exclusive. Then Gordon would announce the other big stories, and those same journalists would look over and smile, as if acknowledging that – yet again – we'd managed to hold back the best stuff, and give them their headlines for the following day.

Once the speech was over, there were perhaps the most crucial forty-five minutes of the day. Everyone would ignore the Leader of the Opposition giving his response and troop outside to the large room leading to the press gallery for the post-Budget briefing. I'd stand with Ed Balls and later Michael Ellam behind the table in the centre of the room, and we'd scan the crowd to see if any especially sharp hacks had made it in, on one occasion prompting a terrified whisper of: 'Fuck me, what's Paxman doing here?'

About a hundred journalists would be standing in front of us, ripping open their Budget press packs and poring over the Budget measures table. Some would start scribbling questions in the margins of the Red Book; others would get out their calculators and work out how much extra tax they and their editors would have to pay.

Then a hush would descend, and Ed or Michael would effectively present the Budget all over again, focusing on the key facts the journalists needed to know, explaining some of the measures in more detail and summarising the overall impact of the package. They'd also flag any measures that we knew were going to prove controversial so neither the hacks nor the Tories could later claim to have 'discovered' them in the Budget small print. They'd then take dozens of questions and answer them properly – not just bat them away press-conference style – with me occasionally chipping in.

This exercise served one purpose above all: it communicated the sense – and usually the reality – that the Treasury knew exactly what it was doing, that there were no hidden horrors and that this was definitely not a Budget that was going to unravel. Not on that day at any rate.

Speaking to journalists who were present at the briefing that followed George Osborne's 2012 Omnishambles Budget, they say the exact opposite was true and any chance the Treasury had of turning the media reaction around was immediately scuppered.

After the briefing, we'd go and catch up with Gordon and tell him what the press mood was, chivvying him up for the important task of ringing round all the daily newspaper editors and senior columnists, something which – in good times – made them write even better headlines, leaders and columns, or – in bad times – made them feel guilty about sticking the boot in too hard.

I'd spend the rest of the day zipping round the press gallery mopping up any fresh questions from the political hacks or taking calls from their economics counterparts. I'd go back to the Treasury where my team of a dozen press officers – all with different areas of responsibility – would be fielding calls from specialist journalists, and I'd sit and brief all the ministers doing the rounds of evening TV news on what issues were coming up and what they should say.

Around 9 p.m., there would be a brief moment of respite. Sarah would lay on lasagne and drinks in No. 11, and Gordon's inner circle would gather to toast him on a job well done and another Budget complete, and he would work his way round the room saying his trademark phrase 'Thanks for all you do', but in a more heartfelt way than normal.

My work for the night was just beginning. I'd watch the late evening news bulletins and wait at Victoria station until midnight to check the first editions of all the papers, where necessary ringing the two or three journalists who'd got something wrong to demand changes for the second edition, or – if one paper had gone big on some obscure aspect of the Budget – fielding calls from all the others worried that they'd missed something.

I'd get home, never risk going to sleep, have a shower and change clothes, and be back in a car at 5 a.m. to meet Gordon in his flat at Great Smith Street for the morning round of interviews. I'd have all the papers piled up next to me, ordered by how much Gordon would like the headline. He'd barrel into the car and – almost by rote – say: 'The papers awful, are they?', then start flicking through them with the occasional approving 'Hmm' at each positive headline or favourable cartoon.

I'd wait until he was in just the right frame of mind, then take him through some of the problems that had emerged and what he should say about them, Gordon scribbling the lines as I talked with his black marker pen, me watching to make sure he didn't get ink all over his hands, shirt or tie. Not for nothing did his special protection officers nickname him Zorro – every plane, car and meeting room he was sat in for more than five minutes would end up criss-crossed with swipes of his pen.

We'd go across the river to do *GMTV* live in the studio, then back to Millbank to do Sky and BBC *Breakfast* just looking down a camera lens, 5 Live with Nicky Campbell, ITN, then the big setpiece interview with the *Today* programme at 8.10 a.m.: Gordon and John Humphrys or Jim Naughtie in the studio, with Nick Robinson sat alongside them. I always had to admire the professionalism it took for Nick to deliver his instant post-interview analysis – often tinged with criticism – with Gordon glowering at him across the desk, and occasionally throwing his papers or his headset down in reaction.

It didn't matter how well the *Today* interview had gone, Gordon would be in a funk afterwards, so we'd do some quick, small interviews to get his head back in the game, one of which would always be with Sumeet from Reuters, an incredibly important journalist for us who also became a good friend.

Even after the demise of Reuters TV, I'd still tell Sumeet to turn up with a camera so we could make the interview look official to Gordon, even if it would only appear as a wire story. More often than not, I'd end up holding the camera. This might have looked odd to other journalists in the building – the Treasury's Head of Communications pointing a camera that clearly wasn't rolling at the Chancellor – but Gordon himself never seemed to notice.

By 9 a.m., we'd be done. We'd head back to the Treasury, I'd sit at my desk and breathe. It was the end of at least two months of intense pressure and – for me – a 48-hour period with no sleep, no let-up and no room for error. Briefing the Budget may be the best job in government, but it's bloody hard work.

16

INTERVIEWS: THE GOOD, THE BAD AND THE UGLY

There's one problem with having the remarkable political longev-ity of someone like Gordon Brown: everything changed around him but he never did. Or maybe he never could.

Gordon grew up at a time when political interviews were an invitation for a minister to summarise the speech they'd just made for the benefit of those who hadn't heard it. He came into politics at a time when ministers or prime ministers facing even slightly awkward questioning could either just walk off the set or berate perfectly polite members of the public.

He spent his years shadowing Tory Treasury ministers leap-ing on their every slip in interviews at a time when they could and did routinely move markets by saying ill-judged things about Britain's currency, exchange rates and so on.

So when he came to government in 1997, Gordon determined to re-invent the political interview. Just not in the way any broad-caster or sane member of the public would be interested in. He determined to prove that it was possible to do political inter-views on the economy year-in, year-out without ever moving the markets and without ever screwing up. He would go on with one mantra and repeat it like a stuck record, side-stepping all possible traps and diversions.

Even on *GMTV*, the ultimate opportunity to speak directly to millions of uncommitted voters, Fiona Phillips used to complain to me that Gordon would sit down on the sofa during the ad break as personal and engaging as he always was in private, but as soon as they went live, his Easter Island game face would be on and he'd be back to drilling out a prepared message.

This got worse before it ever got better, because the more established his reputation became for dead-batting all interview questions and continually contriving a way back to his main message, the more interviewers genuinely did try to wrong-foot him or catch him out. Gordon's reaction wasn't just to keep avoiding those traps, but to start seeing traps that weren't there.

This became Gordon's equivalent of Ed Balls's stammer: an inability to answer questions fluently and naturally because he was thinking too much about the words coming out of his mouth and whether they were going to trip him up.

And whereas Ed eventually realised that the only way he could give a good interview was to relax and not over-think what he was going to say, Gordon could never instinctively allow himself to let go in that way; his default settings were diversionary tactics over direct answers and obfuscation above honesty; to maintain his innate discipline rather than reveal his natural charm.

And that is the paradox: that stubborn commitment to caution may have helped Gordon to become the longest-serving Chancellor for centuries, but it also contributed to him becoming one of the shortest-serving prime ministers. It always made me think of a great defensive boxer who would win plaudits for going ten rounds without a scratch. But if he actually wanted to win the fight, surely he had to lower his guard at some stage and go on the offensive.

What was so frustrating was that when he was good, he could be exceptionally good, but for the most part his interviews will be remembered as bad, and occasionally downright ugly.

That said, the best ones in my time were superb: all what I'd call long-form interviews, where the journalist or broadcaster was able to spend a whole day or a weekend with him, talking informally as well as on the record, seeing him interact with other people and building up a proper picture of him as a man, and then writing or piecing together a broadcast package or newspaper feature on the whole thing. The key for me was getting Gordon to a point where he forgot there was a camera or tape recorder there, and just engaged with the individual talking to him.

Gordon did excellent 'day in the life' pieces for Sky, with Kay Burley and Julie Etchingham, both searching but empathetic interviewers, capable of extracting his funny and emotional sides. Bel Mooney did the equivalent in print for *The Times*, and there were many others in my time who produced brilliantly insightful profiles in that form for TV or newspapers – Martha Kearney, Suzie Mackenzie and the *Mirror*'s Julie McCaffrey to name a few.

They all obviously have something in common, and it's undoubtedly true that Gordon found it easier to open up and relax with female interviewers. Or maybe they just knew better than most of their male counterparts how to put him at ease.

That said, the best three interviews I ever heard Gordon do were with men: a scintillating discussion in his North Queensferry dining room with *The Guardian*'s Ian Jack about his upbringing; forty-five compelling minutes talking about the world economy in the blacked-out studio of the American *Charlie Rose* show; and, best of all, an extended guest appearance with Eamonn Holmes on 5 Live drifting naturally and easily across various topics, both sporting and political.

Eamonn stopped at one point and asked him in all seriousness why he didn't sound like this in all his interviews. It was the only time Gordon tensed up, imagined a trap and reverted to his usual guarded self, including some forced bonhomie: 'Well, maybe you should invite me on more often.'

I thought it was a desperately sad moment, and a reckless part of me wished he'd just seized the opportunity to tell the truth: 'Do you know why, Eamonn? 'Cos I think you're an OK guy, and I think the rest of them are bastards out to get me and maybe I'm wrong about that.'

Now you might well ask, if those long-form interviews worked so well, why didn't we do more of them or, indeed, why wasn't that all we did? The reality is we did as many as we could fit in for each paper and broadcaster, and – for someone like Gordon, who instinctively regarded the demands of the media as wasteful drains on his time and energy – it was always a massive commitment.

Worst of all, those profile pieces didn't always go to plan. One journalist accompanied us on a visit to do a day-in-the-life feature on Gordon and get reactions from the people he met, before doing a formal interview. In reality, he spent most of the day getting reactions from local barmen, and turned up for the interview totally smashed, with no material for his feature at all.

Gordon sensed something was awry when the journalist took a very detailed interest in his diet, and – when I politely asked him to get to the questions – announced that he didn't want to do a normal interview, but was much more interested in having a chat and getting to know the real man, hence his interest in what he'd eaten so far that day.

Gordon, who still had a speech to make that night, gave me his most volcanic look and asked me quite openly: 'What the hell is this about? What's wrong with this bloody guy?' I gave the 'bloody guy' a last chance, going so far as to remind him which questions we'd agreed in advance might be fruitful – that is, the ones for which Gordon had a fairly decent story prepared. But the journo was too far gone. He said: 'I don't want to do all that boring shit. Come on, Gordon, why don't you lighten up for a change?'

That did it. Gordon reared back out of his chair and stormed out of the room, only stopping to tell me that this was bullshit, it was all my fault and I should bloody fix it. And I did, but not in a way sticklers for press freedom might welcome. I wrote the journalist about 600 words of colour from the day, balanced and factual enough that he could stick it straight in the paper, and then provided a dozen paragraphs of quotes in Gordon's name, including the story we'd prepared and a smattering of personal stuff about dietary habits, which he could present as his in-depth interview.

It splashed the paper with a good feature inside. It looked perfectly kosher and there were only three people who knew the reality, although strangely, when Gordon read it, he observed without irony that the journalist had actually done a pretty good job, and we should do more stuff with him.

If that interview could be filed under 'bad', at least it was mostly the journalist's fault. Usually, it was all Gordon's doing and, more often than not, I'd have to provide those 'dozen paragraphs of quotes' after an interview to make up for the fact that Gordon hadn't said anything interesting or newsworthy himself.

One of his even worse habits in newspaper interviews – if he knew the journalist fairly well himself – would be to start very obviously reading out my prepared script for our agreed story, and then – to my horror and the journalist's embarrassment – just hand over the briefing note, and say: 'There you go, all the quotes are there.'

Professional pride would dictate that they'd carry on asking him questions, but he'd start looking increasingly bored and frustrated at the waste of time, and say: 'You've got it all there; that's all you need.' Journalists with heaps of goodwill towards Gordon would come away from an experience like that feeling genuinely hurt and a little offended.

The broadcast equivalent of those 'bad' interviews would come when, for example, the *Today* programme would decide that they really couldn't be bothered just giving Gordon a fifteen-minute platform to recite his mantra for the day about the importance of skills or reform of the Common Agricultural Policy, so would do two questions on that and then change the topic to something completely different.

If Gordon was face to face in the studio, he might just about behave himself when that happened, but if he was doing the interview down the line – in a radio car on a visit, in a sound booth at Millbank or in our little interview room at the Treasury – he would begin miming acts of extreme violence in my direction, while giving the most desultory answers possible or, even worse, protesting about the line of questioning and bemoaning the BBC's failure to focus on important issues.

When those interviews would end, Gordon would wait until a producer's voice had appeared in his headset saying: 'That's it. Thank you, Mr Brown', and then unleash a tremendous volley of abuse, usually just a stream of unconnected swear words. I'm convinced he didn't care that the BBC were still recording at the other end; he wanted them to hear what he thought of their interview. I've always fantasised that someone at the BBC has kept all those clips and carefully spliced them together to play *Cinema Paradiso*-style at John Humphrys's retirement party.

If those interviews were bad, I always consoled myself that it could be worse. I still shudder when I think about the real car-crashes and near-misses.

We were never far away from a Demolition Derby when Gordon had to do rounds of interviews in the Treasury or at No. 10, on foreign trips and at party conference; one broad-cast political editor after another coming into the seat opposite Gordon and giving him a ten-minute grilling. He wasn't particu-larly fond of any of them, and felt downright hostile towards the big three – the BBC's Nick Robinson, Sky's Adam Boulton and ITN's Tom Bradby.

If we could have avoided ever doing these rounds, I would've done, but it went with the job. Once Gordon had set foot in the room, I took up two key positions: standing in front of him when he was having his make-up adjusted so the cameras couldn't film him being powdered and coiffed; and then standing in a fixed position just behind the camera where he could look at me in case I needed to mime the smoothing of his hair or give him a thumbs-up after particular answers.

On a bad day, when each political editor had finished, Gordon would by and large have the same instinct as at the end of those radio interviews – wanting to scream a string of foul-mouthed abuse, this time in their faces – so when he looked at me, I'd purse my lips and jerk up an admonishing finger like a particularly stern librarian, and say calmly: 'Gordon, can I grab you for a moment before the next one – I just need you to sign something', then take him into whatever ante-room we had set up.

As soon as I did, he'd draw his breath to begin a tirade, but I'd shush him again and whisper: 'It was fine, it was good, you dealt with it well, it's all OK. And, I know, he's a bastard, he's a Tory, he can fuck off the next time he asks us for a favour, but let's just do the next one and get through it.' The same routine, every single interview, every single time. I was gone by the time of the 2009 party conference when he let his fury show on camera after an interview with Adam Boulton, but I did think about the other 300 times where that *nearly* happened.

Actual car-crashes in broadcast interviews were fairly rare with Gordon, although the one that's lodged in my memory was during a morning round of interviews at Millbank in 2008, when the first question Nicky Campbell on 5 Live asked him was the apparently innocuous: 'What was the first thing on your mind when you woke up this morning?'

Gordon could've told the truth, which is that his radio alarm went off every morning at 5.30 a.m. tuned into *Wake Up to Money* on 5 Live, so he would have been thinking about whatever they were talking about. One of the biggest irritations of my job was Gordon calling at 5.30 a.m. to say, for example: 'ALL they're talking about on the radio is Equitable Life! Why haven't we got anyone up?'

I'd politely explain that was because he was listening to a programme designed for bankers, and I could in theory ring Ruth Kelly and tell her to get on the phone to the studio, but it might not go down too well. It could have been worse – I dread to think what calls I'd have got if he woke up listening to *Farming Today*.

If Gordon wasn't going to tell the truth to Nicky Campbell about what he woke up thinking about, he could at least have said some other bland nonsense, like what to fix the kids for breakfast, or whether the Boston Red Sox had won overnight.

Anything, but not – oh please God, no – 'Well, to be honest, I woke up thinking about people's household bills, and mortgage payments, and what we can do to help people at this time.' Nicky couldn't believe his luck and took the piss for about five minutes. It was the worst combination of Gordon coming across like he didn't live in the real world, but also as a bit instinctively duplicitous. He knew he'd screwed up and he couldn't focus for the rest of the interview knowing it.

When he came out, he was furious at himself – and obviously at Nicky Campbell and all the Tories who run the BBC – and we had to find a quiet corner of Millbank just so he could punch his palm, sound off a bit and gradually calm down.

But if that was bad, nothing I saw would ever compare to his interview right at the end of his visit to the 2008 Beijing Olympics with the two Sunday journalists who had paid to accompany us on the trip, and thereby subsidised our own flights – Simon Walters from the *Mail on Sunday* and Jamie Lyons from the *News of the World*.

Gordon was in a grumpy mood about having to do the interview ('Jeez, haven't I done enough now?'), and he was upset and distracted by his youngest boy Fraser struggling with a bad cough. But I told him we had to do it because these guys needed to file something for the weekend, and I'd drafted him a nice, easy briefing about how he'd been thrilled by the medal-winning achievements of the British team and he would take that spirit back to his own battles in Britain.

It was innocuous stuff, but perfect for a pair of Sunday papers wanting to throw forward to the conference season and report that Brown was feeling relaxed, upbeat and inspired. Gordon just handed it back to me as we were going in and said: 'I'm not doing this shit. I'm not doing domestic stuff.' Right or wrong, it was no way to go into an interview.

Gordon proceeded to give a performance veering from surly and arrogant to aggressive and offensive, with the redoubtable Simon responding: 'Mr Brown, I've interviewed four prime ministers in my career and this is the rudest behaviour I've ever seen.' There were a few points when I felt compelled to step in, but part of me knew that Simon and Jamie would already be planning to write up the way Gordon had behaved, so any intervention from me would just become part of that story.

The low point was when Gordon looked at the two reporters and said: 'I've given you my time – that's special time – I've been very good to you. You're very fortunate to have this kind of time with me.' I'd never heard Gordon say anything like that to anyone. There wasn't a single strand of arrogance in him – no sense at all of his status – so I was astonished.

When we walked out of the room, Gordon exploded at me for making him do the interviews, and for once I wasn't faking it when I immediately went more berserk than him: 'Oh fuck off!' I shouted back. 'That was ridiculous. There was absolutely no need for it. What the fuck were you thinking? Now I've got to go back in there and try and fix that to stop YOU getting shafted.'

What made me genuinely angry was that – to be frank – I was feeling knackered too, I'd worked my arse off that entire trip, we were nearly at the end, and all I'd asked of him was to be professional, finish the last media job for the trip and do it well. But not only could he not be bothered to do that; he'd caused a massive problem in the process.

When I went back into Simon and Jamie, I think it was the only time when I worked for Gordon that I was actively disloyal to him. They told me they'd have to report his behaviour. In response, I could have promised them every single story I had in reserve for special occasions, delving not into my back pocket but into my black book, but I didn't even bother trying. I just thought: it serves him right.

17

DIRTY HANDS

There are a series of notable firsts when you work as a spin-doctor: the first time you screw up; the first time you deliberately get a front-page splash; your first miracle save to stop a shit story coming out; and, unless you're a very pure soul, the first time you get your hands dirty doing a story you probably shouldn't.

And I'd make a distinction here between dirty and dodgy. Dodgy stories just came with the job. For example, occasionally a very senior figure from HM Revenue and Customs would saunter up to my desk, and say that they'd find it helpful if the *FT* or one of the other broadsheets were to run a story about their intention to close a new tax avoidance scheme which a particular phone company or supermarket was using, just to deter other companies from following suit.

They'd tell me how the scheme worked, and how much revenue was at risk, but then always say: 'Obviously I can't tell you the name of the company because that would breach taxpayer confidentiality.' There would be a pause, then an afterthought: 'Oh by the way, what make of phone is that you're using?' or 'Where do you shop yourself?' I'd say four or five preferences for each, after one of which they'd say: 'Oh they're very good; very efficient, those chaps.' So I'd have the name of the company without them actually telling me, and I'd usually do the same routine when calling a journalist with the story.

Dodgy but not dirty. When I did my first proper dirty story, I could tell the difference. And I didn't just get a bit of mud under the fingernails, I went elbow deep in the drain.

John Major's former press adviser Howell James had been brought back to Downing Street in the role of Director of Government Communications in summer 2004 to try and restore some sense of 'doing things the right way' in the wake of Alastair Campbell's departure and the Hutton Inquiry.

One of his early acts that September was to convene a two-day meeting of departmental heads of communication at the civil service training college in Sunningdale. The first morning and afternoon were impossibly dull, and I spent most of them planning how to escape the following day, giving my PA back at the Treasury, Dawn Goring, a series of messages to send the organisers overnight which would require me to return to London.

However, in the evening, Howell ill-advisedly opened the floor for a frank exchange of views on where the government was going wrong with its communications efforts, and how No. 10 needed to change. Within thirty seconds, it was clear this was going to be dynamite, as one speaker after another laid into the No. 10 operation.

I started surreptitiously taking an aide-memoire: who was speaking and any killer quotes. At the end of the hour, I knew I had a huge story on my hands. I'd like to say that I then wrestled with my conscience and thought about the breach of colleagues' trust, the careers I was going to affect and the damage I was going to do to the government as a whole. But, I didn't think any of that. I just thought this was a story one of the Sunday newspapers would kill for, and it would be the making of my relationship with them.

The next morning, the 'urgent' messages from the Treasury recalling me to London were passed on, I said my goodbyes and made my way straight to Ascot, where I'd arranged to meet some mates for a day's races. After a few drinks, I cold-called David 'Crackers' Cracknell, political editor of the *Sunday Times*, and asked him if he wanted a story. He couldn't believe his luck.

That weekend, the Sunday of Labour Party Conference, the paper's splash was 'Blair spin gurus savage No. 10', 'leaked minutes' from the meeting revealing that it was the PM's closest Cabinet colleagues whose heads of communication had been the most critical. And sure enough, that one story – the first Crackers and I had done together – led to a long and productive working arrangement between us, exactly what I'd been after.

At no stage did I consult anyone else about what I was up to, or really think through what the implications would be. Given there were so many people at the Sunningdale meeting, I naively thought it was unlikely I'd be a suspect and, even if I was, I reasoned that – if the only other person who knew I was responsible was Crackers – no one would be able to prove anything. That was soon put to the test, as the Cabinet Office launched an urgent leak inquiry, not the kind of formality led by civil servants, but a proper investigation led by retired Special Branch officers.

I soon discovered that everyone in government believed I was responsible. Not only was I a suspect, I was the only suspect. Gordon said nothing to me about it, but Ian Austin made clear that I was on my own, saying: 'Mate, if you've done this, and they can prove you've done it, then there's nothing we can do for you.' All I kept thinking was: remember the fire at Peterhouse – avoidance, obfuscation, diversion – you can get through this.

I ended up having three interview sessions, each lasting more than three hours, with the ex-Special Branch officers: two older gents who made clear that they'd done this kind of thing hundreds of times with proper hardened criminals, and they always got to the truth in the end.

I put on a big nervous act in the first session, eventually saying that I had to come clean and hoped I wouldn't be in too much trouble, but … I'd actually gone to Ascot races on the second day, not back to London. They already knew that, having traced my phone records, but it still seemed to throw them that having my illicit jolly discovered was my main concern.

I also volunteered that I'd spoken to Crackers before they could confront me with the fact, saying I spoke to all the Sunday political editors routinely every Friday. And I kept returning to my 'theory' that it was odd that the Head of Communications from the Department for Work and Pensions, who'd been very outspoken in the meeting, was not one of those quoted in the story. That was largely because he'd been very outspoken slagging off Gordon Brown, but the coppers weren't to know that.

Over the course of the nine hours, going over and over the

same questions, they waited for a slip or a contradiction, but I gave them nothing. Eventually, right at the end, one of them said: 'What would you say if I was to tell you that I don't believe you, and I think you've been telling us lies?' 'If you said that,' I responded with bewilderment, 'I'd be outraged, because I'd think: "Why have I wasted all this time trying to help these officers if that's the attitude they're going to take?"'

And that was it. There was no formal report published, but I was told the conclusion passed to Gus O'Donnell and the Cabinet Secretary, Sir Andrew Turnbull, was that I was almost certainly guilty, but they couldn't prove it.

Gordon only spoke to me about the whole affair once, gruffly asking: 'Is all that business over with?', then giving me a long, baleful look, not the only time I saw that particular expression, his equivalent of saying: 'Don't push your luck.' But he added an unnerving rider on this occasion: 'They're out for you now. Blair keeps going on about you. They're into your phone records, so watch who you're talking to.'

Some people will undoubtedly wonder why – if Gordon knew I was guilty of misbehaviour on that and future occasions – he never either formally reined me in or had me moved on. And my answer to that is simply that there was something unspoken between us. Not what people imagine, that he would mutter under his breath about turbulent priests and hope that I would do his bidding, but the opposite.

The unspoken word was from me to him, and said: 'Don't question my methods.' I offered him the best press he could hope for, unrivalled intelligence about what was going on in the media and access to parts of the right-wing press that no other Labour politician could reach. And my attack operations against his Labour rivals and Tory enemies were usually both effective and feared, with me willingly taking all the potential risk and blame.

What I expected in return was simply to have the freedom to take the necessary steps to cultivate those media relationships, whatever that entailed: whether it was forcing Gordon to do the occasional interview he didn't want to, or disappearing to the pub with contacts for half the week, or – on occasion – leaking a good story from another department, not one that would cause them a problem, but just not released at a time of their choosing.

The closest Gordon and I ever came to having this out was in 2007 when John Reid, then Home Secretary – who'd announced he would stand down when Tony Blair left office – was furious that a plan to import Northern Irish-style anti-terror laws onto the UK mainland had been leaked prematurely to the *Sunday Times*. Blair was also angry and they were openly blaming me, not least because my old friend Crackers had written the splash.

Gordon came off the phone after a dressing-down from Tony and John, and said to me, exasperated: 'Why do you do this stuff? Reid's leaving. What's the bloody point?' I just shrugged my shoulders, as I always did, but I was furious at the inquisition and stormed out of the room, thinking: 'Do you know what the *Sunday Times* splash would've been this weekend if they hadn't had that instead? No? Well don't tell me what I need to do and what I don't.'

But if there was another reason Gordon didn't remove me from my position or put me on a shorter leash, it's that – as I showed week after week – I knew how to splash papers and get our briefing to the top of the *Today* programme.

And for perhaps the two dozen memorable occasions when I did that through a black ops manoeuvre or by busting another department's announcement, there were literally hundreds of other occasions when I did it just by getting a mainstream, positive story about the government and about Gordon to the top of the news list; and conversely, hundreds of occasions when I stopped negative stories about the government and Gordon getting in the papers.

Gordon almost certainly looks back and wishes he'd dealt with me earlier, or before it was too late, but at what point, in what week, was he ever supposed to have given up everything else I offered him for the sake of quelling the occasional problems I caused him? That's why he never did.

As for me, with the benefit of hindsight and some greater experience, I never would have done the 'spin summit' story. Not only was it incredibly reckless, but it was a downright shitty thing to do to a few colleagues who'd done nothing more than speak their minds honestly and openly, and – even if it was a bad story for the Blair mob – it didn't do Gordon any favours either, once people worked out who was responsible.

Knowing everything I know now, if I was back in that room in Sunningdale again today, I wouldn't be the one taking notes; I'd be the one intervening at the outset – as someone more experienced should surely have done back in 2004 – to say: 'Do you know what, everyone? I think this is a really bad idea. I don't think we know each other well enough for this level of honesty.'

18

SECURITY

I almost became a spy. Seriously.

After I was accepted onto the Fast Stream, I received a letter a couple of weeks later – with no heading, address or signatory – inviting me to attend a further assessment and selection process, this time at a country retreat, for specialist work within the government, in advance of which I was told to complete and return a twenty-page questionnaire with details of my family and financial history. The letter ended by instructing me not to discuss this invitation with anyone else.

I checked with a friend at the Foreign Office, who confirmed that this sounded like it was from the secret services, and – given the Canary Wharf bomb had recently gone off – he concluded that 'it's probably 'cos they need more Paddies', but then admonished me that if the letter said I shouldn't discuss it with anyone, that included him.

Paying that no heed, I headed down to London that night for a friend's birthday and I took along the questionnaire to show my mates the kind of thing I was being asked, discuss which of them should be my personal referees and generally boast that I was going to be the next James Bond, or – after I'd had a few pints of Guinness – the next David Neligan, if you know your 1920s Irish history. It was a long night on the town and, almost inevitably, I woke up in the morning minus one questionnaire.

I rang the number on the cover letter for anyone unable to attend the centre on the given dates, and explained – to silence at the other end – that I had spilled ink on the questionnaire and needed a replacement. A clipped female voice said: 'Just fill it in as best you can.' 'Ah, but I've thrown it away now.' 'Well, you shouldn't have done that,' she replied. 'We can't offer you a replacement.' She hung up. If the intention was to assess whether I was spy material, they and I both found out in a hurry.

I saw the same form seven years later for the process of 'developed vetting', the screening that every civil servant or special adviser who is going to have access to 'Top Secret' material must undergo. Until I had received my DV status, briefing sessions with Gordon would routinely be broken up by Mark Bowman or another senior official saying: 'Damian, you need to go out for a bit', usually when they'd be presenting some top-secret intelligence.

We spy on other countries to gather some of that intelligence because they are all routinely spying on us. Everyone is at it. Not that anyone obeyed the rule, but we were always told very seriously not to use mobiles in Downing Street because the Chinese and Russians were routinely intercepting conversations, and – God knows how – using live mobile phones inside No. 10 and No. 11 to hack into nearby computers.

On overseas trips and foreign summits, we were routinely issued with new mobile phones for the trip and instructed not to switch on our existing phones and BlackBerrys on the grounds that all phones would be hacked into by various security agencies during the trip. We were also told – especially when visiting China – that we should assume that our hotel rooms and anything we left in them would be searched as a matter of routine by security agents whenever we were out.

One night in Shanghai, at a launch party for Richard Branson's new Virgin airline service to the city, our small gaggle of mostly male Downing Street staff and accompanying journalists found ourselves accosted on one side by a beautiful posse of Chinese girls and on the other side by an equivalent group of Russian blondes. Even before our resident security expert could warn us that their interest was not to be taken at face value, we looked up and saw one of our number disappearing up the stairs to the exit with one of the girls, beaming back at us and doing the 'Chelsea Dagger' dance as though he'd won the lottery.

Needless to say, he woke up in the morning minus his BlackBerry and half the contents of his briefcase, and with a very bad head from the Mickey Finn nightcap she'd apparently fixed him once they'd got back to his room. When that story emerged in the *Sunday Times*, it wasn't my doing, but I helped the journalist get the details of what happened correct, in return for which he agreed not to name the individual concerned. That spared a few blushes, although it didn't go down too well with the other male Downing Street aides on the trip, all forced to deny to their other halves that they were the unnamed guilty party.

Given the prevalence of spying, honey-traps and blackmail operations, it's understandable that the security services put so much emphasis on the vetting process, which – above anything else – is designed to test whether each individual is reliable when it comes to being told top-secret information. If your vulnerability hasn't been thoroughly checked out, you remain the potential loose brick in the wall.

As well as filling in the enormous form on background details, including everything from bank account details to my maternal grandmother's maiden name, I had to supply a handful of potential referees, at least one of which would be interviewed either before or after I'd been seen to check whether I'd answered truthfully. I was then asked who I wanted to do my interview: the choice was described as 'a kindly spinster aunt-type who'll wish you'd settle down and get married or a retired sergeant-major type who'll think you're a poof'. I went for the spinster aunt.

When we sat down together, she looked over her half-rim glasses and said these chilling words: 'Now I've done hundreds of these interviews and this is your first one. My only task is to decide whether you can be trusted to tell the truth, so your only task here is to answer my questions honestly. If you do not, I won't give any indication, but I will write on your form that I cannot recommend you for clearance.'

With that jagged shard in my throat, we began. She started by skipping fairly quickly through the main 'risk' areas: sex and relationships; family and friends; booze and drugs; gambling and money. Based on my answers, she decided what to hone in on, which in my case was sex, family and booze. The next three hours were by turns excruciating and exhausting.

The first focus was on my sexual history and, in probably the worst five minutes of my life, this kindly spinster aunt listed every deviant sexual practice you can think of and asked if I'd ever engaged in them. My answers went something like: 'No... No... No... Erm, no... No... Yes, but only once... No... No... No... Erm, I don't even know what that is. Oh, bloody hell – of course not...'

She then moved onto my partners, testing whether I would be susceptible to honey-traps or liable to bring strangers into my home, and where the risks lay of previous partners suddenly re-entering my life now I'd got this new job. We went through every bit of that history, from long-term relationships to one-night stands: names, locations, details and current status.

Because you have no way of knowing what information the interviewer already holds on you, there is no real option to hide something. You end up telling them everything. The only way that a senior individual could avoid disclosing details of an embarrassing affair is to avoid going through the vetting process full stop.

It was a great relief when she moved onto family, but I realised then that all the background checks had kicked up some concerns. 'Would you describe your father as an Irish nationalist?', 'What about his family?', 'How often do you travel to Donegal?', 'Do you meet your cousins there?', 'Have any of your cousins ever spoken to you about Irish nationalism?' I knew what specifically she was driving at, and – rather than have it crushed out of me – I told her up front exactly what I knew about my dad's cousin who'd served time for IRA-related offences.

After all that, booze was easy. Unlike a doctor, she couldn't care less how much I drank but just wanted to know where I drank, how loudly I talked, whether I took any papers from the office with me, whether I ever lost things and, most of all, could I remember how I behaved when actually drunk. My answers wouldn't have been totally reassuring but they were honest, and

– crucially – they were consistent with those my friend Anthony Glackin gave when she asked him afterwards.

And that was it. She thanked me, I went away and two weeks' later I was told I'd been cleared. I could now be told the secrets that I always had to leave the room for, the first of which concerned the then secret US Terrorist Finance Tracking Programme.

In all the controversy in June 2013 over the US security services accessing people's social media interactions through the PRISM system, it's often forgotten that they had since 9/11 been accessing details of most of our financial transactions through the Society for Worldwide Interbank Financial Telecommunication system (SWIFT).

Clearly that was an invaluable source of intelligence when trying to trace suspects, or identify suspicious money transfers that might indicate a terror plot was being financed, and the British security services were among the beneficiaries of that information when it came to stopping plots in this country. But it also raised uncomfortable issues around America's potential access to the private finances and spending records of prominent politicians and businesspeople around the world.

All that made this a difficult secret for Gordon and the Treasury to be sitting on, even more so when Mervyn King, the Bank of England Governor, was informed. Things came to a head in the Boca Raton holiday and retirement resort in Florida, where the Americans had chosen to host the G7 finance ministers' and bank governors' meeting in February 2004.

Election year in America means every summit or conference hosted by the federal government takes place in a battleground state, no matter how inopportune the venue. It was certainly the oddest summit I ever attended. Finance ministers had to pick their way around the sunbeds surrounding the pool to get from the conference room to the press centre, and the meetings themselves were regularly interrupted by elderly men in bathing costumes looking for the toilet.

Back in the UK, the Hutton Inquiry into David Kelly's suicide had just reported, and – in the acrimony that followed – there was much soul-searching in the UK media about the cost of standing shoulder to shoulder with the Americans in the 'War on Terror'. At that precise moment, Mervyn's conscience told him that he had a duty to blow the gaff on the SWIFT deal, and tell the British people that the CIA had – with the Treasury's connivance – been secretly accessing that financial data.

It's not hard to imagine – in the post-Hutton atmosphere – the damage this could have done to the Labour government, and particularly to Gordon, who'd up to that point largely resisted being tainted with the shitty stick that was the Bush administration.

When Mervyn announced his intentions in a small meeting room in Boca Raton, Gordon quietly told everyone else to leave, aside from the SWIFT expert, Mark Bowman. As Mervyn's aides hesitated, Gordon suggested rather more firmly that we should all 'get out', and Mark led us into the corridor. As he was ushered out, one of Mervyn's aides said pleadingly: 'But I need to hear this.' 'Don't worry,' Mark said laconically, closing the door on us all. 'I think you're about to.'

For the next five minutes, Gordon unleashed a volcanic tirade at Mervyn, very properly saying that he'd be putting Britain's counter-terror operations at threat if he went public about SWIFT and that it would do huge damage to our relationship with America, but adding – perhaps rather harshly – that Mervyn was talking 'fucking bullshit' when he said he had a duty to speak out and that it was his 'fucking ego' dictating his position, not his duty to the country.

However rudely Mervyn felt he was treated – and he enjoyed some cold revenge in his future Mansion House speeches and economic forecasts – there is no question Gordon was right and, as a result of his intervention, the SWIFT deal remained a secret for another two years, until it was exposed by the *New York Times*, and safeguards and formal treaties were put in place governing its use.

Despite the angry confrontation with Mervyn, or very possibly because of it, I'd rarely seen Gordon in such a chipper mood as at the end of that Florida summit. We had time to kill before our flight home and Gordon asked the driver to take us somewhere lively for a drink. American drivers don't do half-measures. If the man wants lively, he'll get lively. He drove us to a resort on the Florida coast and dropped us at the top of a road leading down to a strip of bars on the promenade.

It happened I was on the phone to Ian Austin in London at the time, who said the papers were full of debate about what the outcome of the Hutton report meant for Blair, and inevitably for Brown. Ian had just got to his usual lecture about the need to be disciplined and avoid any controversial press coverage as we turned the corner onto the promenade, and saw what appeared to be an advance guard for the upcoming spring break holiday.

Ian could suddenly hear in the background the crashing of glasses and bottles, the roars and whoops of several parties in full swing in every bar, and a large number of American men vociferously suggesting that the equally large number of American women remove articles of clothing, even though they didn't look like they had much more to remove.

Hearing all this, Ian gently inquired: 'Erm, Damian, where are you?' 'Ah, at a beach resort. We've just got here, but it looks like there's some kind of student party going on.' More crashing glasses. More whooping and hollering. A chant of 'TITS! TITS! TITS!' 'Right,' Ian said patiently. 'And I presume Gordon's not there.' 'Err, yeah, he is, he's trying to get served.' 'Right, right...' Ian said, mustering all his patience. 'Well, can I possibly suggest you get out of there reasonably quickly – like, maybe right bloody now.'

We walked down the promenade and found a quieter bar, where Gordon happily held court, telling stories and drinking a beer. On the bus back to the airport, he sat looking out of the window singing 'The Girl from Ipanema' to himself, and I don't think I'd ever known him more content.

19

THE WASHINGTONIAN

Gordon may have been happy in Florida, but he was always at his most relaxed when spending a week in Washington. If you've never been there, it is an intoxicating city: full of life, but rich in history; burnt-out apartments still left from the 1968 riots a stone's throw away from the plushest ambassadorial residences.

Before I ever became a civil servant, I spent the happiest summer of my life as an intern in Washington, working in the office of Congressman Thomas C. Sawyer, a Democrat from Ohio. His staff told me that he always went on the ballot as 'Tom Sawyer', and could usually count on about 10 per cent extra votes because people recognised the name from somewhere.

I became a minor star in their eyes after somehow ending up in the front row of the Washington Mall Independence Day concert in 1995. I say 'somehow'; I was in fact very drunk, after taking a case of twenty-four beers and – having failed to find any of my fellow British interns or new American mates – drinking them all myself.

So when a rope was lifted and a large group of children charged to get to the front, I simply ran along with them. That was fine until the 'Star-Spangled Banner' and 'America the Beautiful' were played. Twice, on national TV, the camera panned down the front row to see the angelic children sweetly singing, hands on their hearts, and me in my Ireland football shirt simultaneously slurring and miming the words.

That summer was the height of the Newt Gingrich revolution, with Republicans in the ascendancy and Bill Clinton's re-election at that point looking doubtful. Of course, things turned around for him, and I'd like to think I played my part. One day, when travelling at speed round the cavernous tunnels under the Capitol

Hill complex, I whizzed round the corner and knocked Senator Bob Dole flat on his back, the man who would end up losing to Clinton in 1996. I say he never recovered.

One thing I learned in Tom Sawyer's office was the astonishing amount of effort put into each letter from a constituent. The response had to be as personal and empathetic as possible, impeccably researched, guaranteed to win the vote not just of that constituent but all his friends and family. That never left me, and I was amazed when I saw how casual the approach was in Whitehall and Westminster: hundreds of form letters churned out each week without any personalisation.

My next visit to Washington was my first with Gordon. Early in his time as Chancellor, he'd assumed the presidency of the International Monetary and Financial Committee, the key decision-making body for members of the IMF's executive board. While the presidency was in theory meant to rotate between the finance ministers from different countries, Gordon simply assumed the chair's position at every meeting from that point on and used the authority it gave him to steer the IMF round to his agenda.

It also allowed him to spend a full week out there twice a year having preparatory meetings before the spring and autumn summits of the IMF. Obviously those meetings were important but, for a man who famously never took things easy, those weeks in Washington were as close as Gordon got.

For a start, we did much more socialising than usual. On that first visit, I joined the others in the hotel reception, and my eyebrows were raised at the number of women in clingy dresses seemingly involved in an international pilots' convention. I relayed my suspicions to the two Eds when they joined us. They looked incredulous and said they were clearly just the wives of the pilots. When Gordon finally came down, Balls said: 'Damian's got a theory about this hotel to tell you.' Before I could say anything, Gordon said: 'I know, we've got to get out of here, this place is full of hookers.'

That evening, we met Gordon's great friend and adviser, Bob

Shrum, who at the time was heavily involved in John Kerry's campaign for the Democratic nomination to take on George W. Bush in 2004. Bob started tearing into Kerry's upstart rival from Vermont, Howard Dean, saying he was a joke and that his campaign was based on appealing to naive college kids.

Ed Miliband shot me a look, given I'd told him previously I was a huge Dean fan. I thought I'd better speak up: 'Um, I should say, Bob, I'm one of the founder members of the London Howard Dean supporters group, and I'm not sure I go along with that.' There was a great roar of laughter. Ed Miliband said with a big smile: 'You passed the test', Bob clapped me on the back and Gordon shook my hand. As initiation rituals go, it was pretty geeky.

During the daytime, when Gordon wasn't in meetings, and even sometimes when he was supposed to be, Washington meant two things: bookshops and football. He could spend literally hours in Barnes & Noble and other bookshops, reading half the history, politics and economics books, and buying the other half. British tourists visiting the city must occasionally have passed this middle-aged man with wild hair, shirt open almost to the waist, carrying two bulging plastic bags of hardback books, and thought: 'That guy looks just like Gordon Brown.'

For football, we'd drive out to Summers Restaurant and Sports Bar in Arlington on Saturday mornings, Sunday lunchtimes and weekday afternoons to catch any live Premiership or Champions League games. Gordon wouldn't drink, obviously, but it was a rare chance for him to enjoy the atmosphere of watching a game in the pub. And him being there meant the rest of us didn't go too mad.

It was a different story at the end of our spring 2004 trip. I went off to Summers by myself mid-morning to watch Arsenal win the league at Spurs – enjoying several beers and a bottle of champagne; then came back and had farewell drinks with all the journalists heading to the airport; and then holed up in a bar for several hours with my great friend Sumeet Desai from Reuters for more beers, tequila shots and banana daiquiris.

That was all standard fare for a title-winning day, until Mark Bowman called me and said Gordon was expecting me to join him and Sarah for dinner. I could barely speak by that stage, let alone make polite conversation with the Browns. I managed to hold it together until the end of the meal when I did what all good drunk men do, and insisted on trying to pay the bill, physically wrestling it out of Gordon's hands, raising my voice ('I'M getting it, I'M getting it!'), and making a bit of a scene. At least Sarah seemed amused.

Our next trip to Washington, later that same year, made up for all the good days there.

Gordon met us at Heathrow fresh and full of beans from the Labour conference in Brighton, a relatively harmonious occasion compared to normal, despite my *Sunday Times* splash about the spin-doctors' summit appearing that weekend.

Gordon had made huge play in his speech about our obligations to the poorest in the world and was now determined to deliver progress at the IMF. This suited me. He'd spend the flight talking to Shriti Vadera, Jon Cunliffe and his other international and economics experts about negotiating strategy in Washington. I could spend it watching films.

Scattered throughout the plane were the various economics editors of the national broadsheets, and up in business class with us were the legendary Alex Brummer from the *Daily Mail* and Sumeet from Reuters. We landed in bright sunshine at Dulles and, as usual, I had my two phones out and switched on as we were descending, ready for Gordon to ask: 'What's the news?'

I looked at my phones. Thirty-six messages, eighteen voicemails. I went through the texts. Ed Balls: 'Ring as soon as you land.' Ian Austin: 'Ring asap.' Trevor Kavanagh: 'Are you in Washington with GB? A word when you can.' Ian Austin: 'If there are press on that plane, get them well away from GB.' Ed Balls: 'Ensure total discipline.' It's at these moments that three thoughts go through your head: 1. Oh shit; 2. Why does no one take the time to send you a text which just helpfully and succinctly explains what the hell is going on?; and 3. Oh shit.

As we were taxiing down the runway, I rang Ian, who said:
'No. 10 had to announce that Blair's having a heart operation
tomorrow and explain why he's bought a new house, so they've
tried to get on top of it by saying he'll serve a full third term. It's
all being done as a devastating blow to Brown – kills his chances
of ever becoming PM. It's total carnage.' I called Ed, who was as
forceful as I'd ever known him: 'You've got one job – one job –
Gordon and everyone around him needs to be totally disciplined
about this. Total discipline.'

The plane door opened and we walked down into the shut-
tle bus. Gordon approached: 'What's the news?' 'Hold on,' I
replied. 'What's wrong?' he rasped. 'What's happening?' 'I need
to tell you something, but you mustn't react badly. Brummer's
watching you.' 'What is it?!' 'You need to relax. Brummer's watching to see if you're angry or upset, so you need to calm down.'

When I relayed the news, his head started to drop, but he then put
on his famous fixed grin for Alex's benefit and started talking about
what matches were on that weekend. 'Get me Ed Balls,' he whispered. I called Ed and handed my phone to Gordon. A big mistake.
He took my phone with him right the way through fast-track security and passport control, and out into his waiting limousine.

I borrowed someone else's phone in our officials' minibus
and – with difficulty, not having all the numbers – started ringing
round and texting all the officials and advisers with us impressing
the need for 'total discipline'. It was already too late. Somewhere,
somehow, between the plane landing and Gordon's entourage
going into the IMF building, the *Guardian*'s incomparable
economics editor Larry Elliott had managed to get a cracking
quote out of one of our number: 'It's like an African coup – they
waited 'til he was out of the country.'

Once inside the UK delegation office at the IMF – then occupied
by Gordon's former Principal Private Secretary Tom Scholar – the
mood was pitch black. Gordon had a series of meetings scheduled, but couldn't be prised away from Tom's sofa, where he sat
staring out of the window at the street below. Having retrieved
my phone, I called round all the political journalists who had

requested a reaction, sounding as bright and relaxed as I could, explaining that Gordon was busy with his IMF agenda and had no problem with Tony's statement, Gordon occasionally looking darkly at me from the sofa as if I was chiding him.

That evening, as usual in Washington, the media monitoring unit at No. 10 faxed me through the front pages of all the papers. As the *Guardian* splash rolled off the fax machine with its 'African coup' headline, I couldn't believe my eyes. Others at home were having the same reaction, and my phone started to explode again. Ian: 'Have you seen *Guardian*? Who the hell said that?' Ed: 'What happened to discipline?!' Trevor Kavanagh: 'Just seen *Guardian*. An urgent word please.'

I decided not to show Gordon any of the papers that evening, blaming problems with the hotel's fax machine. Instead, we sat at the hotel bar, and watched the first presidential debate between John Kerry and George W. Bush.

That night was the blackest I ever saw Gordon's mood. Within ten minutes of the debate starting, he was rasping criticism at his good friend Kerry. 'Look what Bush is doing – security, security, security. He's defining the election and, instead of challenging him, Kerry's going along with it. He's trying to win on security – he'll never win on security. Where's the economy? Where's jobs? Madness. Madness. He's losing the election here.'

As each question was asked by the debate moderator, Gordon would thump the bar and deliver a word-perfect response for Kerry to deliver, and then thump the bar again and shake his head as Kerry made his own response. 'No, no! Rubbish. You've lost, man. You've lost.' It was a remarkable thing to watch, Gordon gripped by anger and frustration, projecting his own feelings onto Kerry, but still the consummate political genius.

Later that night, a few of us tried to cheer Gordon up over several glasses of wine. I said: 'Look, Blair was forced into making that statement. He didn't want to make it, and he probably doesn't believe it. He had to say it or else he'd have to quit before the election. Nothing's really changed – he's not going to serve another five years.' Gordon just shook his head.

'I've already had seven years. Once you've had seven years in one of the big jobs, the public start getting sick of you. You've got seven years to get people on board, but after that, you're on the down slope. I've tried not to be too exposed, but it's still seven years. The only chance was getting in next year before the election. Tony knows that. Every year that goes by, the public are going to say: "Not that guy Brown, we're tired of him – give us someone new."'

Gordon went through politician after politician – American and British – justifying his 'seven years' theory. I understood his mindset far better after that conversation. I believe he only ever wanted to fight and win one election, serve four years and hand over to the next generation. He believed 2005 was his one chance to do that and Tony's statement had robbed him of that chance.

The next morning, Gordon did his usual briefing for the UK economics editors at the IMF building. As he prepared to go in, he asked what he should say if anyone asked him about Tony's operation. Sue Nye said No. 10 were due to text her when they knew it had been a success and he was recovering, but she'd heard nothing yet. Gordon was only half-listening and, when he sat down with the journalists, he began his briefing by saying: 'I'm sure you'll all be glad to hear that Tony Blair's heart operation has been successful and he's recovering well, and we all wish him the very best.'

Sumeet was hovering at the back of the room, and raised his eyebrows at me as if to say: 'Can I go and snap that?' Having only half-heard what Sue said myself, I gave him a nod. He slipped out and, five minutes later, as Adam Boulton, Nick Robinson and the world's press stood outside No. 10 saying that there was no news yet from No. 10 or the hospital on the PM's condition, the 'Breaking News' flashed up: 'Reuters: Brown says Blair operation "successful"'; 'PM "recovering well"', much to the confusion of Tony's staff given he was still under anaesthetic at the time.

As for the 'African coup' quote, we never did find out who said it. For a while – albeit very unfairly – Shriti Vadera was the prime suspect given her closeness to Larry, her fierce loyalty to

Gordon, and her penchant for over-the-top phraseology. When Ed Miliband arrived in Washington that weekend to help boost Gordon's morale, he was given the unenviable job of getting the truth out of her.

As Michael Ellam, Ed, Shriti and I walked along the street for lunch the next day, Michael and I hung back to let Ed do his interrogation. There was an agonising silence before he finally jabbed a finger towards her and yelled: 'SHRITI-DID-YOU-TELL-LARRY-IT-WAS-AN-AFRICAN-COUP?' 'NO!' she yelled back. Ed turned back to us and said calmly: 'It wasn't Shriti.' He was almost certainly right, but the detective work wasn't up there with Poirot.

As for Gordon's seven years theory, it was ten years until he finally got the top job, and – while you could argue he bucked the trend by initially seeing his popularity rise – it would be hard to dispute that he was on a long-term downward slope. From that point of view, it's worth noting that – by the time of the next election – David Cameron will have been leader of the Conservative Party for almost ten years himself and – thanks to 24-hour news – one of the most over-exposed politicians Britain has ever seen. By comparison, Hercule Miliband will have had just four-and-a-half years in the public eye.

20

LEAD IN THE PENCIL

If Gordon loved Washington, he hated Brussels in equal measure. Which isn't to say he hated the European Union – perish the thought – but he loathed each and every thing about its manifestation in the Belgian capital: the soulless Justus Lipsius building; the self-important commissioners; the endless meetings with their pointless '*tours de table*'; the lunches of soggy salami and rubbery Emmental; and, worst of all, the press conferences with foreign journalists.

He couldn't wait to get out, and he'd wait as long as he could to get in. We'd catch the Royal Flight to Brussels at 5 a.m. on the day of a meeting simply to avoid him having to stay the night before.

Ultimately, Brussels epitomised Gordon's two general hatreds: bastards who wasted your time and bastards who were up to no good. And in Brussels, you found plenty of both.

Take the commissioner for the internal market, Frits Bolkestein, as warm and cuddly a figure as his name suggests. Frits was determined to cause Gordon as much trouble as he could. Every summer and Christmas for years, he tried to curry favour with the UK media by warning the Treasury that it should not infringe the legitimate rights of British citizens to buy as much booze and fags as they wanted from Belgium and France for their own 'personal use'.

We'd retort with accusations that Frits was legitimising the same alcohol and tobacco smuggling gangs who were behind organised crime, people-trafficking and child pornography in Britain, but that was a losing battle. It was the only issue on which *The Sun*, *Mail* and *Telegraph* used routinely to praise the European Commission and call on them to overrule the British government. But it was bitter stuff; during one round of the conflict in the Justus Lipsius building, I had to be pulled apart from Frits's English press spokesman, Jonathan Todd, after he took objection to one of my briefings.

Frits gave us the opportunity for revenge when he launched an inquiry into the cross-border impact of differential rates of VAT on EU competitiveness – in other words, whether Britain's zero rates of VAT were damaging firms on the continent. The big game for Frits was always VAT harmonisation: that is having one rate of VAT all across Europe, applying equally to all goods and services. It makes perfect sense if your goal is making the 'internal market' work more efficiently, and it would also increase the slice of each country's VAT revenues that goes to Brussels.

Nevertheless, we slaughtered him, persuading the British papers that Frits was hell-bent on taxing Britain's books, bus fares, food and children's clothes, and that Gordon alone was standing up to his evil master plan. Even *The Sun* told me to tone it down when I gave them a quote vowing that 'Brown will never let Brussels tax a British baby's bonnet'.

Of course, whenever Gordon 'stood up' to Brussels' plans to harmonise taxes – and went up against all fourteen other member states in an EU negotiation, even on the most obscure issues – it was his proxy for telling the British media and public what he could never say out loud: 'I'm the only one keeping us out of the euro. I'm the only one with the strength to say "No" to Blair on Europe.'

The battle over the single currency had just been fought and won by the time I became Gordon's spokesman in 2003, albeit at the price of him ducking out of the simultaneous internal policy discussions on EU enlargement, feeling he had to let Blair have his way on at least one European issue. It was something Gordon bitterly regretted later on, as the backlash grew against immigration from eastern Europe. 'I had too much going on,' he'd say, 'I couldn't cover anything.'

The next great proxy battle came over the EU budget, where – good European that he was – Tony Blair was inclined to do a deal to increase the budget to pay for the costs of enlargement, even if this meant scaling back the UK's rebate from Brussels. Gordon was naturally dead set against this, because it would cost both money and, more worryingly, votes.

We did our best to scupper the process at Gordon's level. As we arrived for one EU finance ministers' meeting, when he was due to speak out against EU waste, we were told that one of the UK's officials in Brussels had been leaked an early draft of the commission's new budget proposals, containing all kinds of ridiculous spending plans.

After the official talked us through the draft, Gordon took me aside in the corridor and said: 'Do you think that will leak to the press before I speak later?' 'Possibly,' I said. 'Hmm,' he replied with a warning look. 'Be careful – don't do it with any British guys.'

When I asked the official holding the draft proposals if he could give me a copy, he point-blank refused. 'If this gets out, the person who gave it to us could lose their job. I'm not going to do that.' 'I don't know what you're talking about,' I lied through my teeth, 'but you've got nothing to worry about. If it leaks at all, it'll be one of the other delegations that leaks it.'

'I'm not giving it to you,' he said, holding it to his chest. 'Come on, don't be difficult,' I said, grabbing the bottom of the document. 'Please don't,' he said. 'Please don't make me do this.' 'I'm not making you do anything, and it's going to be OK, I promise.' He started to cry, which was a bit of an excessive reaction and made me wonder if he was friends with the source. It also made me feel like a total shit, but he loosened his grip and I took the document away to photocopy.

Half an hour later, it appeared on one of the international newswires, datelined from their Madrid bureau. This was a common tactic: if we ever wanted to leak OECD forecasts or IMF reports, we'd always tend to do so via an overseas bureau of an international newswire to make it look like another country had done the leaking, and then just point the UK press towards the story. And, as in this case, it meant the person feeding us the documents went undetected.

Gordon was able to make merry hay with the material at his

usual briefing for the Brussels-based UK correspondents, and almost took the unprecedented step of volunteering to do a press conference for foreign hacks as well. There was a reason Gordon didn't like doing these: he has very big ears. No, really. He could never get the translation earpieces to fit on him, so would end up throwing them to one side, giving the journalists no option but to ask him questions in English instead.

With most of them, he could never understand a thing and would be reduced to peering at the journalist, trying to decipher some of their words and guess the issue they were asking about, then beginning each answer with: 'I think what you're asking is...'. When he literally didn't have a clue, the answer would begin: 'That is indeed a very important issue, but I would argue the more important one is...'

I was sometimes obliged to stand next to Gordon and pick out the journalists to ask questions at an overseas press conference. This was one of the more thankless of many thankless tasks, as Gordon would turn sideways from the instant a reporter started asking a question, and mutter loudly: 'What's she saying? I don't know what she's saying. You're going to have to tell me what she's saying', all while I was trying to understand the question myself.

The EU budget negotiations were all originally expected to come to a head at a European Council meeting which Tony Blair was due to attend on 16 June 2005, the day after my thirty-first birthday.

I had some bad birthdays during my time working in government, most notably my twenty-fifth. The National Crime Squad had sought a judicial review of the Treasury's decision to deny them the same VAT treatment as police authorities. I had to appear in the Royal Courts of Justice as the nominal defendant; being the resident VAT expert sometimes had its downsides. I arrived at my desk at 6 a.m. and left it twenty hours later – with nary a sip of beer or slice of cake – having spent all day reviewing the case files, and writing an urgent submission for Gordon as he contemplated conceding the case.

By comparison, my thirty-first was a cracker: it was a beautiful sunny day and I took myself off at lunchtime to the Jubilee Tavern, a much-missed gay bar in Waterloo. I filled the jukebox with several hours' worth of my favourite songs and got steadily pissed.

Around 4.30 p.m., as my first friends and work colleagues were beginning to drift in, I started getting calls from journalists coming out of that afternoon's No. 10 lobby briefing. They said there appeared to be a significant hardening of Blair's position against the EU proposals and, knowing that Gordon and Tony had met that morning, they wondered if the two things were connected.

I wasn't going to kill that story, especially after several drinks, so – reasonably straight – I advised anyone who called that: Yes, they discussed it; Gordon's views on this issue are well known; and if Tony's position has shifted as a result, then that is entirely welcome from our point of view. That was all just about acceptable, until *The Sun*'s Trevor Kavanagh asked me whether it would be fair to say that 'Gordon had put a bit of lead in Tony's pencil'.

If not for the several preceding pints, I might have sensed danger in that but, at the time, it sounded good to me, and I gave Trevor the verbal nod. A few minutes later, I got my second call of the afternoon from Phil Webster, the legendary political editor of *The Times* and a good friend of Trevor's, with a nose for a line like Maradona's. 'Hi there,' he said with a chuckle. 'Now I just heard a good line from a colleague which I'd quite like to use … something about Gordon putting a bit of lead in Tony's pencil.' Another chuckle. 'Yeah, OK, go for it,' I said.

Another couple of political editors got in touch to stand up the same line, and all of them used it prominently in their coverage the next day, attributed to a Treasury source. Tony was incandescent, asking Gordon to stay behind after the Cabinet, throwing the papers down on the table, and demanding an explanation. 'It's that bloody guy McBride,' said Blair, 'I told you about him.'

It wasn't often they had a one-way slanging match when it was Tony doing all the slanging, and Gordon was both embarrassed and furious at me. I was none the wiser, having got home in the early hours, not seen any papers, and fallen asleep on my sofa with my phone upstairs in the bathroom. When I woke up near midday, I had twenty-six missed calls on my mobile, a number from Gordon saying: 'This. Is. Gordon. Call. Me. Immediately', and the rest from the various members of staff who were getting it in the ear because I couldn't be tracked down.

When I got in touch, they told me they'd tried to do the customary line when I couldn't be found: 'He's out and about with journalists', but this time, Gordon retorted: 'I'm not stupid. I know what "out and about" means – it means he's asleep or in the fucking pub.'

When I did finally speak to Gordon, he went ballistic, reporting what Blair had said and asking what he was meant to tell him. There was no real defence. I just apologised and said it had all got out of hand after the initial chat with Trevor. Interestingly, Gordon then explained that – apart from anything else – he couldn't be seen as guiding Blair's hand on EU matters. 'It's alright today when they're taking this tough line, but then he'll cave in like he always does on Europe, and Kavanagh will say Brown's to blame as well.'

He was dead right on that, as was proved later that year when Blair did cave in on the UK rebate. And if there's one thing Gordon could never comprehend, it was how anyone could lose an argument in Europe. For all his flaws when it came to dealing with other people, and all his loathing of Brussels, he was by far the greatest diplomat it has seen in modern times.

Not in the corrupted sense of the word – he was the opposite of the smooth-talking, well-connected, multilingual caricatures who make up Britain's diplomatic corps – but in terms of someone relentlessly committed to promoting his country's interests and invariably successful at persuading, or occasionally obliging, others to go along with him, ably supported over the years by his key advisers on Europe, Jon Cunliffe and Ivan Rogers.

At one meeting in Ireland – the day Manchester United played Arsenal in the 2004 FA Cup semi-final – the EU finance ministers were due to discuss who to nominate to be the new managing director of the IMF, with technocratic French banker Jean Lemierre the strong favourite. Gordon's preferred candidate was

Spanish politician Rodrigo Rato, a strong ally of his in IMF meetings on debt relief for Africa and other development issues.

Gordon came running out at the end of the meeting. 'What's the score?' 'United won.' 'Ah, I'm sorry!' he said gleefully. 'Right,' he said. 'They've agreed to say Rato's a candidate and it's evenly split between him and Lemierre. But I've written Charlie [McCreevy, the Irish finance minister] a note to read out if anyone asks him what attributes we're looking for. So get one of our guys to ask about attributes in the press conference.'

One of 'our guys' did, Charlie read out the note as advised, explaining that the EU was looking for someone with good links to emerging markets and developing nations, and with the political skills required to handle difficult negotiations. Sure enough, every paper wrote the next day that Rato was now the clear favourite and Lemierre's candidacy had suffered a mortal blow.

When the UK held the presidency of the EU, Gordon's style of chairing meetings was extraordinary. He would instruct that all country position papers on different issues were distributed in advance, and then would conduct the obligatory *tours de table* by saying to each finance minister: 'We have read your paper. Do you have anything to add?' If they did what everyone does at EU meetings and began officially stating their position, he'd cut off their microphone, and say: 'Thank you, that was all made clear in your paper. We will move on.'

Meetings scheduled to last all day would be over by lunch and with agreement on every issue he cared about along the lines he'd proposed. If he didn't care about an issue, he'd invite two opposing parties to speak first, then say: 'It's obvious we will not make progress today. We will move on.'

He was a force of nature: no tact; no niceties; no indulgence of debate; but always focused on getting results. That didn't always work in his international dealings, and on occasion it was counter-productive, but it was more than a decade of practice for the world financial crisis, when none of the silky diplomatic skills were required, but just a man to bang desks, bash heads and get the job done.

21

GORDON AND THE EDS

In 2008, there was an excellent young broadcast specialist recruited to work for Gordon, named Nicola Burdett. After her first meeting with him, she said: 'God, he's lovely! People are so wrong about him.' A couple of months later, she went to a meeting where he exploded about some NHS issue, and she came out shuddering. Veteran that I was by then, I told her: 'Don't worry, when he can have a good rant in front of you, that means you've made it with him.'

But seeing Gordon lose his temper, and indeed seeing him really let his hair down, was only one of the initiation rites of getting to know him on a personal level. Talking to him about family was another – both the influence of his mother, father and brothers, and the relationship he had with Sarah and his boys.

But, family aside, if you wanted to see what Gordon was really like with the people who knew him best, you had to watch him spend time with the two Eds.

People will often describe the Eds as 'Sons of Brown', which – even without the insufficient age gap – is a lazy misunderstanding of their relationship. I always saw him much more as a college professor simultaneously mentoring but also learning from his brilliant young PhD students; his default setting with the pair was asking them questions and taking notes.

And the quality of those debates could be downright intimidating. Because so many of the decisions they took together required an understanding of complex social and economic theory alongside an instinct for political realities and public opinion, all three possessed the rare ability to operate on both planes simultaneously.

Of all the people who worked with them over the years, I would say only Michael Ellam and Jon Cunliffe were capable of holding their own in both aspects of those discussions, while the rest of us tended to specialise in either the 'economics' or the 'politics'.

It also meant both Gordon and the Eds were equally capable of dismissing some colleagues and opponents as being either 'off in the clouds' and 'not in the real world', or alternatively dismissing others as being 'lightweight' or 'superficial'. That wasn't always endearing if you were on the receiving end.

At the other end of the spectrum, when it came to Gordon genuinely relaxing and enjoying himself – on overseas trips or private dinners and parties in the Downing Street flat – the presence of the Eds was key, simply because he enjoyed their company and their humour so much.

The Christmas parties Gordon and Sarah threw for close colleagues each year were always hugely jolly affairs. We'd eat Sarah's traditional lasagne, and do the usual ritual of exchanging Secret Santa presents, plus receiving a book from Gordon and a tie or socks from Sue Nye. Ed Balls and young political adviser Jonathan Ashworth would lead the singing: 'The Red Flag', 'Bandiera Rossa' and 'The Fields of Athenry'; some Elvis; and at least three full-throated 'Jerusalem's.

But the highlight of those evenings was always Gordon's comedy routine. It was never so much the content of the jokes and anecdotes he told that was so entertaining, but his gradual inability to speak because he was laughing so much under the constant heckling from the Eds.

Anyone who remembers Brian Johnston's hysterics on *Test Match Special* in 1991 will know the kind of high-pitched squeal Gordon used when pleading: 'Come on, you guys, stop it!' Tears streaming down his face, he would finally make it to the punchline of a story about Donald Dewar or union leader Jimmy Reid, and would always, always botch it, the cue for everyone to fall about laughing.

The converse of Gordon revelling in the Eds' company on happy days was that they were always invaluable in turning round his mood and getting him to re-focus on those occasions when he was in the dumps, or when necessary quelling his temper if something had set him off.

There was an interesting difference between them though. If Ed Balls was walking down the corridor and heard raised voices or swearing coming from Gordon's office, he made it his business to find out what the problem was and, having determined that Gordon was over-reacting to whatever it was, would march in to him and say incredulously: 'What's all this racket? What on earth is wrong?'

That almost always succeeded in getting Gordon to calm down and talk the problem through rationally or – more often than not – just drop it entirely. Ed Miliband was different. If he heard some explosion going off as he walked in to raise an issue with Gordon, he'd usually just roll his eyes, ask the office: 'Can you call me when he's finished?', and walk back the way he'd come. Never one to have tantrums himself, he simply couldn't be bothered putting up with what he would see as irrational behaviour.

If the two Eds were sitting with Gordon when some bad news came through and he hit the roof, you'd see the same split reaction: Balls would sit there with a faint smile and say sarcastically: 'Erm, is this going to help?', and if Gordon reacted angrily to that, he'd say: 'No, fine – you go ahead – just wanted to understand your thinking.' Meanwhile, Ed Miliband would roll his eyes, sigh and eventually shout with exasperation: 'For goodness' sake, can we get on with things please?'

If they were 'Sons of Brown', I wish I'd been able to control my own dad's moods the same way. But if there genuinely was any paternal aspect to their relationship, it was most visible when the Eds decided to strike out and seek their own front-line political careers before the 2005 election.

On the night Ed Balls was selected for Normanton, Gordon asked me excitedly how his post-selection interview had gone with *Newsnight*. He looked upset and defensive when I said it hadn't been great and, given I didn't know about Ed's stammer then, it must have made it worse to hear me say blithely: 'He might have been a bit nervous, or maybe it was a bit cold – he just seemed very jittery.'

You could see that same defensiveness when Ed was appointed

to Gordon's ministerial team and faced his first sessions of Treasury questions in the House of Commons. The Tories weren't to know why Ed spoke so hesitantly, so they barracked him pitilessly – a constant barrage of 'Errrrrrrs' every time he got up to speak, and every time he had a 'block'.

Gordon would sit there in a barely disguised rage, glowering at the Tory benches, and I'm convinced that the brutal battering that he used to give George Osborne in those sessions – so bad that George stopped asking him questions for months on end – was fuelled by his anger at Ed's treatment.

Ed Miliband waited until much later – February 2005 – to stand as a candidate, and his selection was far less assured, going up against Michael Dugher, Geoff Hoon's former special adviser, in a Doncaster North seat where Michael had built strong ties. I rarely saw Gordon so agitated as on the March night when the selection meeting was taking place. We were late returning from Brussels and, while usually a stickler for protocol, especially when using the Royal Flight, Gordon had his phone switched on looking for a signal as soon as we started to descend.

Ed's call came through just as we were touching down and, hearing the news that he had won, Gordon let out a great scream of joy and vigorously punched his fist in the air. As a rule, you should never punch in any direction when travelling in a small plane, but upwards is probably the worst move. The collective noise of Gordon yelping and crashing his fist into the roof as the plane touched down brought the RAF steward scurrying back in alarm, and we had to reassure him all was OK.

Gordon being Gordon, the celebration lasted five seconds before he told Ed he should seek out Michael and tell him that Gordon would sort him out a job and an alternative seat. It may have taken a few years, but Gordon was true to his word, giving him a job in Downing Street in 2008, and – not that he needed it – helping him to become an MP at the 2010 election.

I'm sure Doncaster North made the right choice, although – staunch football fan that he is – Dugher would never have made the rookie mistake that Miliband made in December that year, as he sat in the Doncaster Working Men's Club watching Donny Rovers in the final seconds of what was set to be a famous victory in the League Cup over Arsenal.

I took the last step of a desperate Arsenal fan and sent Ed a text saying: 'Very well done, your boys have been magnificent, a fully deserved win.' Most fans in the world would have waited until the final whistle rather than jinx the outcome, but – in his excitement – Ed replied: 'Thanks, we were genuinely the better team.' Cue a last-second equaliser from Arsenal.

Both Eds ascended to Secretary of State level in Gordon's first Cabinet in 2007, and, looking back, it's clear to me now that he envisaged one of them becoming his successor if he could win an election in his own right and step down shortly before the next.

At the crucial party conference that year, when we needed something to stop the void of activity being filled with endless election speculation, I sat in Gordon's hotel suite and he instructed me:

'Build up the young guys. Turn it into a beauty contest about who'll take over from me. Don't for God's sake say I won't serve a full term, but say "Brown doesn't want to go on forever. Brown will start putting the next generation into all the senior posts and one of them will become leader." Then Cameron can't use youth against me. We'll say: "They've got one young guy in charge, and that guy Osborne, but Labour's got all the best young talent coming through."'

I asked him who he wanted me to mention to the media as potential leaders. He thought about it, then reeled off surnames like a football manager naming his line-up: 'Purnell. Miliband. Kelly. Burnham. Cooper. Balls. Miliband.' I replied: 'You've already said Miliband.' 'Both of them,' he said. I was a bit incredulous: 'Really? You want me to say Ed Miliband?' He looked equally surprised: 'You need to watch Ed Miliband, he's the one to watch.'

I could understand Ed Balls being in the list, because the only thing he lacked was confidence in speaking from platforms, in the House of Commons, and doing TV interviews, which – while it was clearly a very big deal – was something he could improve as he gained more experience of what worked and what didn't.

By contrast, for all his academic and emotional intelligence, his confidence and good humour, I'd never seen Ed Miliband as a potential leader until Gordon mentioned him that evening; first, because I'd never seen the drive and ambition he clearly possessed, and second because he'd have to get past his brother, the guy who used to send him curt emails from No. 10 telling him: 'Get this sorted.'

But when I thought about it, more than once when the deliberations were going on about a snap election in 2007, and what that would mean for the timing of the next one, I'd heard Ed Miliband say: 'I'd fancy a post-Olympics election in 2012.' Whether that was 'I' speaking for the Labour Party, or for himself, or indeed for both, was never quite clear.

So it wasn't too incongruous to hear Gordon talking up Ed Miliband's chances in that hotel suite in Bournemouth. Then, with Sarah listening intently, he said to me: 'You know you'll have to choose between them one day. Who will you back?' 'I'm closer to Ed Miliband,' I said, which was undoubtedly true at the time – I didn't send Ed Balls text messages about football matches or gossip to him about which Treasury civil servants might have the hots for each other.

'Don't base it on who you're close to,' Gordon said. 'Base it on who you believe in.'

Looking back, I think it was a mistake for Gordon to say to me or anyone else that we'd one day have to choose between the Eds. People like me who'd always seen them as an indivisible double act began seeing them as separate entities, and – over time – people who were closer to one or the other began identifying themselves as belonging in different camps, with the inevitable rivalry, distrust and sniping that followed.

The team around Gordon, which had always been remarkable for its unity of purpose and single sense of mission, suddenly developed fissures, even before the election that never was, and definitely afterwards. The fact that Ed Miliband zealots later used my forced departure as an opportunity to give anonymous and aggressive briefings against Ed Balls to newspapers and biographers

– despite the damage that would do to Gordon as well – was a sign of how bad things had got, and how much some people were planning for a future in opposition even then.

It would not have been unreasonable for Gordon to say – much as the Milibands' mother did during their contest – that he would never take sides between the two Eds, and he didn't expect any of the officials and advisers who owed their careers to him to do so either. Of course some of them would have defied that ordinance, but they couldn't have done so while Gordon was still in office.

And why didn't Gordon do that? Because deep down, he knew one day he'd probably have to choose himself. If James Purnell or David Miliband emerged as a front-runner for the leadership, determined – as Gordon would see it – to take the party down routes that he had successfully resisted for more than a decade – creeping privatisation and divisive provision of public services, closer political and economic integration with Europe, increasing erosion of constitutional freedoms in the name of security, and so on – then he would have to try and stop that happening.

That would mean backing the candidate that he felt was best able to set out an alternative, positive, Brownite vision and ulti-mately the candidate most likely to win, whether that was Ed Balls, Ed Miliband or indeed Yvette Cooper. When that contest materialised almost as exactly as feared in 2010, Gordon – however uncomfortable it felt – was forced to pick a favoured candidate between the Eds, and use whatever influence he had to try and secure them votes.

By that stage, I was long gone from Downing Street, but people try everything and everyone when the leadership is on the line.

In September 2010, rumours began to circulate that Ed Balls might cut a late deal with David Miliband, where David would accept Ed's position on the pace of deficit reduction and proclaim his attributes as a potential shadow Chancellor, in return for which Ed would withdraw from the race and urge those MPs and members backing him to switch allegiance to David.

My mobile – usually silent those days – started to ring again: Gordon and others close to him urged me that – if I had any influence over Ed Balls or his team (a reference to my girlfriend Balshen, who was helping to run his campaign) – I should tell him he had to reject any deal offered by David, and instead pursue the same deal with Ed Miliband. 'What kind of madness is this,' they asked, 'if he backs David to be leader, not Ed?' I made clear that I wasn't in a position to help even if I wanted to.

As it was, Balls made clear in public he wasn't interested in any deals, and neither Miliband brother was inclined to offer one. So it came to nothing, but did very clearly expose where Gordon had his colours nailed. And just as Ed Miliband can very cogently justify why he felt compelled to challenge his brother, I'm sure Gordon could equally well explain why he felt obliged privately to back Ed Miliband over Ed Balls, while remaining publicly neutral.

Both saw their decisions as means to the most important end – victory in the battle for the direction and soul of the Labour Party. That was all that mattered, even if it meant Ed Balls limping away from the field afterwards feeling just as bruised as David Miliband, something compounded by Ed Miliband's initial decision not to make him shadow Chancellor.

If Labour is in power after the 2015 election, either in its own right or in coalition, with Ed Miliband installed as Prime Minister and Ed Balls as Chancellor, I'm sure they'll invite Gordon to the first Downing Street Christmas party, and get him to tell his 'Japanese Admiral' joke for old time's sake, and perhaps the three will reflect on how far they've come and how much has changed for all of them since they first started working together in Gordon's opposition office twenty-one years before.

And perhaps they can all shake hands then, and let all the fissures of the past be healed, and every bygone be bygone. It would be a shame if they didn't.

22

THE POLITICS OF POVERTY

Shriti Vadera, Gordon's top adviser on international development issues, phoned me up, near-hysterical: 'Well, I want you to know, I've just come off a conference call with Bono, Bob Geldof and Robbie Williams, and they all agreed that you are a total ... well, I won't say the word, I hate that word – but anyway, they all agreed that you are one.'

It was summer 2004, and George Pascoe-Watson had just splashed *The Sun* with the news that there was going to be a 'Live Aid II' concert the following summer, twenty years on from the first, as part of a new charity campaign on world poverty, backed by Blair and Brown. Reading the story, you'd never guess it had come from the Treasury, but Shriti took it upon herself to own up to the three rock stars on my behalf, and they agreed that I was definitely a .... whatever word she wouldn't tell me.

The story was probably a bit premature on my part, but it did no harm, and Bono soon stood it up in an interview with Sky's Kay Burley. For many people in the media, politics and the celebrity world, that story marked the start of a rare year of intense focus on the issues of poverty. For Gordon, just as much as most of the charities in that sector, it was merely the high point of their engagement.

If there was one thing – other than the obvious drivers of personal ambition – that clearly motivated Gordon, one thing that always instantly made him fired up, it wasn't necessarily poverty itself, or unemployment, or lack of education, it was when he looked at young people and thought they'd been given no chances. That dated back to the divisive testing and streaming of his Scottish schooldays.

And his passion for international development issues was

not some affectation to soften his image, or part of some grand economic plan to create new markets in the developing world, or even a way of demonstrating to the Labour Party what his foreign policy priorities would be, unlike that bloody warmonger next door.

No, Gordon had a genuine, burning sense of injustice at the idea that some children are born into the world with no chance of ever achieving their potential as human beings, either because they or their mother do not survive the birth for lack of basic equipment, because they don't get the vaccines to survive infancy or the food to make their bodies grow properly, or – above all – because even if they make it to school age, there are no schools to go to, no books or no teachers.

This was a largely theoretical passion before he visited Africa for a week in January 2005 but, by the end of the visit, after spending hours in packed primary school classrooms in Tanzania, seeing teenage girls in the Kibera slum in Nairobi chanting their demands for 'free education', and meeting a shy twelve-year-old girl who was living with HIV and looked blank when he asked what she wanted to do when she was older, it became something much more heartfelt and personal.

Most of all, as our convoy drove away from a giant sugar plantation in Mozambique – a visit designed to demonstrate the economic potential of the continent if an improved trade deal could be agreed – we passed truck-loads of female plantation workers being taken home after their long day's work. Our press bus belatedly realised Gordon had stopped to talk to the women and we screeched to a halt, the poor cameramen having to run a hundred yards in the heat back to film the encounter.

The women were insistently waving their pay cheques at Gordon and asking how they were meant to get food, clothes, medicine and schoolbooks for their children with the little they were paid for a full day's back-breaking work. It made a huge impact on him.

Ed Miliband was similarly affected, and it was interesting to see him leading the group on that trip in the absence of Ed

Balls: he was a calming influence on Gordon and Shriti whenever they got into a flap; a Godsend for me in terms of getting scripts and press briefings quickly signed off; and a playful presence on nights in the bar, including dubbing me Inspector McBride after I told him I thought something was going on between two of the civil servants in our group, and it turned out they'd been secretly living together for six months.

At the end of one particularly long night in Dar es Salaam, I told the press entourage that we'd be starting at 6 a.m. the next day for a wreath-laying at the local Commonwealth war cemetery. There was a collective groan, a fair bit of swearing, and most of them said they would give it a miss. As Benedict Brogan, then of the *Daily Mail*, passed me by, I said: 'Surely you wouldn't miss a wreath-laying, Ben?'

He caught my look, narrowed his eyes and, sure enough, he was the only newspaper reporter there in the morning, along with a BBC crew doing a *Newsnight* profile of Gordon. Ben listened in to Gordon's interview with Martha Kearney at the cemetery, and splashed the *Mail* the next day with Gordon saying it was time to focus on the future and stop apologising for the British Empire. The other journalists weren't happy, but it was the definition of 'you snooze, you lose'. It wasn't an exclusive; Ben was just the only one who turned up.

The week ended in South Africa, with Gordon due to visit Nelson Mandela at his family compound in the Transkei. It was touch and go whether the visit would take place: Mandela was suffering from tuberculosis and one of his sons had just died of AIDS. But a small plane-load of us set off, with the press entourage left behind, and only the BBC's Mark Mardell and his cameraman accompanying us.

In those circumstances, Mark and I would be expected to give the others a 'fill' on the trip on our return, so they could file stories as if they'd been there, but as we approached the compound in our convoy of jeeps, Shriti texted me that we hadn't yet had explicit permission from Mandela's press advisers to bring cameras into the compound so Mark would have to wait at the gate.

Regardless of the diplomatic niceties, there was no way I was telling Mark he'd travelled all that way to stand out in the sun at the bottom of the road. We were first in the convoy so I asked our driver to speed up and get us there ahead of time. He said the convoy had to stay together, but I said: 'No, we have to be there first to film the arrival.' When we got to the gate perhaps a minute ahead of the rest, arriving at speed, the guards – all carrying machine guns – looked understandably alarmed.

I jumped out and thought I'd just brazen it out: 'Quick, officers, we need to get up to the house; it's the BBC – they need to set up the camera before Mr Brown arrives.' They looked a bit uncertain but opened the gate, and we were able to zip up the last bit of road and clamber out before the other jeeps arrived.

Shriti got out of the lead jeep giving me a stare that could have stripped paint. I mouthed: 'What? They let us through.' She mouthed back: 'I'll fucking kill you', but then smiled as Mandela and his wife Graça emerged to greet her and Gordon, waving happily towards the camera.

We stood in the sun outside while the talks went on for hours, Gordon's protection officers idly comparing notes with Mandela's guards on their choice of weaponry. 'You ever use shotguns?' Gordon's man asked. 'Lot of damage,' Mandela's man beamed back.

When the group emerged, Mark asked how the discussions had gone. Shriti started to shoot lasers at me again, but Mandela was in effusive mood, talking at length about how great Gordon was, but also speaking sadly about the recent loss of his son. It could simply not have been better, and – as we parted – Mark, his cameraman and even the ultra-professional protection officers reached forward to shake Mandela's hand.

I didn't, and while I regret that now, at the time I just thought: Nope, you're here for Gordon, not yourself, and I always wanted to retain the high ground when castigating any Treasury or No. 10 colleagues at my level for 'mixing with the talent' or 'acting like star-fuckers', as I used to say when feeling less polite.

I even applied that self-denying ordinance on handshakes the two occasions I met Arsène Wenger for goodness' sake!

And the reality was that, while working on Gordon's international development agenda enabled us to see extreme poverty in its very starkest forms in Africa, China, India, Palestine and Latin America, it also – more than any other issue we worked on – gave opportunities to mix with some of the richest and most famous people in the world because of their own commitment to those causes, and because Gordon was one of the prime targets for their lobbying.

And if the connections with, or support from, those celebrities enabled Gordon to bring the issues he and they both cared about to a mass audience in Britain, then he would have been a fool to turn those chances down, and – from a PR point of view – I'd have been a fool to let him.

My favourite example came on a conference call Gordon did in 2006 with Angelina Jolie and a handful of journalists from the US and the UK. I was asked to pick two journalists from our side to ask questions. I could have been pious and picked only *The Guardian* and *The Independent* development correspondents to keep things on topic, but I had to remember why I was doing it.

So I called on Andy Porter, then deputy to George Pascoe-Watson at *The Sun*, who said: 'Ms Jolie, you're clearly very impressed by the work that Mr Brown has done on these issues. Would you like to see him become Britain's Prime Minister so that he can pursue these goals at a higher level?' While sounding slightly confused, she gave enough of a positive answer to make the story work, and although the headline and top line may not have advanced our international development agenda with *The Sun*'s readers, the rest of the story did.

But Gordon himself was sometimes torn by this. For all the famous people like Angelina Jolie, Bill Gates, Shakira and George Clooney who genuinely impressed him with their understanding of and passion for the issues, he'd occasionally be appalled – just as he was with many politicians and media people – at the crassness of others.

In Davos one year, he made an impassioned speech calling for people to stop thinking about what could be achieved with the millions resulting from one day of fundraising, but about what could be achieved with the billions resulting from a year of campaigning on debt and aid. To his bewilderment and irritation, Sharon Stone leapt up from the front row, whooping, and said: 'Come on, you heard the man. Get your wallets and purses out. I want to see those cheques. I want to see those IOUs. I want to see who's going to pledge the most in this room.'

When he was asked by Simon Cowell to record a video message for a special edition of the US version of *Pop Idol*, called *Idol Gives Back*, I was the one whooping Sharon Stone-style at the opportunity. But Gordon was distinctly uneasy: 'They're all about bednets. You're not going to solve malaria with bednets. They've got this chance to talk to millions of Americans about poverty, and they're going to bring it all down to bednets.'

That said, he wasn't averse to some reflected glory when it suited him. In 2009, the celebrities who'd climbed Mount Kilimanjaro for Comic Relief were invited to a No. 10 reception with local schoolchildren and, while there was a great cast list due to attend, the real star was Cheryl Cole.

There was an art to timing Gordon's arrival at these things. We'd keep all the celebrities who arrived early in a holding room and tell them they'd be going into the main reception just as soon as Gordon had finished his phone call with the Israeli Prime Minister – always our default excuse when we wanted to say he was busy.

What we'd really be doing was waiting for the biggest star to arrive so he could walk into the reception alongside them for the benefit of the cameras, not to mention the screaming children. But obviously, you couldn't say that to the other celebrities: 'Sorry, guys, just waiting for the A-lister to arrive and then we can go in', or they might be a tad put out.

On this occasion, Cheryl and Girls Aloud bandmate Kimberley Walsh were very late, Gordon was waiting to be summoned from his flat, and the various other stars in the holding room –

especially Gary Barlow – were beginning to get a bit peeved at waiting. Eventually, the back gates of Downing Street swung open, a swanky car pulled in and one of the guards gave a thumbs up.

We got Gordon down straight away and he marched into the holding room, apologising profusely to the other celebrities for the wait. He said: 'We better go and see these kids', but first worked his way round shaking hands and introducing himself, just giving time for Cheryl magically to arrive right on cue behind him.

Except she didn't. He finished shaking hands, everyone started trooping out the door and there was still no Cheryl. 'Can we just hold on, everyone,' I said. 'We just need to warn the kids upstairs that you're coming up.' We really didn't. They were getting almost as bored of waiting as the celebrities, but we needed some excuse to wait.

Colleagues went running all round the building looking for where Cheryl and Kimberley had got to, and one eventually rushed up and whispered that they were on their way; one of our most star-fucking special advisers had intercepted them at the back door and taken them for a quick look round the Cabinet room. I mentally started revving up my chainsaw, but said calmly: 'Oh Gordon, apparently two other guests have just arrived, so let's just hold on for them.'

The eventual moment of Gordon walking in with Cheryl to the screams of the kids was great, all apart from Gary Barlow scowling in the background. It came as little surprise to me when he came out for the Tories at the 2010 election.

But back in 2005, the support from those kind of celebrities and the Live 8 concert, alongside the mass mobilisation of charities and faith organisations around the Make Poverty History campaign, undoubtedly helped get the public support and political momentum required to secure pledges on aid and deals on debt relief at the Gleneagles G8 summit, if not any progress at all on trade.

That summit was a difficult moment for Gordon, seeing Tony Blair, who'd done very little heavy lifting on development issues in the preceding years, claiming all the glory. Gordon also felt that, while the Bush administration owed Blair a huge debt for his support for the Iraq War, he'd used barely any of that capital to extort lasting commitments from them on development.

Indeed, when Gordon used his first meeting with Condoleezza Rice to try and persuade her to back his plan to deliver a massive increase in short-term funding for development, financed by long-term bonds, she not only said the US wasn't interested in the plan but got the White House to complain to Tony Blair about Gordon's 'haranguing' behaviour.

On the eve of Gleneagles, Gordon said quite reflectively that he'd need to keep pushing on this agenda, because if he didn't, no one would. He said Tony would be back on the Middle East and security as soon as Gleneagles was out of the way. That was more prescient than he realised. The 7/7 bombings happened during the summit and all of the momentum on development – as well as the feel-good factor induced by Live 8 and the success of the London 2012 Olympics bid – was totally lost.

In fact, in the wake of 7/7, Gordon felt under increasing pressure to look active on the international security agenda as well, rather than just 'banging on' about development issues. Following the bad meeting with Condoleezza Rice, we would also hear noises from News International contacts that there were concerns at the highest level in the company – i.e. Uncle Rupert – about whether Gordon sufficiently grasped the seriousness of the security situation, and whether he could be trusted to maintain the strength of Blair's relationship with the Bush administration.

On the morning of 21 July, after copycat bombers made their botched terrorist attack on the Tube, I interrupted Gordon's meeting with a delegation of senior businessmen to tell him the news. Alarmed, but perhaps also conscious of the need to look like a man of action on terrorism, Gordon became a whirlwind of activity, barking orders to his office about freezing the bank accounts of the suspects once they'd been identified, making asset seizure orders, handing over any HMRC records to the security services, and telling me to get a press statement ready once all that had been done.

As Gordon resumed his discussions with the businessmen, they could not have looked more impressed at what they'd seen, and how seized Gordon was by the security agenda. By contrast, having concluded that this was one day on which there was zero chance of any journalist needing to speak to me, I went back to my office, closed my door, switched on the first day of the Ashes from Lord's, and relaxed on my sofa.

A big mistake. Half an hour later, Gordon charged into my room with a familiar: 'Damian, where are we?', with the five businessmen following immediately behind. I leapt up, grabbed the remote, switched from the Ashes to Sky News, and bullshitted as best I could about the latest developments, as they all listened intently. All except Gordon of course, who had seen what I'd really been watching and was mentally assaulting me with a large cricket bat.

You can imagine why, when he'd asked me the previous year why I hadn't shaken Mandela's hand, and I said: 'It just didn't feel very professional', Gordon's response was a succinct and scornful: 'Ha!'

23

HONOURS

The late, great John Butterly was a teenager when he took a job working on Glasgow's docks. He never learned to read or write, but, when his tenement building in Dennistoun was threatened with destruction and his family were told their only option was moving into a block of flats in Easterhouse, he became one of the pioneers of Glasgow's housing association movement, which turned back the bulldozers and led to the renovation of thousands of Glasgow's old sandstone tenements.

Dawn Goring was a glamorous, black sixteen-year-old from south London when she turned up for an interview in the Treasury's typing pool not long after Margaret Thatcher had come to power. She was asked what she thought the Treasury did, giving the immortal answer: 'I dunno. Something to do with diamonds?' She got the job and has now worked more than thirty years in administrative positions in the Treasury and No. 10, serving under six chancellors and two prime ministers.

What John and Dawn have in common – other than firm places in my heart – was that, the achievements of their children apart, I never saw them so proud as on the days they went to collect their MBEs from Buckingham Palace. For that reason, I have always been a huge fan of the honours system, and it was a great thrill to see Dawn on the day with her mum, dad and daughter, dressed to the nines and beaming with smiles.

I became even more of a fan of the honours system when I realised what a rich seam it offered for tactical leaks to key newspaper contacts, especially around Christmas when political stories are notoriously thin on the ground.

Twice a year, I would move heaven and earth to obtain a copy of the full honours list from Cabinet Office colleagues, scan it for any interesting names from TV, film, music and sport, and – while I'd be subtle about the actual leaking process, humming a TV theme tune or doing a few bars of a song – it would usually lead to a splash in *The Sun* or another tabloid, and another few months of goodwill for Gordon in the bag.

But it did require a bit of background knowledge. It was no use hoping you'd see the name Status Quo under 'Services to Music' – you had to know who Messrs Francis Dominic Rossi and Richard John Parfitt were. One of my successors discovered that to their cost after going through the 2010 New Year's Honours list when the Quo pair were honoured, and telling the *Sunday Mirror* there were no interesting celebrities on the list.

There were certain things it also helped to know about the system. For example, when Bruce Forsyth was awarded a CBE in 2006, *The Sun* began a long campaign to get him upgraded to a knighthood. I knew that couldn't happen because you usually have to wait at least five years for a higher gong than the one you've received and to have done something significantly new in the meantime. Twice a year, *The Sun* would ask whether they'd be able to claim victory on Brucie, and twice a year I'd tell them, no, it definitely wasn't going to happen.

After I was sacked in 2009, they got some bad intelligence from another source and splashed the Brucie knighthood story in advance of the Birthday Honours. I knew it couldn't be right and, sure enough, they had to wait another two years before the story finally came good.

If the honours system provided some of my best tabloid splashes, it also produced my biggest disappointment – probably the only time going back to my Customs days when I personally tried to drive through a policy change and failed.

The idea of awarding posthumous honours has been around for many years, most notably with the campaign for Bobby Moore to receive the knighthood that many of his surviving 1966 peers received in the years after his death. After all, posthumous honours already exist, but usually only for members of the armed forces or emergency services killed while engaged in acts of great bravery.

In 2008, the Holocaust Educational Trust (HET), led by the unstoppable Karen Pollock – herself now an MBE – began campaigning to see honours awarded to those Britons who had helped Jewish people to escape the concentration camps, often while working in Britain's embassies in occupied Europe, but whose heroic deeds had gone unknown and unrecognised in their own lifetimes.

I started to cause a stir about this internally. Gordon was keen on the idea, both because of his own interest in wartime acts of bravery, but also because he wanted a way to publicly recognise Alan Turing, the Bletchley Park codebreaker persecuted over his sexuality, rather than just apologise in the House of Commons for the way he had been treated.

As always, I also had an ulterior motive. First, I thought the proposal would go down a storm with those supporters of football clubs whose managerial legends would have undoubtedly received knighthoods in today's honours system, but who had died unrecognised: Herbert Chapman, Jock Stein, Bob Paisley and Brian Clough, to name four obvious candidates.

But beyond that, I saw this as something that Labour MPs could get heavily involved in, canvassing nominations in their constituencies for any local heroes whose acts of charity or community had never been recognised during their lifetimes, or even realised until after their deaths; the kind of thing that would lead to local newspaper campaigns and petitions championed by the local MP.

Given the support of Gordon and then Cabinet Office minister Tom Watson, and my own experience of driving through policy changes, I was confident that it would happen. However, I then encountered the combined strength of the senior civil service and Buckingham Palace officials. They were not having it, not under any circumstances.

The debate raged back and forth over a period of weeks: they would list ten reasons why it couldn't possibly happen; I'd challenge all of them; they'd concede two but insist on the remaining eight; I'd challenge again, and so on, like boxers going toe to toe seeing who would drop first.

They argued: 'We cannot impose honours on people who do not have the opportunity to refuse them'; I came back with: 'But you give posthumous honours to police officers and soldiers, no one's able to ask them, and in any case, why not just ask their surviving families, the way you would with organ donation?' Point conceded.

They argued: 'We cannot second-guess the judgements made by honours committees in previous years who chose not to honour these individuals'; I replied: 'But some of them, as with the Holocaust cases, died without anyone knowing what they'd done; and some of them, like Jock Stein, dropped dead in the middle of their careers.' Point conceded.

They argued: 'We cannot make judgements now based on today's criteria and standards and apply them retrospectively to previous eras when different criteria and standards applied.' I didn't know what that meant, but I went for the jugular and retorted: 'If you mean that Alan Turing couldn't get a knighthood because he was a homosexual, and still shouldn't because that was the judgement at the time, then is that really your best argument?' Point conceded.

They argued: 'We only have a set number of honours to award each year; if you want to give some to dead people, you're going to have to exclude deserving living people.' 'Cobblers,' I argued, 'it's not difficult – make it a new, special category, set aside about ten to twenty extra honours per year, and choose the most deserving posthumous candidates each time.' Point conceded.

They argued: 'To whom is Her Majesty supposed to make the award?' 'Are you kidding?' I asked them. 'You already make awards to half the recipients of the Victoria Cross without them physically receiving it.' Point conceded.

Finally, they argued: 'How far back are we supposed to go? Do you want to propose that Boudicca is made a Dame?' 'Again, let's not be daft,' I said, 'but if you want a cut-off point, let's go back to 1917 when the current honours system came into being.' Point conceded.

I thought I had them beaten. The old-fashioned ding-dong of

debate reminded me of the old Treasury tax policy days, and my torment at the idea of losing the argument was giving way to excitement at winning it. However, they had one trump card left to play.

'All this is a nonsense anyway,' they said. 'Receiving a knighthood is simply the conferral of membership of the Order of the Bath. It's like a club. You cease to be a member when you die and you can't make dead people members. For that reason, Her Majesty doesn't want to do it and if the Prime Minister feels so strongly about it, he will need to take it up with her personally.'

I'm not sure the Palace officials or the Cabinet Office ever consulted the Queen, but it was a reasonable bluff. They knew there was no way Gordon was going to raise this with her if there was the slightest chance she would respond that the whole thing was a 'nonsense'. Gordon apologised to me, but said that was the end of it.

The one positive outcome was that the HET succeeded not in getting the existing honours system changed, but in winning agreement to the creation of a special new medal for the 'Heroes of the Holocaust', which has been duly awarded to several individuals since, most of them posthumously.

But the whole episode left a bitter taste in my mouth. Lots of people will doubtless say that the Prime Minister, civil servants, special advisers and the Palace should have better things to do than bestowing knighthoods on dead people, and others will say it's another example of how the whole honours system is a discredited anachronism.

However, I just think back to John Butterly and Dawn Goring, and the pride both they and their families took in the MBEs they received, not for themselves but for what it meant to their families. I cannot see why – in certain circumstances – that pride should not be enjoyed as a consolation by the families of those who have lost loved ones, and long to see their achievements remembered and recognised by the country.

There's another reason it mattered to me, and not just because I'm such a sore loser. It was the strongest civil service rearguard action I witnessed in thirteen years in government. And there was something about it which smacked of the Establishment, which had fought hard to wrest control of the honours system off the Tony Blairs and Alastair Campbells, saying to their successors: 'Hands off, this belongs to us now; these are our knighthoods, we decide where they go.'

There was an interesting postscript to this when a campaign was launched in 2013 to have Jimmy Savile stripped of his knighthood following the revelations that came after his death. It struck me that if Savile or anyone else is ever posthumously stripped of their knighthood, it will knock a bloody great hole in the one supposedly incontrovertible argument that 'membership of the club' ceases to exist after death.

I haven't given up just yet.

24

'THE EVIL THAT MEN DO'

By the time the 2005 general election was approaching and still a civil servant, I was nevertheless committed to the Labour Party and Gordon in a way that many other officials in the Treasury were beginning to find frankly unpalatable.

The final straw, for Gus O'Donnell in particular, was my handling of the Treasury's release of documents relating to the 1992 'Black Wednesday' debacle, when Britain's messy exit from the European Exchange Rate Mechanism cost the country billions and did irreparable damage to John Major's Conservative government.

The documents had been requested under the Freedom of Information Act by the *Financial Times*, and – when I read through them for the first time – I could see how explosive they would be, not because of any one revelation, but because the chaos they revealed and the timing of their publication would play straight into Labour's election rhetoric that the Tories could never be trusted on the economy again.

Given they were papers relating to a previous administration, Gordon was not supposed to have any knowledge about their contents, or any influence over the handling of their publication, but – while I was careful not to speak to him directly about it – I got word to him through Ian Austin, and just reassured Ian that I knew the significance of the papers and would handle them appropriately.

The original timing of the release was delayed, largely as a result of ongoing discussions within the Treasury about the need to protect the identities of civil servants named in the papers and obscure some of the processes involved in money market interventions and the way Britain gathered intelligence about the plans of other European finance ministries.

I became concerned that the longer the delay continued, the more likely the papers would have to be held back until after the election under the rather obscure rules governing what can and cannot be released during the 'purdah' period, when departments are barred from making significant announcements.

Because Sir John Major and the former Chancellor Norman Lamont were also being consulted on the publication, it was quite easy for me to conflate the two things, and get splash stories published in *The Times* and the *FT* saying there was a mystery over the delay and 'fears' that the two Tory grandees were trying to stall publication. I thought that would guarantee the civil servants wouldn't be able to hold things up any longer.

That's how it proved, but all hell broke loose in the meantime as a result of the stories. Sir John went bananas, issuing formal denials and calling for official apologies. When one Sunday paper suggested to me there were suspicions Alastair Campbell was orchestrating the whole thing, I gave them enough rope to run the story as a splash, and Sir John took the bait, going on broadcast news again to accuse Labour and Campbell of pre-election dirty tricks and ensuring the row ran for another couple of days.

By that stage, we were ready to publish the papers on the Treasury website and there was such huge anticipation that most newspapers automatically splashed them, with big inside spreads and commentary. They received a bit of help from me, as I'd gone through the hundreds of pages with a fine-tooth comb in advance and was able to point the journalists to all the best bits – by which I mean the most damaging bits for the Tories.

I was feeling pleased with myself, but the row about dirty tricks still rumbled on. I told Ian Austin I was worried my skulduggery had all got out of hand and asked whether anyone in the Labour Party was pissed off. While warning me to be careful, he concluded: 'But mate, honestly, we've just had a week's worth of coverage about the worst moment in Tory Party history and you think people might be pissed off?!'

Given the Alastair Campbell red herring that was around, I thought my role might have gone undetected, but Gus O'Donnell,

Sir John's press secretary at the time of Black Wednesday, wasn't going to be fooled. I was told later that he shook his head dolefully when discussing my 'disgraceful' behaviour, and told a colleague I was 'the evil that men do'.

It was only years later that I discovered Gus had spoken to Gordon after that episode, told him I'd become too political and needed to be moved. It was put to me rather differently at the time by Ed Balls when he took me for a coffee in Le Club Express on Petty France:

'If you want to carry on working for Gordon long term and see him through to No. 10, you can't carry on as a civil servant. They won't let you do his press work forever. So if Ian becomes an MP in May, Gordon would like you to take his place as the political press adviser.'

There was a long pause. 'But the reason I'm speaking to you, not Gordon, is he doesn't understand what you'll be giving up. You'll never be able to go back to the civil service. Whatever career you thought you were going to have, that will be over. You'll be taking a big, big risk. And if you don't want to take it, you can tell me, and I'll explain it to Gordon.'

I asked Ed what he thought I should do. 'All I know', he said smiling, 'is you seem to enjoy the work, and you seem to like the politics.' Then, not for the last time, he said quietly: 'And Gordon needs you. Without you, he'd be so exposed. *So* exposed.' When I thought of that word, it conjured up the vulnerability of wealthy would-be divorcees without the legal protections of a pre-nuptial agreement. It didn't make much sense at the time, and didn't really until four years later.

I should have taken longer to make up my mind, but I felt like I was part of Gordon's Praetorian guard by then, and going over to the political side would cement that. However good the view, I knew that if I was back in the glass corner office at Customs earning the £100k salary, I'd just sit there depressed the whole time, like General Patton on D-Day.

If I did have any doubts, they disappeared altogether during the course of the 2005 election campaign, when, by dint of my handling the media on the rescue package for staff at the threatened Rover car plant in Birmingham, I spent time with Gordon and Tony Blair as they mixed their government business with their electioneering in the last weeks before polling day.

Part of my enthusiasm was seeing just how rubbish the No. 10 political team's handling of the media was during the campaign, and thinking that I could do a much better job. That was reinforced by the total mess they got into trying to meet the competing demands of *The Sun* and the *News of the World* for a big exclusive interview.

The Sun, edited by Rebekah Wade, thought they'd been promised the first joint interview of the campaign with Tony and Gordon, and were furious to hear that the *News of the World*, edited by Andy Coulson, had been given the interview instead. No. 10 tried to appease *The Sun* by offering an interview with Gordon on his own.

That was fine, except Gordon had nothing particularly to say, and – as we were now in election purdah – he couldn't rely on me or the Treasury to cook up an announcement. We waited in an aircraft tower in Birmingham as *The Sun*'s Trevor Kavanagh and George Pascoe-Watson landed in their special 'election helicopter'. They weren't in the best of moods, and they were even less pleased after thirty minutes of bland platitudes from Gordon about the dangers of voting for Michael Howard.

Trevor was blunt enough to tell Gordon to his face that what he'd given them was totally unusable, while George rolled his eyes and told me the whole episode summed up what was wrong with Labour's operation. Given the failure of the Gordon gambit, No. 10 were eventually reduced to giving *The Sun* Tony and Cherie's first ever joint newspaper interview, leading to the unedifying headline that Britain's Prime Minister was still up to having sex five times a night.

The day of *The Sun*'s non-interview, our small Brown team travelled back to London in a Chinook helicopter with Blair's much bigger entourage. Whether it was the constraints of space or not being able to hear each other talk, they all seemed a bit world weary. I said to Sue afterwards that they didn't look like a team who were up for a full third term. 'That's because they're not,' she said – and this was all before the cash-for-honours scandal hit them the following year.

Compared to the mood in Washington that black night a few months previously, our camp and Gordon personally were buoyant. He'd proved himself indispensable in the last few weeks of the election, so much so that when Alastair Campbell called to speak to Tony during the course of those days in the Midlands, Blair would simply hand the phone to Gordon and let him take all the decisions.

At the end of one day in Birmingham, Gordon asked me if I'd 'sorted things out' with Ed about the job, and seemed genuinely pleased when I said I had. He also said admiringly that it was good of me to come up and help on the Rover story when everyone else was 'having a good rest' in the Treasury, lazy nonpolitical civil servants that they were.

I made the unforgivable error of telling him that it was worse than he thought. While I'd spent the day on the road with him, Michael Ellam, James Bowler, Mark Bowman and others had gone to play golf. 'GOLF?!' Gordon yelled. 'GOLF?!' If I'd said they'd been crocheting swastika cushions, he couldn't have been more outraged.

'We're trying to run a bloody country here, and these guys are off playing golf!!' Sue gave me one of the several variations on her 'Now why on earth did you say that?' look. Gordon went on about the errant golfers for the rest of the day, and wouldn't let it go when he returned after the election, continually saying to Michael, James and Mark that he hoped they'd enjoyed their *golf* while he'd been away. They weren't ecstatic with me.

I spent election evening hosting a party at my house for Treasury staff. I'd joined the Labour Party two days previously, and was all ready to say goodbye to the civil service and go to the dark side. When the result came through from Dudley North that Ian Austin had been elected, I muted the TV, and announced to the room that I was becoming Gordon's political press adviser and my deputy, a laconic genius named Paul Kissack, was becoming the new Head of Communications.

The next morning, I walked away from orchestrating Gordon's return into the Treasury for the cameras, applauded and cheered by all the staff, and walked down the corridor to Ian's old office, a room looking out onto St James's Park sitting next to the Chief Secretary's office and two doors down from Gordon's.

Sitting on Ian's old couch, watching his old telly, and getting to grips with the fact they were now mine, I picked up the bottle of wine he'd left on his desk for his successor, whether that had been me or his Tory opposite number. The accompanying note read: 'Good Luck. Keep out of trouble. Keep out of the shot. And keep having fun.'

I was itching to get into it, but it was a week before Tony Blair would agree to sign the forms accepting my appointment as a special adviser, making clear to Gordon that he wasn't happy at the idea. Gordon gave me a dark look during those days of wrangling with Blair over the appointment, and said: 'They really hate you over there. Some of the stuff they accuse you of doing is just...'

He left the thought hanging. I just shrugged.

MAD DOG ON
THE LOOSE

25

BLAIR AND BROWN: THE COLA WARS

The period between the election in May 2005 and Gordon's succession to the premiership in June 2007 contained one of the most tumultuous fortnights in recent British political history, stuck between two large bookends of boredom, as Tony and Gordon maintained what is best described as a phoney peace.

Of course, this was an improvement on what had come before. The 'African Coup' in autumn 2004 was followed in the New Year by the publication of *Brown's Britain* by Robert Peston. One of the reasons Peston is such an exceptional journalist is that you get so frustrated with him saying he already knows everything you're telling him that you end up dishing up all kinds of revelations simply in the hope of surprising him.

I remember watching Gordon almost kill himself one night in a hotel room in India, when he sat down exhausted on his bed with such force that one of the supporting pillars of the huge, tall four-poster bed cracked. I barely had time to exchange a panicked look with the protection officer before the thick brass beam that had been sticking into the top of the pillar came crashing down onto Gordon's head with massive force. At the very least, I expected him to be knocked unconscious, but he just put his hand to his head, and said blithely: 'Jeez, that's not very safe.'

I remember thinking that if I'd called Peston straight away to tell him that story, he'd have said: 'Well I know, I mean I told him that was going to happen after he turned down the futon. But he just won't listen.' In any case, when it came to writing his biography, Peston clearly got Gordon in revelatory mood, and was able to reveal that he had recently told Tony: 'There is nothing you could say to me now that I would ever believe.'

Gordon's utter sheepishness when the book emerged told us that he had indeed said far more to Peston than his discipline would normally have allowed, and – if we needed reminding – it told us what a dark place he had been in when doing those interviews with Peston the previous autumn. It was highly damaging for Blair given that his trust ratings with the public had already plummeted, and relations between the two men went into the deep freeze.

There was no doubt in our minds then that, if Tony was able to see through his plan to win the 2005 election without Gordon's involvement or assistance, he would be emboldened either to break up the Treasury and leave Gordon diminished and disempowered, or to offer Gordon a move to the Foreign Office and sack him if he refused.

Gordon had privately reconciled himself to accept the latter outcome but resist the former, but at the same time he remained convinced that Tony couldn't manage or win the election without him. And so it proved, with Alastair Campbell, Philip Gould and the two Eds coming together to agree the terms of the truce, signalled by Gordon and Tony sharing an ice cream during a joint campaign visit to Chatham, and then sweet nothings in a soft-focus party political broadcast by Anthony Minghella.

By the time the election was out of the way, Gordon had seen off all attempts to curb the power of the Treasury by increasing the power of the Cabinet Office. The big decisions on NHS funding and the euro – which had genuinely divided them – had been made. Indeed, when Gordon used to say in speeches that it remained our intention to join the single currency when the conditions were right, it was almost treated by the press like a nice ironic gag.

And while Gordon and Tony continued to disagree quite seriously and occasionally heatedly throughout this period on policies ranging from the EU Budget to the pensions system, there was only one major issue or fissure left between them: when was Blair going to go, and at what price?

While the terms of a final truce, handover or surrender remained unresolved, the competing armies of spin-doctors and allies kept up their daily sniping across the border, with the occasional atrocity committed in each other's villages. This, let me admit, was not a particularly edifying period for either side.

For Tony's mob, the message they wanted to convey was that Gordon was insufficiently committed to reform; too in hock to left-wing MPs and unions; unpopular with the swing voters in south-east marginals who had been crucial to Blair's election victories; simply not New Labour enough to appeal to Middle England and not someone people could imagine standing up for their concerns or representing the country overseas. For some of the Blairites, that meant Gordon was the wrong man to take over; for others, it simply meant there was no way Tony could step down any time soon.

By contrast, the message I wanted to convey was that Tony was hanging on to power for the sake of it, enjoying the trappings and the foreign jaunts and the long holidays; a lame duck within his own party, unable to get legislation through without Gordon's support; and ultimately reliant on Gordon when it came to winning the election because the public no longer trusted him. Indeed, after the quickly abandoned experiment at the election with his so-called 'sado-masochism strategy', Tony had stopped even trying to convince the public. In other words, the sooner he went and let Gordon set out his own stall, the better.

The tactics we used were fairly typical for each side. For me, it was leaking any proposals I came across which made Tony look a bit power crazed, promoting his acolytes to shore up his position or planning one last tilt at the windmills of the left; as well as briefing any story I could find – and there were many – which made Tony and his team look like they were enjoying the high life, entertaining ridiculous people in Downing Street, or working out how to feather their nests for the future. I'd also play on the fact that we couldn't get a hearing in many quarters of the media any more because Tony and his team no longer cared what the *Mail* or the *Telegraph* wrote about Labour.

For their part, the Blairites would write memos about Gordon's 'image problem' and commission polling to show it was true, all designed to be leaked. They would play on him not looking prime ministerial, and not being at ease in his own skin. They would brief that every minor controversy around foundation hospitals or the academy programme was the new, ultimate test of Brown's reformist credentials. And time and again, they would orchestrate speeches, policy launches and outspoken interviews by Blair's so-called outriders – Alan Milburn, Stephen Byers, Charles Clarke and the like – attacking Gordon and questioning his succession.

One of the first times I found myself publicly named by the press was when I emailed Sky News to offer them candidates to do the 'before-and-after' analysis of Gordon's 2006 Pre-Budget Report and was told it had already been sorted; they had Milburn and Byers on. I fired back an angry email asking them how putting up two self-proclaimed opponents of Gordon to speak for Labour about the PBR was fair.

I said it was like putting up Norman Scott's dog – Rinka, Scott's Great Dane, whose violent death was blamed on his lover, Liberal leader Jeremy Thorpe, in 1975 – to speak for the Lib Dems. The email correspondence was leaked to the papers, and became a regularly quoted example of my robust approach. I didn't mind that too much, but I did mind the fact that Blair's operation never did anything to stop these characters openly attacking Gordon in public.

Of course, they might have said the same about my activities, but that tells its own tale. While we operated in a different way – they leaked polls and memos, I leaked policy documents; they got Byers to knife Gordon, I gave the *Telegraph* material to knife Blair – I regarded my operations and theirs as equivalent, so it always baffled me when they claimed any moral high ground.

A case in point was at the launch of Labour's local election campaign in Docklands in April 2006: Gordon and Tony putting on a show of unity for the cameras by appearing together in front of a select audience of activists, volunteers and party workers.

As the two of them walked down a narrow corridor to enter the main room where those supporters and a bank of cameras were waiting, I saw Tony's staff stifling laughter as they walked behind. 'Oh my God, what does he look like?' one of them said. I looked ahead, and could see Gordon had clearly run his fingers through his thick, unwashed hair, and now had it sticking up like an outsize cockatoo, just as he was about to step in front of the cameras.

I shouted: 'Gordon! Stop! GORDON! STOP!' He didn't. I was desperate: 'TONY!' Blair turned round. 'Stop Gordon, stop him there! Don't let him go out!' Tony did as asked, and I rushed forward, took Gordon into a side room and flattened out his hair. As I walked back out, Tony's staff looked disgusted that I'd deemed to address 'The Leader' directly, let alone by his first name.

I should explain that if you worked for Tony Blair in No. 10, you generally referred to him as 'The Boss', in the same way you referred to Downing Street as 'The House', two horrible affectations that people had picked up from the special protection officers, who at least had the excuse that the phrases were both short and anonymous if speaking in a hurry or in crowds.

But if you didn't work directly for Blair, civil servants were expected to refer to him as 'The PM', and non-No. 10 special advisers or party workers were expected to call him 'The Leader'. We tried to abolish all those phrases when Gordon was in No. 10, in favour simply of 'Gordon'. I was appalled to hear that, after taking over the party, Ed Miliband's team reverted to an insistence on 'The Leader'. Ugh.

At that local elections launch, we'd agreed that Tony and Gordon would take questions from the attending journalists, and I'd assured the hacks I'd met in the morning that was the plan. When No. 10 unilaterally decided it wasn't, it made me look like an idiot but also made us look complicit in their contempt for the press. So I gave Paul Waugh at the *Standard* a copy of the schedule for the day including the time set aside for media Q&A.

No. 10 were furious about that, but I cared even less than normal, because the hair thing bugged me. At least a dozen No. 10 people ahead of me in that corridor could see that Gordon's hair looked mental and the pictures would invite ridicule, but they seemed to relish the contrast with Tony looking perfectly coiffed and prime ministerial. Was it any worse for me to relish portraying Gordon as transparent and friendly to the media, while Blair looked aloof and evasive?

Anyway, while all this sniping was going on, and on, and on, Gordon and Tony themselves were continuing to have their own private discussions about the succession, and in parallel, Campbell and Gould were meeting the Eds to talk about the practicalities, the policies and the process. But frankly it didn't matter how constructive and amicable the advisers' meetings were, if those between Gordon and Tony remained desultory and hostile.

The Eds would come out of a meeting and cheerfully report back to Gordon that it was all going well; Gordon would come out of his and say that Blair had refused to talk about the hand-over at all, and just wanted to speak about pensions. There was the all too familiar sense for Gordon that, for all the public talk of a 'stable and orderly transition', Tony remained totally unrec-onciled to the idea, and it was just a matter of time before he did what he'd done in 2004, extended his planned end date, and further weakened Gordon's hopes of ever taking over.

The Eds confronted Campbell and Gould with this at their next meeting, and Campbell replied that the problem was that Blair was 'not psychologically ready' to quit Downing Street. It was a dynamite quote, totally in line with my sniper activity since the 2005 election, and evocative of the 'psychologically flawed' description of Gordon supposedly given by Campbell to Andrew Rawnsley in 1998.

After I had a rather long lunch with *Mail on Sunday* columnist Peter Dobbie a few days later, the 'not psychologically ready' quote found its way into that weekend's paper, although not attributed to Campbell. That one column by Dobbie was enough to bring all the talks to a halt, and while I was apologetic about what I'd done, the response I got from Balls and others was a shrug. The meetings had become pointless anyway, so it didn't ultimately matter how they ended, and at least a passing, anonymised mention in a column didn't look as overtly aggressive as the splash that quote probably merited.

Relations went back into the freezer until the Tom Watson 'coup' of summer 2006 and after that had been resolved, we were back to the phoney peace until the day Blair left, with the occasional outbreak of border sniping between the camps, out of either boredom, habit or personal animus.

Looking at that whole period and all that went before, we're left with the ultimate question: how did Gordon and Tony both put up with each other for so long; and why – given all the torment and tumult of their thirteen years together at the top – did one of them not terminate the relationship?

After all, there were any number of fraught occasions when one of them could have cut the rope at a time when the other was dangling from the precipice: if, for example, Gordon had resigned over the Iraq War alongside Robin Cook, or if Tony had backed himself and stuck to his decision to exclude Gordon from the 2005 election campaign.

Some will say it was about some residual personal loyalty and kinship built up over two decades; a marriage they couldn't walk away from. Others will say neither man could have felt secure enough about maintaining control of party donors, the media and the party if he destroyed the other.

And perhaps there's something else: the mystery – very possibly a myth – of what we used to call Tony and Gordon's 'Mutually Assured Destruction', the idea that they possessed information which would turn any attempted fratricide into guaranteed suicide, once the wounded party – with nothing left to lose – allowed what he knew about the other man to become public.

I never heard any open reference to this from Gordon and, among his advisers, it was something we didn't openly discuss, or perhaps didn't want to given it left you feeling that you were playing cards without a full deck. It will probably always remain a mystery, and rightly so.

However, and acknowledging the element of post-hoc rationalisation in this analysis, I would also argue that the reason neither man ever pressed the nuclear button was because ultimately their Cold War was good for the Labour Party. Yes, I'm serious.

Of course there is a common view that all the feuding I've described above and elsewhere, both the genuine disagreements between the two men and the constant sniper fire between their aides and allies, was a disaster for the Labour Party and a dysfunctional mess for the country.

Either they should have learned to work together in harmony, the theory goes, or – if they couldn't – Gordon should have had the guts to challenge Tony or Tony the guts to sack Gordon, rather than letting things fester on for thirteen years. To that theory, I say, with all due respect: bollocks.

The angry, bitter, soap-opera style rivalry between the two men was, I believe, a huge positive for the Labour Party, helping it to win three consecutive terms in office. And if you also believe, as I do, that Labour changed Britain for the better and improved many people's lives during that period, then it follows that the Blair–Brown wars were good for the country too.

My rationale for that is simple. As long as their feud continued, it was the only political story that mattered. No one else, least of all the Conservative Party, could get a look in. And as long as that feud erupted on issues of policy – the euro, NHS spending, tax, foundation hospitals, academies, tuition fees, pensions and so on – it guaranteed that the only debate that mattered in British politics from 1997 to 2007 was Blair versus Brown, and all on issues around the economy and public services too, where Labour wanted that debate to be.

A relatively dry policy issue which would barely rate a mention by the newspapers in normal circumstances could be turned into a front-page story and debated for a week afterwards simply by injecting a bit of No. 11 fury or No. 10 irritation.

Shortly before Tony Blair left office, Andy Burnham – then a rising star minister at the Department of Health – was due to publish a pamphlet setting out the argument for a written NHS constitution. With Andy's agreement, we told *The Guardian* that this would be a key plank of Gordon's reform agenda when he became PM, and by the way, he's a huge admirer of Andy; code for 'Gordon's going to be an even more radical reformer of public services than Tony, and he's going to promote the best young talent to his Cabinet'. A guaranteed splash.

That same afternoon, *The Guardian* also took a call from

No. 10 saying Tony Blair had given the green light to Andy's plans as a key plank of his legacy; code for 'This is stuff Tony needs to do now 'cos he can't trust Gordon to carry on the reform agenda'. Another guaranteed splash! For an hour, standing in Great Smith Street, I argued over the phone with *The Guardian*'s political editor, Patrick Wintour, about which interpretation was correct, presumably with my opposite number in Downing Street in his other ear doing the same.

And there was no middle ground: a political story in that era had to be a triumph for one man and a blow for the other. The idea of Gordon and Tony agreeing on something was obviously not impossible, but it wasn't a story. When I saw the *Guardian* front page that night, and realised the Blairite interpretation had won out, I was incandescent. I had lost out to No. 10, and they knew it. *The Guardian* had sided with them even when they were on their way out; I unleashed a text message tirade against Patrick, and fumed for weeks afterwards.

Yet, in retrospect, it's amazing that a pamphlet written by a junior minister at the Department of Health was able to splash a national newspaper, not because of its contents by themselves, but because of its perceived significance – one way or another – within the Blair–Brown feud. That is what you call dominating the political debate.

And this is why I came to think of the whole feud as akin to the Cola Wars, the long-standing marketing rivalry between Coke and Pepsi. Whatever the heated nature of that rivalry, and the shifting success of one brand over another, the real significance of the Cola Wars is that – for well over a century – they have maintained the position of Coke, Pepsi and their diet equivalents at the top of the American soft drinks market. Coke vs Pepsi remains the only real choice there is, despite being – to the undiscerning palate – essentially the same product.

If one of those brands simply didn't exist, it's unlikely that Americans would just switch wholesale over to the other. People want a choice. It's more likely that – over time – other non-cola drinks would significantly increase their market share, and, as the accepted 'choice' became between one cola drink and some other, very different-tasting beverages, that market share would only increase as more people sampled the alternative.

Similar to Coke and Pepsi, from 1997 to 2007, Gordon and Tony dominated the political market, to the exclusion of the Tory Party and to any other internal rivals for the Labour leadership (the Virgin Cola candidates if you like). They achieved this not only by achieving personal success in their respective roles, but – albeit not consciously – by ensuring that the story of their rivalry and their policy rows was the only show in town for a decade.

As soon as that rivalry disappeared, and in the absence of any other compelling internal soap opera to replace it, Labour was exposed for the first time to viable competition from the Tory alternative and left without the vital grist to make splash headlines out of policy changes. A major reform like the raising of the education leaving age from sixteen to eighteen, guaranteed to create headlines for a week if there had been any Blair vs Brown angle, passed almost unnoticed in 2007 when announced by Brown alone.

Could Brown have done anything about this? Perhaps if David Miliband had been his Deputy PM or Ed Balls his Chancellor, the recipe for soap opera storylines would have been there – the young pretender left in charge over the summer, or the young protégé defying his mentor on economic policy. But it's a brave politician who will willingly sow the seeds of trouble to reap the rewards of media dominance.

I always imagine that, once a year, the CEOs of Coca-Cola and PepsiCo come together at a secret location, drink a can of each other's product and raise a toast to keeping all the others in a distant third place. Maybe one day I'll do the same with the mob I used to fight with in No. 10, and we'll raise a suitable toast to a decade of market dominance and three Tory leaders who could never get anyone to try their product.

Maybe the Tories should have gone down the Dr Pepper route in their election slogans: 'Michael Howard ... what's the worst that could happen?'

26

TAKING ON THE TORIES

'Have you got any Tory friends?'

That, right there, is the single best interview question you can ask any Labour politician, whether it's an aspiring MP at a selection meeting or a Prime Minister running for re-election.

Why? Because for many of them – at whatever level – it makes them pause and wonder: 'What's the *right* answer?' even before they get onto the more difficult point, which is: 'Oh shit, what *is* the answer? Do I have any? What if they ask me who?' Watch for those one or two little pauses, and you know you've got someone uncertain or calculating in front of you, neither an appealing trait.

Apart from telling the instinctive truth, whatever it is, there's only one correct answer to that question, which works for all audiences: 'Probably.'

But there's another reason that question is difficult and revealing. Many Labour people, but certainly not all, can find it difficult to warm to a self-professed Tory because – in their minds – it suggests there's something fundamentally wrong with their values or the sort of life they've lived that's allowed them to choose that path.

Particularly for that generation whose formative years were in the 1980s and early 1990s, if they think: 'Brought up the way I was, seeing life as it was when I was young, how could I be anything but Labour?', then it follows in their minds that anyone who isn't either had a sheltered upbringing or – even worse – had the same formative experiences, but decided to become a Tory.

And that matters because the four main players on the Tory and Labour front benches had their teenage years in that period: Cameron, Balls, Miliband and Osborne, in descending order of age, as well as most of the rising stars and behind-the-scenes heavyweights on either side. Even the hope of a new generation, Chuka Umunna, was a teenager during the Black Wednesday debacle.

Compare Ed Miliband and George Osborne. While the young Ed Miliband would join in his father's dinner party debates about how the left should respond to Thatcher's war against the unions, George Osborne has said on the record – to *Guardian* writer Decca Aitkenhead – that he can't really remember the miners' strike. He was thirteen at the time.

If there's currently more animus than we've been used to seeing over the years between the respective front benches, that gulf between their formative experiences is part of the reason why. The next election will be a fantastic tag team death match between the two Eds, Cameron and Osborne. I can't wait.

I personally have never hated Tories or thought it was inexplicable to be one. My beloved Uncles Bill and John, both sadly gone, were the funniest, kindest men I've ever met. John was a staunch socialist who always explained his beliefs by asking how it was fair for the first son of the Duke of Westminster to be born a billionaire. Bill, by contrast, was Tory to his toes. Having spent a life on the railways, he was contracted to the Communist government of Mozambique, and his first act on taking over his office was to replace the portrait of Karl Marx with one of Margaret Thatcher.

Hating Tories would have meant hating Bill, or my great university pals Chris Spink and Rod Bryce, or my close friend and the 2005 candidate for Sunderland North, Stephen Daughton. So, compared to most people working for the Labour Party in that era, Gordon more than anyone, I didn't feel particularly tribal.

But, to the extent that the Tories represented any threat to Gordon's ambitions, that was where my killer instincts would kick in, not least because Gordon liked to keep a tally of the number of shadow Chancellors he had seen off over the years, and was always itching to take another scalp.

From the moment we saw the emergence of David Cameron at the Tories' 2005 leadership conference, George Osborne at his

side, we were worried. If they were serious about modernising
the Tory Party; if they could succeed in neutralising the economy
and public services as dividing line issues by agreeing with us on
our tax and spending plans; and if – as was evident – they had
the image and freshness to go with it, then they represented a
real threat to Gordon's chances of succeeding Tony, and then of
winning any subsequent election.

This was where Gordon's seven-year rule kicked in. If he was
right that his public appeal was on the wane, and Cameron and
Osborne were determined to turn British politics from a choice
of policies to a choice of personalities, then it would become a
dangerous time. I made a half-hearted attempt to persuade the
press that we were relieved David Davis had performed badly at
the Tory conference, and the man we were really worried about
was Ken Clarke, but they weren't buying it.

So we were left with Cameron and Osborne, and taking them
on became the priority. But while the main Labour attack lines
focused on their posh backgrounds, their tendency to say one
thing and do another, and their remoteness from ordinary life,
that wasn't really my priority. My task was to show they were
incompetent and weak, didn't know what they were doing and
weren't up to the job.

Why? Because it was important to cement that image with the
public for the long-term, but – more immediately – we needed
to show Labour MPs and Labour members that this was what
happens when you put kids in charge; that there was a reason
for favouring experience and solidity over youth and style. We
were attacking David Cameron, but at the same time sending a
not-so-subtle message to those on our own side who were giving
David Miliband the glad eye.

And just as we later found with David Miliband, our job in
depicting the inexperience and naivety of Cameron and Osborne
was made easier because in those early days they so frequently
helped us out, hugely prone as they were to errors and gaffes.

For example, we discovered that whichever junior monkey at
Tory HQ was responsible for managing their online operation

had a bad habit of doing test uploads of key documents before they formally went on the website. When we knew something big was coming, the genius Labour officials who led attack operations and opposition research – Patrick Loughran, Steve Van Riel and Theo Bertram – would sit working away in their Victoria Street offices but refreshing the Tory website every ten minutes to see whether anything new had come up.

Every so often, they'd hit the mother lode, as happened in October 2006 when the Tories gave a test upload to the conclusions of the policy report Cameron and Osborne had commissioned from John Redwood into building a more competitive economy. I scanned through it and it was pretty much the dynamite you might expect if you allowed someone like John Redwood to write what he liked about the economy: abolishing regulation of the pensions industry, introducing a flat rate of income tax and so on.

I ran round to Ed Balls's ministerial office. I was told he was in a meeting but very politely told the office to 'fuck that'. I marched in and talked him through the document. 'Right,' he said, 'let's go and have some fun.' We ran off down the street to Millbank, me ringing ahead to all the broadcasters telling them we had a massive leak and they'd need to put Ed straight on air. The BBC were cautious as always, so I just said: 'Well, wait 'til you see him on Sky, then see if you want him.'

There was no hint of Ed's stammer as he charged round the studios. He was speaking so spontaneously he didn't have to worry whether the words would come out because even he had no idea what he was going to say next. It was great; one of those days when you know your opponents just have their heads in their hands.

If the Tories learned a rather valuable lesson from that – don't let Labour release your documents for you – they learned another a few months later, on a George Osborne venture to Japan: don't make announcements abroad unless you've got a captive audience.

Osborne hadn't taken a press entourage to Japan, and had

instead just given an overnight exclusive to the *Financial Times* that he wanted to build a UK version of Japan's ultra-high-speed magnetic levitating train. He and his team may have gone to bed eight hours ahead in Tokyo thinking the *FT* story was a job well done, but I was just waking up with a whole day in front of me to kill it.

And I did: I spent the morning online researching and distributing to journalists the history of accidents and fires on mag-lev trains, and established the fact it wouldn't even have time to get up to top speed on the route Osborne was proposing. One journalist told me that Osborne texted him and said: 'What's going on with this story? Why has everyone got so down on it?' The journalist replied: 'You've just met the Dog.'

That was, incidentally, the first time I discovered that I was known in the lobby by the nickname 'Mad Dog' or just 'Dog' for short. There are lots of lobby nicknames that aren't usually said directly to the person who owns them, and that was one. Michael Ellam's nickname was 'The Sheik', as in Sheik El-lam, which fitted his Omar Sharif-style personality quite well.

Superficially, what the Redwood and mag-lev incidents had in common is that we were far better at using the internet and doing basic research than the Tories, but it was deeper than that – there was a basic lack of care and competence within the Tory operation. They were a haphazard bunch.

Take the then shadow Cabinet minister for Culture, Hugo Swire. He'd appeared at some arts reception and wondered aloud whether it might not be time to allow the national museums and galleries to start charging for admission, a throwaway thought that was given a favourable mention in the diary column of the *Sunday Times*' culture section.

If you read that column regularly, you'll know it almost always contains some political titbit, so part of my Sunday papers routine was checking it to see if any of our ministers had said anything daft. I saw the Hugo Swire reference and squirreled it away until the following weekend, at which point the *Mail on Sunday* splashed it, and – to my amazement – Swire didn't just have to apologise but was sorrowfully sacked by his close friend Cameron two weeks later.

Obviously what Swire had said was ill judged and lackadaisical, but – again – I wondered why no one on the Tory side was doing the equivalent of my job, reading all the key bits of all the key papers and getting on top of stories like that, in that case getting it corrected and killed before someone like me could exploit it.

There were a few key journalists I could always rely on as good, objective and honest barometers of where we were politically, and – at that time – they were absolutely clear with me: you Brown guys are the only show in town, the only professional operation we deal with; the other lot are not even playing the same game, let alone in the same league.

That was before Andy Coulson. The Tory operation improved beyond all recognition once he was brought in to be their Head of Communications. He may not have had much of a head for politics or policy, not at first anyway, but he had an eye for a story and an ear for trouble, and the Tories immediately became a much tighter and more aggressive ship.

People may look back in future years and see Coulson's appointment as a mistake, but the context is key. At that stage, the Tory operation was a shambles; we were giving Cameron and Osborne the runaround, and they needed to do something about it – otherwise their leadership was going to go down as just another dismal, failed experiment in the long years of Tory opposition.

So if they decided to take a big risk, cut a few corners and omit to ask a few questions when hiring Coulson, that is the reason why. It certainly made sense at the time.

27

LEAKS AND LEAKERS

There is an art to leaking.

Not the kind of leaking where you go to a private meeting with twenty-five other people and tell a journalist afterwards what everyone said. That kind of leaking is for the worst kind of shysters, many of them Cabinet or shadow Cabinet ministers, and – after that first time I got my hands dirty at the 2004 spin-doctors' summit – I barely did a single other story of that nature.

In fact, once my reputation as a leaker was well established, I pretty much stopped attending any non-essential meetings, because if anything did leak out of them, it was odds-on I would get the blame. In fact, it probably made it more likely something would leak because my presence gave people cover. For that reason, I never attended a single Cabinet meeting.

No, the art to leaking is knowing where to look – or who to tap up – to discover information, making a calculated decision about which bits of that information could be made public without causing any blowback, how it should be presented to avoid it looking like a leak, and then finally deploying it – to use the magic phrase beloved of Westminster journalists – with 'no fingerprints'.

Essentially, the entire process of briefing the Budget or PBR is an exercise in that art, including the various bits of skulduggery carried out in the preceding fortnight to try and cause diversions and keep the Budget announcements dry until a few days before-hand. But those were only two events during the year; there were an awful lot of weeks and months to fill between them.

So how did it work in practice? Sitting in my office in the Treasury, I'd scroll through the skeletal version of 'the grid' circu-lated each week by No. 10, an Outlook weekly calendar-style

document which would simply outline on two landscape sheets of
A4 – in as little detail as possible – the main upcoming announcements for the next fortnight: 'Johnson, DoH – Liver Disease' and
so on, with the main story of each day highlighted in bold at the
top of each column.

The purpose of this being circulated was so departments could
avoid their announcements clashing, either in terms of timing
or messaging. You didn't want Alan Johnson unveiling a hard-
hitting campaign on liver disease on the same day Tessa Jowell
was announcing the pilot schemes for 24-hour pubs. It was also a
control mechanism from Downing Street: a way of saying that if
your minister's speech or announcement wasn't registered in the
grid they shouldn't be making it.

Sometimes, these little snippets in the grid would be enough for
me to make a story. If I was able to tell a Sunday hack that the
Department of Health was planning something on liver disease
next Thursday, that might be enough for them to call up some
weary press officer planning to assault their own liver late on a
Friday, and say:

'Hi, I've had a briefing about this liver disease story for next
week, which is all fine – we're probably going to splash it – and
I've got some good quotes from one of your guys and the BMA,
but the one thing I didn't check is which of your ministers is
fronting it up – is it Alan Johnson or one of the juniors? Ah, OK.
And the only other thing is the stats they gave me already seem
to be in the public domain; are there no fresh stats coming out
on the day? Ah, OK. Let me get that down. Thanks very much.'

This was known in Westminster as 'busting the grid', code
for using an overly revealing headline in the grid to decipher an
upcoming announcement. But usually it needed a bit more work
than that, especially when the headline just said something like:
'Reid: Counter-Terrorism' in bold.

That's where I earned my corn. If it was a department where
I had one of my network of 'contacts', junior civil servants who
I'd befriended in pubs over the years, I'd bump into them on their
regular Friday drink, and tap them up to see what was coming

out next week. But as I became a bit better known around Whitehall, it became increasingly difficult to have those conversations unnoticed.

So I'd do the more difficult thing. Because I had access to the Chancellor's office email system – not his personal email, but the official one used for receiving submissions and correspondence – I'd hunt through the folders for Cabinet papers or minutes of Cabinet meetings, and look for a proposal or discussion that might correspond to the upcoming announcement. This could take hours, but I'd usually crack it eventually.

Now came the crucial stage. A reckless or lazy spin-doctor might just print off the relevant document, or copy and paste the key passage, and pass that on to a journalist. That was the sort of thing that brought about leak enquiries, sackings and – in the worst cases – prosecutions, because most of those documents would be marked either 'Restricted', 'Confidential' or 'Secret', the direct leaking of which would have put me in breach of the Official Secrets Act.

So, instead, I'd read the document on screen, absorb all the information and then write it out for myself in entirely different language, as though it was a press briefing. And that was what it would become. I'd sit down with a journalist, or call them up, and talk them through the story as though I was briefing a Budget measure or one of Gordon's speeches.

And – no matter how potentially controversial the story was – I'd brief it in an entirely positive way so that, when it appeared in print, it looked like it had been officially briefed by a minister or spin-doctor from the relevant department. That meant also taking out of the briefing anything that I'd seen in the documents that was obviously damaging to that department, or which undermined their announcement, for example if Tessa's officials were warning her of police concerns over the 24-hour pub pilot schemes.

For the same reasons, I'd also ban the journalist from using the word 'leak' anywhere in the story so that it didn't look unplanned. And that was it. The story would emerge in one paper or another, or – so it looked like a proper briefing operation – in two or three on the same day. The department would be confused and hold little internal inquests to see who'd briefed it, or who'd had lunch with a particular journalist that week, but they'd eventually just shrug.

Of course, sometimes there was a bit more mischief to the art. If I could simultaneously give a good story to a journalist and destabilise one of Gordon's internal rivals or critics, that was all the better.

For several weeks in succession in 2005 when Charles Clarke was Home Secretary and a declared opponent of Gordon's succession to the premiership, I orchestrated what looked like a briefing war between Charles and Tony Blair's anti-social behaviour guru, Louise Casey; each of them in turn appearing to goad the other by making some new announcement on the subject through the Sunday papers, or appearing to claim advance credit for something the other was planning to announce.

There was already plenty of ill-feeling between them, but the Sunday briefings made it both public and self-fulfilling, contributing to Tony Blair's sacking of Charles in May 2006. At a drink with Charles's press team after the reshuffle, they were bitter about Louise's role in undermining their boss and oblivious enough of my own role that they happily supplied details of how Tony Blair had been in tears when he told Charles the news, a bit of colour I obviously then briefed to the papers.

So if that's how the leaking of other department's announcements or proposals used to work in my Treasury days, let me try and explain the more difficult question: why I did it, besides the pleasure of creating a little weekend mayhem for Charles Clarke or John Reid.

It came down to this. For years, Gordon had – hands down – the best intelligence operation on the press of any politician in Westminster, in terms of knowing what different media outlets were planning, thinking or writing before it happened. Other politicians had particularly good connections with certain newspapers or broadcasters, but no one had Gordon's breadth or depth of reach. Much of this he delivered himself through his own strong relationships with editors and proprietors, and much of it was delivered by the Eds through their relationships with key columnists.

But in terms of Gordon's relationship with the actual journalists writing the stories, or with harder-to-reach newspapers like the *Telegraph*, *Sunday Times* or *Mail on Sunday*, that was entirely delivered by the likes of me. And, while Gordon and Ed might have thought I cultivated my contacts just by putting in the hours in the pub, none of that would have mattered if I wasn't also putting in the hours at my computer getting stories for those journalists.

Those relationships are ultimately about the business of selling newspapers. You can be as friendly as you want with a journalist, but – as I discovered myself when my phone stopped ringing in April 2009 – if you haven't got anything useful to trade, then you can't expect a journalist to invest their time or their bar tab in you, let alone share information that you'll find useful.

Gordon never understood that and I never tried to explain it. He'd sometimes say to me: 'How did you get this stuff?' after I'd tell him some crucial piece of intelligence about what the Tories were planning, obtained in return for a good splash, and I'd just say: 'Don't ask.'

I'd see he was a little more suspicious when a potentially bad newspaper story about the Treasury that we'd been fighting all day was suddenly relegated to the inside pages in favour of a front-page splash about an upcoming government white paper. Then he knew not to ask.

And did those ends justify the means? Well, Charles Clarke and others would disagree, but they weren't my concern. Keeping Gordon in No. 11 and getting him into No. 10 was my job, from where – in my mind – he could do what was best for Labour and the country.

And I always asked myself: what would the alternative be if I wasn't doing this; if I wasn't putting in the effort and taking the risks necessary to maintain those relationships; if the Sunday

papers had to find another political story to splash rather than
the one I was giving them, possibly one about Gordon or the
Treasury?

I got to see what that alternative looked like immediately after
my sacking in 2009, when the revelations about MPs' expenses
emerged in the *Telegraph*. It was a disastrous story for all MPs, but
particularly for Labour, given that incumbents are held account-
able for the system, and especially for Gordon, given what was
widely perceived as his slow and inept response to the outcry.

That was in large part because he was not only taken completely
by surprise by the revelations, but also thrown into a total tailspin
in the crucial first twenty-four hours by the *Telegraph*'s decision
to focus the first splash on his domestic cleaning bills. He spent
more time worrying about how to defend his own integrity than
about how to respond to the issue as a whole. David Cameron,
by contrast, seemed remarkably well prepared for the emergence
of the story, and calm and decisive in his response.

A while afterwards, I spoke to a senior figure in the *Telegraph*
group, who said simply: 'The expenses scandal would not have
damaged Labour as badly if you'd still been doing your job.' I
took it as a compliment, meaning I would have handled the reaction better, but he shook his head. 'That's true. But what I mean
is: if you'd still been there, we wouldn't have surprised you with
it and we wouldn't have made Gordon the first splash. It would
have been a breach of trust and a breach of our relationship, and
we wouldn't have done that.'

Exactly the same thing was said to me by a senior journalist
at *The Sun* after their decision to declare their support for the
Tories on the same evening as Gordon's party conference speech
later that year. 'It wouldn't have changed the outcome,' he said,
'but you being there would have changed the entire process, and
probably the timing.'

So is leaking against your own government justified? I would
strongly argue that done in the way I did it, it never did much
harm, and it certainly did Gordon a lot of good. Which raises
what I'm about to say to even greater heights of hypocrisy: me

leaking against every other department was fine, but anyone leaking against the Treasury was asking to be put against a wall and shot.

Gordon's Treasury was almost immune to unplanned leaks, a remarkable record given the length of time he was there. That was in part due to our policy that unless a quote or a briefing came from the Head of Communications, the media special adviser, Gordon or the two Eds, it did not represent the view of the Treasury. All journalists knew we would quite happily dump all over a story if it hadn't come from one of those individuals, even if there was some truth in it.

Our leak-proof reputation was also due – and I admit full responsibility and a fair degree of shame for this – to my Admiral Byng approach to leaks, named after the head of Britain's fleet at Minorca, executed for allowing the island to fall to the French, but primarily – as Voltaire said – *'pour encourager les autres'*.

If anything did appear in the papers that was not from one of our approved parties, I would instantly name a culprit – usually a junior special adviser who'd once been seen speaking to a journalist – and order them to be cut out of meetings and removed from the circulation list for emails until the matter was resolved.

Usually, I was right, but it was the confident assertion and awareness of their guilt throughout the Treasury that mattered, not the actual truth. The effect was simply to put the fear of God into every official and adviser about doing any leaking, and it had the desired deterrent effect. As for the occasional Admiral Byngs, if they were guilty, they never did it again. And if they weren't, they'd usually recover fairly quickly.

When Gordon moved into No. 10, that discipline proved hard to maintain. There were too many separate sources of expertise and authority – and too many people with existing relationships with journalists – to insist that only me, Gordon and his official spokesman Michael Ellam could be considered reliable sources of a 'No. 10' quote or briefing. What's more, while no Labour MP in the old days would have dreamed of describing themselves to a journalist as a 'source close to the Treasury', because that suggests some economic remit, selling themselves as a 'source close to No. 10' was much easier.

My approach to leaking had to change as well once we moved next door. I couldn't bust our own grid, or leak an announcement from another department that we'd deliberately scheduled to get maximum media coverage. But I could still leak some of the small stuff, inconsequential if it had been formally announced to Parliament, but attractive as an exclusive for one paper.

And the big difference in No. 10 compared to the Treasury is the sheer volume of other things that you get to hear about that are nothing to do with government or any planned departmental announcements, from the Church of England to the England football team, which – carefully done, as always – could be worked up into tradable commodities for the press.

Ultimately, if splashing a paper or getting to the top of the *Today* programme gave me a wonderful rush, doing it through a leak added something illicit and dangerous into the drug, and it became an addiction – one I found very tough to give up. When the coalition took over, I found a few of those old junior civil servants I'd befriended getting in touch to say how awful it was having to work for the Tories, and you'll never believe what they're planning to announce next week...

Just say no, kids, just say no.

28

THE ART OF OVERSEAS TRIPS

The closer Gordon got to becoming Prime Minister, the more varied his overseas travel became as he sought to obtain first-hand experience of different countries and continents, and establish relationships with their leaders. And those major overseas trips meant taking with us giant entourages of political broadcast, print and wire journalists.

Before getting into some of those specific trips, it's worth explaining how these things work. Not that we started out as experts; it was not something any of Brown's team had experience of doing before, bar Sue Nye, and her experiences hadn't been entirely happy ones: she accompanied Labour leader Neil Kinnock to Washington in 1986 when he was snubbed by President Reagan, and to Zimbabwe in 1988 when he was held captive in a hut with a dozen travelling journalists while armed soldiers trained AK-47 rifles at them and Neil tried to lead choruses of 'We Shall Overcome'.

As Sue often observed, the key to a successful trip is all in the preparation. On the logistics side, that was about ensuring the schedule was varied and interesting – with lots of nice photo-opportunities – and that all the travel and accommodation arrangements were simple and smooth. Gordon had outstanding logistics and events managers working for him in the Treasury and No. 10, including masters of calm Helen Etheridge, Jo Dipple and Rachel Kinnock (Neil's daughter), and their colleagues Barbara Burke and Lisa Perrin.

But best of the lot was a fiery young lady from the Turkish Republic of Northern Cyprus, Ms Balshen Izzet. She was everything the Treasury wasn't but won over everyone instantly, from Sue Nye to the security guards. The first time I met her, I was mesmerised, and I had the luck of the Irish when we started a secret romance on St Patrick's Day, 2006.

The great strength of Balshen and her colleagues was that they were always thinking not just about Gordon, but about the media entourage. If Gordon was going to get a police motorcade on arrival in a country, would the press bus be allowed in it? Did the schedule allow sufficient filing time for the evening news and next day's papers? And, above all, what was the backup plan if internet access was down at the hotel?

Lots of the irritations that build up between the media entourage and a minister's team on a foreign trip can easily be anticipated and dealt with in advance just by thinking through all those simple questions. The fact they did that allowed me to concentrate on what I did best: coming up with the schedule of stories for the trip.

I had a strict set of rules for how we did this: I needed a good story for the morning we flew out so all the hacks were in a buoyant mood by the time we got on the plane; I needed one strong story for each day of the trip and two belters in my 'back pocket' in case something went wrong; and finally, I needed one decent domestic story – often a bit of grid-busting skulduggery – that I could dispense on the final day or on the flight back as a parting gift to the travelling hacks, just so they felt as looked after and catered for as possible.

When planning those stories, it wasn't enough simply to know that – on Day 3 – Gordon would make a speech and hope that would do the trick; I had to know in advance what the two or three lines of announcements would be in the speech that would be capable of splashing a paper, getting a page lead or going to the top of the *Today* programme, and if there weren't any, I'd tell Gordon he needed to re-write it.

We also had to think out in advance the sequencing between broadcasters, overnight newspapers and newswires. The broadcasters needed a story for their morning bulletins and a different or at least much-advanced story for the evening and night-time news; the newspapers needed a story that would under no circumstances be 'out' back in the UK before 10 p.m. – otherwise they could just as well have sat at home and filed it without the expense of the trip; and the newswires just wanted to put things out as soon as they heard about them.

Having to manage all that while constantly keeping in mind the time difference between the UK and whichever country we were in was – let me be frank – bloody hard work. If we also had the *Evening Standard* on our trip, needing a fresh line for mid-morning, my head would nearly explode.

The only way it could really work was by negotiating with all the various parties and agreeing what information would emerge at what points, and the only way we could have that negotiation was because of the lobby system, the self-policing ordinance which says that political journalists who belong to the Westminster lobby do not screw you or each other over by breaking agreements on the timing, content or attribution of their copy.

And I was bound by those agreements too. If *The Independent* or *Evening Standard* chose not to send someone on a trip, but their political editor called me to ask for a 'fill' – that is a quick briefing on what was happening – it didn't matter how close I was to them or how helpful I wanted to be, I just had to make my excuses and tell them there wasn't much to report. The travelling press would have strung me up by my BlackBerry charger if a newspaper which hadn't 'sent' ever had the same overnight story as all the others that had.

I'd try and establish a shop-steward for the trip – the most senior or respected journalist there – and do my negotiations through them, so anyone who broke any agreements would face their avuncular disapproval. The difficulty would come when one of the broadcasters or newspapers would send a non-lobby journalist to cover the trip, or – worse still – leave it to their country correspondent. To protect my schedule of stories, I usually had no option but to shut them out, sometimes literally.

Gordon once had to conduct a briefing in Beijing for the travelling lobby to a backdrop of muffled shouting and swearing as I held the doors closed at the back of the room to stop the BBC's business correspondent, Nils Blythe – later spokesman for the Bank of England – from gaining entry.

Of course, it didn't always work. There would be misunderstandings or occasional mischief by particular journalists, and the schedule would have to go out of the window. That is where my back-pocket stories would come in: I'd take aside either the broadcasters or the papers – whichever party had been screwed – and say: 'Sorry that happened, but here's an alternative.'

For example, on his pre-G20 trip to South America in 2009, Gordon found himself announcing that he would back reform of the laws on royal succession to allow first-born girls and heirs married to Catholics to ascend the throne. It had nothing to do with the trip, but it was a cracking story, and it got us out of a hole with the broadcasters, whose night-time news line had been bust.

On other occasions, my approach to 'creating' a story was slightly more dubious. In November 2005, we were set to fly to Israel the night before the House of Commons was voting on the detention of terror suspects for 42 days without charge, with Tony Blair facing the prospect of the legislation being defeated by Labour rebels voting with the Tories and Liberal Democrats.

There were growing whispers from 'sources close to No. 10' that, by going to Israel, Gordon was deliberately contriving to miss a vote that was unpopular with Labour MPs, but we hoped to get around that criticism by persuading either George Osborne or Vince Cable to 'pair' with him – agreeing not to vote themselves so as to cancel out the impact of Gordon being missing, a courtesy that opposite numbers will occasionally extend to each other if there is a good enough reason.

As we sat in the VIP holding suite at Heathrow, with the press already on board the flight, word came through that neither Osborne or Cable would play ball, and that the Labour whips and No. 10 were insisting that this meant Gordon would have to stay behind for the vote. Quite aside from this being a pain for Gordon, it was a potential nightmare for my management of the press entourage.

With no Gordon, there would be no opportunity for a good chat with the hacks on the plane or the 'Day 1' story he would brief during that chat. Instead, we'd have a bunch of cheesed-off journalists wasting a day in Tel Aviv while all the action went on back in London.

So, instead, I persuaded Gordon and Sue that we should fly out, wait until we landed, and only then 'discover' the instruction from the whips' office. That way we'd be able to do the chat on the plane, give the hacks an Israel story to write and – as a bonus – ensure that they could report the drama of Brown being summoned back to London for the cliff-edge vote.

We executed it perfectly, right down to me being quoted in several papers saying: 'Guys, I think we may have a bit of a problem. It looks like Gordon has to go back home' after our flight landed, and briefing the sequence of messages left by the whips while we'd been airborne. Sure, it cost the taxpayer an extra return flight for Gordon, and his presence made no difference to the outcome of the vote, but the hacks were happy and that was all I cared about.

There was another complicating feature of those overseas press entourages: the Sunday papers. Unless it was very obviously in their timeframe, the Sundays wouldn't usually send anyone on the trip, but if one or two Sunday hacks had persuaded their bosses to let them go, the pressure on them to deliver at least a strong page 2 lead for the weekend was massive.

On one trip to India in early 2008, we had two Sunday hacks with us, and I reassured them that I had a great line for them: Gordon was going to come out hard for Ken Livingstone, his former bitter enemy, who was standing for re-election as Labour's Mayor of London. It may not sound much, but in the politics of the day it was deemed significant, and they both seemed happy with the story.

As Gordon began his exclusive briefing, reading out the script I'd written him, one of the hacks started looking visibly faint. I thought it might be the heat or Delhi Belly or last night's drinks catching up with him, but when I asked him if he was OK afterwards, he said: 'You said he was going to come out hard for Ken. I thought you meant he was going to attack him, not endorse him. I've told the desk I've got a guaranteed splash.'

He looked through Gordon's words again, desperately trying to find some nuance that would fit with what he'd told his news desk, but just kept shaking his head. There was nothing I could do, but it was a reminder to me to be careful with the wording of my trailers.

If all that sounds like we focused far too much on the needs of the media, I'd say you're damn right we did. After all, they were the buggers effectively paying for the trips. Chartering a plane or, less preferably, block-booking dozens of seats on a scheduled flight was always the most expensive aspect of any overseas visit, and the way we paid for it was by inflating the fares charged to the press to subsidise the travel of Gordon and his team.

There was one aspect of that arrangement that always intrigued me. If we chartered a flight from BA, Virgin or one of the occasional private airlines we used, then all the food and booze we'd normally consume on a flight was obviously thrown in as well. That meant if the galleys were still full of unopened bottles of champagne, wine and beer when we were on our return flight from Japan, Santiago or Cape Town, that was all booze already paid for by the hacks just waiting to be drunk.

Well, that was no situation for shrinking violets. I'd explain to the cabin crew that – rather than everyone sitting in their seats occasionally having their glass topped up while watching one of the Bourne films – we were going to hold a proper end-of-trip party on board, and would happily serve our own drinks so they could have a break.

We'd start slowly, usually with Gordon and Sarah coming back to join us for a relaxed chat, but after they went to bed, or in Gordon's case, off for a good, uninterrupted eight hours of work, the hard drinking would ensue. I'd kick things off with a quiz, then there'd be hours of standing around swapping war stories and jokes, a bit of singing, and eventually a core group of stalwarts settling down for an all-night session of poker,

Scattergories, charades or whatever other game we felt up to, all while steadily draining what was left of the booze.

There were some civil servants and journalists who fastidiously refused to take part, but a hardy few of us used to come off those flights – often in the cold light of the morning at Heathrow – absolutely plastered. It made for outstanding bonding, even with those journalists sensible enough to get some sleep, and generally meant that, even if there had been tensions during the trip, they all felt they'd had a good one.

Of course, besides the fact they were paying for the trips, there was another very good reason for making sure we geared everything around the media entourage. Simply put, if not looked after, they have the capacity, incentive and pack mentality to destroy you on a foreign trip. I always disagreed with Tony Blair's description of the press as 'feral beasts', but one thing's for sure – if you didn't feed them properly, you'd soon find your boss on the menu.

And a foreign trip is so fraught with potential gaffes, snubs, misfires, examples of excessive spending and rows about what is on or off the record, that an angry entourage of journalists can easily spend an entire trip giving you a kicking, and – if you cut off all contact with them in response – they'll just report that as well, with accompanying analysis that the pressure of the job was clearly getting too much and leading to increasing worries back home.

Sometimes bad days on trips are inevitable: such as the occasion when Gordon did a briefing at the G8 summit in Japan about the need to tackle the world's waste of food, and then found himself at a luxurious thirteen-course banquet laid on by the hosts that same evening. The press got hold of the menu and it was Sayonara Sapporo.

Sometimes, you can even have two or three bad days in a row, as Gordon found on a trip to Washington in 2008, when the row over scrapping the 10p tax rate was starting to blow up at home. Gordon was in a foul temper anyway, preoccupied with the emerging financial crisis, and every time he spoke to the press – whether in formal briefings or supposed off-the-record chats on the plane – things got worse and worse. My schedule of stories

ceased to be of any value on those days, when the only story was
Gordon's mood and the pressure he was under.

But the worst thing you can do in those circumstances is
start isolating yourself from the press or dismissing them all as
bastards. That couldn't really happen as long as I was around
because I regarded myself – to use the journalistic term – as
'embedded' with the entourage on those trips, and, because of the
constant engagement with them I had, there was always a subtext of saying: 'OK guys, you've had your few days of fun – it's a
fair cop – can we get back to normal now?'

And that suited the hacks too. No one wanted to go back to
the days when Tony Blair refused to come to the back of the plane
to speak to them; that kind of access is invaluable no matter how
bad relations get. And they didn't want to lose the supply of good
stories and useful information that Michael Ellam or I always
provided.

It was telling that probably the worst foreign trip Gordon
ever had came after I'd been sacked and Michael had left, when
– despite the best efforts of our replacements – Gordon had
become consumed in contempt for the press, a feeling recipro-
cated by many of the travelling journalists. His trip to New York
in September 2009 was a real low point at a crucial time, with
Gordon needing a boost to take him into the last party conference before the election.

A leaked story about Gordon's five snubbed requests for a
one-to-one discussion with President Obama was compounded
by a further report that the eventual meeting they'd had – much
heralded by Gordon's new spin-doctors – had actually been a
snatched conversation when walking through a United Nations
kitchen.

The papers were merciless, and Gordon's reaction told me
everything about what a low ebb relations had reached; he sent a
text message to one of my successors saying: 'Cut off all contact
with *Telegraph*, *Guardian* and BBC', the three outlets who had
broken the story.

Incidentally, the witch-hunt for the source of that snub leak was conducted with a level of intensity, suspicion and anger that made my 'African Coup' inquest on a previous Washington trip look like a game of Happy Families. There were many suspects, and it was commonly assumed to be a Foreign Office or embassy staffer disaffected with Gordon's gauche behaviour to his American counterparts and possibly serving the interests of their much smoother immediate boss, David Miliband.

That wasn't correct. The leak came from a source close to Douglas Alexander, then Secretary of State for International Development.

With friends like that...

29

THE EDITORS

Despite the way Gordon and the Eds demolished the hierarchical structure of the Treasury, we still believed in pay grades when it came to dealing with newspapers.

My pay grade was the political and economics editors on every paper, and all the individual reporters beneath them. For the two Eds, their pay grade equivalents were the columnists and, on Budget Day, they'd divide phone calls to all the Polly Toynbees and Jonathan Freedlands between them.

After I was sacked, one senior *Guardian* columnist bemoaned the fact that I didn't ever return her phone calls. That was because it wasn't my job, much as I would have liked it to have been, and part of the discipline of Gordon's media operation was that everyone stuck to their task so there was no confusion and mixed signals.

And Gordon's task – his pay grade equivalent – was to keep on board the newspaper editors. He would regard them as equals, whereas he treated proprietors, like Rupert Murdoch, Lord Rothermere or the Barclay brothers, more like he would the Pope or Simon Cowell.

He was always the first to send a new editor a text message congratulating them on their appointment and inviting them into Downing Street for breakfast. And equally, he was the first to text them and commiserate when they faced the near-inevitable axe.

I sat in on countless breakfasts, lunches and dinners between Gordon and newspaper editors. It was very important for me to be there because – while Gordon's account of what had been *discussed* at such events was photographic – his account of what had been *agreed* was notoriously unreliable.

People think of his 1994 Granita restaurant summit with Tony Blair as a once-in-a-lifetime misunderstanding, where Gordon thought they'd reached a deal on a future handover date, and Tony thought nothing of the sort.

The reality is that it was the same story at every meeting he ever had with an editor, business leader or foreign dignitary. Gordon would come away talking enthusiastically about the vows they'd just exchanged; his dining partner would walk away picking their teeth and trying to remember what Gordon had been banging on about. So, after each such occasion, I would call up my opposite number on the paper, do a post-mortem, and agree what had been agreed.

Every newspaper editor I ever met at those events appeared to be driven primarily by the bottom line: was the paper making money?; how were sales, views and advertising revenue doing?; was the business model sustainable?; where could costs be cut? All of which obsessions you could understand in an industry more ruthless than Ancient Rome.

Beyond that, many of the editors cared deeply about their prestige within the industry – winning awards and such like, getting big stories ahead of their rivals; and some – but by no means all – cared deeply about their access to and influence with individuals in power, not just in government, but in business, sport and showbiz, and about being able to publicly flaunt that influence.

Of all those I met alongside Gordon, let's just say there was a spectrum in how they behaved. At one end, you had the likes of Richard Desmond, one of the more hands-on proprietors, and Andy Coulson.

Gordon was obliged by Tony Blair to go and meet Desmond at the *Express* headquarters in Blackfriars, near my old Customs building. Blair had told him he thought Desmond could be persuaded to endorse Labour, but the stumbling block was his dissatisfaction with the government's tax policies. Gordon took Ed Balls and me with him.

Gordon tried his usual opening patter with editors: 'What are

your big issues at the moment?'; 'Any big campaigns?'; 'How's
the circulation doing?', all a perfect opportunity for Desmond
to launch into a debate about their long-running campaign on
inheritance tax. But he didn't seem interested.

Instead, he launched into a bitter tirade about the rules on sales
of capital assets, which he said were preventing him making various planned property moves. Gordon tried to engage him on the
detail, and Desmond immediately fetched the *Express*'s accountant to join the conversation.

We were left with the slightly troubling sight of Desmond, the
accountant and Gordon taking themselves off to one side to go
over the details of the property transactions and work out why
the capital gains tax charge was so prohibitive. The traditional
cast-iron rule that 'ministers cannot involve themselves in the
affairs of individual taxpayers' was becoming rather rusty before
our eyes.

Ed Balls tried to maintain some semblance of propriety
by opening up a conversation with the rest of the table about
marginal tax rates, employing his own favourite opening gambit:
'What do you think average wages are in Britain?' (Answer: a lot
lower than you or Tony Blair think they are.) That debate was
progressing reasonably enough when Desmond returned to the
table and began a rant about the state of the NHS.

Gordon tried to reply meaningfully, talking about what we
were doing on hospital infections, but again, Desmond didn't
want to know. 'Oi,' he said to Peter Hill, the editor of the *Daily
Express*: 'Show Gordon your X-rays.' He explained that Peter
had been in hospital for a colonoscopy and before Gordon had
quite absorbed what that meant, he was being passed some
grainy images.

'I don't believe this,' Desmond laughed to Peter. 'Gordon
Brown's looking up your arsehole. The most powerful bloke in
Britain and he's looking up your arse!' To his credit, Ed Balls
leant over and said to Gordon: 'Right, we're leaving. Right now.'
Gordon was more polite and explained he had an urgent meeting
at the Treasury, and we left, more swearing ringing in our ears as

we went. We went down the lift and walked out in silence, before Gordon and Ed turned the air blue themselves around the theme of 'Fucking Blair.'

If that was bad, an even more excruciating meeting was Gordon's breakfast with Andy Coulson in No. 11 in 2004, when Andy was editor of the *News of the World*. At least Desmond was interested in some issues of public policy, if only to the extent they affected his tax bills or Peter Hill's arse, but Andy simply wasn't.

While it was de rigueur for Gordon and Tony to meet the editors of all the national newspapers, Andy appeared completely baffled as to why he'd been invited in, even though he edited the one with the biggest circulation. He explained that the paper was driven by sport, celebs and scoops, and sat blankly as Gordon tried to interest him in various things the Treasury was doing. Even Gordon didn't think anything had been agreed after that meeting.

At the other end of the spectrum, you had the likes of Paul Dacre.

Dacre and Gordon clearly had a very strong relationship, although – because all their meetings took place behind closed doors – no one was ever quite sure how they interacted with each other in private, or how open, warm or personal they were with each other. It was a little like Gordon's relationship with Tony Blair, bar all the shouting.

But one thing was always clear: no *Mail* reporter, columnist or leader-writer ever told me they'd been instructed to go soft on Gordon as a result of their dealings; and Gordon never told me that we were to put any particular scoops in the *Mail*'s direction. The business of running the newspaper was entirely separate to whatever personal relationship they had.

On one occasion, the two men agreed it would be a good idea if Gordon set out his emerging thinking on the issue of 'Britishness' and how it could best be celebrated to a group of Dacre's editorial staff. So Gordon, Ed and I trooped over to the *Daily Mail* HQ in Kensington for lunch.

It was a tough old crowd: columnists Simon Heffer, Melanie Phillips and Stephen Glover; and City editor Alex Brummer. Dacre gave Gordon the floor, and he hadn't got much more than ten minutes in before Heffer started chuntering that he'd never heard so much rubbish in his life. Gordon ploughed on, but Heffer became steadily angrier, eventually intervening.

'This is just utter nonsense. You're going on about these great British institutions: the monarchy; the church; the NHS; the Army. These are English institutions, not British.' 'Tell that to the Highlanders at Alamein', shot in Ed Balls, at which point Heffer threw down his napkin, said he had far better things to do than listen to any more of this nonsense, and walked out.

It didn't get a whole lot better after that: Melanie Phillips said the whole crisis of Britishness was entirely Labour's doing thanks to its obsession with multiculturalism; Stephen Glover politely doubted whether this agenda would solve Gordon's problem with Middle England; and Alex Brummer explained people were rather more interested in the value of their house.

Even if it was a bit of a waste of time, I couldn't help but admire the way that Paul Dacre rocked back in his chair and let the whole scene unfold, a gentle smile on his face, as if thinking: 'You want intellectual debate; here it is. You want to know what the *Daily Mail* thinks; we're going to tell you.' It was the definition of speaking truth to power.

Much as I admired Dacre, he also effectively scuppered one of my greatest plans. Traditionally, the thirty-year rule dictated that the government's official papers, minutes and internal documents would be published by the National Archives three decades later; usually by that time all the politicians mentioned in them were long gone.

I sat in the pub one night shortly after the 'election that never was' in 2007, and worked out that if we reduced the limit to fifteen years, and started issuing quarterly publications from 2008 in order to catch up, Labour could go into what would now likely be the 2010 election holding out the prospect that, if we won, we would be the only government ever to publish the secrets of our own time in office while still in power. I proposed it to the team working on Gordon's constitutional review package, and they loved it: transparency; liberty; freedom of information; it ticked every box.

Obviously I didn't give a cobblers about any of that, but I did have a very clear vision: first that, at a time when relations with the press were at a low point, Gordon would be giving them an extra three major events in the news calendar for the next five years, in addition to the one current annual release of papers; and second, that this meant – if we got the timing right – we'd go into the 2010 election having seen all sorts of secrets revealed from the years of Thatcher's government, from 1979 until perhaps 1987.

However, Gordon was nervous about leaping into it and instead asked Paul Dacre to lead a review, which meant both a delay and a total lack of control over the outcome. When his recommendations emerged in 2009, the plan was broadly similar to what I'd proposed but on a much slower timetable, and with the royal family exempted, which defeated some of the long-term news value.

There were others I would put in the same 'engaged but impossible to influence' category as Paul Dacre, editors who were not only totally unimpressed with the power of the politician in front of them, but happy to challenge them both in private and in their papers on why they weren't doing the right things with it: the Sunday Times' John Witherow and the Telegraph's Tony Gallagher to name two.

For all the talk about the overly cosy relationship that existed in the past between editors of News International titles and senior Labour ministers, the likes of John Witherow prove it was certainly no corporate policy. But did News International titles have more control and influence than other papers over New Labour? Over Tony Blair's operation, I would definitely say yes. You only have to look at the standard triumvirate for any major Alastair Campbell briefing – Phil Webster at The Times, Trevor Kavanagh at The Sun, and Catherine MacLeod at The Herald – to work out where their priorities lay.

And we were sometimes the same. We kicked off Gordon's first party conference as leader in 2007 with a typically under-stated splash in the *News of the World* (Brown: 'I'll scrub the wards clean') based on an article I'd written in his name about tackling hospital superbugs. It was a great hit, but as Vincent Moss, the laconic political editor of the *Sunday Mirror*, said to me that evening: 'Keep riding that tiger – see how far it takes you.'

In general though, we tried to spread the exclusives around and to ensure that News International titles had no more influence than the other main newspaper groups. However, you could argue that was because, whereas Tony and Alastair were largely in thrall to the Murdoch empire, we were obsessed with keeping every paper on board, and getting every proprietor and editor onside. I would plead fair cop to that.

As a final thought, you may have noticed something about some of the anecdotes above: the absence of Ed Miliband. As Ed himself might say, let me tell you something. He was the only person who routinely rolled his eyes in boredom if I asked him to be part of Gordon's entourage for a breakfast or dinner with a newspaper editor. He never instinctively thought the media were that important; he didn't obsess about them or pretend to understand all their ins and outs.

That revealed itself, for example, at his first meeting with Rebekah Brooks (Wade until 2009) in 2010, back when he was a candidate for the Labour leadership, and she was still – below proprietor level – the most powerful person in the British media. Now, most politicians with a decent knowledge of the press would have known about Rebekah's long-standing desire to have children, happily now fulfilled.

In 2010 though, it was a sensitive subject, which made it all the more surprising that Ed should launch into a cheery 'How are the kids?' gambit at the end of their meeting. She tried to let Ed off the hook with the response: 'My god-children? Oh, they're great. Thanks for asking.' 'No,' Ed persevered. 'I meant, how are yours?', finally receiving the terse response that she didn't have any.

I was told that story by someone present as an illustration of Ed's failings, but – once I looked past the awkwardness of the moment – I thought how refreshing it was to have a leader of a political party who hadn't memorised every detail of the personal lives of his media counterparts, and who, by extension, wouldn't spend any longer than necessary worrying about what they wrote about him in their papers. It's certainly worth a try.

30

POLITICAL FOOTBALLS

Personally, I can't stand watching football. I hate every single second of it unless Arsenal and Celtic are 3–0 up in added time, or Spurs and Rangers are losing by the same scoreline, and as soon as that brief moment of euphoria is over, I go back to worrying about the next game.

Years of experiencing only the fear of losing or of seeing enemies win has stripped me of any enjoyment of the game in general. I would rather sit through a Kieslowski retrospective than watch any football match not involving those four teams, and I hate talking about football in general.

This put me in a strange position of siding with those who rolled their eyes at the obligatory obsession with football that pervaded Labour politics, and Gordon's Treasury in particular.

And to be clear, this was no confection, unlike David Cameron's supposed love of Aston Villa or Tony Blair's for Newcastle. Gordon had a simply encyclopaedic knowledge of football and a ravenous appetite for any game he could watch.

Just because he could, he once threw a reception in Downing Street for all the sports editors of the daily and Sunday papers, and that great football writer, Paddy Barclay, decided to grill him on ancient Scottish football results to test how deep the passion went. After five minutes, he conceded defeat, saying to me: 'That guy knows his bloody stuff.'

If there were footballers or managers at an external event or on the invite list for a Downing Street reception, Gordon could not be prised away. And they all came away impressed by him and his knowledge. When I had the ultimate honour of stopping Arsène Wenger at a charity reception, so Gordon could say hello, Arsène couldn't have looked less interested in the prospect, but came away twenty minutes later beaming at the conversation they'd just had about economics.

When he met Roy Hodgson, the current England boss, at a Downing Street reception, Roy was so taken with their chat and with the nice letter Gordon sent him afterwards congratulating him on keeping Fulham up, that he replied 'as a long and faithful Labour supporter', saying: 'I was so impressed that you were so knowledgeable about so many current football matters. I hope that is not presumptuous of me to wish you every success in this difficult political climate and that your stay as Prime Minister will be a long and fruitful one.'

What spare time Gordon had up in Scotland he poured into not just supporting Raith Rovers, but pulling strings behind the scenes at the club, sometimes becoming a bit too involved. I rang him in October 2006 and said I'd had a call from a Scottish journalist who'd heard the bizarre rumour that Gordon was seen in a pub car park in Kirkcaldy after midnight apparently negotiating contract terms with Trinidad international Marvin Andrews. Gordon was silent, then said: 'Have they got photos?'

Raith was Gordon's only Scottish team, and – as someone sensitive to such issues – I can confirm it is a myth that he is a secret Glasgow Rangers fan. As much pleasure as he always took in Celtic being beaten, I never saw him take any interest in what the other lot did.

He kept his English affiliations much closer to his chest. He'd grown up following Spurs' push-and-run side of the 1960s because of their large contingent of Scottish players, but that had clearly waned over the years, and – even if just out of loyalty to his great friend Sir Alex Ferguson – Manchester United's result was always the second one he wanted to hear after Raith's.

In May 2004, to Gordon's extreme annoyance, he was told we'd be flying back from America during the Man United–Millwall FA Cup Final. He got Sarah to record the game, and put us all under strict instructions not to say a word to him about the result when we landed. As we touched down at Heathrow, I went to remind the travelling journalists not to say anything, at which point the pilot came over the intercom and announced that Man United had won 4–0. Even back in economy class, you could hear Gordon's anguished scream from the front of the plane.

Nevertheless, even if he was something of a closet Man United fan, Gordon was too canny ever to confirm it or even put himself in a situation where he'd be seen in public watching them. Instead, he saved all his clumsiness about football for the oldest rivalry of the lot: England versus Scotland.

Two facts are absolutely clear. First, Gordon is as fervent a Scotland fan as you could ever wish to meet, following them to the 1982 World Cup as part of the Tartan Army even before he became an MP, and feeling so ill from drowning his sorrows after their exit that he gave up his thirty-a-day cigarette habit immediately and never smoked again, although he replaced the habit with an addiction to Kit-Kats; not quite thirty a day, but not far off.

Second, and steeped in his long-standing resistance of Scottish nationalism, Gordon has absolutely no time for Scottish people, or Welsh and Irish come to that, who define themselves by their loathing of England. The first time he shouted abuse at me directly was not over any screw-up but because I said I was supporting Turkey against England in a crucial Euro 2004 qualifier.

Those two facts should not be mutually contradictory. But by God, we managed to tie ourselves in knots over them. The first time was entirely my fault and a rare occasion when my confidence in just writing things in Gordon's name without referring them to him was ill placed.

I was asked by a *Sunday Telegraph* reporter – ahead of the 2006 World Cup – for Gordon to name the best England game he'd attended. The answer I gave was totally reasonable: that, for the atmosphere rather than the result, it had to be the England vs Scotland game in Euro '96, when Gary McAllister missed a chance to equalise for Scotland from the penalty and Gazza soon afterwards scored a 'great goal' at the other end.

The journalist totally stitched us up, presenting it as Gordon's surprise choice of the 'favourite goal' he'd ever seen, but even so, I should have seen that coming. There was hell to pay in Scotland over it and much piss-taking down south, too, that this was a sign of how desperate Gordon was to appeal to Middle England. I felt gutted, even more so because Gordon couldn't exactly explain that his press adviser routinely signed off articles, quotes and recipes in his name without him seeing them.

During the World Cup itself, I invited Peter Dobbie and Simon Walters from the *Mail on Sunday* to come in and do an interview with Gordon while he watched one of England's matches. Given the beers being consumed during the match, the interview was a bit hairier than normal, with Simon at one stage asking Gordon whether he would have taken Britain to war in Iraq, and telling him three times that he didn't believe him when he answered: 'I supported Tony's Blair's decision.' As Simon leant forward, saying: 'I don't believe you' more loudly for a second and third time, Gordon was about to explode, but to Simon's huge chagrin, Dobbie stepped in to move things on.

The piece came out fine but, again, it caused lots of irritation on one side of the border and piss-taking on the other, and when it was shown to a focus group in a south-east marginal – the audience Gordon continually struggled with – they hated it, saying he came across as false and dishonest saying he supported England. And this was the problem: every time Gordon was told people thought he was lying about being pro-English, he felt obliged to go further trying to prove it.

The nadir came in India the following January, when, after a great day with the Premier League promoting a new TV deal to screen Premiership matches in the sub-continent, Gordon told the travelling press that he would make it his personal mission to bring the World Cup back to England in 2018, persuading every country in the world he visited to get behind the bid.

He wanted World Cup 2018 to be his equivalent of Blair's London 2012 Olympics, but was also still hoping the Scottish FA could be persuaded to make it a joint bid. When Nick Robinson did a follow-up interview asking him who he would be supporting if the bid was successful, Gordon did the 'clever' answer he'd prepared if it was a joint bid: 'I'll be supporting the hosts!' Nick said: 'Even if they play Scotland?' Gordon just smiled and said: 'Scotland will do very well.'

The whole thing was done in a jokey atmosphere in a park full of Indian kids playing football but hearing it I knew we had a massive problem, even if Gordon was oblivious. Nick made a beeline for the other journalists to tell them what had been said, as I got in the car with a smiling Gordon.

We began the crawl through the early evening Mumbai traffic back to the hotel. Almost immediately, one of the other press officers rang and shouted down the phone: 'We've got a major problem here. All the papers are very excited and they're all ringing their Scottish desks to tell them the story.' 'OK, mate,' I replied calmly, holding the phone as far away from Gordon as I could, 'take it easy and keep me posted', as if he was telling me the cricket score.

'What's the problem?' Gordon said. 'Nothing,' I lied. 'I heard someone say "problem" – what's the problem?' he said, getting slightly irate. I sighed. 'OK, now don't go mad, but we're just going to need to do a bit of handling on your Nick Robinson interview 'cos of you saying you'd support the hosts in the World Cup. It's fine but we'll just need to clarify it a bit so it doesn't sound like you'd support England over Scotland.'

There was a terrible moment of silence before the storm. Now, in the cars Gordon usually used in London he could have raised the enormous file of papers he always carried above his head and crashed it down onto his lap or legs in an act of furious self-flagellation, occasionally resulting in them scattering over the floor in front of him. I hadn't seen him do that particular manoeuvre many times, but that's because I tended to avoid giving him bad news when travelling in cars.

On this occasion, he raised the pile of papers and brought it crashing down, but because we were in a much smaller car, it whacked off the top of the passenger seat in front of him, almost taking the head off the armed Indian bodyguard sat there, and then scattered over the front seats like outsize confetti at a particularly ill-tempered wedding. Gordon simultaneously let fly a blood-curdling 'FUUUCK!'

The driver swerved the car in panic, while the bodyguard faced the existential dilemma of dealing with an attack on the car from the VIP he was meant to be protecting. Gordon was oblivious to the fact that we now had a very nervous driver and a very confused bodyguard with a gun at his side, and continued his rant, having quickly decided that I was to blame.

'This is all your fault! Why have you done this to me? I'm too tired to do all these interviews. You've made me do too much.' 'Oh come off it,' I replied. This was no time to be angrier than Gordon, not with the bodyguard still looking for someone to shoot. 'Anyway, it's done now,' I said, 'let's just get back and deal with it.' It was an achingly slow journey back to the hotel, Gordon staring out of the window in complete silence, the bodyguard handing back pages of A4 paper in little batches, and me thanking him and apologising profusely every time.

I told our press officer that as soon as the hacks got back to the hotel Gordon would come and speak to them and explain what he'd meant. When he did so, it was the most propitiative I'd ever seen Gordon before the press. Nevertheless, they all still wrote the story and it splashed all the Scottish tabloids, just a few weeks before the elections up there.

We tried to make up for that in Brazil a couple of years later when Gordon met the great football star Socrates. We'd agreed in advance that the pair would make headlines by agreeing that the goal scored by David Narey to put Scotland 1–0 up against Brazil in their 1982 World Cup game was a fine goal, and not, as it had infamously been described by the Tartan Army's hate figure Jimmy Hill, a 'toe-poke'.

Socrates's previously fluent English appeared to fail him when the cameras began to roll, and as Gordon asked him to agree that Scotland's strike was not down to 'luck', Socrates thought he was arguing that Scotland had been unlucky to lose the match 4–1. He looked bewildered, and insisted defensively that they could have won by much more.

After watching Gordon come a cropper so regularly on his specialist subject of Scottish football, the last thing I ever thought I'd do was let him loose on a story about cricket, a far-away sport about which he knows nothing. But we were back in India in January 2008, my final-day story had fallen through and I'd already used all my back-pocket items; I was forced to improvise.

Some spin-doctors might have conjured up an apology for the Amritsar massacre, or a new policy on visas for Indian students, but I was not such a man. The Indian cricket team had just beaten the Aussies in Perth to end their record-equalling run of consecutive Test wins and I sold Gordon on the idea that he should propose reviving the tradition whereby Commonwealth cricketers – such as Sachin Tendulkar – could be nominated for knighthoods, like Sir Don Bradman or Sir Gary Sobers.

I say that I 'sold' Gordon on the idea. More accurately, I told him that I'd already briefed it, it had gone down pretty well and I'd written him a briefing note on the subject which he should read in case any of the hacks asked about it.

Gordon looked a bit baffled when I was telling him this and didn't seem much the wiser when he sat down to give a press conference to a few hundred local journalists alongside the Indian Prime Minister. At the last minute, too late to warn Gordon, I discovered that my civil service counterparts from the Foreign Office and No. 10 had briefed the cricket story to the Indian press, who were both excited and divided about it.

In all the time I did the job, I was rarely more nervous than waiting for the Q&A to begin. But Gordon had my briefing

Surely he'd read my briefing note. The first question came: 'Mr Brown, we are very interested in your idea to give knighthoods to Commonwealth cricketers, can you explain how this will work in practice?' My heart was in my throat, as Gordon adopted his trademark rictus grin and fished into his suit pocket for my note.

To my immense relief, he was magnificent, hailing India's triumph in Perth, tickling the crowd with some barbs about the Aussies, and then – I could feel my stomach tighten – singling out for praise, with a glance down at my note, 'Sa. Chin. Ten. Dul. Kar.', each syllable carefully enunciated as though he was counting to five in Ancient Greek.

'A magnificent cricketer,' he continued. 'One of the greatest ... one of the greatest...' Please say 'batsman', please say 'batsman', whatever you do, don't say 'bowler', I thought, mentally preparing my lines about Gordon's appreciation for Sachin's under-rated off-spin if he went the wrong way.

'Perhaps the greatest batsman of all time.' Phew! And hurray Gordon! The assembled crowd of guests and journalists cooed with approval, albeit with some anti-colonial murmuring when he went on to propose that it would be right for Sachin to be recognised through the British honours system.

The press conference ended, and I was feeling very chuffed with my work until the press liaison officer from the British embassy took me firmly by the arm, escorted me to a huge group of Indian journalists and said dryly: 'Mr McBride will answer all of your questions about Sir Sachin.'

I'd done briefings after Budgets and Gordon's conference speeches, but this was by far the largest I'd ever conducted. It went well enough though, even when one particularly animated correspondent who quite liked the idea said: 'But after the way they have behaved over the years, does Mr Brown really think any Australian deserves a knighthood? These are not gentlemen, they are bastards.'

'Ah,' I said – on a roll by now – 'but Mr Brown might argue: would any true cricket fan in India disagree with a knighthood being granted to Mr Richie Benaud?' There was a great sigh of approval. I felt like the other Socrates.

The questioner replied: 'I have to say, we had no idea that Mr Brown was such a cricket buff.'

31

CONFERENCE

What must be recognised above all about modern party confer-ences is that the vast majority of people spend the three or four days in Manchester, Brighton or Blackpool alternating between extreme excitement or abject stupor fuelled by drink, lack of sleep and occasional sex. The atmosphere is like an 18–30 holiday in Spain with the odd speech thrown in.

It seems strange that some of the most politically significant moments of recent years could have occurred in that atmosphere, but occasionally we're all capable of taking life-changing deci-sions when very drunk or tired. Anyone who's proposed marriage, had an affair or punched a best friend during a wedding weekend would know the feeling.

Now, of course, most of the senior politicians at these events are too busy and disciplined to get themselves under the influence of booze, sleepless nights or the horn, but they can only function as effectively as the team around them, and if that team are off their heads, inevitably that tends to weaken the boss.

By contrast, a team that can embrace all the temptations and privations of conference but still function effectively will find it the best possible place to win friends and influence people. It will come as no surprise that I took to that task like a dipsomaniac duck to a pond of piña colada.

In fact, it was a lot like the rest of my life – drinking all day but still doing loads of work, staying up far too late and getting up far too early. The difference at conference was that everyone was acting the same. I felt like the naked rambler stumbling into Cap d'Agde. The problem was that – in my excitement at everyone joining in – I'd then indulge even more, always last to go to bed in hotels which would happily serve you until dawn.

At my first, in Brighton 2005, the only two people left standing in the early hours were me and one of Charles Clarke's press advisers. I hate to admit this but, after one hotel bar closed, we were reduced to picking up other people's discarded pints and drinking those instead. It was eventually and very gently suggested to us by a police officer that we might consider heading to bed. When we got back to the main hotel, the bar still looked quite lively so we went in there for another.

Gloria De Piero, still then at *GMTV*, sidled up and – as kindly as she could – explained the reason it looked busy was that all the morning broadcasters were setting up for their set-piece interviews with Tony Blair, who would be coming down in five minutes. 'I think you two standing at the bar with pints isn't quite the backdrop he's hoping for.'

Manchester was always the worst for drink, just because – besides the lively nightlife outside – the bars at the two main hotels, the Midland and the Radisson, were cavernous and perfect for late-night, large-scale singing sessions. This made for the occasional morning to forget, but one I never will.

Sue Nye had the unenviable job on conference mornings of facilitating the several breakfast meetings Gordon would have booked in his room with newspaper editors, union leaders and Labour-supporting celebrities. Breakfast was always the best time for these meetings with both Gordon and the suite immaculately scrubbed – before he suffered from the ravages of a day at the laptop, and the suite became littered with discarded print-outs and Kit-Kat wrappers.

Sue also had the even more unenviable job of making sure that the various people who needed to sit in on these meetings were up and ready to do so, marching along the corridor and banging on doors like a holiday rep, shouting: 'Twenty minutes 'til Eddie Izzard' or 'Tina Weaver's waiting downstairs'.

One such morning in Manchester, she couldn't get any answer out of me and I wasn't answering my mobile. She asked Gary, one of Gordon's special protection officers, to let her into my room to check if I was even there. I was. Spread-eagled naked on the bed – fortunately face down – having come in about two hours beforehand, stripped and collapsed.

Sue walked straight out, and asked Gary if he could give me a shake and wake me up. As I was told afterwards, he took a look, came out, shook his head and said: 'That', pointing into the room, 'is not in my job description.' Sue ran down the corridor to the suite Ed Balls was sharing with Yvette, and told him he was the only person available to help.

At this point, given there was quite a bit of noise outside, I became vaguely conscious. When I felt Ed grasping me by the shoulders, shouting quite loudly and giving me a good shake, I became about a quarter awake, but unfortunately – in my addled and still drunk state – my mind interpreted what was happening as some amorous play-wrestling from a female bedmate.

I started to roll over and try and pull 'her' onto me with a winsome 'C'mere', at which point Ed sharply lurched away from the bed with a loud 'Good grief!' As I fully woke up, it was difficult to work out what was happening. I could see my bedroom door was open, apparently with several people whispering outside; I could hear the bath-water running, with lots of irritated swearing coming from the bathroom; and I was stark naked with my clothes in front of the bed.

As I sat up, Ed emerged from the bathroom with a face like thunder and hurled a binful of cold water over me, shouted: 'Now for fuck's sake, get up!', and stormed out. When I was sat in on Gordon's breakfast with Patience Wheatcroft ten minutes later, my mind wasn't quite on the job.

There was another reason that I was a natural for the demands of conference in that era, because – to the extent that every one of them repeated the same Blair–Brown drama as formulaically and ritualistically as a WWF wrestling contest – I played my same part each year (Fat Baddie No. 3) with gusto and conviction, always managing to convince the audience that this time the outcome might be different.

It never was. Each year, we'd come in with Tony under pressure, probably assisted by some unhelpful splashes from me in the Sunday papers; Gordon would make an ecstatically received speech appealing to Labour's soul and adding to the pressure; and Tony would then deliver an even better-received speech dashing Gordon's hopes and putting him back in his box. And on some occasions we'd have the added drama of an 'intervention' from Cherie.

Brighton 2005 played out exactly like that and started with Cherie's intervention. The famous BBC TV news producer Paul Lambert (aka Gobby) shouted to Cherie as she was exiting a hotel doorway: 'Is this your last conference?' Cherie beamed back and said: 'There'll be lots more to come, darling.' It was a wonderful, spontaneous moment to launch the conference. Although perhaps it wasn't. I've never confirmed it but I was told by a BBC contact that they'd done several takes to get it right.

Many people, including her husband, think that Cherie should always have been *hors de combat* when it came to the Blair–Brown wars; that for a journalist or a political opponent to have a go at her was just a cowardly means of going after Tony Blair.

I never saw it like that because I never saw Cherie as a mere 'politician's spouse', any more so than Hillary Clinton was to Bill. I think, more than anyone who's ever been in her position in British politics, and all credit to her for this, Cherie was a player; a more ardent, active and indeed aggressive promoter of Tony's agenda and ambitions than even I was of Gordon's. When those two things conflicted, that made her fair game as far as I was concerned.

So I didn't have much compunction about the splash in the *Mail on Sunday* that 2005 weekend, saying that Customs had pursued Cherie over unpaid VAT and customs duty on pearls she'd brought back from China, which made her look simultaneously filthy rich, out of touch and a tax-dodger. The original story, written the previous fortnight, hadn't been briefed by me, but I'd given the paper some assistance with this follow-up about the Customs investigation.

I went into the Labour Party press office at the conference centre that morning, full of No. 10 staffers, and there was silence.

I tapped away at a computer, took a break to fetch a Diet Coke, and, on my return, found a copy of the *Mail on Sunday* left on my keyboard like a souvenir. I tossed it back in the pile of newspapers and carried on working. Half an hour later, I went out to take a call, and the paper was back on my keyboard when I returned. I continued working in silence.

The people in that room – and many beyond – clearly thought that story was beyond the pale, but to my mind, if Cherie was going to be on the pitch, she could expect a few rough tackles, and she certainly gave as good as she got, as her orchestrated interventions at the 2005 and 2006 conferences showed.

In 2006, coming off the back of the summer coup by Brownite supporters against Tony Blair and the uneasy truce that had resolved it, Gordon had a difficult speech to make at the conference trying simultaneously to plead for unity and reconciliation but also to remind people why he was still the right man to take over the following year when Tony would stand down.

He executed it superbly and I bounded up the stairs to the press area in Manchester, ready for some pats on the back about how it had gone. Instead, there was a rush of hacks towards me, all with gleeful faces, asking me for my reaction to what Cherie had said. 'What did she say?' I said calmly. 'She stormed out during Gordon's speech and – as he was saying how great Tony was – she shouted out "Well, that's a bloody lie."' I turned and walked back down the stairs.

I went into Gordon's 'green room' in the pop-up backstage area. He was drenched in sweat, necking a can of Coke, bear-hugging anyone who would have him, thrilled at how the speech had been received in the hall. He gave the usual 'What are they saying?' greeting when I came in, but this time delivered with a beaming smile, presumably expecting even his harshest media critics to be giving him grudging praise.

I pointed that we should move away from the Labour officials and Treasury advisers milling around, in case he had a meltdown. He knew something was wrong. 'What was it? What was it?' he said, as if a line in the speech must have gone down badly.

I waited, and then told him what Cherie had done. He faintly smiled that instinctive way you do when you hear awful news: scared, incredulous, willing it to be a joke.

Then the rage boiled up from his chest. He suppressed a roar of anger, but slumped sideways into the makeshift wall with a force which made me worry it would collapse. 'So that's it now, that's the only story,' he said. 'She's killed us, she's killed us.' I had no doubt that by 'us', he meant not just himself, but everything the conference was supposed to symbolise about the party's reconciliation.

Later on, I said to him: 'But look, people are saying this is outrageous, how's Blair going to respond; he's got to say something to put it all back together.' With remarkable prescience, or just years of experience, Gordon said; 'Naw, he'll just tell some bloody joke, and dismiss it all. And it'll all be "Good old Cherie".'

Sure enough, the next morning, Tony's office called Sue Nye and informed her that Tony would indeed be making a jokey reference to the incident at the start of his speech, and Gordon should be ready to smile. He grinned on cue when Tony said: 'At least I don't have to worry about her running off with the bloke next door', but I knew how he was feeling inside. The coverage of his speech had been more about Cherie's reaction than the speech itself.

That night, in Gordon's suite in Manchester, we could hear the sounds of laughter, music, singing and popping champagne corks coming from the suite and balcony above where the Blairs and their staff had their rooms. We sat there in silence feeling utterly sick.

With Tony gone and the decision whether to call a snap election in the balance, the 2007 conference was a break in the pattern but in 2008 it was back to normal, with the boot on the other foot: Gordon coming in under massive pressure with his Blairite rival – David Miliband – expected to throw down the gauntlet; Sarah Brown the one making a crucial intervention; and Gordon emerging unscathed.

However, 2008 was also my last conference and the point I

realised that the game was truly up for me as an adviser to Gordon. In some ways, I was at the peak of my abilities. I remember standing at the bar scanning the room at the Unison-sponsored disco at the Midland Hotel – always a riotous affair – and seeing from about 25 yards away that an extremely pretty girl was chatting to Ed Balls.

My antennae started twitching. I wasn't worried about how pretty the girl was. After all, Yvette was nearby and Ed's not that sort of bloke. I was just worried about how relaxed a mood he might be in, what she might be asking and what he might be saying. Sure enough, as I got closer, I recognised the girl as one of the best undercover reporters in political journalism, with a number of high-profile scalps to her name then and since.

I approached the pair and said to the hack cheerily: 'How are you? Where's your secret camera?' Ed looked at her, looked at me, and remembered an urgent appointment on the other side of the room. Given we'd never met, she shook my hand and said with a smile: 'Just doing my job.' 'So am I,' I replied. I'd willingly bet not a single other Labour person at that conference would have known that journalist's name, never mind what she looked like, and none of them would have regarded it as their job to prop up the bar at a disco scanning the room for signs of trouble.

But, at the same time, my reputation was going before me by then. On the night of Gordon's conference speech – at another reception – Nick Robinson revealed to me that *Newsnight* was going to be reporting that Ruth Kelly and Geoff Hoon were both resigning from the Cabinet in dissatisfaction at Gordon's leadership.

That news not only had the obvious ability to overshadow Gordon's speech, but would – if true – trigger immediate talk of a coup. Simultaneous resignations don't happen by accident. I leapt into crisis mode and, working with Sue Nye, established that Geoff was definitely not resigning, and that Ruth had told Gordon she was going some weeks previously but had agreed to wait until after conference for it to be announced, something Gordon had bizarrely failed to tell us.

It appeared Ruth had let that slip to the wrong person at a dinner that evening, word had got to *Newsnight* and they were planning to run it alongside the Geoff Hoon rumour. Neither we nor Ruth's people were in a position to deny she was going, so the only thing possible was to confirm it but explain the background and make clear it was with Gordon's blessing.

As *Newsnight* was going on air, I called every political editor of every newspaper, explained the situation, and said whatever *Newsnight* reported was bollocks. I then went back to our office in the Radisson hotel, worked out a press statement with Ruth's press adviser, Julie Crowley, and phoned it round all the political editors, who were now hastily updating their second editions.

Around 2.30 a.m., I got a call from a friendly journalist, who told me there was an atmosphere brewing among the hacks in the Midland Hotel bar. There was some briefing from the *Newsnight* team that we'd 'got at' Ruth and Geoff to spike their story, and people were now wondering whether this in fact had been – and might still become – an attempted coup.

I grabbed Julie and said: 'Come on, let's go and kill this before it gets out of hand.' We headed over to the Midland and, with my first pint for several hours in hand, I went carefully through the events of the night, took the hacks through the press statement, fielded their questions and got Julie willingly to confirm it was all correct. By the end of it all, the journos were disappointed that the story had been strangled, but at least satisfied they'd heard the truth.

Over the next couple of days, the story began to circulate that Ruth had been bounced into resigning after I'd given the lobby a '3 a.m. briefing' saying she was going; the timing of the briefing said with raised eyebrows to suggest I'd revealed the news after a long night on the booze, even though I'd been as close as I ever got to stone-cold sober. The briefing even obtained the name 'Peronigate' after the *Telegraph*'s excellent Iain Martin wrote a fictional parody of the event.

The whole controversy was obviously bollocks, made all the more annoying by the fact no one could provide any sensible explanation for why I would want to bounce Ruth into resigning and thereby create a massive storm before the round of interviews Gordon was going to do the following morning. People might have disagreed with how I did my job, but I took umbrage at them implying I was shit at it.

The fact was, by that stage in my career people could believe just about anything they heard about me, and I'd become a name and a face that was known and despised by Labour people I'd never met. On the last day of that 2008 conference, I walked into the bar at the Radisson, where four middle-aged men in suits were sat in a row on barstools. I didn't recognise them, and don't know to this day whether they were union officials, obscure Labour MPs or someone else entirely.

But, as I entered the bar, the first one said to the others: 'Oh, look who it is.' As I walked past him, he called me the worst word in the English language. So did the second, the third and the fourth. What got me was not just the abuse from people I didn't know, or the embarrassed and shocked looks from other drinkers, but the fact I just had to ignore it and pretend I hadn't heard, or maybe that I didn't care.

A few days later, I told Sue I genuinely wanted out; I was done; I just didn't want to do this any more; I felt totally burnt out. After five years I'd got to the stage where every morning felt like the exhausted hangover after four days of conference. With no Ed Balls to throw water over me.

32

THE FAMILY GUY

People might think of someone like Gordon Brown as being totally driven by politics and power; that – if he was in a film – he'd leave a broken-down bus of orphans by the side of a volcano to make a lunchtime brush-by with Bill Clinton.

But as driven he was, when I knew him, nothing mattered more to Gordon than his family, both the one he grew up with in North Queensferry and the one he started there with Sarah. He constantly put his family before politics and, while that's a thing that every politician *should* be able to say, the truth is very few can. Certainly not many who were as senior as Gordon for so long.

I was with Gordon at an EU finance ministers' summit at a hotel in The Hague in autumn 2004 when he got a call from his brother to tell him that his elderly mother – who had been ailing – was in a worsening condition, and that it was best they all planned to be in Scotland that coming week. Gordon slumped against an alcove in the reception area, staring out of the window lost in his grief.

At that moment, Nicolas Sarkozy – then the almost fully risen star of French politics – came bounding into the reception area from his morning run, followed by a scrum of cameras, security guards and officials. He approached his beloved friend Gordon and started joking that tomorrow they would have to go running together, or have a game of tennis, because he and Gordon were 'great men' who had to be in training for the challenges to come.

The French press loved it, and I would bet that 99 per cent of politicians in the world – given the cameras, the badinage and the warmth from the French president-in-waiting – would have swallowed whatever they were feeling, leapt up and responded in kind. Instead, Gordon just sat there, head inclined, and waved Sarkozy away with a few half-nods and smiles.

His beloved mother, Elizabeth, died a week later.

That moment came back to me in 2007 on the night of Gordon's first party conference speech as Prime Minister, with speculation growing that he was preparing to call a snap election. We'd received word that the *Times* splash the next day would accuse Gordon of plagiarising many of the lines in his speech from American politicians, in particular John Kerry, an occupational hazard when both men were using Bob Shrum as a speech consultant. It was the angriest state that I'd seen Gordon in, and the only time I ever saw him angry in the presence of Sarah.

I think, under any circumstances, that story would have driven him wild, because it was a basic challenge to his integrity, always something he found impossible to absorb. But this story went further by accusing him of plagiarising the line that his parents had given him his 'moral compass'.

That was a line Gordon had first conceived and written for the eulogy given by his elder brother John at his father's funeral in 1998. If you felt as strongly about your family as Gordon did, and you'd been accused of plagiarising the most important line you wrote for the eulogy at your father's funeral, you might have hit the roof the way he did.

There were only three of us with Gordon in the room at that moment: me, Sue and Sarah, and we could do nothing but stand in silence watching him sat hunched in his chair, punching the desk in a powerless rage, almost grief-stricken about the insult to his family, barely caring about the Labour Party conference, his upcoming decision on whether to call an election or anything else at all.

It told me something that Gordon was willing to be so angry in front of Sarah on that occasion but never on others. She and the boys were always an instant pacifier of his moods, as were his two brothers and usually the two Eds. But there was no point in disguising from Sarah how angry that *Times* story made him, because she knew exactly how he was feeling – this was about family.

After Gordon and Sarah had lost their first child, Jennifer, in

2002, the subsequent joy of Sarah discovering she was pregnant or going into labour with their sons John and Fraser was always tinged with worry about whether everything would be OK, and that was the case in July 2006 when I flew up to Edinburgh to handle the media for the birth of Fraser. But everything went like clockwork: I announced to the Press Association that Sarah was in hospital, got the doctor to make a statement about the success-ful delivery, and then organised the photo-call for Gordon and Sarah's departure with the newborn baby.

The only drama that week came when I got back to London, and Sue called to tell me I was being investigated by the Treasury for sexual harassment. 'What?' I yelled. 'Who of?' The answer was Balshen ... who I'd been secretly dating for four months.

A press office colleague had supposedly just happened to see on Balshen's phone a rather clucky text message from me about the new baby, thought it inappropriate and took it to the HR department.

Rather than just asking Balshen or me about it, they alerted the new Treasury Head of Communications, Chris Martin, who alerted the new Permanent Secretary, Nick Macpherson, who alerted Sue Nye, who had the common sense to ring me. Within an hour, our secret relationship of four months was common knowledge across the Treasury. Poor Balshen was mortified, but it at least brought us closer together in mutual irritation at some of the idiots and busybodies we worked with.

As for Fraser, the whole of the Treasury fell in love with him when Gordon and Sarah brought him around; a small wee fellow, but with huge dark eyes and a lovely curious expression. Four months after he was born, my mobile rang in the late afternoon: *The Sun*'s George Pascoe-Watson, an immaculate gentleman and professional in all things.

'Hi there,' he said. 'Bit of a sad one, mate, but the Scottish desk have had a phone-in saying that Fraser is being treated for cerebral palsy. Which is obviously devastating, but we've got to look into it, so that's why I'm calling. Obviously, if it is true, we will do this any way we can that's acceptable to Gordon and Sarah; the last thing we want is to cause any unnecessary upset.'

'OK,' I replied, 'well, if it's true that's honestly the first I've heard of it, so let me check it out.'

As I walked down the corridor, my phone beeped from George: 'Sorry, not cerebral palsy – cystic fibrosis.' Whatever this was, it wasn't just someone having a punt. Incidentally, it's worth saying that nowadays the reaction of any spin-doctor to that call would probably be to say there's no public interest in this information and to seek an immediate injunction against its publication, but those tactics were largely unknown back in 2006 and it never entered my mind or anyone else's as an option.

The 2006 Pre-Budget Report was only a week away, so Gordon was in a planning session with the Eds, Ian and others. I asked Sue for a word and, as soon as I said it was about Fraser, she put her finger over her lips and ushered me back down to my office. 'Barely anyone knows,' she said, 'all those private meetings we've been putting in Gordon's diary are for Great Ormond Street. That's why he's been so distracted.'

She went back to the office and broke up the meeting. Gordon, the Eds and Ian all piled down the corridor into my office. Gordon's expression was a strange mix of thunderous anger and deep sadness, and he spoke very softly. 'Are we sure that they know?' 'Well, it's one fact, isn't it?' I replied. 'That's the story.'

'No,' he said, 'the story is "Gordon and Sarah: more heartbreak"; "Another tragedy"; and it's not fair – it's not a heartbreak, it's not a bloody tragedy, there's nothing wrong with Fraser; he's as healthy as any other boy, he'll just need to look after himself when he's older, he'll just need to exercise and keep his lungs clear. He'll be fitter than any of us!'

The room was silent. 'What do you want me to do?' I asked. 'Well, I'll tell you one thing,' he said, anger beginning to mount, 'I'm not having my son – my son's health! – treated as some exclusive bloody story for a newspaper. Sarah and I will put out a statement now, and say this is the diagnosis, but there's nothing wrong with Fraser and we couldn't be happier.'

I looked around the room for support, but the looks I got

back were of the 'You're on your own here' variety. 'Gordon,
I know what you're saying and I agree, but we can't really do
that, otherwise next time there's anything like this, *The Sun*
won't even bother checking with us; they'll just run the story.
And they'll say that's fair enough 'cos we can't be trusted not to
do a spoiler.'

'A spoiler?' he screamed. 'This is my family! I don't give a fuck
about *The Sun*! I'm not having my family used as newspaper
exclusives. We put out a statement; that's the end of it.'

Now the looks from the rest of the room were 'I wouldn't push
this one if I were you'. 'OK,' I said, 'but we're going to at least
have to tell *The Sun* that's what we're doing.' Gordon and the
others went off to write the statement, while I closed the door
and rang George. Professional as always, he just said: 'OK, let me
pass that on, but don't do anything in a hurry.'

There were further phone calls from *The Sun* but they made no
difference. Gordon came back down the corridor half an hour later
with a finalised statement, and Yvette Cooper was lined up to do
interviews afterwards; although I said we should wait to put out
the statement until after the early evening news so as not to cause
chaos beforehand at the BBC and ITN.

That also gave me time to do what I personally believed was
necessary – despite Gordon's anger about the whole thing – to
make sure our relationship with *The Sun* wasn't permanently
damaged and to ward off any suspicions from other newspapers.

I called George back and told him when I planned to issue the
statement and what it would say. 'OK?' I asked him. 'Got ya.
Thanks, mate,' he said. That was my tacit nudge and wink to
tell him *The Sun* had about thirty minutes in which to break the
story, not as they'd hoped on the morning news-stands, but still
online and on Sky News.

I then rapidly called round, in descending order of how suspicious and angry they might be, the *Mirror, Mail, Telegraph,
Guardian, Times, Standard* and *Independent*, and did a whirlwind script, telling them on 'strictly operational terms' (i.e. for
information and planning purposes, not for direct use) what was

about to emerge in our statement and why, but emphasising that
The Sun did NOT get the story from us and were pissed off we
were spoiling it.

It's worth pointing out that this was in an age before the ubiq-
uity of Twitter accounts, so even if I was taking a risk with some
of those operational conversations, it wouldn't have been easy for
any of the journalists to do much with the information they had.
I then tipped off the BBC and ITN in similar terms and waited
for the news to break on Sky, which it did with a mock-up of The
Sun's front page, and George at Millbank to do the analysis.

While it was a chaotic and traumatic couple of hours, I think
we handled the story about as well as we could. Gordon and
Sarah were upset that something very secret had suddenly become
common knowledge and a subject of public debate while they
were still learning about the condition themselves. But they didn't
blame The Sun at the time, and they were grateful that they'd
been able to handle it in their way without any overly aggressive
reaction from the paper. That was why relations with The Sun
carried on pretty much as normal.

It was only when the allegations over phone-hacking emerged
years later that Gordon put two and two together and made five.
He was utterly and wrongly convinced – and enraged – that The
Sun had become aware of the story as a result of the voicemails
being left on his phone from family members discussing matters,
and wishing Fraser well.

Even if Gordon over-reached by making that allegation public in
2012, with The Sun responding that there was a 'legitimate source'
for the story connected to Edinburgh Infirmary, it remains the
case that his significant behind-the-scenes role in urging along
the newspaper editors and MPs who exposed the phone-hacking
scandal was largely driven by his anger over the idea that the
Fraser story had been obtained through those highly personal
voicemail messages from family members.

Indeed, when reporters from the New York Times first began
researching their September 2010 article which re-ignited UK
interest in the scandal and alleged Andy Coulson's complicity,

their initial conversations with me and others in Brown's circle revolved almost entirely around the Fraser story.

If there was a more immediate repercussion, it was to harden Gordon and Sarah's position about the boys appearing in public when they went over to No. 10, and settle that argument between Gordon's various advisers in favour of the entrenched position taken by Ed Balls, Michael Ellam, Ian Austin and me that the kids should never be 'used' in publicity.

After Fraser's birth, there had been a brief lapse in the other direction, with a card issued by the Browns thanking people for sending flowers or cards featuring a photo of the family posing together, which went on to appear in every newspaper. But from 2007 onwards, we maintained cast-iron rules; when we went into No. 10, Michael issued a formal notice to editors that they were not to publish any pictures of the children. Any newspaper that subsequently did so – and there were a couple – received an immediate censure from the Press Complaints Commission.

Occasionally, I'd be called up by a journalist saying they had the most lovely shots imaginable of Gordon playing in the park with John and Fraser, that it would be tragic not to use them, that it would change perceptions of Gordon entirely, and I'd just say: 'Sorry, no can do.'

I knew myself from watching him with the boys around Downing Street or in the garden in North Queensferry how much he doted on them, and how his mood, tone and energy levels were transformed when they were around. He'd be on the phone on a Saturday with me in one ear and John in the other. Occasionally, he'd get confused and ask me in a baby voice: 'And what are *The Observer* doing?' I'd say: 'Are you asking me or John?', and he'd revert to his normal tone and reply incredulously: 'Why would I ask John what's in *The Observer*?'

Every so often, a new adviser would come on the scene or someone like Piers Morgan would visit, see what Gordon was like with the boys and try their utmost to unpick his resolve. They'd look at our private polling which showed that a significant part of the population didn't even know Gordon had children, and would tell him it was a no-brainer that he had to get the boys 'out there', not least because of how damned cute they were.

But I always took the line that to do so would not only be wrong in terms of protecting the boys' privacy; it would also be a disaster with the media because it would look as though we had changed our mind purely for PR reasons. Gordon and Sarah both remained firm on the issue, to the extent that Gordon decided publicly to make a virtue of it at the 2008 Labour conference, preparing to use the line that – in obvious contrast to David Cameron – 'my children are not props, they are people'.

I felt massively uncomfortable about the line, not least once we knew Sarah was herself going to appear on stage to introduce Gordon, but also because I thought the rule in this area should be that you do what you feel is best for your kids, but don't question another parent's decisions. After all, Ed Miliband has ended up including his kids in publicity shots whereas Ed Balls and Yvette always refuse – neither has the 'right' answer. I fought hard to get the 'props' line taken out, but I was told repeatedly that not only did Gordon like it, so did the focus groups who had previewed the speech.

To my surprise, it didn't cause too much of a fuss, except with Quentin Letts from the *Mail*, who berated me afterwards for the hypocrisy of using that line on the children while simultaneously using Sarah as a warm-up act. I agreed with every word he said. That Christmas, Cameron's card to Gordon was famously signed: 'From David, Samantha and The Props!' It was only when you saw the indentation in his underlining of 'props' that you could tell how angry he must have felt.

When I had to quit No. 10 a few months later, doing so at the weekend may have saved me the indignity of a public exit but it also removed the opportunity to say goodbye in person to a great many people, most sadly of all John and Fraser.

Over time, first John and then both of them came to know me as 'the French soldier': if they came into the corridor or my office, I'd come to attention, march up to them, click my heels and then request their orders in a loud, exaggerated French accent. I'd always do that routine and it made them laugh like crazy. But how do you tell two kids that the reason the silly French soldier isn't here any more is because he sent some silly emails?

I could barely watch the coverage after the 2010 election and I found the idea of watching Gordon's exit from No. 10 too painful for words. But I brought myself to do it, and was as surprised and moved as everyone else when the boys came out with him and Sarah. I listened to all the commentators say: 'Why didn't we see more of them while he was in office?', and just smiled.

33

GOING TO THE MATTRESSES

The day had gone so well.

George Osborne was in Tokyo, lying in the smouldering rubble of his announcement that he would build a version of Japan's mag-lev train in Britain, and I was having an evening drink in Victoria, receiving grudging texts from even right-wing hacks that unless the Tories got their act together we would shred them as soon as Blair's mob got out of the way.

Then Phil Webster, political editor of *The Times*, called. Of all the journalists I ever dealt with, Phil had the most telltale greetings. A chuckle meant good news; a quick 'Oh, hi mate' meant he needed an urgent bit of information or clarification; and a relaxed 'How are you?' meant he fancied a decent run round all the issues on his train back to East Anglia. At 6 p.m. on 31 August 2006, it was a low-pitched, elongated 'Ah, hiiiiiii'. Oh shit.

'What's up?' I said, trying not to sound too worried.

'Well,' he said, 'we've done an interview with the PM tomorrow and it's pretty strong, it's the splash, and you'll start getting calls on it pretty soon. I can't tell you the line but all I'll say is we were told in advance this would be the line, and we checked afterwards that they definitely wanted it to be the line, and they were very clear. So I know you've had a good time on all the George stuff, but keep your wits about you 'cos you're going to have a long night.'

Other hacks soon told me that the two crucial lines were that Tony would not be setting down any timetable for his exit and that certain people had to stop obsessing about dates. Everyone was planning to do it up as yet another hammer blow to Brown's chances of becoming Prime Minister, with Blair seemingly determined to stay on until an alternative successor could be found.

I called Gordon and told him. Compared to Washington in 2004, he didn't seem devastated and betrayed, just utterly uncomprehending and resigned. 'What do you want me to say to the hacks?' I asked him. 'I don't know ... I don't know. Just don't answer your phone for now.'

Ed Balls called shortly after. 'Are you getting loads of calls?' he asked. 'Yeah, but Gordon said not to talk to anyone. Are we just shutting it down?' Ed sighed: 'I don't know. There's no controlling this. We've been telling all the backbenchers it's all going to be OK and they just need to give Blair time. They're all going to go nuts now. I'm not sure where we're going to end up.'

He also told me not to answer any calls, and make sure nothing came out of the Treasury or the Brown team which could take on 'African coup' status. I didn't quite refuse to answer calls – I'd never done that before and it would have drawn more attention if I'd started then – but I just said as plainly as I could to everyone who called that we had nothing to say.

That same night, a group of West Midlands MPs met for a curry to mark the end of the summer recess, with Gordon's staunch ally Tom Watson in a fury over the Blair interview. There were many MPs present who, regardless of their past affiliations, wanted rid of Tony Blair as soon as possible, given the number of voters in their constituencies and councils who would never vote Labour again as long as George W. Bush's wingman remained in Downing Street.

What followed can only be described as the most perfectly conceived and almost perfectly executed British political coup of recent decades. Within a week of refusing to set a timetable, Tony was forced to announce publicly that he'd be gone within a year. And it's an indication of how brilliant a coup it was that I knew not a thing about it; indeed, no journalist, no spin-doctor, no one in Brown's inner circle or Blair's ever had the slightest clue what the next move would be or who from.

Tom kicked things off by coordinating a letter from a group of MPs calling on Blair to quit. He signed the letter himself and allowed a frenzy to mount about whether he could retain his junior post within the government having done so, thus ensuring everyone was paying attention when he then quit. Further letters and resignations followed. Indeed, over a 48-hour period, every time we thought the pressure exerted on Blair had reached its peak, the ringleaders would amaze everyone by coming up with another group of Labour MPs calling on Blair to quit, while a dwindling band of Blair loyalists could be found to go on TV and defend him. For two days, we sat in the Treasury watching the whole coup unfold on TV like the O. J. Simpson car chase.

Impressive as it was, there was something alarming and somewhat anarchic about it all. There is a story, thought to have been leaked by Douglas Alexander, that Gordon – alarmed at the open warfare on his television screen – said: 'We've got to stop this', and that Ed Balls responded: 'We can't stop it.' It is entirely true, but it didn't have the imputed meaning as evidence of their complicity in the plot.

In reality, Gordon was genuinely appalled at the rising level of vitriol on either side – MPs, ministers, Labour-supporting columnists were all at each other's throats. Even if it was clear that the rebel side was winning out, Gordon had reached the point where – if Blair was forced to resign – he thought it would be impossible to stitch everything back together and reconcile the two sides. When MPs like Vernon Coaker, who defined the non-aligned centre of the party, were so obviously furious at the actions of the plotters, you could tell the Labour Party was in very serious danger of falling apart. But Ed was clear with him: we're not in charge of this; it's not ours to stop.

The only thing that could be done was for Gordon to approach Tony and try to find some formula that would take the momentum out of the crisis, urge unity and stop moderate MPs feeling forced to take sides. Gordon drove in through the back gate of Downing Street to avoid the cameras en route to meet with Blair, but as he emerged from his talks, the snappers were surrounding the exit. Sue told him to make sure he didn't look unhappy at the outcome. A bad thing to say to Gordon. He lurched in the opposite direction, flashed his trademark spontaneous grin, and his apparent laughter at the success of 'his' coup and the carnage within the Labour Party became the defining photo of the week.

Meanwhile, Douglas was wheeled out on camera by No. 10 to be the voice of compromise and unity, telling the rebels that they did not represent the mainstream view of the Labour Party and that the country wasn't interested in their internal wrangles. Tom Watson must have felt like Mel Gibson's William Wallace, covered in blood on the battlefield, on the verge of victory, having to look back and watch the posh horseman from Paisley wave goodbye.

As briefings started to emerge of an imminent compromise and truce between Brown and Blair, I received an angry phone call from a colleague of Tom's: 'Is this stuff on Sky coming from you?' 'No, of course not,' I said. 'I haven't said a thing for a week.' 'Well, can someone tell Gordon to wake up? We've got Blair on the edge of the cliff; we need to stamp on his fucking fingers. What's this bollocks about a deal?' 'I don't know,' I said truthfully, 'but Gordon thinks it's all gone too far.' 'OH FOR FUCK'S SAKE!' he said, and hung up in frustration.

It's not a popular view, but Gordon saved Tony that day; he got him his final year in power, for all it was worth. And he was right to do so: the unceremonious, immediate ousting of Labour's most successful leader would have been a terrible scar for the party to bear, in the same way that Margaret Thatcher's removal affected the Tories for decades afterwards.

Of course, that was not quite the end of the story. The following Saturday, I was making calls in the garden at Gordon's home in North Queensferry as he prepared to do the Sunday Andrew Marr interview the next day – part of his deal with Blair to project an image of unity. Gordon was insistent that we keep our side of that deal, even though my counterparts at No. 10 were unleashing blistering briefings to the journalists writing reviews of the week in the Sunday papers.

A call came through from my old Peterhouse contemporary Jonathan Oliver, at the *Mail on Sunday*, and I assumed it would be just another request for a response to the vitriol from Blair's mob. It wasn't: 'Hi there, it's only a little fishing expedition, but we've got a contact claiming that Tom Watson was in St Andrews last weekend before the coup was launched, and we're just wondering if he might have seen Gordon, given that's quite close to Kirkcaldy. Could you ask?'

I rang Tom. He said: 'But how do they know I was in St Andrews ... oh fucking hell – Lord Snape.' He said before he'd travelled to Scotland the previous weekend, the only person he'd mentioned it to was his predecessor as MP, Peter Snape, ennobled in 2004 by Tony Blair. 'But you didn't see Gordon, did you?' I asked. Tom groaned. He said his family had stopped to drop off a present for baby Fraser. 'We were only there twenty minutes. Sarah and Siobhan [Tom's wife] were there the whole time. Even if we'd wanted to talk about Blair, we couldn't.'

I went into the kitchen to see Gordon and told him what was happening. He shook his head in almost amused disbelief. 'So stupid ... we watched fucking *Postman Pat* was all.' I was so worried about the impact if we told the truth that – for the only occasion when I worked for Gordon – I offered him the liar's way out: 'Look, only we know for sure that Tom stopped here so why don't we just say he went straight to St Andrews and you never saw him? We could get away with it.'

He looked at me sharply: 'Never do that. Never ever do that. The truth might hurt you, but it's the lie that kills you.' Jonathan couldn't believe it when I rang back and volunteered the information that Tom had indeed visited Gordon, and talked him through the details. Of all the briefings I've ever done, that one left me feeling sick, and it felt odd to get a big cheery 'Well, thank you very much – I must buy you lunch' at the end.

We got totally battered in the Sunday papers, and Gordon's interview the next day with Marr was regarded as one of the worst examples of a politician being duplicitous on camera until he topped it again after the election that never was the following year. In subsequent polling, Gordon's reputation for honesty and integrity had been severely damaged. Nevertheless, however pyrrhic the victory, there was no doubting both the immediate and ultimate effectiveness of the coup.

But the art of the coup goes both ways.

Knowing how to withstand a putsch is just as great a skill as prosecuting one. And – whether through endless practice at the other end of the rifle sights or simply because of his own unprecedented longevity within the Treasury – Gordon proved himself the Charles de Gaulle of Downing Street when it came to surviving assassination attempts.

As the 2006 coup showed, momentum is everything: to succeed, the plotters must keep pushing the leader to the edge of the cliff. And the crucial determinants of that momentum are the media: if they say it's fizzling out, then that becomes self-fulfilling; if they say one more bad day will make the leader's position untenable, then it usually will.

But those media judgements are no objective science; they are a collective view formed by the most influential people at different outlets – the editor, political editor and key columnists – based on their conversations with each other and with key players on different sides. That is why, no matter how bad the coverage became during Gordon's time at No. 10, it was still vital for us to maintain strong and friendly relationships with those key people.

But as well as having that extensive and close set of press relationships, Gordon also had easily the best political intelligence operation of any of his contemporaries, and that too was crucial in terms of his survival. But it didn't happen by accident.

We would routinely place moles on the ministerial teams of suspect Cabinet ministers and cultivate contacts within their camps. At our different levels – special advisers, backbench MPs, ministers – we would take talkative, sociable types out for drinks or dinner, and test the water by privately venting and exaggerating our own concerns about the future. And above all, we would all keep our eyes and ears constantly open for unusual couplings or hushed conversations.

As a result, when the first major coup attempt came along in September 2008 – a Blairite assault led by John Reid's diehard rump of supporters – Nick Brown, Gordon's Chief Whip, was chairing conference calls and going through the 'secret' lists and plans of rebels signed up to the plot a full fortnight before they moved into action.

Of course, that kind of intelligence was only of value because we knew exactly what to do with it. Once we knew what was happening, when, and who was involved, the main goal of the Brown team was to make the whole enterprise look shambolic and doomed to fail, thereby shaping the media coverage and putting others off from joining.

At the 2009 local elections, just after my departure, the plan for the coup was for James Purnell to resign, followed by Caroline Flint. Once the crisis point had been reached, David Miliband would also dramatically resign, urging Gordon to step down or face a leadership challenge. So the key to defeating the coup was simply to delay Caroline's resignation, at which point – when the expected announcement didn't happen – Miliband got cold feet, and Purnell was left high and dry.

With David Miliband's various abortive coups, there was a certain crude art to inducing their failure. I was often personally criticised for over-reacting to some new Miliband manoeuvre, unnecessarily 'ramping it up' as people would say. But given David's tendency to treat rebellion like a reluctant bather inching his way into the sea at Skegness, it made sense to shove him right in at the outset, on the grounds that he'd run straight back to his towel and not try again for at least six months.

But if David Miliband's behaviour was rather easy to predict and influence, there were other Cabinet ministers under Gordon who were much less predictable and were always a concern when attempted coups were in motion: the likes of Alan Johnson, Jack Straw and Alistair Darling, all with the seniority and Cabinet status to do huge damage, even just by remaining silent.

In January 2010, former Cabinet ministers Geoff Hoon and Patricia Hewitt wrote a strange joint letter calling on Gordon to hold a leadership contest to clear the air. To this day, many people feel that they did so with tacit encouragement from their good friends Alistair Darling and Jack Straw, but whether that was true or not, Geoff and Patricia seemed to have no clue as to what to do after they'd published their letter and the supposed coup became something of a media laughing stock. Ed Balls was one of those who took to the airwaves to blast the pair and call for the party to get a grip ahead of the election. Perhaps out of guilt, Darling and Straw both strongly protested to Gordon over the Balls attack.

Once the test of a coup's momentum becomes the response of key Cabinet ministers, every hour that ticks by without those responses piles pressure on the PM, as it did when Gordon and others were silent during the summer 2006 coup.

So our priority was always to know where each minister was and have a guaranteed way of getting a message through to them. If the response came back that they couldn't be reached or they were in a meeting, then they were either part of the plot or they were waiting to see how it would unfold. Either way, they were no use. However, if they did respond, we would throw the gauntlet down by telling them they were next up on the TV round at Millbank and dare them to refuse.

At the very least, we always had to put doubt in the mind of a wavering minister or MP: what if Gordon gets through this and I looked disloyal when he asked for help? That pressure increased if all they were seeing on their TV and hearing in the Commons tea rooms was one loyalist after another giving unstinting support to the leader and criticising the plotters, something Blair simply didn't have in sufficient numbers to get through the 2006 coup unscathed.

However, as Blair found on that occasion and as Gordon found in June 2009, there comes a point when you need to sue for peace in order to save yourself. The only answer then is to negotiate, perhaps not with the plotters directly but with influential Cabinet ministers or party figures, asking them what it will take to settle things down.

With Gordon, it meant drastically revising his planned 2009 reshuffle, most notably keeping Alistair Darling in post, rather than replacing him with Ed Balls, and also accepting that he would change his style of government, his way of running No. 10 and his engagement with MPs.

While the scandal surrounding my sacking clearly didn't help Gordon's cause at that time in 2009, it didn't help either that he shortly afterwards lost one of the other 'fat men' he kept around him for protection: Tom Watson, who felt so battered by the attempt by *The Sun* and others to implicate him in my scandal that he'd removed himself from Westminster and told Gordon he wanted out.

I remember one journalist from *The Sun* warning me the weekend I was sacked that the paper was going to be giving it to me and Tom both barrels the following day. I said: 'Look, I'm fair game here, but Tom seriously had nothing to do with it. It's bonkers everyone dragging him into this.'

He said there was nothing he could do: 'I'm under orders from the top, mate. Revenge for what he did to Tony in 2006.' Now you'd think anyone who looked at that 2006 coup would realise that Tom was a dangerous enemy to make, and definitely not someone whose life you'd try to destroy … unless you were sure you could finish the job. They didn't.

The 2006 coup led to the 2009 *Sun* onslaught against Tom Watson that led to his retaliatory war on News International over phone-hacking in 2011. And God only knows where that will eventually lead.

34

ASIAN PERSUASION

If Gordon loved America and was inspired by Africa, India and China always made him think.

He was simultaneously gripped by the pace of change in both countries, and their relentless desire to overtake the rest, but hugely perturbed – on an economic, political and personal level – by the vast inequality on show, feeling there was something not just undemocratic and unfair, but downright unsustainable about the social strata in those countries.

In Africa, when he went to the slums in Kenya or South Africa, that is what the local press wanted to ask him about at their press conferences: what were his impressions; what was he going to do about it? In India, let alone China, his trips to the poorest areas were usually of zero interest to the local media, despite the profound impression they made on him.

This was part of his frustration on our first trip to India in January 2007, when I had to inform him shortly after landing that our agenda, including my carefully worked-out schedule of stories, had been thrown completely out of the window because Jade Goody had made racist comments towards Shilpa Shetty in the *Celebrity Big Brother* house.

I don't think Gordon knew where to start asking who or what all those things were, so he went for the catch-all question: 'What the fuck are you talking about?'

This was, after all, a man who, on being told later that year he was going to join *Big Brother*'s Jermaine Jackson on the Hope Not Hate campaign bus in Glasgow, strolled confidently up to Jermaine's Afghan wife Halima, shook her hand, and told her how much he loved her music.

I explained everything about Shilpa Shetty and Jade Goody

carefully, but he was still baffled about what it had to do with him or our trip. 'Well,' I said, 'it's turned into a diplomatic crisis between the two countries, it's the only thing our hacks are interested in, and you're Johnny-on-the-spot.'

Our travelling press entourage, who'd been working out how they might persuade Gordon to give them a quote on the row, were delighted when I instead presented them with a full statement from Gordon saying we treasured our friendship with India, and when it came to how people should vote in the eviction battle between Shetty and Goody, 'a vote for Britain is a vote for tolerance'.

I think every one of the hacks – except the poor *FT* – got a byline on their paper's splash the following day. It was Cobras all round at the bar that evening and the assistance we gave on that story probably helped us get an easier ride – at least in the English editions – when Gordon committed his 'supporting the hosts' gaffe on World Cup 2018 later in the trip.

By contrast, our Indian hosts appeared mortified that the visit had become overshadowed by the *Big Brother* row, and when a massive press scrum gathered during Gordon's worthy but indecipherable speech on trade relations in Mumbai, they assured us that they would – with the assistance of the Indian police – hold them back until he had left the building.

As the crowd of cameras and microphones gathered at the bottom of the staircase leading up to the dais, and a small army of police wielding wooden lathis stood above them, you could see trouble coming. So with my Indian counterpart and translator, I went to the top of the steps and said: 'If you can please make a path for him to go through, Mr Brown will take one question on the *Big Brother* issue – he only has time for one question – then we must go to the next event.'

There was a murmur of agreement and a parting of the scrum below the staircase – immediately bolstered by the police – but then an almighty row ensued as the journalists tried to agree which of them would ask the question. This was still going on as Gordon finished his speech and went to leave the dais. I ran up to him and said: 'It's one question only. Go to the top of the stairs, pick whoever's shouting loudest, give your *Big Brother* line, and then we're out of here.' Gordon, as ever, did as instructed but for one thing. He picked the only guy with a microphone who wasn't waving his hand.

'Me?' the surprised journalist said. 'Erm, Mr Brown, erm, what are the chances of a trade deal that India can accept?' Gordon, delighted at this turn of events, started reeling off a summary of his five-point plan to revive the Doha trade round, while the assorted Indian tabloid and TV journalists began a small-scale riot. I stood in front of Gordon to prevent him going down the stairs and bellowed: 'One *more* question!' Fortunately, this time, it was about *Big Brother*, Gordon gave a flawless answer and everyone was happy. Except Gordon obviously, who thought I'd screwed the coverage of his trade speech.

The following year, we were back in India and then on to China in 2008 to review preparations for the Beijing Olympics, and talk about UK–China business links. The trip got off to an inauspicious start when Sue Nye, Michael Ellam and I contrived to miss the police motorcade from No. 10 escorting Gordon at rapid pace to Heathrow.

This was very bad news: if Gordon had to spend an hour at the airport waiting for us, we'd hear about it not just for the duration of the flight, but every day afterwards. We managed to persuade the police to slow down so our car could catch up. However, as a consequence, we arrived at Heathrow late, directly under the flight path of BA38 arriving from Beijing, which promptly crash-landed short of the runway.

There were days of speculation as to whether the security system surrounding Gordon's motorcade had been responsible for some kind of electronic failure on the plane. Until that was ruled out as a cause, Sue, Michael, the cops and I lived in fear, not of the public finding out we'd nearly killed 152 passengers and crew, but of Gordon finding out we'd deliberately slowed down one of his journeys.

That 2008 trip was three years since Gordon's last visit to China and he was stunned at the speed of transformation even just in that space of time.

It's a common theme among politicians, journalists and businesspeople. They go to China, see the science-fiction skyline of Shanghai and the vast factory complexes in Shenzhen, then return a short while later and find them all unrecognisable from the last time due to further development. Most people who experience that feel rather overwhelmed and star-struck, as though this is the only future and we must all rush to be part of it.

By contrast, I'd say Gordon was deeply troubled, both because it raised profound questions in his mind about where Britain's competitive advantage would lie in the decades to come, and also because even then – before the financial crisis – he could see world economic growth becoming so dependent on demand from China that a serious shock there would bring everyone's house down. That was partly why he was so worried at the potential he saw for social unrest and instability.

In Shenzhen in 2005, when we were taken round a factory manufacturing Sky digi-boxes as an example of British design and Chinese manufacturing working together, Gordon – who was already stunned by the poverty of the satellite towns we had passed en route – became distinctly uneasy about the separation of male and female workers, the apparent youth of many of the females, and – most of all – by the fact that all the workers were effectively tied to their work stations.

To his credit, when he met the local Chinese party chief afterwards, Gordon didn't duck the issue but made clear that, for all the city's global success, it was important that all its citizens and workers were able to share in the benefits, and that the improvement of their rights and working conditions needed to be as much a priority as further growth in the years to come.

It was impressive enough that the embassy officials present began whispering heatedly to their Treasury opposite numbers that this was NOT the way you did things in China, although when I observed to them that the party chief and the Chinese officials didn't seem too put out, they said that Gordon's interpreter had been diplomatic in what she passed on.

We were back in China in summer 2008 for the close of the Beijing Olympics, with a press entourage who were – to say the least – pleased to get that gig. My duties to them were even more sacred than normal: I had to make sure that, as early as possible each morning, I'd sorted out the stories for the newspapers and evening bulletins so that they could write or record them, file them and then go and enjoy a day watching Olympic events without getting any heat from their news desks.

As an exercise in looking after the entourage, that was probably my finest hour, not least because every night, I was up until the wee hours with Sumeet Desai from Reuters and the effervescent Jon Craig from Sky, men to whom the concept 'last orders' did not exist when 'on tour'.

We even overcame the biggest press row I ever witnessed, when Pippa Crerar, an *Evening Standard* reporter who was a one-person entourage for Boris Johnson, asked to sit in on Gordon's morning press briefing one day. She did so on strict lobby terms – agreed with us all – that she could listen but was not allowed to file anything for that day's edition back in London.

Gordon did a terrifically engaging and enthused briefing with the top line that, while the independent Honours Committee would have to make their judgements, he would be strongly supportive of a knighthood for Chris Hoy and major honours for other successful competitors. The press loved it, but sure enough, that afternoon, the *Standard* splash was: 'Arise, Sir Chris'.

Our hacks went ballistic and, despite Pippa's protests that it was all an accident, they nearly lynched her. But I gave them some additional quotes from Gordon and did a bit of back-pocket action so at least they had something exclusive for the following day.

On the night of the closing ceremony, almost everyone with a British passport in Beijing gathered in the special 'London House' venue set up by the 2012 Games organisers and cheered Boris as he did his flag-waving in the Bird's Nest stadium.

Gordon approached me on his arrival at London House and

said: 'Boris has got loads of jokes; we need some jokes.' I told him firmly: 'No. He's the star turn. You've just got to stand there next to him and enjoy it, just like everyone at home will be enjoying it. Remember, it's Cameron who'll be going nuts; it doesn't matter to you.' Gordon did exactly that and, for once, people saw him just smiling and laughing naturally as Boris did his 'wiff-waff' routine.

It turned into a wild night: a mix of celebrities, athletes, politicians, journalists, businesspeople and officials all getting increasingly trashed and turning the place into an impromptu nightclub. At one stage, I was walking near the VIP area when Jackie Chan's publicist grabbed me, pointed at the film star working his way towards Gordon in the corridor, and said: 'Jackie wants to meet Mr Brown.'

Now I should point out that one of my constitutional roles working for Gordon – shared with Sue Nye, depending on the occasion – was to stand a foot behind him at all parties and scan the crowd. If someone was approaching him from right or left, or he was about to walk into them, I'd pinch the relevant elbow and whisper in his ear their name and any other crucial information. Often this would just be a reminder in case he knew the face but was struggling for the details, so, for example: 'Cheryl Cole, Girls Aloud, recovering from malaria, don't mention Ashley.'

Gordon would then greet them warmly and reference the other information, and especially with celebrities and journalists, they'd feel special and at ease with him right from the off. It didn't always go to plan though. Once, he was approaching a group at a No. 10 lobby reception including Sumeet. Gordon had been interviewed by him two dozen times over the years, but he could never get his name right.

I said: 'That's our friend Sumeet ahead. SUH-MEET. He's just come back from honeymoon, you sent a card and flowers to his wedding.' 'What's the name?' Gordon asked. 'SUH-MEET. SUH-MEET,' I said. I don't know what went on in Gordon's head in the next half a second, but he charged into the group and roared: 'SHAMBO! Congratulations!'

Anyway, back in Beijing, I ran and grabbed Gordon's right elbow and whispered in his ear: 'Coming at you. Jackie Chan. Huge film star. Martial arts.' Gordon rasped: '*Crouching Tiger?*' 'No, action comedies, *Rush Hour*.' Gordon didn't quite get it, and greeted Jackie as if he was Ang Lee. 'Jackie, it is an honour to meet you. Your films are so important to us in Britain, and we have learned so much from you about your culture. When will you next be visiting us?'

It clearly did the trick. Jackie immediately said he wanted to sign up as the first volunteer for London 2012. I turned to his publicist and asked if there was anyone else he wanted to meet: Boris? Seb Coe? He replied: 'David Beckham?' I felt a little hypocritical given I was always angrily accusing other No. 10 colleagues of being 'star-fuckers' but going up to Becks in the VIP room, and saying: 'David, would you like to meet Jackie Chan?' was easily the coolest moment of my career.

Despite that temporary lapse in professionalism – and despite the lateness of the hour and the ocean of booze I'd consumed – I then had to commit the most calculated and professional of fouls. I got a tip that ITN were planning to run a story on that evening's *News at Ten* – based on a call from a viewer – that the Tourist Board animation played at London House that night to promote the 2012 Olympics had included a fleeting glimpse of some modern-art portrait of Myra Hindley.

All I could think was this. When that story appeared at 5 a.m. Chinese time, the news desks on every paper and every other broadcaster back in Britain would wake up their extremely tired, possibly incapacitated member of our media entourage, and say: 'Weren't you at London House tonight? I need 500 words on this for second edition in the next half hour.'

I could just have alerted Boris's people or the Games commit-tee, but it wasn't in their interests to have the story in any first editions, and they owed no responsibility to the No. 10 entou-rage. They'd have just thanked me, prepared a statement for ITN and left it there until 10 p.m. UK time.

I couldn't let that happen. I checked whether No. 10 or DCMS

had any involvement in the production or vetting of the animation and, once I'd established we didn't, I quietly worked my way
round each of our hacks, saying: 'Sorry mate, you've got some
work to do, but I'm saving you a job later.' I explained the story,
said it was for Boris's people and the Games committee to explain
and respond, but if they needed a No. 10 reaction, here you go.

As it turned out, even though it caused a mini-meltdown in
London House that night, the fact that news desks back home
were told the story early and knew everyone had it meant that
no one went too big, and it fizzled out quite quickly. But our
entourage were hugely grateful to me for the service, and – rightly
or wrongly – that was all that mattered to me at the time.

After I was sacked the following year, Boris wrote an excoriating article in the *Telegraph* about the night he came face to face
with Brown's attack dog, suggesting that it had been one of the
No. 10 staff who'd spotted the Myra Hindley portrait, and that
I'd done my best to wind it up with the press simply because
London now had a Tory mayor and my 'relentless, brutal, tribal
viciousness' dictated that I should try and destroy a great night
for Britain.

Over my career, I was guilty of many moments of relentless,
brutal, tribal viciousness, but I don't think that night really qualified. I was just trying to stop the *Telegraph*'s Rosa Prince and all
the other journalists in our group getting woken up at 5 a.m.
A few months after Boris's article, I wrote to him asking if he'd
attend an event at Finchley Catholic High School, and I took
the opportunity to apologise for the London House incident but
explain a bit of the context. He wrote a very nice letter back,
saying he accepted my explanation and that it was all water
under the bridge.

The London House incident would have been a sour note on
which to leave one of my favourite foreign visits – even if I didn't
see a single moment of the Olympic sport myself – but before
we left Beijing, I came across the pile of letters that had been
prepared for Gordon to sign officially congratulating the medal
winners on behalf of the country. They were all identical: the only

changes from one to another were their names, their events and the colour of their medals.

I imagined being one of the athletes opening their letter and being quite pleased, thinking it was a nice thing to hang over the toilet back home, but then literally comparing notes with their colleagues on the journey home and seeing that no thought had gone into them at all – they'd just been mail-merged from a spreadsheet and signed without a glance. By the end of the flight, I'm sure half of them would have been used as paper aeroplanes.

I sat down and spent several hours re-writing all seventy letters, personalising them with details of the great rivals beaten, adversity overcome, proud families back home, anything I could find that actually tried to sum up what they'd achieved and for whom. I then sat with Gordon next to me, talked him through every letter and he either signed them or told me to make changes on screen, especially where he'd watched the medal won himself in the stadia or on TV.

We reached the end but I asked Gordon if he also remembered the girl he'd been excited about who wouldn't settle for silver and crashed her bike trying for the gold. 'The BMX girl!' he said excitedly, 'Sharon? Sheila? Shona?' 'Shanaze,' I told him – not a name Gordon was ever going to find easy. 'Well, you're only supposed to write to the medal-winners, but I think you should write to her too.'

He did and that became our seventy-first letter. A couple of years later, Shanaze Reade said in a newspaper interview that one of the things that persuaded her not to quit the sport after her Beijing heartbreak, but come back and compete again, was getting a letter from Gordon Brown after the event praising her courage and saying her determination to win and refusal to accept second place made her his personal hero of the Games.

That's how I choose to remember Beijing.

35

BECOMING THE LEADER

Way back, during Christmas 2002, I was talking to a young shining star in Customs, Rebecca Hall, about life in the Treasury. She asked me whether it was frustrating working with Gordon, given he must be bored stiff of being Chancellor and was so obviously desperate to be Prime Minister.

Even though the extent of my relationship with Gordon at that stage was limited to our great corridor conversations: 'Betting Guy. How are the horses?', I wanted to impress her, so I advanced the theory that his burning ambition when he came into politics was less to be Prime Minister than to be leader of the Labour Party. Obviously one might follow the other, or the two might go together, but you can only have one burning ambition.

I don't know why I said that, or even whether I actually thought it, but when we formally embarked on planning the leadership campaign and everyone was treating it as a bit of a boring formality to go through, I remember getting myself stirred up for it by saying: 'Come on, this is big, this is about his life's work.'

By early 2007, there were only a few remaining possibilities for where the challenge for the leadership might come from, if it came at all, and Gordon had been genuinely pleased and heartened by a conversation at No. 10 where Tony openly went through the list of all his potential leadership rivals, dismissing every one of them as either not ready or not up to it.

If David Miliband or Alan Johnson stood, they would be viable candidates, but David was playing it too cautious as always and Alan appeared happy to settle for a shot at the deputy job. There would inevitably be a candidate from the left, unless Gordon bought them off with commitments on union rights and Trident, which he wasn't prepared to do.

There was also the prospect of a wrecking-ball effort from one of Gordon's critics, a Charles Clarke or Frank Field presenting their candidacy as an opportunity to ask him tough questions. But if they made that their offer, we'd just say they were doing the Tories' work for them, and they'd never get enough nominations to get on the ballot.

And then there was John Reid.

Edinburgh Gordon and Glasgow John went way back, and could hardly have been more different characters. When they were both in the Commons in the late 1980s, Reid was drinking heavily and drawing flak for his occasional fighting and carousing, while Gordon was also busy every night, but largely in the business of firing out parliamentary questions and press releases as shadow Chief Secretary to the Treasury.

Reid stopped drinking in 1994 and became a heavyweight politician, but Gordon never saw him much differently from their first encounters and I daresay Reid continued to look at Gordon the same way too. As Reid rose up the ranks, the enmity grew unabated; in parallel, the personal rivalry grew between me and my counterpart in Reid's office, a Labour special adviser named Steve Bates.

Bates was a class act with a superb eye for a story, respected by the hacks and feared by his Tory opposite numbers. He is one of those (along with Tony McNulty) with a legitimate claim to have invented the phrase 'Hug a Hoodie' to characterise David Cameron's infamous 2005 speech about thugs needing love. He certainly fed it to the *News of the World* – among others – for their splash headline, which enabled the myth to take hold that Andy Coulson had come up with it.

But Bates was also ambitious for his boss, and that meant attacking Gordon. Even by my standards, he went too far one week when I was told by a contact on the Andrew Marr programme that Bates had fed them suggested questions to ask Gordon. It was customary if your minister's opposition shadow was on Marr to provide an attack briefing to the programme, but I'd never heard of anyone pro-actively doing it to a minister on their own side.

As we got closer to the leadership election, those MPs closest to Reid were clearly taking soundings about levels of support for him among the backbenchers, donors and party members, and Bates organised lunches and dinners to do likewise with groups of journalists, at least one or two of whom at every event could be relied on to feed back to me every word that had been said.

Those 'soundings' climaxed in a dinner at the London Marriott Hotel at County Hall attended by a large group of Westminster's most influential journalists and columnists, each in turn offering their opinion about Gordon's candidacy and John's chances of challenging him.

I decided, carefully and tentatively, to unearth from my black book some of the stories I'd gathered over the years about Reid's escapades from the 1980s and early 1990s. After all, the stories about his past were going to come thick and fast if he had a chance of becoming Prime Minister, so I figured that I'd see whether he and Bates were ready for that level of scrutiny.

Coincidence or not, no sooner had the first call been made by the first newspaper following the first story I'd given out, than Reid announced he would be resigning as Home Secretary when Tony stepped down, with accompanying briefing that this was the end of his career in front-line politics.

I got a call from a journalist friendly with Reid and Bates. He discussed the news with me, then said: 'So you can call off the dogs now.' I asked what he meant. 'You know what I mean; there's no need to go for him now.' I said I had no idea what he was talking about.

The field was now clear for Gordon, although we still had to staff, launch and run a leadership campaign: all a chance for some easy media coverage; some much-needed outreach to Labour MPs, members and party staff; some further opportunities to 'sell' Gordon to the public; and inevitably some disastrous PR screw-ups.

One of our priorities was to introduce people to a bit more of Gordon's back-story: the fact he still lived in the ordinary town where he grew up; went to a fairly ordinary school; faced massive adversity with his eye injury and long-term hospitalisation as a youngster; and was inspired in his politics by the social justice preached by his father and the poverty he saw as a boy. The subtle message: he's not like that posh bastard Cameron, you know.

We did some excellent paper and broadcast profile pieces up in North Queensferry, the best of them with Nick Robinson for the BBC *Ten O'Clock News*, only ruined by the fact that, when Nick alluded off camera to his own awful accident as a youngster, Gordon pretty brusquely changed the subject, as if openly rejecting the opportunity to bond with a guy he'd written off as a 'bloody Tory' long ago.

We also did a Sunday Andrew Marr special from Gordon's old school; a great interview but no one noticed because between me setting up the shot and going back into the impromptu control booth Gordon's trousers had ridden so far up his legs, he looked like he was wearing Gieves & Hawkes Bermuda shorts. The exposure of his ivory white shins proved rather distracting for audiences.

After that, we always had strict instructions for Gordon that he had to check his shoelaces were done up, his socks were pulled up and his trouser bottoms were pulled down before any cameras started rolling.

A few days later, I was waiting for him to arrive by car to open a new school in Sheffield, and he emerged from the back seat having followed all these instructions both rigorously and vigorously, except between yanking down his trouser bottoms and yanking up his socks, he'd managed to pull one sock over the trouser leg almost up to his knee, creating a rather splendid one-legged knickerbocker effect.

Jo Dipple, his political events chief, came out of the car on the other side, and made a very weary and wobbly beeline for me, while an oblivious Gordon greeted the head teacher, head boy and head girl. 'What the fuck is that?' I said to Jo. She just shook her head with the dead-eyed look of someone who'd spent three hours in a car with Gordon in a bad mood.

We waited until the cameras had stopped shooting before I

alerted Gordon about the sock. 'Did anyone see?' he asked, a little sheepishly. 'I think they were all looking at your face,' I lied. The day wasn't over. At the end, Gordon had to cut open a huge balloon net to launch the new school, and approached the task a little gingerly given the high winds.

As he cut the tape, the netting broke loose and wrapped around his arms and head. I was faced with the horrifying spectacle of Gordon struggling manically to free himself, becoming more entangled in the net and the trapped balloons as he thrashed around, while dozens of beaming children yelped and cheered. Eventually, Gordon broke free, almost falling over in the process.

Amazingly, the video footage wasn't that bad, with Gordon's struggles obscured by the balloons, but when I approached the stills photographer he was chuckling to himself looking at his shots. They were as bad as possible. Jo had been looking after the snapper and, while equally horrified, she couldn't help burst out laughing as we looked at each fresh picture of Gordon's contortions.

Eventually, the snapper said to Jo: 'You know what, you've been great today, and you got him to do everything I asked; plus I've already got the sock picture. So I won't send out the worst ones.' Jo gave me a look which said: 'See, I might not have seen the sock, but I still know what I'm doing.' Indeed she did.

Unfortunately, Jo wasn't in charge a few days later when Gordon's campaign was formally launched in London. His socks, trousers and shoelaces were immaculate, and there wasn't a balloon in sight, but somehow he managed to end up with half his face obscured by one of the autocue screens for the duration of the speech.

And yet it seemed the more of these kind of mistakes happened and the more Gordon looked unpolished and unmanicured, the more the public seemed to warm to him and to the contrast with the glitz and smoothness of Tony Blair and David Cameron.

It was an entirely different story when it came to his efforts, or I should say the efforts foisted on him by some of his more focus-group- and poll-driven advisers, to broaden his appeal beyond the mainstream political news pages and broadcasts to some of their 'softer' target media, including women's magazines, rather than doing the kind of 'laddish' things I'd been getting him to do – things he was very good and natural at – like talking about sport.

This was what came to be known publicly as 'Project Volvo', although frankly if anyone had used the words 'Project Anything' around me concerning Gordon, I'd have told them to stick it up 'Project Arse'. I didn't tend to go to those meetings, or any of those geared around polls or focus groups.

Frankly, there was always a very large divide between those of Gordon's advisers who went on gut instinct about the way he came across and just wanted him to do things he was comfortable with and be his natural self (the bits fit for public consumption at any rate), and those continually warning him that he faced an image problem which was eventually going to cost him votes, particularly with women and especially in the affluent south east, and urging him to present himself in a different way, use softer language, smile more and so on.

As Life President of the 'Be Yourself' contingent, I'd rail against the pressure that Gordon was put under by the 'Image Problem' collective, for example when he'd suddenly remember at the most inopportune times in interviews that he'd been told to smile more. But, to be fair, my opponents would simply counter that you couldn't cheat the evidence from the polls and we weren't going to beat Cameron in a personality-driven election unless Gordon made changes.

That tension was never resolved, and one of the reasons it continued was that Gordon himself could never settle on what he thought the basis of his 'appeal' should be: he was happy to take and try to meld all sorts of contradictory advice, but he never cared enough about what he called 'that image stuff' to actually work out what he thought was best. And stick to it.

During the pre-leadership period, the nadir of this tension came when Gordon was due to give an interview to *New Woman* magazine, leading to the famous Arctic Monkeys fiasco. The worst aspect was that they'd given us the 'quick fire Q&A' in advance so we could veto any questions he refused to answer. Compared to most of the questions, 'James Blunt or Arctic Monkeys?' was pretty innocuous.

'Who's James Blunt?' he said to the four of us in his room, receiving the simultaneous answers 'Twat', 'Fucking Tory', 'He's shit', and 'Oh, I quite like him'. Gordon heard only one word: 'He's a Tory?! I'll say the other lot. At least I've heard of them. Are they Tories?' 'No!' times four.

Cometh the interview, cometh the question. Gordon said: 'Ah, I'm not a fan of either really, but the Arctic guys.' The *New Woman* editor was gently amused: 'Why? I thought you'd be more of a James Blunt man!' He didn't explain why he wasn't, but said: 'I usually listen to music just to wake me up in the morning, so I need loud music. At least the Arctic Monkeys would wake you up.'

Much as I was down on the whole interview, I thought that was pretty well handled. But no. The introduction to the *New Woman* profile was all about what a surprising man Gordon was, and concluded – not even in quotes – with: 'And he wakes up to Arctic Monkeys!' Cue the ridicule of an entire nation.

And that's how myths are born; the fact he never said it didn't make a difference. But you could argue he got his fair comeuppance. If he'd just been himself, he'd have said: 'Neither, I listen to Bach', but the fact that he was actively trying (or being told to try) to project a more modern, relaxed image had led him down that path.

At least the leadership campaign was back to Gordon's comfort zone: trooping round meeting halls and university campuses; opening schools and hospitals wherever we went; and holding a series of fairly desultory hustings sessions against the would-be challenger from the left, John McDonnell MP. We were in two minds whether we wanted John to get the required nominations to go to a formal ballot, just so Gordon could look as centrist as possible, but given Leon Trotsky would have looked fairly moderate next to John, there wasn't much to be gained from it.

We were all on a train coming back from another long day-trip when Sue Nye got the call that the deadline for nominations had closed, Gordon was the only candidate and was therefore leader-elect of the party without the need for a ballot. She came off her mobile with a huge beaming smile, filled Gordon's wine glass, raised it to him and said: 'Gordon Brown, it is my pleasure to tell you that you are the new leader of the Labour Party.'

There was a joy and exhilaration on the train at that moment, and at the campaign headquarters when we got back, which was never quite there when Gordon was installed as Prime Minister a few weeks later. Maybe that was because of the formality, pressure and importance of the latter occasion; or maybe I was right after all when I told young Rebecca from Customs back in 2002 that it was the leadership he craved most of all.

Either way, I felt the same exhilaration myself. Gordon had done it. He'd seen off every other contender – Milburn, Reid, Clarke, Johnson, Miliband and dozens of others whose ambition had fizzled out on the back benches or in the junior ministerial ranks.

He had survived thirteen years, ten of them in government, as the main contender – and consistently the public's favoured choice – to succeed Tony Blair as Labour leader. It was an astonishing feat of personal discipline, political resilience and total commitment to the cause, and to have been there and done my bit in the crucial last years was my own greatest achievement.

36

WHAT WE LOST THE DAY WE WON

There are only four people alive who know what it feels like to walk over the threshold of 10 Downing Street for the first time as Prime Minister. Only eleven men and one woman have known that feeling at all in the past seventy-five years, and – remarkably – only five of those as a result of winning a general election outright.

But I can almost guarantee none of those individuals had a stranger start to the day than facing the wall in a near-empty room and booming out their old school motto: 'I WILL DO MY UTMOST', while a rotund, red-faced spin-doctor yelled back: 'SOD OFF, YOU SCOTTISH GIT!'

Sue Nye and I had joined Gordon and Sarah in the large ceremonial room between his office and mine on the Treasury's second floor where he was rehearsing the first speech he'd make outside Downing Street as Prime Minister. The speech had been weeks in preparation, and the final draft had been given a double thumbs-up from the various focus groups who'd been shown it, particularly the school motto. I hated the use of focus groups at the best of times but, on this occasion, it really got under my skin.

Obviously it helped to know that a representative sample of swing voters liked the speech but it still meant that a dozen individuals, their friends and families would hear Gordon supposedly speaking from the heart about the most important moment of his working life, and think that he was just some shyster who'd asked them to decide what he should say. It was the opposite of the principle drummed into me by Congressman Sawyer's office in Washington that you win elections one person at a time.

Nevertheless, it meant Gordon was in confident mood about the speech. Now he just needed to deliver it properly in front of the vast bank of cameras waiting outside No. 10 to see Tony Blair's exit and his arrival. Given that – as well as the cameras – Iraq War protestors were gathering outside Downing Street, and news and police helicopters were constantly circling overhead, we suggested Gordon try the speech a few times with us heckling him and generally making a racket so he could get used to the distractions he'd experience later.

Sue's heckles were straight out of children's panto: 'Booo!', 'Hiss!', 'You're a very bad man, Gordon!', but I tried to inject a bit of realism: 'You stole my pension, Brown!', 'You're a bigger bastard than Blair!', 'Tell us about Bilderberg!' and so on.

Every so often, I shouted something that would get under his skin ('Where's the gold, Brown?'), and he would stop and give me a long, deathly stare. On occasion, he even shouted back. 'Why's there blood on my hands?' he demanded, in response to one traditional heckle. 'You signed the cheques, Brown!' I boomed back in my protester voice, albeit with a bit of feeling as a veteran of the 2003 Hyde Park march against the Iraq War.

Sue stepped in and told Gordon forcefully: 'Excuse me! You can't stop and have a debate with one of the hecklers if you don't like what he says. That's the whole point of this', and we carried on.

It was all useful preparation, and we were kicking ourselves over the coming weeks that we didn't do the same to prepare Gordon for his first Prime Minister's Questions.

He was used to speaking to a packed House of Commons for his Budget speeches, but they were generally heard in total silence. And while he was used to an occasionally raucous atmosphere for sessions of Treasury Questions, there were usually a maximum of 200 MPs present and he had no difficulty dominating the chamber.

So, despite his twenty-four years of parliamentary experience, Gordon was totally unprepared for the first time he faced a wall of noise from packed opposition benches and couldn't hear himself speak, developing an elongated version of Foghorn Leghorn's stammer as he repeated the first phrase of each sentence again and again, waiting in vain for some quiet.

It's no coincidence that, more than three years later, Ed Miliband prepared for his first ever Prime Minister's Questions simply by having his aides scream and shout at the top of their voices as he delivered his questions. Good thinking on his part, although it says something pretty dismal about the culture in the House of Commons that he had to do so.

Nevertheless, Gordon's unhappy afternoons in Prime Minister's Questions all lay before us on the much happier Wednesday of 27 June 2007, as he left the Treasury for the last time, every single official filling the corridors, stairwells and the reception area downstairs, to shake his hand, wish him luck, applaud him out and shed some tears. I was told that, on the way to Buckingham Palace, Gordon did too.

There was a lot of crying in the Treasury in those last few days before Gordon left. For the few civil servants making the transition to Downing Street, like Jon Cunliffe, Leeanne Johnston and Helen Etheridge, it was a case of painful goodbyes. For others, who'd expected to go across, the tears were of disappointment – and no little anger – that the move which their effort, brilliance and many sacrifices had helped deliver for Gordon was being denied to them.

To my huge irritation, Balshen was one of those told she'd have to wait and see what opportunities emerged. The subtext was that, as essential as she'd been in managing Gordon's events, visits and media appearances, it might look as though I'd pulled strings for my girlfriend if a No. 10 civil service job was immediately created for her. And I couldn't kick up too much of a fuss, or else – in some minds – it would have proved the point. As it was, Ed Balls took advantage of the indecision and snapped her up for a more senior role at his new Children, Schools and Families department.

As well as the civil servants left in limbo, some of Gordon's Treasury special advisers were rather cruelly left to wait and see how many vacant slots would be available once he had finished trying in vain to persuade some of Blair's key No. 10 advisers to stay and support the succession.

Rightly or wrongly, Gordon was desperate to show unrecon-
ciled Blairites that he was not going to trash Tony's legacy, and
was indeed willing to pick up his torch. Having lost ministers like
John Reid who'd decided to step down with Blair, trying to get
Tony's advisers to stay on was the next best thing, but it was a
huge and rather humiliating waste of time, and caused unnecessary angst for some of Gordon's longest-serving aides.

As for me – even though dozens of people claimed in April
2009, either on the record or anonymously, that they'd warned
Gordon not to take me with him to No. 10 – my position there was
never in doubt, and the view was that Michael Ellam and I would
complement each other perfectly, he as Prime Minister's official
spokesman and me remaining as the political press adviser.

Nevertheless, when the day came, I couldn't drag myself away
from the Treasury. I left a good luck card and a bottle of whiskey
on my desk for my successor, Alistair Darling's excellent special
adviser Sam White, who unfortunately didn't do the press job for
long. I put half my possessions and old papers in moving crates to
go to No. 10, and half in bin bags to go on the skip.

But then I just sat in my empty office, watching the TV and
waiting for Gordon to arrive at No. 10, sending my usual abusive
texts to fellow Brown press officers and advisers who kept opening the door or appearing on screen. What made it worse was
that I knew some of them were trying their best to get 'in the
shot', either to make themselves look important or just to show
off to their families, but either way making us look like rank
amateurs to our new No. 10 colleagues.

Gordon eventually arrived from the Palace and delivered
his speech flawlessly, despite all the noise from the helicopters,
hecklers and flashing cameras. Once inside, he summoned all the
staff to one of the large state rooms and arguably made a more
impressive speech.

Given that a lot of the civil service staff wore their loyalty to
Tony Blair on their sleeves, it was a sceptical audience, but he said
he knew this was a day of great sadness for them, having to say
goodbye to Tony, Cherie, Euan, Nicky, Kathryn and especially

Leo, whom many of them had known since he was a baby, and he knew also that they'd had to say goodbye to a great many friends among Tony's advisers and that they too would be sorely missed.

When David Cameron made a similar speech to No. 10 staff on the day he became Prime Minister, his only reference to his two predecessors was to joke that a civil servant had told him he and Nick Clegg were already getting on better than Blair and Brown, and he hoped to set the bar a bit higher than that. While some officials laughed, many others thought it deeply crass, given that they had worked hard for both men over the years, knew more of the realities of their working relationship than Cameron ever would, and didn't like to see them dismissed in such an offhand way.

By contrast, Gordon's speech transformed attitudes to him among the No. 10 staff, not just in terms of what he'd said, but the amount of thought and care he'd put into it. Although, as they all soon discovered and not entirely to their pleasure, one of his best or worst habits was putting huge amounts of thought and care into every single speech he made; a luxury that the demands of life in No. 10 simply didn't afford.

As Gordon settled in at No. 10, his two big speeches for the day complete, I continued sitting alone in my Treasury office into the early evening, taking calls from hacks about everything from the impending reshuffle to what Gordon would be eating for dinner that evening. Eventually Sue called me and asked where I was in the familiar tone she used when I was clearly not where she thought I should be. 'I'm still in the Treasury,' I said. She sighed: 'Well, you know you work here now, don't you? And there are No. 10 people rather anxious about meeting you.'

After all that work trying to get Gordon into No. 10, I felt a real aversion to going there myself, not because I was scared or daunted, but because it meant leaving the Treasury, a place I genuinely loved and had come to regard as home, to the extent that, afternoons at Arsenal aside, I preferred to spend my weekends there.

I called Balshen and told her I had to leave shortly, and couldn't face walking through the press office to say goodbye. She came round, and burst into tears as soon as she saw the empty office, which set me off too. We had a good cuddle and told each other it would be OK. I left after that, but I had to go and sit on a bench in St James's Park for half an hour before I felt composed enough to go in the back door of Downing Street. I didn't want to disappoint my old foes turned new colleagues in the No. 10 press office by not looking like the 'Mad Dog' they were expecting.

There's no getting around the fact that, by this point, many of the No. 10 civil servants who'd worked under Tony regarded me with something between distrust and hatred, given how many nights and weekends they'd had ruined as a result of my activities and lots more where they probably felt I was to blame, even if I wasn't. In particular, there was always a sense that the Brown camp had played a role in escalating the Lord Levy cash-for-honours scandal, which we definitely didn't. But when your colleagues and friends are having their homes raided at 6 a.m., you tend to want someone to blame.

Nevertheless, all the staff I met that first evening were totally professional and friendly when greeting me. I was looked after by the exceptional Head of News, Emily Hands; introduced to the press office brains trust of Brendan O'Grady, James Roscoe and Ruth McAllister; and put in an office with old Alastair Campbell acolytes Paul Brown and Martin Sheehan, two lovely chaps, both effortlessly superb at their jobs planning the government's grid of announcements and speeches.

Paul had on his wall the *Mail on Sunday* splash denouncing the fact that the 'chief burier of bad news' was to be awarded an OBE, that honour proving 'how debauched and discredited this government has become', according to rent-a-quote Liberal Democrat MP Norman Baker. I eventually owned up to Paul that I was responsible for that story and he thanked me, saying it was one of his proudest moments – both receiving the gong and there being a front-page story about it.

As my tour continued, I was shown the 'stand-alone computer' through which No. 10 staff could use personal email accounts which were otherwise blocked by the Downing Street servers to avoid foreign intelligence services using them to access the No. 10 network. 'We don't discuss this publicly,' I was told; 'we don't want people going on about "second Downing Street email systems"', the existence of which had been hotly disputed during the cash-for-honours scandal.

What I wasn't shown that day was the secret underground tunnel to the Whitehall nuclear bunker. It was only after a series of staff departures in 2008 that I was told I'd finally made it onto the list of key officials and advisers who would be bundled off to safety along with the Cabinet and the monarchy when the bombs dropped so that we could restore good government and repopulate the country once the smoke cleared. By that stage, I'm afraid my reaction was: 'Do I have to be?'

The other consequence of the mass exodus of the Blair family and advisers from No. 10 was the sheer volume of material that they'd left piled up to go in the skip: files, letters, lanyards, chipped mugs, stained ties and other detritus. I had a good root around in the rubbish to recover any serviceable books, stationery and memorabilia. My prize find was Tony Blair's GQ Politician of the Year Award from September 2003, a lovely piece of slate and glass, which now sits on my mantelpiece at home.

Late into the evening, all the long-term Brown staffers who'd made the trip over to No. 10 gathered to watch the 10 o'clock news and have a drink.

There were handshakes and hugs, and a feeling of genuine pride and relief both that the day had gone so well and that we'd finally made it. Gordon was not for basking though, interrupting one minor burst of mutual congratulation to ask for all his documentation on the next day's reshuffle and say: 'Right, what time are you all in tomorrow? Can you be in for 6 or 6.30?'

Sue's face beamed, savouring the moment: 'Oh yes, Prime Minister.' Gordon responded by returning some of the choicer heckles from earlier in the day.

It was a happy moment alright, but – looking back – it's clear to me that we lost something that day. Some people have argued we lost our raison d'être; that Gordon had sought power for its own sake and didn't know what to do once he had it, rather like the politician played by Robert Redford in *The Candidate*, winning the Senate race only to say: 'What do we do now?'

There's another argument that we lost control; that Gordon's previous reliance on set-piece moments like the Budget, and the drawn-out decision-making that led up to them, was fundamentally unsuited to the fast-paced and usually random nature of events in No. 10. In the Treasury, he could afford to invest time and care into every speech he made because he made fewer of them, they were less varied and, most importantly, he had more time to spare.

I think there are elements of truth in both arguments, but they are nevertheless post-hoc explanations of the events that followed, and neither might stand up if Gordon had made the right decision in October 2007 and pressed ahead with his plans for a snap election.

For me, what we lost the day Gordon became the Prime Minister was something more fundamental, as apparent during the first months of the 'Brown Bounce' as it was in the doldrums that followed. We lost the Treasury. By which I mean that, in the Treasury, Gordon had his various 'guys' and 'girls' in every key position who knew how he worked and what he wanted; who knew when to refer issues to him or the Eds, and when to take decisions themselves.

These were relationships built up over a decade of long days and late nights working on Budgets, spending reviews and Mansion House speeches, or attending EU, IMF and World Bank summits. Gordon knew them by function if not by name, and he trusted them. Those perfunctory acknowledgements of staff as he passed them in the Treasury corridors may have been comical at times, but they helped make the organisation under Gordon a finely tuned machine.

The bulk of the staff Gordon took with him into No. 10 were political advisers – filling the gaps left by Blair's outgoing team – with a broad mix of policy, communications and political respon-sibilities. By contrast, he took barely more than a handful of civil servants with him from the Treasury, waving goodbye to dozens of individuals with trusted experience and tested know-how, including all the key Treasury experts who shadowed departmental spending and policy.

When you saw the difference exceptional civil servants like Jon Cunliffe and Michael Ellam made to Gordon's ability to function effectively in No. 10, you couldn't help but think how much he could have done with a few more Cunliffes and Ellams making the journey with him. Not that there is any doubting the quality of the civil servants he inherited in No. 10, but what they lacked was that knowledge of his working methods, and what he lacked was the same level of trust and confidence in their judgement.

Gordon's response was to lurch into micro-management; and the response of his new staff was to let him, assuming that was just the way he worked best. When practised every day, on every issue, that inevitably ate into Gordon's time, energy and mood, as well as his capacity to see the big picture.

Take his preparation for just one potential topic at one session of Prime Minister's Questions. In the Treasury, a civil servant could have said to him: 'Here's what you need to know … Here's what you need to say', and he would have written it down and had the confidence to trust them. In No. 10, he could hear exactly the same thing but then feel the need to ask a dozen more questions to gain that same confidence, filling his head with all kinds of unnecessary detail. It was hugely time-consuming and usually counter-productive.

As a side effect, it meant that people who were generally good at helping him cut through the nonsense and focus on the key messages – me included – avoided PMQs preparation like the plague. If you got trapped in there, it was half of Monday or Tuesday lost. It was a terrible use of time for the extremely talented individuals who were obliged to sit through the whole thing – Ian Austin, Patrick Loughran, Theo Bertram and James Bowler most of all – and I personally got in the habit of only showing my face fifteen minutes before I knew Gordon had another meeting scheduled.

I'm not suggesting Gordon either could or should have gutted the Treasury of its best officials; the civil service wouldn't have allowed it. But if half the time he devoted to trying to persuade junior members of the Blair entourage to stay on in No. 10 had been spent negotiating the secondment of even a dozen more trusted Treasury civil servants into key No. 10 roles, he would have been better off. After all, if he'd recorded his 2009 YouTube message on expenses with Balshen behind the camera, she'd have laughed at him before the rest of the nation did and told him to do it again without the smiles. She might even have asked: why are we doing this on YouTube?

But if Gordon lost the Treasury on 27 June 2007, it's also worth noting that the Treasury lost him, with equally significant consequences. Gone was its own sense of purpose, gone was its own rigid control of the Budget process, gone was the leadership and authority that Gordon and the Eds gave it, and – if I say so myself – gone was its control of the media.

THE
ROLLERCOASTER

37

THE HACKS

If I ever caught a colleague who wasn't supposed to speak to the press having a chinwag with a hack, I wouldn't ask them what they'd been saying, I'd ask: 'What terms were you speaking on?'

'What?' they'd invariably reply, at least the first time.

'Well, you know. Was it in your own name or as a source? Was it "on the record" or "off the record"? Was it "not for use" or just "no fingerprints"? Was it "on background" or just "operational"? Was it "you can't act on this" or just "you didn't get this from me"? You know, which of those?'

'Um, I don't know, it was just, a chat? What does that count as?'

I'd roll my eyes, put my arm round their shoulders – some with a tighter grip than others – and explain that if they didn't know the difference, they had no business speaking to the media, which funnily enough, they didn't anyway, so please don't do it again, otherwise I'll have to tell Gordon.

Some of them would get wise and the next time I'd catch them, they'd say confidently: 'Ah, that was entirely "not for use".' 'Blimey,' I'd respond, 'that sounds big – what were you telling them?'

The main purpose of those tactics was not just to control what messages and information came out from Gordon's team to the press, but to persuade everyone else in the operation that there was a reason we exerted that kind of control: these were dangerous characters, these journalists, and if you didn't know exactly what you were doing, you could come a cropper.

In some ways, I was too successful at those scare tactics for my own good. In the small and close-knit Treasury team, I contributed to the speech-writing, the policy development and the political strategising. But as part of a quite large team of advisers in No. 10, I found myself increasingly confined just to dealing

with the media. When my colleagues introduced me to strangers at parties or receptions, they'd always say by rote: 'This is
Damian. He looks after the hacks.'

Indeed, 'How are the hacks? What's the mood?' went from just
being one of Gordon's catchphrases to being the default greeting
from everyone in the Brown operation to me – whether it was
on an overseas trip, a regional visit, at party conference, after a
questions session in Parliament, on the day of a Gordon speech,
or just when I was passing them in the No. 10 corridors.

So, compared to the Treasury, I felt a much-diminished figure
in No. 10 in terms of my responsibilities, and could only really
get involved in the work everyone else was doing through my
influence over Gordon.

Sometimes, if I saw a bunch of Gordon's strategic policy thinkers and civil servants going off to a meeting room, almost out
of spite I'd get hold of their agenda, wander in and see Gordon
while it was going on, get him to take five decisions and – by the
time all the policy wonks scurried happily back to their desks
filled with a sense of purpose – there would be an email from me
in their inboxes saying: 'I had a quick chat with Gordon. This is
what he wants...'

Obviously, if I'd wanted to, I could have engaged more with my
other colleagues, shared my instincts about Gordon's preferences
and worked with them for the collective good, but – and I do
curse myself in retrospect for this – I had that terrible combination of laziness and impatience which meant that I resented any
time spent in a meeting room which could be spent on the phone
to, or in the pub with, a journalist doing what I regarded as my
proper and more important job.

So I allowed myself to be pigeon-holed as the guy who looked
after the hacks.

I should stress that this went far beyond the skulduggery I got
up to with journalists in terms of leaking stories and information
in order to kill more damaging stories, or gather media intelligence, or stymie Gordon's rivals. What it included were all sorts
of other help that I provided openly and in good conscience. It

could be anything, depending on the journalist involved, and it could be any time of day or night, usually starting with the *Standard*:

6 a.m.: 'Hi matey, that line the *Today* programme are running out of Brussels? We like it but we can't get any detail and Miliband's people are in the air, so if you want to do us a quick 250 words from Gordon, that would probably be our splash. We'd need it by 10 a.m. though? Thanks, grand.'

9 a.m.: 'Dog! Quick favour. I'm talking at some PR industry lunch today, and I've just noticed there's a table full of Centrica and all that crowd, and another table full of bloody green charities, so can you just talk me through where we are on energy policy and the environment and all that?'

Noon: 'Hi mate, the editor's got a bunch of our shareholders in this afternoon and he's asked me to be there. They're bound to ask me what the plan is on the banks, so can you just give me some bullets in an email in shareholder-speak on where we are with everything?'

3 p.m.: 'Now then, I've got to do a two-page write through on the week from hell, mainly on donations, so I just need whatever colour you can give me plus some analysis about where it all goes. Have you got half an hour now, or shall we do a pint this evening?'

6 p.m.: 'Hiya, listen, nightmare day. Everyone's off apart from me, I've got a cracking interview with Foxy that I'm still writing up, so I haven't looked at Gordon's transparency bollocks yet. Can you just do me a 600-word summary with the key quotes and what it all means? By half-six?'

9 p.m.: 'Are you still in the office? Do me a huge favour. I've got this work experience girl with me and I've taken her to the Red Lion giving it the big 'un about all the history, and no bugger's in here. So can you come over for a pint and do the whole Downing Street bit? Cheers, I'll owe you one.'

Midnight: 'Hi Damian, are you still out? *The Guardian* did well for you on that transparency stuff, eh? I'm not sure we even got it in. Actually, no, we got a few paras at the bottom of the donations story. Now, the reason I'm calling is: have you seen this line in the *Express* about Gordon and the McCanns – the desk just asked me to check it. That's bollocks, is it? OK, I'll stand them down.'

3 a.m.: 'Morning, sorry if I've woken you up. I'm doing the overnight at Millbank, and the bloody news desk – having told us they didn't want a bulletins piece on the transparency speech – they've seen the *Guardian* splash and decided they do. So can you just talk me through it quickly?'

That cycle would begin all over again the following day, alongside which I'd be fitting in my own pro-active briefing of stories, my extra-curricular skulduggery, and discharging the odd one-off requests for Gordon to record messages for leaving parties, or sign framed cartoons for auctions, or say hallo when someone's kid was shown round Downing Street that afternoon.

Part of the reason most of those round-the-clock requests continued to come to me over the years was because I never passed them on and always dealt with them immediately. I prided myself that if a journalist rang up and said: 'You're probably going to need some time on this one, but I need a summary of where you guys stand on the Severn Barrage', they'd get it right there and then.

Michael Ellam and I could have had a decent arm wrestle about which of us knew more than the other about the background and policy on every conceivable issue, but certainly no one else in the whole of government would have come close, and that made us invaluable not just to give a briefing to the minister going on *Question Time* each week, but to the dozen hacks filing stories each day.

The other reason those requests came to me was because, at its simplest level, I understood what the hacks needed. The one going to brief shareholders would get six factual bullet points, including external criticism of what we were doing, rather than a eulogy to our plan. The one wanting an objective, spin-free 600-word digest of the news lines from a speech would get exactly that and nothing more, something they could simply copy and paste into their story if they wished.

Just as I operated on the basis that Gordon's overseas trips were organised for the benefit of the hacks who were accompanying us, and by extension the British public who saw and read their reports, I regarded my function in No. 10 simply as providing the hacks with a service, and imagined myself to be the person 'embedded' in No. 10 on their behalf.

To that extent, I regarded the journalists I worked with every day as akin to colleagues, even when they were giving Gordon and the government an enormous kicking. And like any colleagues, the more we got to know each other, the more those relationships extended outside of work. I attended stag-dos, weddings, Arsenal matches, Bruce Springsteen concerts, karaoke sessions, double dates, birthday parties and Christmas lunches with journalists, and why the hell not? That was our spare time and, as far as I was concerned, it only ever made it easier for us both to do our jobs.

Now, I'm conscious this is exactly the kind of thing which – in many people's minds – confirms the diabolical picture painted by Peter Oborne and others of a political class that has become far too close to its media counterparts over recent years, and a generation of political hacks practising what Oborne calls 'client journalism', where access to the information held by government is exchanged in return for positive coverage. What hope in that world for the fearless, independent investigative journalist seeking simply to report and sometimes expose the truth?

To which my considered response would be: 'Cobblers.'

If that model held true, then the coverage Gordon received over the years would have been correlated to the strength of his relationship with different newspaper editors and proprietors, and mine with different political journalists. Yet many of those relationships stayed entirely constant – Gordon's with Paul Dacre, or mine with George Pascoe-Watson, for example – even as the coverage in the *Daily Mail* and *The Sun* shifted considerably.

What newspapers and individual journalists wrote about

Gordon was – by and large – only correlated to the standing of the economy, his standing within the Labour Party and his standing with the public, and in his last years in government, all three. If I was doing my job well, I could affect the tone, balance and prominence of that coverage, but I couldn't dictate its overall thrust, and I certainly couldn't ensure that it would be positive.

The only thing I could dictate and ensure was that – as long as I was doing my job in the way I did it – we would always maintain a sensible, grown-up and businesslike relationship with the press, where Gordon could continue to get an objective hearing, no matter how bad things were, and where the press would not actively look to screw us over unless we totally deserved it.

As for the idea that the closeness that developed between members of the press and members of the political class stopped the former doing their job and representing their readers effectively, that is again not borne out by the evidence. Rebekah Wade's attendance at a Chequers 'pyjama party' didn't stop *The Sun* leading its political coverage the very next day with an excoriating attack on Gordon for pressing on with ratification of the Lisbon Treaty, written by George Pascoe-Watson.

And as I found out only too well, all the services provided, favours exchanged and personal relationships built up with political journalists over the years didn't stop them sticking the boot into me as hard as I deserved in the days after I was sacked. In fact, I'll always admire the resolute professionalism of the Sunday hack who called me up that Saturday and said:

'First thing, are you OK? Good. Second thing, am I mentioned in any of the emails you sent to Draper as a source of any stories? Good, well in that case, the third thing is don't read my paper tomorrow 'cos I've got to knock sixty shades of shit out of you. And final thing, do you want to meet up for a pint next week?'

And that what it was about. With a handful of exceptions who became genuine friends, the journalists I dealt with were just businesspeople. I ceased to be of any value or significance to them the day I was no longer in a position to service their needs or trade anything with them. But in my view, that was far better than being one of the hundreds of other spin-doctors for Labour and the Tories alike, who lived a much quieter life but were never of any value or significance at all.

There is another reasonable criticism of the relationship I had with the hacks and the effort that I put into maintaining it – which I recall Steve Richards among others making – that this was no substitute for, and was probably an almighty distraction from, the need to establish a clear and coherent media strategy for Gordon as Prime Minister.

But I look back at Gordon's time in No. 10, or at the least the two years when I was there, and I ask myself: if we could never come up with a clear and coherent political strategy and stick to it from two months to the next, what hope did we ever have of establishing an accompanying media strategy?

In the Treasury, it was relatively easy: we had clear objectives for all the major set-piece moments we had across the year, as well as broad objectives for the parliament as a whole, and we built our political and media strategies around them. And on a micro-level, we were also able to deliver media strategies extremely well for many of Gordon's smaller set-piece moments inside No. 10 – reshuffles, overseas trips, summits and the like.

Indeed, it's interesting that one of Gordon's big constitutional plans that never saw the light of day was to establish an annual 'State of the Union'-style address from the Prime Minister to Parliament, setting out what had been achieved and announcing new policies in each area, as if trying to recreate the strategic planning and set-piece management processes that had worked so well in the Treasury.

But if anyone had come to me before we went to No. 10 and said they wanted me to draw up a comprehensive six-month media strategy with objectives and messaging and delivery plans and key moments and milestones and an evaluation plan, I could have done it, but I'd equally have complained: 'This is all very well but what happens when the next bomb goes off?'

We soon found out.

38

RIDING HIGH

After the success of Gordon's first speech outside Downing Street and his well-received reshuffle the following day, we were off and running, and could start to focus on delivering the short schedule of planned announcements, events and speeches before the summer recess, many of which revolved around 'firsts': Gordon's first Prime Minister's Questions, his first overseas trip and so on.

But the night after he'd gone into No. 10, we got our first surprise: a thwarted bomb attack on London's Haymarket, followed by another shambolic effort the next day at Glasgow airport. When Gordon and his new Home Secretary Jacqui Smith addressed the media and public over subsequent days, their unshowy style and calm demeanour went down well. We didn't need to highlight the difference with Blair's overblown rhetoric and emotion for others to point out the contrast.

The key to getting Gordon to come across in that unvarnished, businesslike way wasn't to tell him that was the image or tone we were going for – it was to tell him nothing, and just let him be his normal self. My 'direction' before he did interviews in those days was just: 'Walk up to the microphone, say your piece, take two questions, walk back.'

And for all the criticism we got from some quarters about his dandruff, his unkempt hair and his skew-whiff ties, the public didn't seem to care, and it simply burnished his reputation for being an honest, hard-working bloke who cared more about doing the job well than how he looked. Boris Johnson without the jokes, if you will.

That image of him was encapsulated when he went on his first holiday as Prime Minister at the start of August. We kicked off his break with a trip to visit the Olympic sailing venue at Weymouth – including the obligatory photos of Gordon looking over-dressed and awkward in beige jacket and navy slacks while strolling among his fellow holiday-makers.

We announced that Gordon, Sarah and the boys would be staying in a small holiday cottage at a secret location near Weymouth, a suitable contrast with the private Caribbean resorts of Tony Blair's summer holidays. The only people who were downright disgruntled about this were the Downing Street staff and protection officers who used to accompany Tony on those luxury holidays and now had to set up shop in a small conservatory in Dorset.

In America, they believe that the President should be able to exercise all his powers at all times – right down to Air Force One functioning as a mid-air White House and the constant presence of the 'nuclear football' allowing him to destroy the world from a small suitcase. In Britain, we send our leaders away on holiday with a laptop, a satellite phone, and a couple of clerical and secretarial staff.

But, in fairness, these were no ordinary staff. The 'Garden Room girls', so called because of their office adjoining the Downing Street garden, and the private office 'clerks' were fixers nonpareil. If Gordon wondered aloud: 'What was that war thing with the English guy playing an American?', he'd have the *Band of Brothers* book and box set on his desk, and its creator Stephen E. Ambrose on line two, within five minutes. And yes, I know Ambrose is dead, but that never stopped the Garden Room girls.

As well as those staff, his team of protection officers and his family, Gordon also had me for company in Dorset, at least for the first week. It was generally agreed that, if anyone had to give up their own holiday to join Gordon's, it should be me. I had no family commitments and no holiday plans of my own, and I was best placed to deal with any disturbance caused by unwanted press intrusion once the media worked out where he was.

Most importantly, the entire office and Sarah knew that if there was a single bad story in the papers, or any emerging issue with a hint of crisis about it, Gordon's first instinct would be to ring every other person trying to take a break to see what they thought, quickly followed by an urge to rush back to London and deal with it. So my primary job was to calm him down about any media stories that emerged and reassure him they didn't require his attention.

Ed Balls – who plays the drums very well in his spare time – used to reflect in musical terms that there were two types of people around Gordon: amplifiers and dampers, and his reactions to external events depended on what kind of person was around him at the time. If he was wound up about something inconsequential and you either argued, agreed or – worst of all – asked him more about it, you were just turning up his volume. If you immediately changed the subject and told him he needed to focus on the next and much more important thing, you were damping it down.

I will always maintain that the person most to blame for the Mrs Duffy incident at the 2010 election was not the person who arranged the chat with her, or the person who was supposed to take Gordon's lapel microphone off, or even Gordon himself, but the aide in the back of the car who had three opportunities to change the subject and get Gordon focused on his upcoming Jeremy Vine interview, but instead made the cardinal sin of asking him: 'What did she say?', classic amplification which invited the killer quote about Mrs Duffy being 'a sort of bigoted woman'.

It didn't make it any easier to listen to the Mrs Duffy recording knowing that – just as it was me sent down to Dorset to do the damping at the start of Gordon's holiday – it probably would have been me in the back of the car with him on that day, if I hadn't got myself sacked by then. I like to think I would have seen the red light on the microphone as well; I always had a good eye for trouble, except when it was coming for me.

The afternoon that we arrived at the cottage, I went tramping round all the neighbouring fields to examine potential vantage points for long-lens photographers, and identify all the parts of the property where Gordon and Sarah could be overlooked. I returned a bit exhausted and muddy, and instructed them: 'Right, that bedroom window, that side window and that bit of the garden – all of them are overlooked so make sure you're fully clothed at all times.'

Sarah took careful note; Gordon muttered that the press were bastards – even though at this point none of them had even worked out where he was, let alone sent snappers down there. I was keen to get away and check into my hotel before it got dark, but Gordon insisted I stay for dinner and opened a bottle of wine. He was in a happy and chatty mood, and got into an animated discussion about whether José Mourinho would stay at Chelsea another season.

Then Peter, the private office clerk, popped his head round the door: 'Gordon, I've got the office on, they say it's urgent.' Gordon slammed his wine glass down, as if cursing himself for having a drink before the day was through. 'Is it another bomb? Get the news on. Why isn't the news on?' He zipped through to the impromptu office set up in the conservatory and I watched him through the window listening intently to the person on the other end of the phone, then barking orders back at them and at the staff in the conservatory. He gestured me in, hand over the mouthpiece on the phone and said: 'Foot-and-mouth disease. Bloody foot-and-mouth.'

This was not going to be a question of damping Gordon down and telling him it didn't need his attention. He set up an immediate conference call with the Chief Vet, Debby Reynolds, and Hilary Benn, the Cabinet minister for farming and rural affairs. He told them he'd head back to Downing Street in the morning to chair a meeting of the COBRA emergency committee, named after its original secure location in the basement of Downing Street, Cabinet Office Briefing Room A.

You could hear the collective groan from London as those civil servants who hadn't yet escaped on holiday realised they would now be stuck for the duration of the crisis. I was in the same boat, but my more immediate priority was knowing that I was sitting on an enormous news story as the first editions of the newspapers were almost ready to go to print.

I had no mobile signal in the cottage so ran up the steep path to the A-road, standing on the hard shoulder and beginning a set of nine almost identical phone calls to the political editors of the national daily papers. I hadn't written out a script but the conversations all played out the same:

'Hi mate, massive story for you in case you want to crash it into the first edition. But I don't want to see anything on Sky or online. Right? OK. Foot-and-mouth outbreak in Surrey, near Guildford. One farm so far. Symptoms reported yesterday. Test came back positive today. Cows. About fifty. Yeah, five-zero. Testing neighbouring farms to see if it's spread...

'Gordon's spoken to the Chief Vet, and he's coming back to London in the morning to chair COBRA. Yeah, I know! Massive. Debby Reynolds. Like the actress but with a 'Y'. No. 10 spokesman quote: "We are doing everything in our power to identify the source of this outbreak and control its spread. We are determined to protect the British farming industry." Right, got to go. Talk later.'

Next, I called the BBC, then ITN and then Sky, giving them all a 10 p.m. embargo so they could all break it at the same time. Then – just so they could be the first to break the news to their editors – I called the political editors from all the Sunday papers. I was up on the hard shoulder for about two hours shouting over the traffic, and didn't even have enough battery left to light the road in front of me when I stumbled back to the cottage in the pitch dark.

Gordon was still working away, so I reassured him the media were impressed by the grip he was taking, and finally headed back to my hotel at midnight. I was back at the cottage at 5 a.m. for the drive back to London. I asked the protection officers in the driveway: 'Gordon up yet?' One of them gestured up at the bedroom window I'd warned Gordon about, where, sure enough, he was peering out into the morning gloom naked from at least the waist up.

He barrelled into the back of the car with a cry of 'Let's go!' as if we were in *The Sweeney*. There were times I dreaded long car journeys with Gordon, when he was in a grumpy mood with little to do but gripe about how long everything was taking, what a waste of time it all was, and eventually asking the unanswerable question: 'Why are you doing this to me?' – his version of 'Et tu, Brute?' – uttered with the weary desperation of a man realising his most trusted staff were wilfully trying to sabotage his political career, physical health and sanity by filling his day with useless demands.

Often, when attending a visit with Gordon, you'd see fellow staff members step out of the car with him, carrying the blank look of an American soldier released from a Vietnamese prison camp in the mid-1970s, relieved the ordeal was over but unsure whether life could ever feel the same again, just muttering under their breath: 'Tailback. M6. Very long. No phone signal. Very bad.'

Fortunately, the two-hour race from Dorset to London that day was not such an experience. In fact, it was everything that was good about Gordon as a leader and man of action. I asked whether he'd slept. "No, I was reading all this stuff."

He had in his hand the 187-page report by Dr Iain Anderson into the government's disastrous handling of the 2001 outbreak and the Royal Society's report into the science of the 2001 outbreak. Every single page of both reports was covered in scribbles from his black felt-tip pen, and he had an extra twenty-page note just consisting of his scribbled action plan for the next twenty-four hours.

He seemed to get through half that action plan just in the course of the journey, barking instructions and questions at officials and ministers, all lifted from his study of the two reports, about footpaths, bridle paths, cull zones, exclusion zones, buffer zones and export restrictions.

It was reminiscent of the Treasury at times: 'Get me a horse-racing guy at Culture', 'Get me a tourism guy at Business', 'Get me a VAT guy at HMRC'. At times he had a mobile at each ear so that two ministers or officials at different departments could receive the same orders. I texted culture buff Stewart Wood – another of Gordon's long-standing special advisers – saying it was like being with The Wolf from *Pulp Fiction*.

When we got back to Downing Street, Gordon convened the COBRA meeting in the Cabinet room and stood like a four-star general over the table with maps of Surrey spread out in front of him, Debby Reynolds calmly describing the likely epidemiology of the outbreak and Gordon issuing instructions on the size of the cull zones.

Every time he asked how many more livestock would be slaughtered if he stretched the cull zone further, his voice would drop, as if the affected cows were listening at the door, but he was determined not to repeat the mistakes of 2001 when an insufficient initial response led to the outbreak growing out of control. I asked him later if it affected him ordering those slaughters, especially when the cattle were probably not infected. He screwed his face up as if to say 'Don't be silly', but then muttered quietly: 'You feel sorry for the little ones.'

When he made his statements to the media during the course of that day, he looked a mess, but no one watching him would have been in any doubt that he was in charge, in control and totally the right man for the job. For all the complaints about Gordon being a micro-manager, there were times like that crisis when a bit of micro-management was required. And it not only succeeded but went down hugely well with the public, even after it emerged that the cause of the outbreak was lax security at the government-owned medical research laboratory at Pirbright.

It was driving the Tories mad. Who would have thought that their effort to turn the battle between Brown and Cameron into one based on personality would work in Gordon's favour, with people at that point preferring the competent old curmudgeon over the young bloke going on about sunshine?

I heard that frustration for myself when listening in on one of Gordon's calls to Cameron during the crisis. The tone was pretty friendly, with lots of affirming of each other's points, and towards the end Cameron asked Gordon almost pleadingly when he thought things would stabilise sufficiently so Gordon could go back to Dorset and Cameron could go back to Brittany.

His exact words were: 'I can't go away until you do, and we

won't get a holiday at this rate. But you really have to go away first.' Gordon laughed and said he'd let him know, but he couldn't go away until they'd had confirmation that the outbreak was definitely contained.

The call ended, and Gordon immediately ran into the outer office and shouted at me: 'That was personal, that was private. You don't say a word about that to anyone.' So not only was the call civilised, but Gordon's reaction indicated his desire to build a decent working relationship for the long term, not allow the likes of me to jeopardise it for short-term political advantage.

Later the same day, Cameron did a series of TV interviews very critical of Gordon's handling of the crisis, apparently using information he'd learned from their phone call. Gordon was furious about it and – even before the political tide turned between them – he felt some real acrimony towards the Tory leader.

That made events interesting a few months later when they were forced to come together and process through to the House of Lords to hear the Queen's Speech, always an odd occasion when the politicians who have been throwing vitriol at each other for months in the House of Commons apparently turn into long-lost friends when walking down the corridor.

Gordon's strength of feeling about Cameron was at a level by that stage that we were worried he'd simply ignore him on the walk through, and that any enforced attempt at bonhomie would have looked so false as to be counter-productive. So my suggestion was simply that as soon as they come together, Gordon start briefing Cameron about some serious issue relating to Pakistan and keep it up all the way through.

It worked a treat on the television. Gordon looked like a serious-faced schoolmaster giving a boy a short lecture about Byzantine pottery as they strolled through the corridor, while Cameron looked baffled but nodded attentively as if he was hanging on every word.

As I say, the best direction you could ever give Gordon was: 'Walk that way, talk ... and don't worry about smiling.'

39

PRESIDENTS AND FIRST LADIES

As an experiment, I once separately asked the Eds which character they would aspire to be in American drama series *The West Wing*, and which character they thought they currently best resembled. They both gave Leo McGarry for both answers, the wise old chief of staff, perpetually rolling his eyes at the shortcomings and idiocy of his colleagues, but forever inspiring both them and the fictional President Bartlet to greater heights.

The West Wing was broadcast in the UK from September 2000 until August 2006, and the gripping battles it depicted between principle and pragmatism have helped fuel a worship of American politics in today's Westminster which is neither very healthy nor particularly accurate, alongside similarly romanticised notions of the Roosevelt and Kennedy administrations, and the idolatry of the Lyndon Johnson portrayed by his biographer Robert Caro.

It follows that nothing tends to bring modern British politicians to their knees like an encounter with the US President, in a way that would make the young Monica Lewinsky blush. I'd like to argue that Gordon Brown was different, but the best I can ultimately say is that the record was mixed.

At his first meeting with George W. Bush – a Camp David summit at the end of July 2007 – Gordon very deliberately set out to maintain a respectful tone but a suitable distance, to show the British public watching back home that this marked the end of the cosy deference of the Blair years.

Camp David itself is an astonishing place, a vast area of woodland in Maryland which looks and feels every bit the military base that it is, right down to the army-style canteen area for staff and the hundreds of camouflaged guards eerily dotted in random positions around the woods, standing stock still alongside the trees for hours at a time.

Gordon arrived by helicopter on the Camp David lawn, determined to be as formal as possible in his opening encounter with Bush. Easier said than done. Bush put him in an open-sided golf buggy to drive him up to the lodge, and decided to do a few 'playful' circles on the lawn, vaguely aiming towards the waiting press.

As the buggy leant heavily towards the passenger side on one circuit, I could tell from Gordon's fixed grin and very tight grip of the vehicle's rigging that he was hanging on for dear life. As bad photo-opportunities go, falling out of a golf cart on your first official visit to the President would rank pretty high, and my heart was in my mouth until they sped off out of sight.

The talks behind closed doors were friendly enough, and Stewart Wood and Michael Ellam came out to give me some colour from the evening meal. I would concentrate on giving that stuff to the hacks the next day while Michael would stick to officially briefing the contents of the meeting.

The next morning, I did my colour briefing at the entrance to an enormous aircraft hangar alongside the lawn where the British press entourage were sheltering from the sun, waiting for the press conference to begin. I talked them through the exchange of gifts, some of the lighter parts of the conversation and the full menu.

Every summit needs a name that sums up its character. Blair's first with Bush at Camp David became the Colgate Summit, after Bush revealed they used the same toothpaste. It summed up the way that Blair had translated his famously warm relationship with Bill Clinton into an immediate rapport with Bush; a sign of things to come.

The British hacks were hoping there would be something from my colour that would work as a name for the summit, and – without looking like I was pointing too hard – I lingered over the words 'Roast Beef' from the menu, and there was a general murmuring of content. It was perfect: robust, unfussy and distinctively British.

Gordon stuck to task at the press conference. Bush addressed him as Gordon; Gordon addressed him as 'Mister President'. When Bush went for bonhomie and personal praise, Gordon stuck to talking about what they'd discussed and agreed. All in all, the 'Roast Beef Summit' couldn't have gone better, and we knew we'd done our job when the only criticism in the UK press was from those diehards who thought Blair's closeness to Bush was a good thing for Britain.

Our next encounter in Washington in April 2008 was with prospective presidents, when the two Democratic rivals, Barack Obama and Hillary Clinton, and their Republican challenger-in-waiting, John McCain, came to the UK ambassador's residence for one-to-one meetings with Gordon, partly because of his unofficial role as world authority on the emerging financial crisis. Saying 'I've been discussing these issues with Prime Minister Brown' was useful ballast for a candidate when asked about their credentials as a leader on the economy.

However, Gordon was pre-occupied with the brewing row in the UK over the imminent abolition of the 10p tax rate, and on the day of the three meetings we got word from the UK that Angela Smith, a Labour MP, was planning to resign her junior position as an aide to Yvette Cooper in protest. We were left with the incongruous spectacle of Gordon having to spend time in Washington on the phone to London trying to persuade an MP he barely knew not to resign, while one of the prospective next leaders of the free world sat in an ante-room waiting for him to finish.

Perhaps because of his irritation and anger over that nonsense, Gordon was again in a very businesslike mood when he met the three candidates, and there was no obeisance on his part, even with the two Democrat stars. His snap verdicts after the meetings were fascinating:

'McCain – very ideological. He sees everything in military terms. You talk about the economy, and he starts talking about the threat of China, and he means "threat".

'Obama – bit light. I don't think he really gets what's happening with the economy; talking about how we need to reform for the future and all this stuff, he doesn't get how serious things are now.

'Hillary – so sharp, unbelievably sharp, probably more than Bill. Totally understands what the risks are if we don't get all this stuff sorted, said she'd support whatever we had to do.'

When Obama visited London three months later, having beaten Hillary for the Democrat nomination, Gordon was stunned by the transformation. After their private talks about the economy and foreign policy in No. 10, Gordon came out saying: 'He's done some bloody homework, that guy; he's on top of it all now, totally gets what's happening. He's really impressive, really impressive.'

Obama himself was full of confidence, and exuded a natural charm and warmth that melted everyone he met. I don't know whether US presidents are trained to do this, but he did something that Clinton and Bush had both done before when walking around Downing Street.

All three were used to seeing people peeping out of office doors as they passed, hoping to catch a glimpse of the big guest without breaching the careful stage-management of these visits. Obama, like Clinton and Bush before him, made a point whenever he saw an office door crack open of stopping a little theatrically and saying: 'Hold on a second, who's hiding in there?' before going in to say hallo to the star-struck civil servant, shake hands and pose for photos.

But there was another transformation too on that visit: Obama's staff – previously friendly and eager to build relationships with their No. 10 counterparts – now had their eyes on the future. They'd pretty much written off Gordon, and were now focused on building a relationship with Cameron and stealing a march on presidential rival John McCain by showing that Obama could work equally well with the Republicans' supposed allies in the Tory Party.

When that happens, if you're the British Prime Minister, you need to take it on the chin, and wait for the inevitable moment when the American President or candidate who was riding high suddenly needs all the support he can get, or until world events

take a turn and you become important to them again. If you do
the opposite – try and force the relationship, or look upset or
angry that you're being given the brush-off – then you risk only
making things worse.

Gordon unfortunately fell into the latter category, and – bar
the success of Obama's visit to the G20 summit in London –
their encounters from 2008 onwards looked rather undignified
from the point of view of the UK press, culminating in Gordon's
humiliating efforts to secure a one-on-one meeting in New York
in September 2009.

When Obama won the presidency in November 2008, Gordon
and his staff went to great lengths to persuade the Tate Gallery
that George Frederic Watts's famous 1886 painting *Hope*, which
had inspired Obama's second book and one of his most famous
speeches, should be loaned to the White House for the duration
of his presidency as a gift from Britain.

It would have been a fantastic gesture and a great story, but the
response came back from the White House that the gift would
go down badly. They wanted to get away from the 'Hope thing'
and show Obama was down to the hard business of working
to resolve the financial crisis. Plus the book title *The Audacity
of Hope* was lifted from a sermon by Pastor Jeremiah Wright,
inspired by the painting, and they weren't keen to remind people
of Obama's closeness to the controversial pastor.

Undeterred, Gordon tried again on his March 2009 visit to
Washington: he presented Obama with a pen-holder carved from
the ancient timbers of HMS *Gannet* – a nineteenth-century anti-
slavery ship; a nod to the famous Oval Office desk, made from
the wood of HMS *Resolute*, presented by Britain to America to
commemorate the ship's role in fostering good relations between
the two countries.

It was hard to see what could possibly go wrong with that
gift, until we saw what Obama had got for Gordon in return: a
collection of twenty-five DVDs, all great films without question,
but definitely a present with something of the Christmas Eve run
to the petrol station about it. Bits of the British press lapped up

Gordon's apparent humiliation, although the American media and talk shows took the new White House to task for being bad hosts. It was certainly not the finest hour for their wonderfully named assistant chief of protocol, Randy Bumgardner.

Either way, it arguably did us a favour; when Obama attended the G20 summit a few weeks later, he and his team went out of their way to be warm and helpful.

Personally, I had three crucial roles in relation to that summit. The first was staying as far away from it as possible, given that – following the October 2008 reshuffle – I was supposed to be keeping a low profile and wasn't to be seen mingling with the media at major events.

The second was negotiating with Jamie Oliver and his vast army of 'people' about the Downing Street dinner that would be served for the G20 leaders during the summit. I'd had the idea of inviting Jamie's apprentices to cook the meal – in keeping with the summit focus on jobs – and Gordon's broadcast adviser Nicola Burdett and I were trusted to make sure that all ran smoothly.

That's 'trusted' in the modern sense, as in the rest of No. 10 making clear that: 'It's your idea, you deliver it; if anything goes wrong, it's your fault.' As it was, everything went perfectly, we got great coverage out of it and Jamie's people were even accommodating when I very gently asked them to change the dessert on the menu from 'rhubarb crumble' on the grounds that I didn't want the G20 being labelled the 'Rhubarb Summit'. They did Bakewell tart instead.

My third job, and one I genuinely relished, was taking over the media management for Sarah Brown's engagements with Michelle Obama, particularly a joint visit to a Maggie's Cancer Care centre for mums and kids affected by cancer.

Sarah couldn't get any official support from the No. 10 press office on the grounds that she had no official government function and all the media special advisers were busy supporting Gordon, so she ended up relying on me and Balshen, who took leave from her job working for Ed Balls to help out on a voluntary basis. I hadn't worked with Balshen for two years by that stage, and I missed our double act on visits and events, so it made it all the more enjoyable.

The best compliment I could pay Michelle Obama is that there was no difference between her when the cameras were on and when they weren't: she was one of the most personable, friendly, empathetic and downright funny characters I came across in my career, and spread smiles and happiness throughout every room she walked into, and to every mum and child she met.

But the person I admired most that day was Sarah. Over the years, I'd come to know her as a deeply intelligent, cerebral, private person with a simply ferocious passion for the causes and people close to her heart, most of all her family.

That day in April with Michelle, it was her town, her husband's summit, Maggie's was her charity – one she'd been patron of for years – and the visit was for the benefit of her national press. But she had the class, grace and humility to know that Michelle was the star in that situation, and the good media sense just to allow Michelle to shine without trying to force herself into every camera shot.

And, of course, that's what she always did for Gordon. He was always the star and, whatever she did to support him, it was always to enhance his story, not become the story herself.

She was no less fiercely loyal to Gordon than Cherie was to Tony; the difference was that while Sarah was happy to express that loyalty privately – including giving Gus O'Donnell the cold shoulder after the help she suspected he'd given some of Gordon's hatchet job biographers – Cherie was never happy *unless* her loyalty was expressed publicly, with her face the one all over the papers, rather than Tony's.

I remember one of my first encounters with Sarah, years ago on an overnight trip, when she asked me to help unload the car. On the way down, she mentioned a recent *Evening Standard* article about the key people around Gordon. I'd briefed the article and – rather naively – when the journalist had said: 'And of course, I'll put you in there', I was pleased to let them.

Sarah said: 'I love those pieces, because it's always interesting who's mentioned and who's not.' She let it hang, then said: 'And you can tell it wasn't a press person who's briefed it because you and Ian Austin are mentioned, and you'd never mention yourselves.' It was her subtle way of saying: 'Remember who you work for and why you're here; it's not for yourself.'

When she was sworn at by Matthew Freud for failing to deliver Gordon for a photo-stunt with Blair and Murdoch at Davos, and when she saw media people constantly staring at her tummy amid rumours she might be pregnant again, she never screamed and told them all to bugger off the way most of us would want to do. She just shrugged and got on with it, because that was the life, and what mattered to her was whatever was best for Gordon and her boys.

It was little wonder that when the Tories came into No. 10, they asked for access to her emails, diary and contact book in order to study what they called 'best practice' for setting up Samantha Cameron's private office. They were refused permission, but it was a telling fact about what kind of 'first lady' they envisaged that Mrs Cameron would be.

But Sarah will always be a tough act to follow, precisely because, just like Michelle Obama, with her it was never an act.

40

MAGGIE AND ME

I was born and raised in Margaret Thatcher's Finchley constituency. My closest cousins were born and raised in her hometown of Grantham. As a young boy, I thought all towns somehow claimed Mrs Thatcher as their own. That was before I visited Glasgow and Derry.

At eleven years old, I went with my mum to see Cliff Richard perform at the 1986 centenary celebrations of St Paul's Methodist Church in Finchley, with Maggie delivering a thank-you speech. As we waited to make our exit afterwards and Maggie worked the crowd, she tried to glad-hand my mum. Barbara McBride, Latin teacher *sine pari* and local stalwart of the National Union of Teachers, simply ignored her. Maggie bent down and shook my hand instead. After she'd passed, to my eternal shame, I said to my mum: 'She's got children too, you know.'

Maggie was always a divisive figure in our house. At the 1983 election, my dad – a volatile character at the best of times – tried to stop my mum leaving the house to vote Labour, convinced as he was that only Maggie stood between us and Russian enslavement courtesy of Michael Foot and the Campaign for Nuclear Disarmament. Four years later, by contrast, he was in the street telling the frail old woman who lived opposite – Mrs Webster – that if she went with the Tory activist offering to drive her to the polling station, he would never collect her pension again and it would serve her right if she starved to death.

When I joined Finchley Catholic High School as a fifteen-year-old, anti-Thatcher feeling ran high, not so much because of the poll tax but because of a particularly bitter year of murders in Northern Ireland triggered by the killings on Gibraltar, for which she was – rightly or wrongly – blamed. This was in a school where the semi-organised violence of the St Patrick's Day's 'Ireland versus the Rest of the World' games made my football matches at Cambridge look like croquet.

When it was announced that Maggie would be coming to open our new technology block that year, our popular Irish deputy headmaster, Kevin Hoare, addressed all the boys and told them that – while he understood the strength of feeling – we had a responsibility to the school to behave in a civil and dignified manner. The message was taken on board, but nevertheless a dozen boys from across the school were locked up for the afternoon because they were considered too incorrigible or militant to be trusted. I was distraught not to be one of them, as were some of the teachers.

Incidentally, nothing in my Nationalist upbringing prepared me for the confusion I experienced in July 2007 when Gordon made his first trip to Stormont as Prime Minister, and I encountered first the thoroughly lovely Reverend Ian Paisley – introducing himself to all Gordon's officials as he waited for his meeting and greeting me like a lost brother when I told him my dad was from Donegal; and then Martin McGuinness and Gerry Adams – who turned up ten minutes late and ignored me and everyone else in the waiting room, all part of their refusal to acknowledge our right to be there.

It was a confusing month all round. In those early weeks, when Gordon was winning plaudits for his style of government, we deliberately invited comparisons with Maggie's tough leadership, Stakhanovite work ethic and un-showy presentational style, and, to my slight surprise, the press lapped it up, not least because of the contrast with Cameron and Osborne presenting themselves as the rightful 'heirs to Blair'.

I arranged all Gordon's earliest interviews in Maggie's old study overlooking Horse Guards Parade. This gave the impression that Gordon had set up his office in the 'Thatcher Room', eschewing the sofas in Tony Blair's den. In reality, I'd just put a phone, computer monitor, some old Cabinet papers and books on the desk for the sake of the cameras, but if any of the hacks had bothered to follow the wires on the phone or the computer, they'd have seen they weren't connected to anything.

After Gordon's cancellation of his holiday to take personal charge of dealing with the foot-and-mouth crisis, the comparisons kept coming. Gordon was instinctively wary of the 'up' because of the inevitable 'down'. He once chided me quite fiercely after I referred to the emerging idea of him acting as 'father of the nation', telling me: 'Don't ever say that to the press.'

However, the 'Thatcher thing' appealed to him, and he talked with great animation and amusement about his first encounter with her after he became an MP in 1983, when she summoned him into her office in the House of Commons to 'discuss' one of his speeches, poured them both enormous whiskies, told him she thought it was a shame that such an intelligent young man should be so fundamentally wrong about every issue, gave him a half-hour lecture and sent him on his way.

The idea started to percolate around Gordon's staff – except Sue Nye, who was horrified by the whole thing, not least out of loyalty to Neil Kinnock – that Gordon and Sarah should invite Maggie for tea or dinner in Downing Street, but we needed some valid reason to do so, otherwise it would simply look like we were pushing the comparison and revelling in the discomfort it was causing Cameron.

This is where I came in. I knew that one of the Sunday political editors was an acquaintance of Richard Stone, Maggie's favourite artist, and, shooting the breeze in the pub one afternoon, we came up with the idea that Gordon could commission a portrait of her to hang in Downing Street. It wasn't as simple as that though: we needed to explain why there should be a portrait of her as opposed to, say, Harold Macmillan or Clement Attlee; and we needed someone to pay for it.

I had a good look round the Downing Street estate, and worked out that the only two portraits of twentieth-century politicians – beyond the standard photos of prime ministers and cartoons of chancellors on the respective main staircases of No. 10 and No. 11 – were a large photographic print of Churchill next door to the Cabinet room and a painting of Lloyd George in the No. 11 meeting room.

This allowed me to argue a rationale for commissioning the portrait, on the basis that Lloyd George was the victorious PM at the end of the First World War, Churchill at the end of the Second, and Maggie at the end of the Cold War. A wealthy Tory benefactor was found to finance the painting, Richard Stone said he was willing, and we were able to present the whole proposal to Maggie's office and invite her in to make it official. They were naturally delighted.

We kept the whole visit as quiet as possible until the day, but when the news and photos emerged – with Cameron at the height of pressure within his own party over grammar schools and the sliding Tory poll ratings – all hell broke loose.

While there were a few Tory commentators who criticised Gordon for 'exploiting' Maggie, and a lot of Labour voices furious at him for going anywhere near her, the general reaction from the media was that it was a fantastic coup for Gordon, a devastating (albeit silent) comment from Maggie on the Cameron project, and likely to prove a huge hit with swing voters. And so it proved: Labour's lead, Gordon's personal poll ratings, and the focus group reactions were beyond anything his pollsters, Deborah Mattinson and Stan Greenberg, had seen before or ever hoped for. If the snap election wasn't a certainty before, it looked cast in iron after that day.

On the day in question, as Maggie was saying hallo to some of the old 'Garden Room girls' who'd worked with her, Gordon asked me if I wanted to be introduced, given my Finchley history and the role I'd played in engineering the visit. I thought of my old mum and dad, I thought of the 1980s Irish hunger-striker Bobby Sands, I thought of the miners, and I said: 'No, it's OK.' It was the only time during that whole episode when Sue Nye smiled at me.

Nevertheless, when – shortly afterwards – we had the most serious of many overnight scares where rumours were flying around that Maggie had been taken seriously ill, and her office couldn't be contacted, I was given the job of writing the media and parliamentary briefing note that we would use if Gordon, the family and the Palace decided she should have a state funeral. Someone else was given the opposite job of writing the explanation if we didn't.

In my briefing, I didn't mention her gender on the grounds that I felt being the 'first' of anything shouldn't be a qualification in itself; I didn't mention how she changed the country, given the strength of feeling in many parts of it that she did so for the worse; and I didn't mention the Falklands, on the grounds that John Major or Tony Blair shouldn't then be expecting state funerals for the various wars they had prosecuted when there was no threat to Britain involved.

I simply stuck to my Cold War argument that – like Winston Churchill before her – she had led Britain at a time of enormous peril for our country and the world during the fragile and unpredictable events of the 1980s and played a crucial role in our final victory. That, I thought, was an argument around which Gordon could rally most people, if definitely not all, in what would have been one of the most difficult decisions for a Labour Prime Minister to take.

Thankfully, he never had to, and she not only enjoyed a few years more but was able to see Richard Stone's portrait unveiled in No. 10 in November 2009, several months after my own departure from Downing Street.

Needless to say, I wasn't invited but the whole event was a sign of how things had changed in the space of two years. Gone were the comparisons between Gordon and Maggie, or her rumoured favourable view of him, and gone was the pressure on Cameron. Indeed, David Cameron was not only present at the unveiling, but requested to come in the back door of No. 10 so that there wouldn't be a picture of him looking presumptuous on the doorstep a few months before he expected to be there not as a guest, but entering for the first time as Prime Minister.

If you'd predicted that in mid-September 2007, I would have said you were mad.

41

TOO MANY MISTAKES

Gordon had one very special phrase when in a particularly angry mood, rarely used because it could only be said when he was within punching distance of a chair, headrest, wall or other suitable, non-human surface. It would generally come at the end of a long day when every person he'd encountered had been utterly useless and everything he'd done had been a waste of time.

He would sit silently reflecting on all this, then slowly punch the surface in front of him very hard three times, and utter the mantra: 'Too. Many. Mistakes.' If you were next to him, you just shut up and looked out of the window. There was literally nothing you could say which could help.

The election that never was in autumn 2007 was the greatest misjudgement of Gordon's long career, utterly changing the way he was perceived and defined, but it was the product of six other major mistakes, and it's important to understand how cumulatively they turned the eventual, terrible decision he made into the only option he had.

The fact is that we always envisaged an early election, by which I mean it was never the idea that Gordon would hang on until the last minute in 2010.

The plan was that he'd come in, establish himself and the new, younger Cabinet; get a short-term bounce simply because he wasn't Tony Blair; probably stabilise into level pegging with the Tories by the end of the year; and ride into an election in early 2008 appealing for his own mandate.

That appeal – and remember, this was before the banks started collapsing – would couple the usual promises around economic stability and strong public services with a big aspiration agenda, the centrepiece of which would be the abolition of tuition fees and big cuts in inheritance tax and stamp duty, and a major constitutional reform programme covering the House of Lords, the voting system, war powers and MPs' outside income.

That package would be designed to keep most of those who voted Labour in 2005 in the red camp, while trying to win back a lot of old Labour voters who'd gone Liberal Democrat because of Iraq. The best-case scenario was the same or a slightly larger majority. The worst-case scenario was a coalition with a Menzies Campbell-led Liberal Democrats, forged over the constitutional reform programme.

What that plan didn't envisage was that Gordon would have such a good start in the job and such a large bounce in the polls, without needing to announce any of those planned reforms.

Accepted wisdom now says it was a massive mistake not to have ruled out an autumn election as soon as the speculation started. But the fact is Gordon's pollsters, Deborah Mattinson and Stan Greenberg, were telling him this was a unique and unforeseen opportunity: his ratings and Labour's were beyond anything they'd thought possible, and they would surely never get this good again.

It may have been a mistake to let the speculation continue, but it would have taken Elijah's foresight, Solomon's wisdom and Job's patience to say it at that stage.

The first genuine, avoidable mistake, if we were ever going to go for it, was not announcing the election before the party conference season began, in order to catch Cameron and Osborne off guard, and set the agenda with our manifesto launch. The Tories were already panicking and we should have capitalised.

Shortly before conference season, Gordon was in fantastic form at a party in Shoreditch House thrown by News International's Les Hinton for his partner and adviser to Gordon, Kath Raymond. When Cameron, Osborne and Coulson came in – seeing Gordon surrounded by the great and good of the Murdoch empire – their faces collapsed.

I winked at Coulson at the bar: 'We'd better make the most of this, mate. It's going to be all work the next few weeks.' 'Yeah?' he said, trying to gauge whether I was serious. 'We'll see,' I said.

But the reason there was never a chance of us going for it before conference season was the worst one of all – money. We couldn't call an election and still go ahead with conference as normal: MPs would all want to be in their constituencies instead; the TV companies wouldn't be able to give it the blanket coverage they normally would; and ministers would be barred from making policy announcements. We desperately needed a 'normal' conference to raise the revenue required to finance the campaign, including the opportunity to schmooze wealthy donors. The party certainly couldn't afford to refund all the members, media, businesses, charities and others who had already paid to attend or book rooms, receptions and advertising.

This was one of many areas where Tony Blair had a huge advantage on Gordon: he was a highly proficient and effective fundraiser, even without the assistance of Lord Levy; Gordon was pretty hopeless. It was a strange paradox that the man who had no difficulty instructing presidents, premiers and sultans across the world to commit billions to the fight against poverty often felt simply too embarrassed to ask some millionaire businessman for a few bob.

So the conferences went ahead, and – even though I was very conscious that the 'will he, won't he' coverage of Bournemouth was a turn-off to the voters – it was easy to get carried away in the heady atmosphere, as even the right-wing press fawned over Gordon. People marvelled that not only did the *Telegraph* throw its first party at a Labour conference in living memory, but Gordon stayed for an hour, compared to barely ten minutes at *The Guardian*'s afterwards. Even ultra-Blairite special advisers said to me: 'How have you managed this?'

When the post-Bournemouth polls showed massive Labour leads, the narrative started to emerge from the Tories that their objective was now simply to eat into Labour's majority, and show that some of the more prosperous south-east marginals which had stuck with Blair in 2005 were turning Tory, holding out the prospect of victory next time round. They knew as well as we did that, despite what was happening in the rest of the country, Gordon was still struggling to cut through to voters in those marginals, mainly because of their hostility over taxes and transport costs.

At the same time, a narrative started to emerge from the left that, if he went for an election, Gordon would be gambling with the seats of MPs who'd been elected only two years previously, and in a very hard-fought election at that. Many argued that if Labour's majority was reduced by even one seat, that gamble would be exposed as both a failure and a huge folly. When I ridiculed this idea in front of a group of colleagues, they all looked at me as if I didn't get it, and Ian Austin – one of that 2005 intake – said: 'They're right, mate – Gordon would have to resign if that happened.'

Letting that consensus take hold in the party, the media and in Gordon's inner circle was the second massive mistake, and I take my share of the blame for that.

We left ourselves in the ridiculous position whereby every private and public poll conducted in those weeks showed that Labour would win a clear majority, but that itself was not enough. When people later mocked Gordon, saying: 'So you didn't look at the polls, realise you were going to lose, and cancel the election?' he was telling the truth when he said 'No!' We would always have won.

But the same polls showed that Gordon was going to shed at least a few south-east and Midlands marginals. And once the consensus took hold that any reduced majority would mean Gordon had to resign, that became a larger and larger problem.

On the Sunday of Tory party conference, 30 September 2007, around a dozen of Gordon's close advisers gathered at Chequers for yet another discussion about the impending decision. For most of us, it was our first time there and Gordon started the day with a tour of the house and the gardens.

It's a beautiful warren of a building: a child's dream, full of ancient, precious artefacts and military equipment, and made for playing hide and seek. Gordon and Sarah mainly used it at weekends to entertain other families with children: the kids would go swimming in the long, narrow pool, while their parents ate lunch.

Gordon was very tickled showing us the Rubens painting *The Lion and the Mouse*, which Churchill decided one night needed a bit of work, touching up the mouse with some brighter colours so it was easier to pick out. As always when Gordon told anecdotes, he had to deal with heckling from the two Eds, and Miliband in particular was on fine form during the tour, mimicking a Jewish patriarch being shown round his grandson's house: 'Nice place you've got here, Gordon, nice bit of real estate.'

Eventually, we got down to business. There was a clear hierarchy around the grand dining table. The main players were the Eds and Douglas; then the polling experts; then the party chiefs. Strange to say, some of Gordon's longest-serving staff – the ones who worked with him day-in, day-out, like me, Sue and Jonathan Ashworth – were largely silent observers. Some of his most trusted advisers like Michael Ellam and James Bowler were excluded as civil servants.

Gordon said: 'Right, I want to go round and flush out all the reasons why we *shouldn't* go for it.' There was silence, eventually broken by Ed Balls: 'Well, just to play devil's advocate...' One after another, those round the table offered desultory arguments against an early election.

Douglas Alexander: 'Voter registration's going to be a problem – lots of kids who've just started at university won't be registered to vote.' Ed Miliband: 'It'll be dark in the mornings and the evenings – lots of people will just stay home rather than vote in the dark.'

Gordon called a halt to the discussion, and moved on to all the reasons we should go for it, receiving a much more enthusiastic response. I made my one contribution to the discussion. 'Well, from a media perspective, I think we've got to think about the reaction if we decide not to go for it now – they'll absolutely slaughter us.'

Ian Austin looked down the table at me and said: 'Hold on, the worst possible reason to go for it is what happens if we don't.' There was a murmur of assent. I remember immediately thinking: 'Isn't that the best possible reason to go for it?', but I didn't say it out loud and the moment passed.

It seems inconceivable to me now that we didn't have a more substantive discussion about the potential media reaction and the resulting impact on Gordon's reputation if we didn't go for it, but perhaps that simply reflected the fact that we all thought that we were. Nevertheless, it was the third major mistake and one I hold a great deal of responsibility for.

The next day, George Osborne promised in his speech to the Tory conference that he would raise the inheritance tax (IHT) threshold to £1 million, paid for by a new levy on non-domicile residents.

It was a sickening moment, first because we knew how popular it would be in those south-east marginals where our problem lay, but also because we'd come so close to neutralising IHT as an issue before then. Gordon had two options in his last Budget in March 2007: one to cut the basic rate of income tax by abolishing the 10p rate; the other to give married couples and civil partners a combined IHT threshold, effectively doubling their tax-free allowance.

This was where the Budget scorecard process could occasionally work against good decision-making. The income tax proposal was relatively straightforward, whereas every time we looked at the IHT proposal, we came up with new reasons why it might not work: what about recently widowed individuals, what about war widows, what about non-married partners, how far back could you go if you wanted to make it retrospective, and how much more would that cost?

We ended up convincing ourselves that there was too much risk of the IHT measure unravelling on the day, whereas the income tax cut was an easier sell, even if that also unravelled over time. It was the wrong call, and one of the other major mistakes that affected the election decision.

Nevertheless, at the point Osborne made his speech, I was confident I could turn it into a tale about panicky Tories making it up as they went along. After all, it was on my specialist subject and the sums didn't come close to adding up. But the hacks writing the story out of Blackpool had Tory spin-doctors and the cheers of the conference hall in their ears, and I literally couldn't get a hearing. The Labour press officer we had up there – the excellent Iain Bundred – said it was hopeless.

I am absolutely certain that if Osborne had made that announcement in the Tory manifesto during the heat of an election campaign or indeed in a Budget speech, it would have unravelled, because those type of announcements tend to come under greater scrutiny and be reported with a greater sense of detachment. It reinforces why it was a mistake not to call the election before conference season.

The fifth major mistake came the next morning when Gordon flew to Iraq. The idea that it was an attempt to distract attention from the Tory conference was nonsense, but there was an element of calculation: he wouldn't have been allowed to travel there during the election purdah period and if he didn't get out beforehand, there was a risk of it becoming an issue during the election campaign that he still hadn't visited the troops since becoming PM.

We just didn't see the backlash coming. The Tories wheeled out John Major to complain about the 'cynical timing', and a story that should have been covered by the journalists travelling with Gordon to Iraq became another story reported out of Blackpool, with predictable results.

After Gordon's return from Iraq and the success of the Tory conference, the mood in the inner circle had discernibly shifted, along with the polls. Advisers and MPs who'd previously been urging him to go for it had started to play devil's advocate more convincingly and, to cover their backs, Gordon's pollsters were also more frequently pointing out worst-case scenarios about drastic reductions in Labour's majority.

It didn't help that – without doubt – some of the MPs and

advisers who had Gordon's ear were clearly thinking about their own futures and shifting their positions accordingly, either because their seats were quite marginal or because they were too associated with Gordon to survive a change of leader if he was forced to resign.

One of Gordon's greatest strengths was identifying when people were 'in it for themselves' and judging their advice on that basis. It may sound self-centred, but his rationale was simple and fair: his staff and allies would rise or fall with him, so any ambitions they had should simply be invested in his. I first heard him use the expression back in 2003, reacting to a *Guardian* interview where Douglas Alexander had painted himself as neither Brownite nor Blairite. And I heard it many times thereafter.

But that week, Gordon was giving too much credit to an awful lot of subjective advice, which was the sixth mistake. Inappropriate as it would have been, he should have asked the likes of Michael Ellam what they thought, or listened more to long-serving advisers and friends like Bob Shrum and Sue Nye who he knew only had his interests at heart. He could have listened to me tell him that every journalist I spoke to was convinced we should go for it. And he certainly should have listened more to Ed Balls.

Ed was the one resolute voice throughout that wobbly week saying Gordon should definitely go for it. With the exception of Tom Watson, he was the only person who consistently argued that Labour could increase its lead over the course of a campaign, insisting that we'd wipe the floor with Cameron and Osborne. 'These guys are amateurs. They've never fought a general election – they don't know what it takes. We'll just say: "Are you really going to trust this pair of jokers to run the country?"'

But by Friday 5 October, with Balls away in Yorkshire, the inner circle gathered in Alastair Campbell's old office, a thick net curtain shielding us from the cameras outside No. 10. We heard Deborah Mattinson present the latest, unchanged polls from marginal constituencies, and sat waiting for Gordon to announce the inevitable.

You'd have forgiven him for lashing out at those who'd urged him along at every stage and were now counselling caution, but he just seemed stoical. Finally he said: 'Right, well, does anyone have anything else they want to say?', like the lawyer of a condemned man hoping someone in the courtroom will produce an alibi. Everyone looked at the floor.

Finally, Bob Shrum spoke up. He'd been in what we used to call Gordon's dusty bin since the *Times*' accusations of plagiarism in Gordon's conference speech, so it took a lot of guts to say what he said: 'Well, if the worst comes to the worst, and you only get three more years, there's a lot you can do in three years. Jack Kennedy only had three years.' Gordon didn't look up, walked out of the room and didn't look back. And that was that.

The last mistake didn't contribute to Gordon's decision, but it certainly exacerbated the impact and every single bit of the blame lies with me. If it was possible to make an already disastrous news story even worse, my media handling of the announcement on Saturday 6 October delivered.

The basic plan was for Andrew Marr to come in on Saturday afternoon and pre-record an interview, so Gordon could explain his decision and try and look relaxed about it. Nobody else in the BBC would know this was happening, but extracts would be released to all broadcasters for the Saturday early evening news. People have argued we should have done a full press conference, or a round of TV interviews with every broadcast political editor, but those were destabilising for Gordon at the best of times. In this situation it could easily have led to a public meltdown.

The timing of this plan was a huge problem for the Sunday papers, every one of which was doing a minimum of four pages of coverage on the impending election decision, with expensive polls and 'Should he, shouldn't he?' columns. The announcement on the Saturday was going to come as a complete surprise to them, and if it stayed that way until the mid-evening news, it would have meant whole pages or sections having to be pulped, columns having to be re-written and so on.

I believed – and still do – that the long-term damage that would have done to our relationship with the Sundays would have been huge, and it was my top priority that Saturday to prevent them turning implacably hostile to Gordon. Why? Because whenever anyone asked me: which is the most important paper for you – meaning is it *The Sun* or the *Mail*? – I always answered 'the Sundays'.

The Sundays have the resources, the quality of journalists and columnists, the size of readership and the competitive impulse to kill any politician they decide to target. Plus fifty weeks of the year, you can usually guarantee that the best Sunday splash will be the top story across all the broadcast media. I always knew it would be too debilitating to spend every weekend fighting that kind of fire. That's why – quite frankly – I always did my best, partly through my leaking activities, to make sure at least one or two Sunday papers had a belter of a splash that was nothing to do with us.

So, on the Saturday morning, I tipped off the political editors of all the Sundays that an announcement was coming, on the understanding that this went no further than their editor, news editor and lead columnist so they could reshape their pages, coverage and columns. In general, senior journalists tend to respect those kind of heavily conditional tip-offs – no matter how explosive the information – for the obvious reason that they want the same consideration again next time round.

Given those same political editors had to explain at great length in their pages how and why the decision had been taken, I also did what I always did best, giving them 'the colour': who was in the room when; who said what; which room we were in; what Gordon had for breakfast.

That gave me the licence to spin the line that Gordon's mood had been moving against an election for some time, even before the Tory conference. I recast the desultory devil's advocate lines I'd heard at Chequers as serious and influential concerns: Douglas was worried about disenfranchised students; Ed Miliband was worried about people having to vote in the dark.

Both with the tip-offs and that colour, I was doing all I could to turn a terrible story to our advantage, in that – even though the coverage would be awful – the Sunday papers would be grateful for our professionalism and courtesy, and that would be good for long-term relations.

As far as I understand it, and rather disappointingly, one of the Sundays tipped off the Tory press team, they tipped off all the broadcasters, and thus exploded the mother of all shit-storms. Andrew Marr arrived to do his secret, exclusive interview with every camera in London outside No. 10 filming him going in, and Adam Boulton, Nick Robinson and others reporting what Gordon was about to tell him.

It created a sense of utter chaos, shambles and farce around the announcement, and ensured the broadcast coverage was as bad as it could possibly have been, presented by political editors visibly incandescent that Gordon hadn't done interviews with them. I walked into the room where Gordon was getting ready for Marr, and Douglas didn't even bother to stop his rant about how dreadfully I was handling things, all in the name of helping my 'mates on the Sundays'.

And yes, that was why. And yes, it was a disaster. But I will always maintain that I was right to make those Sunday relationships my priority that day. I don't think Gordon would have had any chance of surviving until 2010 if the Sundays had come after him hard every week after that.

There was one final mistake that weekend, but not of consequence to anyone but me.

The Sunday headlines were predictably brutal and while all their huge 'write-throughs' included my colour, they also had very hard anonymous quotes from 'insiders' attacking the pollsters, Douglas and, to a lesser extent, Ed Miliband for changing their mind about the election. There was an uncomfortable proximity between those quotes and my 'No. 10 source' quotes about what Douglas, Ed and others had said at Chequers, but I wasn't too worried.

Gordon called to ask how I thought the story was developing for Monday. He sounded totally disconsolate, but – as always on big days like that – he gave me my marching orders in terms of briefing:

'The one thing we have to do is make sure we don't fall apart ourselves. Some of the stuff in the papers today – these guys all blaming each other – we can't have that. Make clear I'm the only one to blame; I take full responsibility. Keep saying that. Don't let the papers make it civil war. You're the only one that should be speaking to them. Tell the papers that; you're the only one with authority to speak.'

I had not the slightest indication from Gordon that he thought I was to blame for any of the briefing. You might argue he was being subtle about it, but Gordon didn't do subtle.

As I was walking down to Arsenal that afternoon, I took calls from two journalists. I started delivering my script, but they came back with phrases like: 'Are you saying anything yourself?' 'There's a lot of flak coming your way' and 'People are sticking the boot into you quite hard'. It took me a while to realise 'you' didn't mean Gordon, which was how I usually heard it; they actually meant me. 'Me?' I kept saying. 'Me? What have I done?'

One of them told me openly that the briefing against me was coming from Paul Sinclair, Douglas's acolyte, who informally looked after Gordon's interests with the Scottish press. 'He's given us off-the-record quotes accusing you of briefing against people, but saying you're the biggest one to blame, all the media speculation was your fault, you fucked up the announcement yesterday.'

Feeling angry and reeling a bit, when Ed Miliband called I started ranting at him about how ridiculous it was that I was being accused of briefing against people.

'But where's all the briefing coming from, Damian?' he said. 'They've got all these details of the meetings we had; that must have come from you.' 'Of course that stuff's from me,' I said, 'that's just the colour – that's harmless, but that's not the same as these lines blaming Douglas and you for the whole thing.' 'Well, where's all that coming from, Damian?'

'I don't know where it's coming from, but of course it's not from me – you know I wouldn't brief against you.' 'I don't believe you, Damian,' he said, something in his voice and tone reminding me of Hal the computer in *2001: A Space Odyssey*, 'I think you're lying.' 'Ed, for God's sake, don't say that. I'd never brief against you.' 'That's the trouble, I don't believe that's true.'

Despite being known to bend the truth occasionally, I've always hated being wrongly accused of lying, so I came back aggressively: 'Hey! You can't say that, Ed. I'm not going to have that.' 'I can't help it, I think you're a liar.' 'If you keep saying that, you know we're finished, I'm not having that.' 'I don't care, Damian, I think we are finished.'

The call ended. I was totally stunned. Eight years of working together, four years of real friendship, all destroyed in two minutes, and over something that wasn't true. And my mistake? I didn't care enough to do anything about it; I didn't care enough to complain.

I should have gone to Gordon and demanded that he vouch for me, remonstrate with Paul Sinclair and tell Ed Miliband to apologise. I should have said if he didn't, I'd quit. Instead, I just thought: 'Sod 'em. Idiots. They can say what they like.' That reaction just reinforced the impression I was guilty and set me down a dangerous path where I didn't care when I got the blame for things I hadn't done. Occasionally, if it was a good story, I actually revelled in it.

Three years later, Steve Richards's biography of Gordon came out, repeating the accusation that I'd briefed against Douglas and Ed that weekend, with one source ludicrously claiming that they caught me in the act and I told them I was acting on instructions from Ed Balls. If I'd had any reputation to protect by that stage, I'd have sued, but as it was, I just sighed.

To my surprise, I was called up by a Labour MP on that day who I'd not heard from in years – not someone who'd been prominently involved in the election discussions – who said: 'I know you're getting it in the neck again for all that briefing, and I just want to say sorry; it was me who did Douglas in – it was just payback for 2006 – and I'm sorry you got the blame.'

I called a friend who was working on Ed Miliband's leadership campaign at the time and told him the conversation I'd just had, without naming the MP. If I was somehow hoping that would lead to a reconciliation, or at least some closure, I was disappointed. My friend came back and rather sadly said that – when he'd told Ed the story – he'd just shrugged and said: 'Oh well.'

The reality was I don't think Ed or Douglas particularly cared whether I was guilty or not. I was just an Admiral Byng: a convenient person to blame to create the perception that they'd been wronged by someone close to Gordon and Ed Balls, allowing them to get some distance from the sinking ship in No. 10 and some victim status with Labour MPs. And it worked.

Meanwhile, poor Gordon was left to despair that the whole sorry litany of mistakes had not only devastated his credibility with the media and MPs and wrecked his hard-won reputation as a man of strategic genius and iron resolve, but had ripped apart his close-knit circle of advisers.

But over the many months he had to reflect on those mistakes before the start of the financial crisis, he must have learned something. When every other world leader was not just wobbling but panicking about what to do, it was Gordon who brought all his old strategic genius and iron resolve to bear in preventing total meltdown. If he'd gone for the election in 2007 and been forced to resign afterwards, he wouldn't have even been there.

So perhaps it wasn't such a mistake after all.

42

NEW PEOPLE

There was a strange atmosphere in No. 10 in the immediate aftermath of the election decision: the staff were almost determinedly cheerful, like Christmas Day on a hospital ward; and Gordon – typically when he blamed himself for something – was quiet, sheepish and sweet to everyone.

It was only over the coming weeks that the gloom really set in, as we endured what I would describe as the most appalling run of bad luck, but what the media, the opposition parties and those good old 'told you so' Blairites simply revelled in as evidence that Gordon's government had become the most incompetent in history.

My mantra during that period was: 'Let's just get to Christmas.' If we could keep our heads down and make it to the seasonal firebreak, Gordon could disappear for a fortnight, come back refreshed and our narrative would be: 'New Year, Fresh Start.' But it seemed like Christmas would never come, and every new week was worse than the last.

We had the report into the fiasco of Scotland's May elections with Douglas Alexander under pressure to resign, his sister Wendy – leader of the Scottish Labour Party – also under pressure over dodgy donations, and likewise Peter Hain. We had Anthony Seldon's book on Tony Blair's last six years in office, which depicted Gordon and the Eds in a dismal light and quoted Blair saying they made him feel like an abused wife.

We had a further leak of foot-and-mouth from the Pirbright laboratory, the ongoing crisis over Northern Rock, a Commons defeat over detention of terror suspects and the rumbling row over Gordon's use of the phrase 'British jobs for British workers' back at Labour's party conference.

We had retired chiefs of the armed forces making a coordinated assault on Gordon for supposedly breaking the 'military covenant', and Gordon shooting himself squarely in the foot by again being seen to prevaricate and over-calculate about whether to attend the signing ceremony for the Lisbon Treaty, something which made the normally unflappable Michael Ellam tear his hair out.

Worst of all for me were, first, the loss by HMRC of two discs containing the entire child benefit database – how could my old department do that to us? And second, the revelation in the *Mail on Sunday* that eccentric businessman David Abrahams had unlawfully used a 'jobbing builder', a lollipop lady, his solicitor and his personal assistant as proxies for donations to the Labour Party, including more than £100,000 since Gordon had become PM.

Right at the outset of that scandal, the widely liked and admired General Secretary of the Labour Party, Peter Watt, fell on his sword – albeit with some encouraging pats on the back from colleagues – but the resignation of one person taking 'full responsibility' just leads to a media frenzy for the next. Scandals need scalps, and one is never enough.

Incidentally, I once saw how this works in practice. I'd stayed on after Treasury Questions in April 2004 to watch Home Office minister Beverley Hughes deliver her resignation statement, admitting she'd inadvertently misled Parliament by saying she hadn't been warned about bogus eastern European visa applications. Home Secretary David Blunkett sat next to her almost in tears, but at least they both must have thought that was the end of the matter.

Not a chance. As we exited the press gallery, I watched the political lobby gather in a tight circle outside, like commandoes planning how to take the next building. 'Right, Bev's done. We all going for Blunkett?' A collective 'Yep.' 'What are the angles?' They worked out the various vulnerabilities in Blunkett's position, split between them the jobs of checking them out and then dispersed to get on with it. It was both impressive and frightening to witness. They didn't get Blunkett then but he remained under fire, and they got him on another visa mishap, coupled with a sex scandal, a few months later.

In contrast to that row, and as always in these kind of moments, we retreated to establish the facts on David Abrahams before saying anything, and then Gordon made clear within No. 10 and the party that only I would speak to the press about the story, just to make sure we stuck to one clear account and narrative, and had no contradictions or mixed messages.

For what seemed like the whole week, I stalked around one of the large empty offices at the Horse Guards end of Downing Street, mobile phone in one hand, iron poker from the fireplace in the other, dealing with hundreds of press calls on the issue and punctuating my briefings with ever more elaborate swishes and thrusts.

I was in my element, but the truly hard part of the week was experiencing up close the reality of a group of people from Gordon downwards determined not to be dragged down by the scandal, and full of mutual suspicion and mistrust.

Whereas I regarded it as my job to kill the story as quickly as possible and ensure there were no more scalps, because those were my orders from Gordon, many others feared that all I cared about was protecting him and – as much as possible – trying to shift the blame onto those who were in charge when Abrahams was first recruited in 2003.

So one minute I'd agree with Lord Triesman, former chair of the Labour Party and shortly about to become chair of the FA, that I'd return the calls that had been made to him by *The Times* and *Daily Mail*. The next minute, one of his friends would call and say that under no circumstances was I to speak on Triesman's behalf, and that I'd be sued if I tried to implicate him.

It was a tough time, and the worst of it was that – as everyone was frantically protecting themselves – poor Peter Watt was left at home with a newborn child with no one calling to check how he was getting on or what he was going to do next. From those kinds of omissions, personal resentments grow, and Peter went on to deliver a stinging account of his time with Labour before the election.

We finally made it to Christmas, battered, exhausted and almost terminally damaged by the events of the previous three months, a period cruelly crystallised in the House of Commons by Vince Cable when he talked of Gordon's transformation in the public mind from Stalin to Mr Bean.

But, in that period, I also saw Gordon's private transformation from a man who blamed himself for the election debacle to a man who felt everyone around him was letting him down, even his most loyal and longest-serving staff. We were used to hearing him shouting: 'I need new people!' when he was exasperated or angry, but now he was saying it soberly and seriously.

And it was a massive mistake. However bad things were over that three months, it at least built a real camaraderie among the Downing Street staff – old Blair civil servants and former Treasury staff alike – fuelled by long days under the same cosh, a rich vein of gallows humour and huge Friday night drinking sessions. Someone like Katie Martin, a shrewd communications strategist who arrived the week after the election decision, *only* knew that bad period, and yet by Christmas felt both fiercely committed to Gordon and fully bonded with the rest of No. 10.

In those circumstances, bringing in a whole cast of people with no experience inside government as our supposed saviours was always going to be counter-productive, as some would struggle to find their feet in an atmosphere of rolling crisis management while the existing team of civil servants and special advisers, hitherto loyal and dedicated, were made to feel like chopped liver. For Gordon, it risked half his staff not knowing what they were supposed to be doing and the other half losing their motivation to do it.

Nevertheless, Gordon was determined to have some new toys for Christmas, and January saw numerous comings and a few notable goings among the No. 10 staff. Most importantly, Tom Scholar – an exceptional civil servant dealt the rawest of deals – went back to the Treasury and was replaced as chief of staff by Stephen Carter, an external PR man recommended by Brunswick's Alan Parker.

Carter was a nice guy, clever and confident, with an excellent background in corporate communications. His main problems were that he didn't have the slightest clue what job he'd been brought in to do and, whatever job it was, it wasn't one he was qualified for. In terms of managing the fragile and sensitive network of personal and political relationships within No. 10, he was like Frank Bruno performing brain surgery in his boxing gloves.

I got an early and somewhat formative taste of his people skills when he called me into his office, said he had huge respect for how I worked, didn't want to interfere in any way and looked forward to working with me. Well that was good, I thought. The same afternoon, I got a call from a lobby hack saying: 'I'm not sure how to tell you this, but that guy Carter's just offered me your job.'

Hmmm. It's a sign of how vulnerable we Gordon 'lifers' felt by then that my instinct wasn't to go to war with Carter over that because, if it was true that he was trying to replace me or offering other people my job, he might well be doing so at Gordon's instigation. I just did my best for a few weeks to look as indispensable as possible: splashing papers with positive stories; bringing in top-quality media intelligence; even turning up on time for trains.

Reassuringly, I wasn't the only one having problems with Carter. Despite, I'm sure, being told by everyone that he needed to try and get on the good side of Sue Nye, Carter said the one thing almost guaranteed to do the opposite, telling Sue he understood her role as being 'Gordon's sort of "office wife"'. What Gordon's actual wife would think of that, let alone Sue's husband, he didn't say.

Carter's reaction to those teething problems with the existing staff was to insist on bringing in lots more new people, who'd owe their jobs to him. In fairness, some of those who joined around that period – the likes of David Muir, Richard Lloyd, Mark Flanagan and Nicola Burdett – were excellent additions in specific areas like political strategy, digital communications or broadcast media, but for every one of those, there were others with ill-defined roles who just made No. 10 even more dysfunctional and poorly managed than it had been before.

Carter also began bypassing all the normal channels for getting things done, instead doing everything himself. I was walking past his office one day when I saw a very junior lobby hack coming out, so junior that I didn't even have to worry about him being offered my job. I asked Carter what he'd been doing there, and he explained that the guy had written a story making a passing reference to him which wasn't quite accurate, so he thought he'd get him in for a chat and tell him he should always call before mentioning him in a story again.

I didn't know quite where to start explaining to Carter why that was a ridiculous use of his time, so I just rather tersely said that we all got lots of stuff written about us, but what mattered was what they wrote about Gordon. I said if he wanted to spend his time talking to journalists, it would be better if he did some positive briefing to senior political editors and columnists.

He took umbrage at being chastened and that was the die cast between us. Stories began popping up in PR Week, not a magazine I spent too much time worrying about myself, giving inside accounts of tensions inside No. 10, with very detailed guides to who was doing what and managing who, and a common theme that the 'old guard' were being sidelined in favour of Carter and his new hires.

I put up with a few weeks of that, then started returning fire through the newspapers with stories about Carter's taxi bills or the wages of his PA and so on. It was the sort of stupid, destructive, internecine warfare played out in public that either the No. 10 chief of staff or the press adviser should have stopped immediately, except, in this case, we were the ones doing the fighting or were at least the leaders of our respective 'old' and 'new' factions.

And once these things start, they get a life of their own. It becomes the topic of gossip when junior No. 10 staffers meet junior lobby hacks in the pub, and stories start to appear which neither 'side' is responsible for, but which exacerbate the tensions between them.

By right of seniority, and Gordon's decision to go down the 'new people' route, Carter should have won the battle but eventually Gordon himself had started to tire of his Christmas toys. The nadir came in June 2008, when the long-rumbling row over Wendy Alexander accepting an unlawful donation (of just £950) from a Jersey-based businessman came back to the fore, after a Scottish parliamentary committee censured her.

I was in Gordon's office, which adjoined the Cabinet room, with him and Wendy's brother Douglas as they discussed how to handle the issue. It was far from clear whether Wendy would or should have to resign over some minor criticism over a small mistake in relation to a tiny donation, but the bigger concern was that she and Gordon had made entirely contradictory statements about the timing of a referendum on Scottish independence, and there was a danger of both issues rumbling on unresolved over the summer if she stayed in post.

Anyone who blanched at the idea of Ed Miliband taking on his brother for the Labour leadership would have actually fainted if they'd heard Douglas dispassionately advising Gordon that his sister had to quit to avoid further damage, but make clear it was just about the donation, nothing to do with the referendum. If I was sometimes cold blooded about how I did my job, I had nothing on Douglas that day.

In that tense atmosphere, Carter came in and handed Gordon a print-out of what he described as 'where I've got to with Wendy on letters'. Gordon scanned the pages with a rapidly furrowing brow, as it dawned on him that Carter had been engaged by email in a protracted and difficult negotiation with Wendy about what she was and wasn't prepared to write in any resignation letter.

As potential stories go, a leaked email from Gordon's chief of staff telling the head of the Scottish Labour Party how to explain her decision to resign is pretty high up on the splashometer, and there was enough ill-feeling at Wendy's end that such a leak was a distinct possibility. Gordon erupted: 'BY EMAIL?! BY EMAIL?!

ARE YOU MAD?! WHO TOLD YOU TO DO THIS?!' If a
nuclear bomb had gone off across the street at the same time, we
wouldn't have heard it.

Carter tried to calm him down, but Gordon just told him to
get out. It was very, very rare for Gordon to shout directly at the
subject of his anger, and I saw it as a pretty clear sign that he was
sick of Carter and knew he'd made a mistake by hiring him.

But the fault didn't lie with Carter. He was the right man for all
sorts of jobs – just not that one, not with that boss and definitely
not at that time.

And on reflection, throughout this entire period we were missing the real problem. No amount of people, old or new, could ever
be an adequate substitute for the two Eds in terms of enabling
Gordon to function effectively, Ed Balls in particular, and giving
him advice that he would trust.

There were times working for Gordon when you could allow
yourself to think – given this was one of the most powerful people
in Britain and he was asking your opinion – that you were in
some way a person of influence. That illusion was inevitably shat-
tered each time he'd listen to everything you had to offer, stare
at you sullenly for a moment or two, then say: 'Get me Ed Balls.'

Even after the Eds left the Treasury in 2004 and 2005, they were
always around the place, and there was no sense of Gordon having
to cope without them. But once they were Cabinet ministers with
their own departments to run after 2007, they didn't have the time
to spend sitting in Gordon's office working through issues, speeches
and strategy, let alone the time to manage the way that No. 10
operated, or take decisions and sign things off in Gordon's name.

I was prepared to do that myself when it came to media issues,
but I was one of the exceptions, and – when we reverted to relying exclusively on Gordon's decision-making – we ended up
with a bottleneck around everything from policy issues to diary
management, which neither Stephen Carter nor anyone else was
capable of resolving.

If the experiment with 'new people' proved a rather time-
consuming and attention-distracting dud, it also had a damaging,

long-term effect in terms of our communications. For the first time in sixteen years since becoming shadow Chancellor, Gordon had lost control over who was authorised to speak to the press on his behalf.

The rigid discipline of the Treasury was long gone. Even his ability to instruct No. 10 and the party that only I was allowed to speak about the Abrahams donations was a thing of the past. As soon as we had the proliferation of No. 10 and Downing Street sources that were quoted during the 'old' versus 'new' briefing wars, there could be no restoration of that control.

That's partly because once a lazy or unethical journalist knows you've lost that control, they don't need too much encouragement simply to make up a quote to support their story, or at least get a quote from somewhere or someone and give it a 'No. 10 source' attribution. That will sound shocking to many people, including the majority of journalists, but I knew it happened because, in my Treasury days, I frequently read stories by certain hacks where my own quotes had been re-imagined as coming from No. 10 or the Home Office or even Buckingham Palace.

The only way to prevent that is by being able to assert with confidence – as we did in the Treasury – that if a quote wasn't from Gordon, one of the Eds, the Head of Communications or the political press adviser, then it was made up. Once we were in No. 10, and that list of people grew to double figures, it became open season.

43

THURSDAY NIGHT LIES

People forget that Gordon Brown had some very successful election nights as Prime Minister.

Well, one. When we were riding high after Gordon's takeover, we won the Sedgefield by-election triggered by Tony Blair's resignation as an MP, but – more surprisingly – we romped home in Ealing Southall, a seat that both the Liberal Democrats and Tories had been confident of taking from Labour before the Brown bounce kicked in, with the Tories especially appalled to get only a 0.9 per cent increase in their vote share compared to the 2005 election.

What made it doubly sweet was that they had chosen to alter the ballot papers for their candidate to say 'David Cameron's Conservatives', thus making his personal brand the basis of their appeal. What made it sweeter still was that it was the most high-profile chance we'd had to show the power of the Brown machine against the Tories, and we monstered them.

Our campaign chief, Tom Watson, had secured a photo of the Tory candidate, Tony Lit, posing with Tony Blair at a Labour Party fundraiser just over a month previously, along with a copy of the cheque he'd signed to the party that night. Tom had the photo in his back pocket for weeks, but – no matter what problems we faced during the campaign – he resisted the temptation to use it too early.

He reminded me of a Victorian sergeant-major, his men nervously leaning their rifles on bloody sandbags as the enemy attacked, saying calmly: 'Wait for them, lads ... Wait for them!' When he finally said 'Fire!', the Sunday before the vote, I managed to get the photo onto almost every broadsheet front page and on page 2 of every tabloid.

That said, given later events, it's interesting to note that Tom and I almost fell out over the distribution of the photo, since he thought it should be an exclusive for the *News of the World*. It's also interesting that I was so paranoid at that stage about doing party political business even from the stand-alone computer in No. 10 that I sneaked into the Treasury with my old pass to email the photo round to the Sunday newspapers from one of their many stand-alone terminals.

Watching the Sedgefield and Ealing Southall results announced late on 19 July 2007 was as good as elections ever got for us, and every Thursday election or by-election night after that was a fearsome test of the spirits, not just because of the results but because of the inevitable panic, dark moods and mischief they triggered among Labour MPs and ministers.

I spent the 2008 local elections, an utter disaster as Labour slipped to third place with a national vote share of 24 per cent, in Labour's HQ at Victoria Street. My job was to give briefings and lines to the succession of ministers and MPs trooping off as cannon fodder for the live election night broadcasts. Their first question was always: 'How bad is it?' You could tell a lot from their reactions when told. Those loyal to Gordon said: 'Fucking hell.' Those who weren't just raised their eyebrows and sighed.

Harriet Harman chaired a succession of hourly conference calls with regional organisers from around the country, her customary grimace growing ever more pained. Each new forecast of a council in the heartlands where Labour was going to lose control was greeted with gasps by the room like a roll call of the dead: 'Oh, Oldham! Agh, Wolverhampton! Hartlepool? Surely not Hartlepool!'

I slept on the floor at Victoria Street that night and skulked back into No. 10 wondering how much longer Gordon or any of us would be there. Over the previous few weeks, a consensus had taken hold among the advisers that, if we lost the London mayoralty, Gordon would probably have to go, and – while the discussions with him about it were more abstract, using phrases like 'Some people will argue' – there was little doubt in my mind that Gordon felt the same way.

If he didn't go, he would almost certainly be ousted acrimoniously, not least after Ken Livingstone laid the blame for Boris's victory in London at his feet. Gordon's last service to the party would have to be to step down with dignity and call for a unifying and constructive contest to succeed him.

We thought that he'd also have to say – possibly in agreement with the Queen – that whoever the new leader was, they would be given a chance to set out their stall for a few months but with the guarantee that they would call an autumn general election to let the people decide, as Gordon should have done the year before.

When the news came through on Friday night that Boris had won, I simply told the hacks who rang me that we'd see what happened on Monday. Not for the first time, as Gordon counselled opinion that weekend, there was a split between the MPs he spoke to and his other advisers.

For the most part, the former were dead set against him quitting simply because the prospect of a general election any time soon seemed like madness for the party when we'd just polled 24 per cent and career suicide for those in marginal constituencies.

Matters only got worse the following week as MPs already reeling from the results came back to London reporting that dozens of their constituents were bringing in their April pay packets, furious that their income tax bills had risen, as the abolition of the 10p rate kicked in. Gordon's stubborn insistence that they were not net losers only made things worse.

These were dark days. Gordon couldn't do or say anything right, and the party was in open revolt. But, God rest her soul, Gwyneth Dunwoody – who'd died two weeks before the local elections – probably saved Gordon that spring. Internal hostilities were temporarily suspended as Labour attention focused on holding onto Gwyneth's seat in Crewe and Nantwich. Even though the campaign and the result were disastrous, it gave Gordon a small firebreak and gave Alistair Darling time to rush through a panicked increase in the income tax personal allowance to reduce the number of 10p losers.

The Glasgow East by-election in July was different. If the waters were muddied in Crewe and Nantwich by the 10p shambles and Labour's ill-judged 'Toff' jibes against the Tory candidate, there was no doubting Glasgow East would be viewed simply as a referendum on Gordon in his own backyard: a safe seat he couldn't afford to lose.

When word reached Labour's Warwick conference – attended by every union leader and Labour Party bigwig in the country – that we were indeed going to lose it, it was arguably the moment of greatest danger to Gordon's premiership, at least until the botched Purnell coup of June 2009.

In the heated atmosphere that Thursday evening, the union leaders were of one mind: there was no point trying to negoti-ate an agreement on policy-making and workers' rights with a Labour Party run by Gordon Brown because he wasn't going to be running it in a week's time. So pointless did they find the situ-ation, they were quite prepared to pack up and collapse the talks.

If they'd done so, it would have been completely self-fulfilling; the ultimate sign Gordon had not just lost one of Labour's safest seats but totally lost control of his own party. Gordon's political fixers, Joe Irvin and Jonathan Ashworth, and his loyalist MPs performed heroics that night, persuading their union opposite numbers to stay round the table.

The key message that worked was: 'If Gordon has to go, what do you think will happen next?' It didn't take much imagination: Labour would tear itself to pieces in a contest between Blairites determined to seize back the throne and the left determined to stop them; the press and the public would demand an immediate general election; Cameron would win a clear majority and drive through boundary changes; and Labour would be back out of power for a generation.

'Après moi, le déluge' always has a persuasive effect, even when people are bloody sick of the 'moi'. I helped this process by briefing the hacks hard that David Miliband and Harriet

Harman were already on manoeuvres: Miliband courting wealthy donors to fund his leadership campaign, Harriet touring the bars of Warwick talking about her 'moment'. At that point, it didn't matter whether either thing was true, which they weren't; what mattered was that people heard the drumbeats of a Labour civil war. Rightly or wrongly, Gordon survived Warwick and limped into the summer holidays.

As for me on those three torrid election nights between May and July 2008, I did the only positive thing I could do and determined to turn the very awfulness of the results into a way of enhancing our relationships with the political media. In simple terms, I became the only spin-doctor in government or opposition who ever reliably told the truth on election night.

It may come as a surprise, but very few politicians or spin-doctors do actually tell outright lies, and it's something of a shock when you find out they have. I mean, why take the risk of being caught out telling a lie when you could simply avoid, obfuscate and divert?

When I was hurriedly spreading my mischief about Miliband and Harriet the weekend of the Warwick conference, I wouldn't lie outright; I'd just point a journalist in an erroneous direction by asking a question: 'Are you hearing this rumour about Miliband asking Lord Levy to bankroll his campaign? Won't that be a massive story?'

But election night is when all pretence of being even halfway honest goes out of the window and – almost by convention – politicians and spin-doctors tell the most blatant lies. To understand that, it's first important to grasp what they know on election night and how they know it.

On the big Thursday election nights in May or June, when hundreds of party members are knocking on doors getting out the vote, ticking known supporters off at polling stations, or observing the count at the town hall, the information they are gathering is being constantly fed back to regional organisers, then on to party headquarters, and then tapped into central computers. At by-elections, where entire towns are flooded with party activists, the detail gathered is even greater.

The information gathered on the day is put together with the data they already know from postal votes and phone canvassing, and, by processing all that, each party headquarters will generally know fairly early in the evening which seats and councils they'll win and which they'll lose, and be able to estimate their national share of the vote down to the first decimal point.

As the night goes on, those numbers and estimates are refined, but rarely by very much. Labour Party election experts like Theo Bertram would listen to me and others note optimistically that 'the early results don't seem as bad as you're saying', smile in a sympathetic way, and say: 'Well, we've never been wrong before.'

But even though spin-doctors and ministers on both sides know almost exactly how good or bad their results are, tradition dictates that the triumphant party will tell the newspapers and broadcasters off the record that things aren't looking as good as they'd hoped, while the defeated party will say: 'Bloody hell, guys, it's even worse than we feared.'

This is explained by spin-doctors of all parties as an exercise in trying to get expectations into 'the right place', by which they actually mean lying to people so the media's expectations are in an entirely wrong place.

Why do they do that? Well, simply because – when the actual results emerge – they hope Nick Robinson and David Dimbleby or Adam Boulton and Kay Burley will spend the following day saying: 'There will be some relief in the Labour camp that their vote held up as well as it did' or 'The Tories are admitting even they were amazed by the scale of the victory.'

In his later years in office, Tony Blair's spin team turned the opposite way entirely, telling journalists they'd done much better than they actually had, simply in the hope that the first editions of the papers that people saw in the morning weren't as bad as all the rest of the coverage to come.

There was a disdain for the press in all this behaviour that used to irritate me. We saw the same thing with Alastair Campbell in 2005 writing one of his ridiculous top-secret memos designed to be leaked shortly before the election warning that Michael

Howard could win because Labour voters assumed victory was in the bag and were planning to stay home.

So, when I was in charge of this process, I made a conscious decision to do the opposite. I met at the Pimlico Tandoori restaurant around 9 p.m. on each disastrous election night with a handful of political editors, had a curry and told them exactly what the result was going to be, then got them to pass it on the others. And I told them: if I'm wrong, never believe another word I say to you.

They'd then be in the bizarre position of calling my Tory counterparts and saying: 'So we understand from the Dog you'll be on 44.2 per cent or thereabouts, and you're going to gain Solihull and Bury', and they'd respond: 'Don't fall for that old rubbish. Are you kidding? Not a chance!' And of course, within a few hours, I'd be proved right and my opposite numbers would be exposed as blatant liars.

What purpose did that serve? Well, at the time, it did precisely zero to improve the coverage of those elections; in fact, it only ensured that the first editions of the papers had a fairly accurate sense of the dimensions, duration and crimsonness of each bloodbath.

But, it ensured – at least at that time – that Labour was still seen as having a more professional and honest press operation than the Tories, it ensured that our flows of intelligence and trade with the media remained open, and it meant that the party and Gordon were still being listened to and reported in a reasonably fair and objective way, no matter how bad the polls looked.

My election night honesty was only one part of the way I maintained those relationships, but it was a symbolically important one. And, of course, the odd times when – as at the Warwick conference – I thought I needed to bend the truth to protect Gordon's interests, it meant I tended to be believed.

44

FOR THE GLORY OF GORDON

My dad was very fond of shouting things out in public. An entire cross-Channel ferry found out about Bob Willis's eight for forty-three to win the 1981 Headingley Test because my dad was relaying every wicket with growing volume and elation from his transistor radio.

When I was very small, our trips to Sainsbury's would stop for ten minutes while he screamed about the Highland Clearances or the Famine to any fellow shoppers he heard making anti-Scottish or anti-Irish remarks. He'd berate me or my brothers in public if we said a word out of turn on the walk to church. And – while I wouldn't always understand the reasons – I'd regularly hear him hurl abuse at passersby with whom he had ongoing grudges: ex-pupils, former colleagues, old friends.

But what I remember most of all, and in retrospect much more fondly, was him seizing me by my tiny arm the many times we visited an ancient church or cathedral, pointing to the detail of the masonry or frescoes in the highest alcoves, or getting me to feel the intricacy of the wooden and stone carvings of statues beyond the point the eye could appreciate them, and shouting: 'Do you understand? Done where only God can see! For nothing but the Glory of God!'

If I felt he was sometimes a hard man to please, it was just because I often didn't grasp what pleased him. The only time he saw me captain Peterhouse at Cambridge was against the whipping boys in our league. We beat them 11–0, and I scored five of them. As I came off to greet him afterwards feeling proud of myself, he walked straight past me, shook the opposition captain's hand, and – with tears in his eyes – said to him: 'You were magnificent; you kept your team going the whole game; you never stopped running.'

It was the same spirit drilled into me by my mum when she taught me cricket, read me 'Vitai Lampada', and explained that you were measured by playing the game with the same passion, effort and determination whether you were coming into bat at 300 for one or at eighty for nine.

To look at my sporting or my political records – the very antithesis of playing the game in the right spirit, respecting my opponents and taking defeat on the chin – you might think I owe an apology to my mum and dad for not listening to a word they said, but they would know better. They would look at the long, dark days I spent in Downing Street during 2008, and know I did them proud.

Now don't get me wrong: No. 10 itself is the best place to work in the world, and being the political media adviser probably one of the best jobs.

Walking through the black door each day felt like a thrill: the Cabinet room and Downing Street garden straight ahead down the corridor; and each room off to the side or up the stairs with its own history of famous meetings, summits, banquets or interviews. And – whether we were in No. 10 or out on the road – the days themselves in 2008 were often thrilling.

In March I helped to ensure the first Anglo-French summit between Gordon and President Sarkozy took place at Arsenal's Emirates Stadium, when I convinced a sceptical Gordon that he should use the soundbite suggested by his genius foreign policy adviser Tom Fletcher that we wanted 'the Entente Cordiale to become an *entente formidable*'. It made Arsène Wenger smile!

In August in Afghanistan, we were driven at high speed from Kabul airport to the presidential palace with a squaddie telling me how to fire his rifle if he was incapacitated or killed, then swooped back to the airport from the British embassy, flying low and twisting sideways over the rooftops in a machine-gun helicopter, because of fears of a Taliban missile attack.

Everyone else was deliberately downbeat and under-stated about the whole experience afterwards, and nodded sagely when talking about the brave members of the armed forces who did that kind of thing every day. I just sat there grinning, my inner thirteen-year-old saying: 'That was fucking awesome!'

Yet, for all the occasional excitement that 2008 brought, and for all that I loved spending every day in No. 10, most of the year felt like one long exercise in dealing with the shit that was happening, trying to stop other shit from happening and shouting at the colleagues who kept adding more shit to the mix: 'That's quite enough shit for now, thank you.'

This is where, God bless him, I have to thank Alastair Campbell, because as well as his No. 10 'grid system' providing me with many years of good stories to leak to journalists in the No. 11 days, it was absolutely fundamental to the whole waste management challenge within No. 10.

Of all people, I'd have been forgiven for being sceptical about the grid precisely because I knew what a good source of potential leaks it was. But my rationale was similar to Campbell's: every government faces leaks; they're annoying, but they're rarely fatally damaging. What is fatal is the government losing grip over what it's announcing, how, when and most importantly why. If the price you pay for the grip that the grid offers is the occasional unscheduled Sunday paper splash, it's worth every penny.

Not long after David Cameron's guru Steve Hilton left No. 10, he gave a lecture at Stanford University and unveiled a one-foot-high bundle of paper to his students, which he said represented just four days' worth of documents circulated to Cabinet committees. He said: 'This just shows you the scale of what you're up against in trying to control these things. The idea that a couple of political advisers read through all this and spot things are bad, things that are contradictory, is just inconceivable.'

But that's precisely why the grid system was put in place, so political advisers didn't have to do that. Many Westminster people wrongly think of the grid as simply a news management tool, with a series of announcements, speeches or events plotted to dominate each day's coverage and give narrative structure and themes to the week, fortnight and months ahead.

That's the way it was used when originally conceived for

Labour's 1997 election campaign, and the way some businesses now use it to plan the launch of a new brand or product, many of them advised by ex-Labour folk who've taken the corporate communications shilling.

However, within No. 10, the far more important role of the grid system was doing precisely what Steve Hilton concluded was impossible: giving political advisers an easily digestible paper titled 'Upcoming Business' and detailing every government announcement or important external news item for the next fortnight. The grid itself was simply a tabular summary of this longer document; that's what I would see in the Treasury and use to try and decipher those upcoming announcements.

The 'Upcoming Business' paper was compiled and circulated by the great Paul Brown in No. 10's Strategic Communications Unit each Thursday evening, and would then form the basis of a Friday morning meeting to go through each item in the grid line by line.

At different times under the Labour government, those meetings were chaired by special advisers like Alastair Campbell or Gavin Kelly, ministers like Ed Miliband or Liam Byrne, and civil servants like Jeremy Heywood or Michael Ellam – what mattered was that whoever was chairing the meeting had the personal clout to sort any problems out themselves, or the influence over Tony or Gordon to tell them when they needed to weigh in.

The meetings were attended by every No. 10 civil servant or special adviser within the No. 10 Policy Unit responsible for shadowing different government departments, almost all the communications staff, and all the key civil servants in Gordon's private office. They were the only meetings I used to attend on a weekly basis in No. 10, and the only regular occasions after 'the election that never was' when Ed Miliband and I would see and speak to each other.

They were also a model for a well-run meeting: no agenda, no apologies, no presentations, no minutes, no any other bloody business; just an hour spent investigating the meaning, purpose, impact and timing of every item on every day for the next fortnight. And because each item would get at least two airings before it was due to be announced, it was inconceivable that something would be announced without No. 10's knowledge and explicit agreement.

Here is a real-life example: the Ministry of Justice under Jack Straw submitted an item to Paul Brown one Wednesday in 2008 saying they'd be issuing a consultation paper a week on Tuesday on options for improved management of cemetery land; something Paul translated into the grid as 'MoJ: Cemetery Management'. That was enough for Gavin Kelly and Dan Corry to raise their eyebrows and ask curiously: 'What's this about?' Paul was told to get a copy of the consultation paper and dig out the Cabinet sub-committee meeting where it had been discussed for the next week's meeting.

Next Friday, four days before the planned consultation, Paul was able to put a lot more detail in the 'Upcoming Business' paper about the proposal, at which point everyone in the room erupted. 'Hold on a minute, one of the options is to dig up old graveyards in high-value areas, incinerate the bodies, and sell off the land?! Are you fucking kidding?! Get it out of the grid now, and tell Jack Straw's office this consultation is not happening in any form at any time, full stop.'

And why is that example particularly relevant in the context of Steve Hilton's complaints? Because a similar item labelled 'Forest Management Consultation' was allowed to slip through unnoticed and unchallenged by anyone in No. 10 in October 2010, leading to the great row and rural rebellion in 2011 over the planned 'privatisation' of England's forests.

This was around the time Hilton and his policy team had stopped attending the grid meetings because of their animus with the Tory press team, which – when I think back to attending those grid meetings in Ed Miliband's office in 2008 despite the froideur between us – seems rather childish and dysfunctional.

And if people in those positions are not prepared to suspend their own personal feelings for the one hour it takes every Friday to come together as a team and stop potential problems materialising, they are never going to be willing to do the infinitely more mind-numbing, energy-sapping and soul-destroying work that I had to do for hours each week on my own trying to neutralise and nullify problems that had already emerged.

On one day, it would be some obscure bit of legislation we were enacting with a consequence that no one could possibly have foreseen, let alone intended. On another day, it would be something a junior minister had said at what they thought was a private meeting that you prayed to God had been taken out of context.

These stories were the antithesis of the grid. They were the gloop: no planning, thought or preparation would have gone into any of them; they would always come along at the worst possible time; and – while having every capacity to do so – they were the last thing you would ever want dominating the news agenda.

If I was lucky, I'd be told about them by another Whitehall press office or by one of our own No. 10 policy advisers: they'd have spotted the potential problem themselves and we could sort out our response before anyone else did. If I was unlucky, the call would come from a journalist, meaning we had a story to kill; if I was having the day from hell, that's because they'd been tipped off by the Tories, meaning we had a political row on our hands.

The keys to dealing with that kind of story were time and control – the more of both the better. If Ed Balls called up at 9 a.m. on a Monday and said a lawyer in his department had just realised their new safety legislation for children's playgrounds was going to mean a ban on climbing frames in pub beer gardens, that was fine. If it was 3 p.m. on a Saturday with the Tories offering that same story round all the Sunday papers, we had a major problem.

Obviously the easy thing for me to have done over the years would have been to say: talk to the department, it's their legislation; or what the minister said in that meeting is a matter for him. I could have ducked the responsibility, or at the very least passed it on to someone else. But I regarded dealing with these kind of stories and stopping them becoming 'news' as one of the most integral parts of my job, just as surely as trying to get one of Gordon's speeches into the headlines.

But what made the gloop such hard work was that, precisely because the story could be about anything and come in any form, there was no set method or routine for killing it. All I could do was work backwards and ask myself: 'What makes this the *Mail on Sunday* splash? What's their headline?' And then I'd focus simply on making that line untrue.

So if the *Mail on Sunday* rang me and said: 'We understand that nurses who receive free cabs home after late shifts are in future going to be taxed on them as a benefit in kind', I'd need to go back two or three rapid phone calls later and say:

'Not true. We think some idiot from the revenue office near the Royal Free misinterpreted the guidance, so HMRC have told him he's screwed up, and sent out fresh guidance to clarify the position, just in case anyone else makes the same mistake.' 'Well, when did they send out the guidance?' 'I'm not exactly sure, but definitely within the last fortnight.'

That would be a minor lie-without-lying. I wouldn't be exactly sure at which second within the previous ten minutes an urgent email had gone out from HMRC to its revenue offices, but I was right to say it was within the last fortnight.

Those kinds of stories were relatively easy, albeit frantic. We could always say some daft action a department had taken had already been unpicked or that amendments had already been prepared to undo the unintended consequence of some legislation. Even if a newspaper still ran the story, it was unlikely to be the splash the next day.

More difficult were the stories based on unassailable facts: missed targets; rogue quotes; wasted money; leaked memos; letters that had never received a reply. Things that would just make the government, ministers or Gordon himself look like shit. Sometimes I'd just have to accept that the story was too good – by which I mean too bad – to get on top of, but it was rare that I'd accept defeat so easily.

More often, I'd say to the journalist, obviously provided I knew and trusted them: 'Looks like a fair cop. Shame though, I had a little exclusive I thought you'd like for tomorrow, but if you've already got your splash, I'll give someone else the other story.' I wasn't actually proposing a trade-off, but it would take a brave journalist not at least to ask what the other story was about, so they could weigh up what was better. So they usually would.

That was where things could get murky. If I had an exceptionally strong and revelatory new policy announcement, then briefing that was an option – but it was also a bit of a waste.

More usually, if there was a really shitty story that I knew was due to become public soon – a Freedom of Information release, some bad statistics, a damning report – I would take the view that this was the best time to get it out, if it helped obscure some bit of gloop in the process. It was what you might call burying bad, unplanned news under worse news that we were prepared for.

Obviously I wouldn't just dish up that alternative story in full; I'd provide a rough outline and say: 'If you think that would definitely be the splash instead of your story, I'll give you all the details.'

And say what you like about media ethics, what exactly is the hack meant to do in that situation? Turn down a better, more damaging story than the one they've got? Maybe take both stories, hold one back, and splash them both? Or split the front page and do a 'Government in chaos' headline? Or even, my goodness, expose the No. 10 adviser shamelessly trying to manipulate the press?

Well, take your pick, but in the real world, any journalist worth their salt would just say: 'Nice doing business with you', and go off and tell their editor they had two belting exclusives for tomorrow's paper, the first of which is guaranteed to dominate the morning news agenda.

I'd estimate that I spent at least a hundred days within 2008 engaged in that desperate effort to keep the gloop out of the newspapers, or at least get it off the front pages, and on the vast majority of occasions, I succeeded. But it was the oddest form of 'success' to experience.

Doing the job I did for as long as I did, I engaged in huge numbers of thankless tasks: cleaning up Gordon's hotel rooms after he left them in case the cleaner was an aspiring journalist; spending hours briefing ungrateful, arrogant or air-headed ministers about what to say on *Question Time* or *Any Questions?*; and taking what Ian Austin described as 'no votes' phone calls from members of the Foreign Press Association for an overseas paper, as in: 'Why do you bother, mate? There are no votes in it.'

But right at the top of the list of thankless tasks were those long days and evenings spent simply stopping stories from appearing in the newspaper. I'd sometimes leave No. 10 after midnight – too late to get a drink, too late for the Tube – and walk down to Victoria to buy the next day's papers.

I'd flick through the one I'd been dealing with all day, turn every news page until I got to the lifestyle or the business section, and know I'd achieved my objective: I'd achieved nothing. I'd sometimes have spent eight or nine hours that day calling and emailing, threatening and cajoling, permanently damaging relationships with other departments, flogging my guts out just to ensure nothing happened and no one noticed.

On other occasions, where I'd dealt with something entirely myself, I'd stand at Victoria and realise that only the journalist and I would ever know what I'd done and how hard I'd worked to kill his or her story, and they were the last person who would thank me. I'd sit on the night bus back to Finchley, feeling sorry for myself, unappreciated, isolated and a little distraught at the idea I could be doing exactly the same thing tomorrow. And the next day. And all weekend.

I'd go on the Saturday night press call, where advisers from all over Whitehall would be told what was on the front pages of the Sunday papers and be told by me and others what their ministers should say if asked questions about them the next day. The No. 10 press officer on overnight duty would read out the headlines on each splash, and I'd feel like shouting: 'Do you know what that almost was?' when we'd get to a paper whose gloopy story I'd spiked. But I was never one for revealing my methods.

Instead, at all those times I just used to remind myself what my dad would shout in those churches: 'Only God can see! Just for the glory of God!' Not that I was fool enough to believe God gave a damn about what appeared on the front of the *Express*. He's more of a *Telegraph* man.

But my dad's words were a reminder to me why I really did what I did, and why I kept coming back to do it again every day, and why I never, ever slacked off or left the responsibility to someone else. It was what I'd dedicated and subsumed my life to every day of every week for the last five years: just making sure Gordon was protected and defended at all times.

My morning equivalent was waking at 5.59 a.m. every weekday, always with a feeling of sheer terror as the pips introducing the *Today* programme came on and I waited to hear the first news bulletins. If we'd briefed a story and it hadn't made it on, I knew Gordon would call and go wild, demanding to know why I'd failed. But far worse were the mornings when we hadn't briefed anything, and the sickness in my stomach was just a fear of the unknown: what if I'd failed to stop a bad story appearing; what if I'd let Gordon down?

Did he appreciate it? Did he even know? Those were never questions I asked myself because frankly they didn't matter. I wasn't doing the job to be thanked or praised. I wasn't doing it – as my mum taught me – for a ribboned coat or a season's fame. I wasn't doing it for myself.

I was doing it out of devotion, out of loyalty and out of some degree of love; and I not only wanted to destroy his enemies, I also came to despise any of his so-called friends who were in it for themselves rather than for him.

45

THE FORCES OF HELL

23 February 2010 – I'd been almost a year out of Downing Street, almost eight months into my job working for Finchley Catholic High School and had almost entirely disappeared out of public consciousness. I was killing time in the Tally Ho pub in North Finchley before my usual Thursday evening quiz in Whetstone, when I looked up at the TV, saw my face on Sky News, and thought: 'Ah bollocks, what's happened now?'

The 'Breaking News' banner whooshed up on the bottom of the screen: 'Darling says "Forces of Hell were unleashed" on him in August 2008.' Of all the abusive responses that filled my mind at that point, I'm glad to say the one that won out was from the old media professional still beating away inside me:

'Will Alistair ever do ONE fucking interview where he says something positive about the Labour Party or the economy, or does he set out to create bad headlines every single time?'

I wrote that out as a text message to send to a few old colleagues and trusted journalists, stared at it for a bit, sank what remained of my pint, let the rage die down and pressed delete. I might have been learning very slowly, but at least I was learning.

I had a wry smile as my phone started to fill up with texts and voicemails from a huge number of journalists I'd not heard from since the week I'd been sacked, as well as the smaller number who'd kept in touch. I resisted the urge to spend the evening re-acquainting myself with the strangers and instead just sat there thinking. What is it with Alistair? Why does he always do this?

As far as I was concerned, he was either catastrophically inept or misguided when it came to his public interventions in – as opposed to his private relationships with – the press; or he was just totally out for himself and didn't care about the impact on the government as a whole.

Alistair said later he just told the truth as he saw it, and felt that was the best course. His supporters were obviously expecting the public to appreciate him for it – not that it ever appeared to do him much good when it came to his poll ratings as Chancellor.

Before 2008, I had always got on well with Alistair and his family. I stayed at their home a couple of times in Edinburgh, including the night before Robin Cook's funeral. I offered his eldest son work experience in the Treasury. I sat up watching TV with his wife, Maggie, who generously agreed to switch over from *Newsnight Scotland* so I could watch *NYPD Blue*.

And when Gordon decided to make Alistair his Chancellor, I drafted and doled out the press briefing which said it was important the markets knew there was no going back to the years of chopping and changing chancellors every few years, and that – as the ultimate 'safe pair of hands' – people could have confidence that Alistair would stay in post until the next election.

I was no enemy of Alistair's and in his early months in post, I bent over backwards trying to help his special advisers, talking them through how to brief the Budget and feeding them all the best attack lines we had saved up for use on George Osborne.

When Osborne gave a hideously bad interview to *The Guardian*'s Decca Aitkenhead in September 2007, I was straight onto Alistair's office, pointing out the worst lines and suggesting how they could use them in Treasury Questions. I can distinctly recall saying gleefully: 'They must be bloody mad giving an interview to Decca Aitkenhead – what did they think was going to happen?!'

Among my many commandments of being a press adviser, one of the higher placed was: 'Thou shalt under no circumstances do an interview with Camilla Long, Decca Aitkenhead or Petronella Wyatt.' They're all excellent journalists; it's just that no good has ever come of a politician doing an interview with any of them.

Roll forward to the end of August 2008. We'd just returned from the success of the Beijing Olympics and the political season was about to begin in earnest. I'd had a good Friday afternoon doing my rounds of the Sunday hacks, and began my evening routine phoning the daily political editors to see whether there was anything cooking in the tomorrow's papers. Andy Porter from the *Telegraph* sounded brisk. That was never a good sign.

'Yeah, there is something I need to check. Were you guys all on board with this interview Alistair's done with *The Guardian*?' I tried not to sound too disturbed. 'Erm, not sure which one you mean? Who's it with?' 'It's in the magazine, he's done it from his holiday in Scotland ... with Decca Aitkenhead.' A small nuclear bomb went off in my head. 'But I assume you guys must have OK'd it because it's quite heavy on the economy, you know, "the economic situation is the worst for sixty years". 'Does he mean the world economic situation or Britain's?' I asked. 'He doesn't say,' said Andy. 'And is that the top line?' 'Yeah, "Britain in grip of worst economic crisis in sixty years, admits Darling".' 'Splash?' 'What do you think?'

Whatever the truth about the economic situation, this was a massive crisis. Gordon was busy telling the press, the markets and the public that the world was facing a major financial crisis, but because of our historically low debt levels and the early and decisive action we were taking to maintain liquidity and confidence, we were better able to withstand the global recession than other countries and better prepared than we had been in previous generations.

That was the script that even the most junior minister knew to deliver, let alone the Chancellor. Andy asked if we wanted to comment, and I said no. I asked him if everyone had it, and he said that it was just in the *Telegraph* and *The Guardian*.

I phoned Michael Ellam, then Gordon. Michael was incredulous but phlegmatic. Gordon was equally incredulous, but rather less than phlegmatic. Nevertheless, both were clear there was only one course of action: we had to agree a joint line with the Treasury that there was no split between our position and theirs.

The key was to explain that Alistair had been misquoted and misinterpreted. He meant that the world economy was facing its

most serious crisis in sixty years – no one disputed that – but what
The Guardian hadn't reported was his clear view, often expressed,
that the action we were able to take in Britain, because of our
stability; our low levels of debt, inflation and unemployment; and
our decision to stay out of the euro, was going to protect the
country from the worst damage seen in previous recessions.

It was going to be difficult to turn this round, but at least the
message was simple. Gordon went away to phone Alistair, and
Michael and I called our opposite numbers at the Treasury with
two instructions, probably more subtly worded by Michael than
the way I delivered mine:

'First, you need to tell Decca to get out there and make clear he
was talking about the world economy and that he was confident
about Britain's prospects, and tell her if she doesn't, you're going
to have to dump on the whole story. Second, you need to get the
transcript of the interview together to make clear he was quoted
out of context.'

The Treasury press office immediately washed their hands of
responsibility for the interview, and said it was all down to Alistair,
Maggie and his political media adviser, who had assured them it
would just be a personal profile. Spin-doctor's Commandment
No. 8, sub-clause (b): '… especially if Camilla, Decca or Petronella
tell you it's just a "personal profile".'

A friend in the press office also tipped me off that when I saw
the photos accompanying the interview, I would flip: Alistair
posing on the beach with black storm clouds behind him, and
dangling out of a small fishing boat in a fluorescent life-jacket as
it washed up onto the rocks.

If that wasn't bad enough, the point I knew beyond doubt
that this was a total amateur-night shambles was when I was
told that the Treasury couldn't do a transcript of the interview
because the only person who'd recorded it was Decca. That was
when I exploded: 'What the fuck are you guys doing? This is
the Chancellor. The Chancellor! His words matter. Even if he's
making papier-mâché hats on fucking *Blue Peter*, you have someone there with a tape recorder. This is bloody basic!'

Nevertheless, despite the mutual acrimony, there was at least agreement from Gordon and Alistair, and at all levels of both teams, about what our response should be: that what Alistair was talking about – even if we couldn't prove it – was the world economy. And that was the script Michael and I spent our Friday night, all day Saturday and all day Sunday delivering.

The idea that anyone was authorised by Gordon to do 'background briefing' against Alistair – or that anyone unleashed the attack dogs against him – is not only totally untrue, it wouldn't have made any sense. Our one objective in terms of media and public perceptions was to show that Alistair had been misrepresented and that he and Gordon were in full agreement. You couldn't say that to journalists but then add: by the way, Alistair's really fucked up and he's going to get the chop.

Now people might point out that I've freely admitted in this book to several other occasions when I did or said things without Gordon's knowledge or approval, hence it's not inconceivable I could have done some freelancing on this occasion too. But if Gordon gave me a script and a set of marching orders, I followed them to the letter. I didn't add little private postscripts or give my own take.

That's partly because I valued my job and my testicles, and wouldn't have retained either for long if Gordon felt I was disobeying his instructions. But it's also – and this is crucial – because no journalist cared what I personally thought. Take the dozen or so hacks who called or texted me for the first time in ten months on the evening of Alistair's 'Forces of Hell' interview. While they wanted a comment then, I'd ceased to be of any value before that night because I was no longer the voice of Gordon Brown.

So when I was doing the old job, if I'd ever rung a journalist and said: 'This is Gordon's position ... but, by the way, here's what I personally think' and said the complete opposite – 'Alistair Darling needs to be sacked' – not only would I have been failing to get the story Gordon wanted and incurring his wrath in the process, but the journalist concerned would have stopped regarding me as a reliable conduit for Gordon's views.

In that forty-eight hours, I had journalists I regarded as trusted friends ringing me up and saying: 'Come on, off the record, Gordon must accept this is a disaster – look at the BBC – it's dreadful for you guys.' And all I kept saying was, of course the news is going to be like that if they're going to misrepresent the interview and say Alistair was talking about Britain, but he wasn't. They would sigh, almost disappointed that I was maintaining what was effectively a lie.

So instead they'd do what all good journalists do, and keep phoning round every Brownite MP or former adviser until they found someone they could vaguely describe as 'close to Gordon Brown' to give them an anti-Darling quote; and in their copy, they would simply assert that the interview had caused dismay, irritation and anger in No. 10, all of which was both true and obvious.

If relationships and trust between the Brown and Darling teams were already fairly strained before that day, they were pretty much broken thereafter. And the truth is I didn't always help things.

At one point, when my 'exiles' team from No. 10 won the Treasury quiz, I took the microphone and – to vociferous boos – said: 'Well, you've really fucked it all up since we left.' Just before the 2008 Pre-Budget Report, I sent the old Treasury Head of Communications, Steve Field, a text saying: 'Steve, for God's sake tell that clueless prick J-C you don't piss away your only good story three days early', full knowing that J-C Gray had inherited Steve's phone number and would get the message himself.

But I was resentful myself of the way that – almost overnight – I began to be ignored by Alistair, Maggie and their kids when we'd pass in the corridors in Downing Street. On a professional level, I would tear my hair out at the way my opposite numbers would publicly exacerbate our problems.

I was walking to Arsenal one day in autumn 2008, when one of the hacks – a mischievous soul – called me in a state of hilarity. He said: 'I'm sorry to laugh 'cos you're going to hate this, but I had a massive hole on page 2 for tomorrow, so I gave Alistair's people a call and said: "I'm getting more noises about the reshuffle"; they said "Is that from No. 10?" and I just went "Hmmm – possibly"; and they've gone bloody bananas. I've got all these quotes about how Alistair won't be the fall guy for Gordon's failures, and it's Ed Balls this and Ed Balls that, it's fantastic stuff! We might end up splashing it!'

Hilarious indeed. I naturally declined to do a No. 10 source response and he cheerily said he didn't expect I would, but then concluded: 'Just to be serious though, Damian, Darling does need to go. I'm serious, because the entire lobby thinks that operation is now a joke. And you can't have the Treasury being regarded as a joke. And what I've just done there, I mean that's fish in a barrel stuff.' 'OK, I'm off to the football.' He laughed again: 'I know, I know, I'm not asking for a response, I'm just telling you.'

The reality was he was exactly right. I knew the Treasury and I knew Treasury communications, and I'd worked in both success-fully. I could tell when it was all working well and when it was an absolute shambles, and I still had huge numbers of friends on the inside confirming my impression that the latter was now the norm. All the sense of grip, purpose and professionalism that had been there under Gordon and the Eds had disappeared.

Gordon recognised it too, which was why he was running the whole response to the financial crisis from inside No. 10 and why he was desperate to find some way of getting Ed Balls to take charge at the Treasury. Balls himself was resolute: he wouldn't even discuss the economy with Gordon unless it was in an open way with Alistair at the table, which just increased Gordon's frustration.

He also repeatedly turned down Gordon's entreaties to come to No. 10 in a 'First Secretary of State' capacity, the role that Peter Mandelson ended up in from June 2009, because he saw it for what it was: an attempt to get him running the economy by the back door, which he wasn't prepared to do.

The only way Gordon could put Balls in charge was to make him Chancellor, and that was exactly the bullet he planned to bite in his 2009 reshuffle, which he imagined coming off the back of a successful G20 summit and a boost in the polls. In that scenario, Ed would have a year to get the Treasury back in shape and deliver a successful pre-election Budget.

But then there was the debacle of my exit, followed by the expenses scandal, terrible local and European election results, the abortive Purnell coup, and the concessions that Gordon had to make to Harriet and others as the price of staying in post. So Alistair survived.

Miraculously, even after I'd left, Alistair's policy decisions, speeches and Budget statements continued to get hideous media coverage, and his poll ratings as Chancellor remained dire. So, laughably, his people started blaming other No. 10 figures for his continuing problems, or alleging that I was still pulling strings behind the scenes.

If there's one thing I learned over the years, it's that strong press advisers with good media intelligence were blamed for a lot of stuff they hadn't done. And it was weak press advisers with no media intelligence who did the blaming. If a minister read negative coverage and asked their adviser where it was coming from, they would obviously never admit they had no clue and no control, let alone tell the minister that the media just didn't rate them; not when it was easier to assert as a fact: 'It's that bastard McBride trying to do you in.'

Don't get me wrong. In some cases, with some ministers, they'd be right. But in Alistair's case, it became a self-inflicted and self-fulfilling obsession.

At some point, I believe he or his people must have realised that the only time he didn't get negative coverage was when the story was about him being under pressure, undermined and attacked, and everyone being after his job; even better if it was an interview where he said all that himself. Then at the very least he got some sympathy for his plight and admiration for his resilience.

I lost count from 2008 onwards of the number of MPs and hacks who said to me: 'Well, Alistair says the proof you were briefing against him was that Andy Porter had that "sixty years" story in the *Telegraph* on the same day as *The Guardian*, and did it in the most negative way possible.' I used to wonder how he could possibly be so clueless, but it would have suited his supporters' political agenda to assert that victim status, and to claim that all the terrible headlines that followed his Decca interview were somehow my fault.

So, in February 2010, while I felt a little irritated to be falsely accused of briefing against him, and a little angry when Sky cameras turned up the next day outside my mum's house and a *Sun* reporter appeared at the Finchley Catholic High school gate asking kids whether I taught them, at least I'd stopped feeling confused about why Alistair felt the need to drag me through the mud again, instead of talking about – I dunno – how the economy was on the mend.

He didn't care what impact generating those headlines had on Gordon and the government, let alone me. All he seemed to care about, to me, was his own reputation and image, which by that stage was well established as 'poor Alistair, who had to put up with so much, and hadn't got the credit he deserved for his role in resolving the financial crisis'.

Spare me.

46

THE DAVID MILIBAND CONUNDRUM

Given he was at a pretty low ebb when we broke for the summer in 2008, Gordon was in a remarkably good and positive mood for the first week of his fortnight in Suffolk.

In fact, when Andrew Rawnsley's book *The End of the Party* emerged two years later, quoting an anonymous source saying Gordon had 'hated every minute' of his time near the seaside resort of Southwold and couldn't wait to get back to Scotland, it was the one bit of definitive proof that – with no disrespect to Andrew – at least one of his key sources was wilfully making things up.

Gordon loved the house Sarah had chosen – owned by photographer Dave Hogan, whose portraits of celebrities were on every wall – and it was perfect for the kids to run around, for entertaining guests and for Gordon to go jogging with his new personal trainer, Millie.

As usual, I went down there for a few days – staying in a village a few miles down the road – just in case we had any initial problems with the local press or paparazzi. Shriti Vadera was also down and the days followed a nice pattern, where Gordon would exhaust himself playing with the kids or doing his workouts, and then sit outdoors in the early evening to shoot the breeze with me and Shriti.

Well, it was Gordon's version of shooting the breeze: quite involved discussions about political, economic and media strategy with him taking notes, but with a glass of wine in hand and the occasional diversion to talk about football or the latest book he'd devoured.

Gordon also kept returning to one of his favourite pursuits: fantasy reshuffles. He would never talk about who to get rid of, but loved talking about the ex-Cabinet ministers he could bring back, and the possible recruitment of non-politicians, particularly from the celebrity world.

Over time, I learned not to take all of these discussions seriously, but occasionally, I'd realise Gordon was genuinely intent on trying to get the likes of Alan Sugar, Fiona Phillips, Simon Cowell or Lorraine Kelly to take on government roles. He finally succeeded with Lord Sugar, but could never persuade Fiona or Lorraine to take the title Baroness. I'm not sure he ever asked Simon Cowell.

But the name he mentioned more than any others that week was Peter Mandelson. 'What would you think?' he'd ask with a big grin, not interested in what I personally thought, but in what the press would make of it. And I told him repeatedly: they would absolutely love it.

It was incredible even to hear Gordon say Peter's name in a pleasant tone. Before that year, his reaction to almost any unexpected bad coverage or political criticism would be to narrow his eyes and say ominously and angrily: 'Mandelson'.

It didn't matter how irrational this was; if anything, the more impossible it was that Peter had anything to do with a story, the more it smacked to Gordon of his cunning handiwork. The only surprise when HMRC lost the child benefit disks was that he didn't accuse Peter of stealing them. If he was brought back to Gordon's Cabinet, I knew it would be a truly sensational tale, like Captain Ahab going swimming with Moby Dick.

Enjoyable as those evenings were, I wanted a bit of a break myself, so I spent Tuesday 29 July having a wander round the pubs of Lowestoft, watching *The Dark Knight* at the cinema, and generally feeling like it was one of the better days of that year. Always a dangerous thought.

In fact, no sooner had I marvelled that my phone had barely rung all afternoon, than I got a call from a lobby journalist tipping me off that *The Guardian* seemed quite excited about an article by David Miliband they were carrying the following day. 'Thanks very much,' I said, and called up one of Miliband's aides.

'Is this article anything we need to worry about?' I asked. 'One of the hacks seems to think it's causing a bit of excitement.' 'I don't know why they think that,' they said. 'It's very positive about everything; all about how we'll win the next election – just attacks the Tories really; there's no problem at all. We sent it to Jonathan Ashworth earlier and he didn't have any comments.'

If Jonathan, who was holding the fort in Downing Street, was fine with it, then that was good enough for me. He had a nose for trouble like Lassie's. I didn't even bother telling Gordon about it on the basis it was no reason to disturb his evening.

My phone started to ring again around 9 p.m. when the article appeared on the *Guardian* website. Of itself, it looked relatively innocuous, but – as ever with David's articles – the treachery was between the lines: criticism of 'exaggerated claims of success' at a time when Gordon was under fire for hailing the end of boom and bust; demands for a 'radical new phase' for Labour, and for the party to offer 'real change, not just in policy, but the way we do politics'.

It was always an oddity of these things that he seemed to have no desire in communicating his meaning plainly to the public or even to most *Guardian* readers, the vast majority of whom would, I assume, have been a little annoyed if told that those lines were designed to be understood by the Westminster cognoscenti, not by the likes of them. There was something of the art-house auteur about him.

Rather more blatantly, the article set out all the ways Labour should oppose David Cameron, but omitted any mention of Gordon Brown. And if there was any doubt how the whole exercise was meant to be perceived, *The Guardian*'s very heavy splash story accompanying the article removed them.

Still, I couldn't work out why Jonathan had cleared the article and not warned anyone. The answer came through: he hadn't and didn't know what I was talking about. And if that was deliberate misinformation, I could understand why. It was early enough when I'd called Miliband's people that if we'd demanded to see a copy of the article at that stage, we could have insisted on changes being made, which would have made him look weak and defeated the whole object of writing it.

In the morning, there were a series of hasty conference calls, including with Gordon, to decide how we were going to respond. Usually there was a pretty clear consensus about these things, but on this occasion the advice was split. Douglas in particular was insistent we should be relaxed, and say we agreed with every word David had written and had no quarrel with how he'd written it.

Knowing what I knew about the way the article had been briefed, I thought that was impossible naivety from Douglas and I mean *impossible*. By contrast, Ed Balls was adamant that we all knew what David was up to, as did every Labour MP, and there was no point kidding ourselves; the only question was a tactical one about how to respond.

Gordon himself was as equivocal as the advice he was getting, saying things like 'Don't go too heavy', which suggested a relaxed response, but then 'Put him in a position where *he's* got to come out and clarify what he meant', which suggested ramping the pressure up a bit. Ultimately, the marching orders weren't clear, and when told that some backbench MPs were already on the rampage against David, he just sighed that there was nothing we could do about that.

I was effectively left to make my own judgement, and – whether it was right or wrong at the time – the way I responded became a bit of a template for how to deal with David's interventions. Talking to the lobby hacks, they were a bit baffled that there seemed to be no coordinated follow-up from the Miliband camp: no one calling up to brief them on what it all meant and what the next steps were; and no serious figure doing a round of broadcast interviews.

It was as though he'd lit the blue touch paper, but forgotten to connect the fireworks. Or, if I was being generous to David, perhaps all he or his supporters were looking to do was sow a little seed over the summer and see what it had grown into by the time of party conference.

Given that was the case, it suited me to present this up front as a full-blown coup attempt – the first shots in a Labour civil war – and say that everyone was anxiously waiting for David's next move. When, inevitably, nothing happened, it looked like he'd bottled it. Worse for him, he felt obliged to come out and explain that wasn't his intention at all, that people had misinterpreted his article and that he had full confidence in Gordon's leadership.

Put together with David's failure to challenge Gordon for the leadership in 2007, the whole episode helped to form an impression of him in the media as being over-cautious and over-calculating, lacking that crucial level of ruthlessness required to seize the crown. And when we came to party conference that autumn, that impression of him proved self-fulfilling beyond my wildest hopes.

Even though we'd trounced the attempted Blairite coup in September, the atmosphere at the conference in Manchester was raw. The leaders of that coup sat prominently in the bar at the Radisson Hotel the first night we arrived, and many Labour MPs and party organisers made a point of being seen to go and sit with them out of solidarity and sympathy.

There was much whispered discussion about the fact that the *Mirror* – never seen as a paper to agitate against the leadership, and still on good terms with Gordon – had thrown over several pages of their weekend edition to a David Miliband interview and profile. Those things don't happen by accident, and at the very least, it was seen as them nailing their future colours to the mast.

The whole conference was therefore set up as Gordon's make-or-break speech to save his leadership versus David's best opportunity to convince the party and the country he would make a better alternative. Gordon grasped his moment with arguably the speech of his life, while David just grasped a banana and let his chance slip by again.

While people remember the banana photo best from that conference, the story that damaged David most at the time was the BBC's report that he'd got into a lift with an aide, who chided him that his speech only deserved a 'six out of ten', to which David had supposedly responded: 'I couldn't have gone any further. It would have been a Heseltine moment,' a reference to the idea that by wielding the knife against Margaret Thatcher, Michael Heseltine guaranteed he could not succeed her.

When Nick Robinson drew me to one side at *The Guardian*'s party that evening to tell me the news, I was beside myself. It was over-cautious, over-calculating David in a nutshell. Nick wouldn't tell me how they got the story, but it became clear that a BBC employee had been in the lift with them.

It still made absolutely no sense that David and his aide would have had that conversation in front of anyone, until I was told that the chap in question had been wearing a scruffy T-shirt, jeans and trainers, and, of course, some people think you can say what you like in front of people dressed like that.

If that makes David sound a little arrogant and haughty, well – as far as I was concerned – he certainly had his moments. I always thought he could stand in a conversation with Barack Obama and the Dalai Lama, and still look over their shoulders to see if anyone more important was around. That disengagement would trip him up even more damagingly during the 2010 leadership election when he left his campaign staff to call MPs and ask for their votes because he couldn't lower himself to do it.

But none of David's self-inflicted wounds that week in Manchester would have mattered as much if Gordon's speech hadn't been such a success, and I had a job to do on that front too.

The morning of the leader's speech to conference is a lot like a Budget Day in terms of the routines of walking the *Standard* and the broadcast political editors through its content and structure in advance, thankfully without the need for as much secrecy.

I had two priorities for those briefings: the first and simplest was – without mentioning David Miliband's name at all – to get into their heads that the key quote in the speech was 'No time for a novice', the line worked out by Ed Balls the evening before. They all liked it, Nick Robinson chuckling and saying: 'I wonder who that's aimed at.' Sure enough, when Gordon delivered that line, the cameras cut right on cue to a stony-faced David Miliband. Perfect.

My second priority was to make the idea for Sarah Brown to introduce Gordon – which had been in the back of people's minds for a while and discussed in earnest early in the conference – look like a totally last-minute, spontaneous decision on Sarah's part, and one that would come as a genuine surprise to the hacks and the Labour members.

So the way I briefed that on the morning was to say: 'Sarah's woken up with this idea. It might happen, it might not. We're trying our best, but Harriet Harman was due to introduce Gordon so we need to persuade her to stand down. Have the cameras primed just in case, but don't do any advance speculation.'

Briefing the *Standard* over the phone on one of the Radisson's balconies, I went a bit further and totally fabricated the idea – albeit I said 'not for use' – that Harriet was pissed off about being replaced, and we therefore weren't sure if it was going to be possible, fingers crossed and all that – all simply to cultivate the sense that this was a very last-minute, totally thrown-together decision.

Unbeknown to me, Harriet was on the floor below and heard every word. She was naturally furious, given she'd been actively encouraging Sarah to do it. Sometimes I just didn't help myself: what I regarded as harmless white lies designed to tell a wider story seemed like gratuitous and totally unnecessary slanders if you were the person on the receiving end.

But in terms of the overall presentation, I did my job: the broadcasters treated Sarah's appearance as a big surprise and she gave an incredible performance. Gordon had a great speech written, but it was the combination of Sarah's introduction and David's dismal week that put him in exactly the right mood to deliver it.

You would think that David would have come away from that week both smarting and determined to do things differently next time around. But a few months later, he bottled it again after the 2009 local elections, and by that point, most lobby hacks felt they could write the script for his timid attacks and panicked retreats by rote.

Perhaps David had simply given up on the next general election by that point, and assumed that the leadership contest that followed would be his to win almost by default. He didn't count on the fact that his brother had clearly inherited all the ruthless genes in that family.

And it does raise a basic question: when is ruthlessness in politics a bad thing?

We applaud prime ministers who are ruthless in their reshuffles, especially when it comes to getting rid of well-liked but ineffective ministers, or sacking colleagues they regard as friends. We applaud their ruthlessness when they realise a policy announced by one of their departments is a pig's ear and intervene to demand it is ditched.

We also bemoan a *lack* of ruthlessness when a politician like David has the chance to kill off an unpopular leader, or when a Prime Minister like Tony Blair has the chance to sack a troublesome Chancellor, but they hesitate to strike, leaving long enough for the moment to pass and often for the problems to grow worse.

But, conversely, when we see political ruthlessness demonstrated through the suppression of dissent, the manipulation of the media and the knifing of rivals, it's usually seen unequivocally as a bad thing. People talk angrily about such politicians and their advisers behaving like gangsters.

Frankly, I always thought there was a lot to learn from studying a walk of life, much like politics, whose most successful practitioners usually combine their mental strengths and business skills with a bit of brute force and some ruthless competitive instincts. As Al Capone once said: 'You can get more with a kind word and a gun, than you can with just a kind word.'

And if I could offer my simple view of why David Miliband will be remembered in political history for failing to live up to his potential and achieve his great ambitions, I believe it's because – when it came down to it – he just had no gun.

Come to mention it, a few more kind words to Labour MPs would have helped as well.

47

THE ART OF THE RESHUFFLE

A reshuffle is just a Budget, but with human beings instead of taxes.

The Prime Minister organising it, and the team helping him, need to know a hundred or so people inside out: their strengths, weaknesses, pros and cons – just like Budget measures.

They then need to bring this altogether into a coherent, convincing package with an overall narrative and a few big stories for the media, and they need to convince everyone on the day – politicians, press and public – that they know exactly what they're doing.

Tony Blair had a bad habit of botching the re-jigging of his ministerial teams, so much so that the starting point for the press in reporting his reshuffles ended up being: 'Will he botch this one or not?'

I had a minor but crucial role in that process. Early on the day of a Blair reshuffle, I would sow a few seeds with the press about switches we were fairly sure were going to happen, because they involved either members of the Treasury ministerial team or Gordon's close allies. On a day when each member of the press is desperate to be the first to speculate about something that will later prove correct, having a text from me saying: 'Des Browne – Defence' was gold-dust.

Most importantly, it established the credibility of my intelligence. So when I subsequently started to spread a bit of gossip – some well sourced, some pure guesswork, some pure mischief – I would tend to be believed.

I only needed to do a tiny bit of that – a text message saying 'Hold on re Des; it all hinges on Charles Clarke' or 'Blair wants to make some gender history so Ruth Kelly in flux' – and that was all believed too, occasionally because it was true. By then, the whole thing would start to be seen as botched and the shambles would become self-fulfilling, as ministers watching the TV thought: 'Well, if everyone else is digging their heels in, why shouldn't I too?'

As the French Resistance showed, you only need to set off a couple of small bombs to make the whole railway grind to a halt.

My rationale wasn't quite as clear as the Resistance's though. At its most basic level, I was just trying to make the Blair mob look as though they couldn't run a whelk stall, let alone reshuffle a government; and I was also trying to make it look as though Blairite ministers were able to run rings round him as the price of their loyalty. And since I would join the hacks in rolling my eyes at the perceived incompetence, there was also the implication that it would all be different under Gordon.

And it genuinely was. Gordon's reshuffles were planned and delivered with the same precision as his Budgets, and with the same focus on handling the media, not just making the decisions.

The key to the process was an enormous magnetic whiteboard in an office adjoining the Cabinet room, on which a table would be drawn with the name of every government department and a number of slots under each name representing the ministerial positions.

The names of every current and potential minister were then written on individual magnetic plates, in black and red felt-tip respectively. Then there were some extra names, written in blue: people from outside Westminster entirely who might be brought in as ministers via the House of Lords.

Like the old Budget scorecard, none of these names were ever rubbed out entirely. We had to keep track of every person currently in a job or who might be expecting one, so we knew who Gordon needed to call – either with good news or bad news – on the day of the reshuffle.

If you didn't do that, you could end up in the position Tony Blair found himself in with Angela Eagle in 2002, forgetting the Home Office minister existed, giving someone else her job and effectively sacking her from the government by mistake – and without informing her.

The key individuals in charge of the reshuffle grid were the two Sues: Sue Nye, who was expected to think through all the political and personal implications; and Sue Gray, the Cabinet Office civil servant, who was expected to keep track of any issues around the overall number, grading and allocation of posts, and any security issues regarding particular individuals or jobs.

For example, Sue Nye would remind everyone that if we move this Cabinet minister to that department, we'll have to move that junior minister somewhere else because they absolutely despise each other, following that unfortunate incident at party conference in 1996.

But Sue Gray might then gently point out that we couldn't move that Cabinet minister to that kind of sensitive position because he was considered somewhat high risk from a blackmail point of view. Gordon, with his occasional Queen Victoria tendencies when it came to his ministers' private lives, would always need reminding why they were considered high risk and screw up his face in horror when told.

Incidentally, my favourite Queen Victoria moment of Gordon's came when I told him on the plane returning from South America in 2009 that the *Express* had splashed the fact that Home Secretary Jacqui Smith's parliamentary expenses included a claim for a pornographic film downloaded to her home TV.

Before we could even get Gordon to focus on what to do about the story, we had to deal with his utter bewilderment that those channels just before BBC Scotland on his Sky box were all porn channels, and that you could use them to download X-rated films, particularly when Stewart Wood started listing some of the more famous parody titles. *Shaving Ryan's Privates*, in particular, attracted a horrified 'What?!' from Gordon.

Back in 2007, when Gordon wanted to make Jacqui Smith the Home Secretary in his first Cabinet, we had to inform him that he was taking something of a risk given that – if asked a direct question – she would confirm that she'd taken cannabis in the past. When he decided to go ahead and give her the job, we thought we could make a virtue of her honesty and encourage others to follow suit, part of the new spirit of transparency in Gordon's government.

So whereas usually the instruction would go out from No. 10 that if the *Mail* rang around the entire Cabinet asking them if they'd taken cannabis, every minister's press adviser should say: 'We don't respond to surveys', we told them all this time to be upfront about it.

Obviously I hoped that process would also put more pressure on Cameron, Osborne and Michael Gove to answer or at least flounder over the million-dollar question which no journalist ever quite asked in the way it needed asking, despite my many entreaties for them to do so: 'When did you *last* take Class A drugs?'

However, my wheeze fell apart when three of our own Cabinet ministers wouldn't answer: the first because – as a point of principle – he refused to talk about his life outside politics; the second because he said, while he'd never taken drugs, he didn't want to open the door on the rest of his private life; and the third because he said if he answered the cannabis question, he'd have no good reason not to answer the million-dollar 'Class A' question.

But before we'd even get to the personal lives of the Cabinet, we'd build the grid from the bottom up, filling the most junior ministerial positions. And here's where an uncomfortable truth would emerge. There would be at least a dozen post-holders where no one in the room, least of all Gordon, had the slightest clue how they were performing in their ministerial roles.

Gordon or Sue would go round the room asking for views. If they'd ever featured in a Quentin Letts or Ann Treneman sketch from the Commons – favourably or unfavourably – I'd pipe up. If they'd ever featured on one of Nick Brown's lists of suspect individuals or alternatively driven through a difficult bit of legislation that Gordon was keen on, Jonathan Ashworth would chime in.

But all too often, we just drew a blank, in which case that minister's fate would usually hang on whether the whips' office thought they were a good performer in the House or not, or whether – when Gus O'Donnell phoned the head civil servant in the relevant department – he received a good report about how much work they got through. A laconic response like: 'Well, I wouldn't *usually* look for them at their desk on a Thursday afternoon' could be damning.

In addition to the vacancies created by the loss of those unfortunates, there were younger junior ministers who were known not to have cut it at all, older ones who'd given up on further promotion and were clearly treading water, and a handful who'd signalled in advance they'd prefer a quieter life on the back benches or in the House of Lords.

With luck, we'd therefore always end up with a fair few positions which we could fill with rising stars from the 2005 intake; or with individuals who'd been highly rated before resigning over Iraq, tuition fees or terror laws; or those who expected to get their jobs back having resigned in the 2006 coup against Blair; or finally with Gordon's odd collection of outsiders – individuals like Sir Digby Jones and Admiral Lord West – rather mockingly dubbed 'GOATS' because of Gordon's 2007 use of the phrase 'Government of All the Talents', a phrase which I insist worked well at the time.

As well as filling vacancies, the junior ministerial positions presented some opportunities and some awkwardness. There were always some people who considered themselves 'waiting on the runway' for a Cabinet position who were gravely disappointed when they found out they were staying put, and equally some rising stars who were delighted to be told they were being made the No. 2 in a department, and therefore in a prime slot for take-off next time round. Arguably, being on the runway is the worst position in British politics, and it's a very dangerous place for prime ministers to leave someone for too long.

Once the junior positions were sorted out, we'd move onto the real headlines – any changes or new faces at Cabinet level. Gordon's major chance to bring fresh blood into senior positions and to create new positions and departments came in 2007, and he did so with a fair degree of ruthlessness, although – again – we took a lesson from the Budget: if there were any unpleasant surprises, they had to be discounted by the media ahead of the day. Margaret Beckett may have been disgruntled to get the chop as Foreign Secretary in 2007, but no one was expecting anything else.

The grid was now full, but that wasn't the end of the process. We would look across the departments and see patterns and problems to be sorted out: a department that was too male dominated; an ambitious or troublesome Secretary of State with no trusted Brown allies keeping an eye on them; or alternately, a Brownite with too many old 2006 plotters in their ranks. We had to look at people's mates too: it was no use thinking Alan Johnson would be happy with his new job if his closest ally, Gerry Sutcliffe, had been shafted.

On the actual day, once the science of putting the whole package together was complete, it was up to Gordon – with the Sues literally at his elbow – to do the hard work of delivering the good and bad news, and to make sure there were no changes of plan. Once the grid had been worked out, just like the Budget scorecard, it was sacrosanct. If anyone refused to accept even a junior position, we had reserve lists and fallback plans, but we never made the mistake of starting from scratch.

For me and Michael Ellam, our job was delivering the anti-botch: surprising the media with the timing and speed of the changes; being definitive about when things were happening and then beating our own projected deadlines; and crucially – especially in 2007 – removing the theatre of a procession of ministers going in and out of Downing Street, and delivering the whole plan via Gordon's Commons office and by telephone. What we lost in terms of a photo opportunity we gained twice over in terms of avoiding the kind of 'Whitehall farce' headlines endured by Blair.

Just like his Budgets, Gordon can look back at his reshuffles and say that – even if he made some minor mistakes which caused problems down the line, combining the jobs of Defence Secretary and Scottish Secretary for example – he executed them all near-perfectly, with the notable exception of his cold feet over replacing Alistair Darling in 2009.

Besides that one, I regret to say Gordon's biggest and costliest mistake was his failure to bite the bullet and get rid of me entirely in his 2008 reshuffle when he had the chance, and when I was urging him to do so. As it was, I ended up half in, half out – a solution which satisfied no one, least of all me, and which left me with idle hands in early 2009.

I had come out of the 2008 conference determined to leave, and said as much to Sue, Michael, Stewart and others in the days immediately afterwards. But while they all sympathised and agreed that I needed to find a way to lower my profile in media terms, there was a nervousness about what it would mean for Gordon and the No. 10 operation if I was no longer around, and no little concern about what would happen to me if I was out of work and had nothing to do all day but drink.

The whole October 2008 reshuffle was a balancing act. At my level, if I was going to be sidelined as part of the reshuffle, then it couldn't be seen as a victory for the Stephen Carter contingent, so he would have to leave No. 10 too, albeit with a peerage and a made-up ministerial job as compensation.

Higher up the food chain, after the recent manoeuvrings of David Miliband, Gordon wanted to shore up his defences by promoting Nick Brown to Chief Whip, and restoring ministerial roles to Tom Watson and others who'd been untouchable since the 2006 coup.

In order to do that without inviting massive criticism, he needed his changes at Cabinet level to be impeccably Blairite and 'reformist'. That meant promotions for Liam Byrne, Jim Murphy and John Hutton, and then the icing, the cherry and the whole cake, the return of – and proof of reconciliation with – Peter Mandelson.

Gordon had been toying with the idea of offering jobs to Alan Milburn, Stephen Byers and even Charles Clarke, just to show he was a totally changed man and wanted the broadest tent possible, but – as he said himself – 'If I bring back Mandelson, I don't need to bother with that bloody crowd.'

I didn't know it at the time, but as part of Gordon's negotiations with Peter over his return, there had been some discussion about who would be running the show in No. 10, and whether characters like me would still be wielding any influence, let alone wielding the knives we used to aim at Peter. It was inevitable that his return – formally as Secretary of State for Business, informally as Brown's new chief *consigliere* – would be linked to any down-grading of my role.

That was all the more reason why I just wanted out. From my point of view, it would avoid the embarrassment of looking like I was hanging around when my job had disappeared, plus I quite liked the kudos of Peter demanding my head before he would return. And from the point of view of Gordon and his standing, it would look strong, ruthless and decisive, and help manage the wider Cabinet balancing act of trading off Blairites versus their enemies.

But Gordon wouldn't hear of it and not enough other people he trusted were pointing him in that direction. There was a clear feeling that my contacts and relationships with the media were too impor-tant for Gordon, and that I was one of the few experienced people left in the No. 10 set-up who could be relied on to calm him down and keep him focused on the stuff that mattered. Plus Gordon just felt a debt of loyalty to me and wouldn't see me cast adrift.

Indeed, when I saw how difficult he found it even to tell me that I would be going into a made-up back-room role focused on 'strategy' and would need to stop my day-to-day briefings with the press, it was obvious he would have found it impossible to go further at that stage and sack me entirely, when – as far as he could see – my only offence was to have pissed off his enemies.

He told me he was sorry and that he knew I'd only been doing my job, but that too many people were now saying it was impos-sible for me to maintain my front-line role. He reeled off names, all said with a scowl: 'Harriet... Purnell... Darling... Douglas', and then almost with a sense of disbelief, 'Even bloody Ed's complain-ing about you.' By then, I didn't have to ask which one.

He asked what I thought of my proposed successors as special advisers on the media – Michael Dugher from Geoff Hoon's office and John Woodcock from John Hutton's. I told him I got on well with Dugher, but I'd clashed with Woodcock because of

Hutton's open defiance of Gordon over the unaffordable recommendations in Adair Turner's review on the future of pensions. But I said they were both excellent, I'd support them however I could, and – more importantly – wouldn't do anything to undermine them. 'Good,' he said, then as always wanting to finish on a positive note: 'At least you won't have so many lunches with journalists now – you can lose some weight!'

Unlike most people who've had bad news at reshuffles, I had the luxury of knowing in advance, and I'd booked Balshen and myself on a weekend trip to Champagne in France organised by our good friend, a PR adviser to Michelin-starred chefs, Kirsty Stanley-Hughes.

We boarded the Eurostar at St Pancras on Friday 3 October just as Adam Boulton announced in Downing Street that I'd been sacked, and it became apparent during the journey that many of the passengers in our group were feeling uncomfortable as they read reports about the reshuffle on their phones: 'Do you think he knows?' Balshen heard one of them whisper.

When we got to the other end, Kirsty announced a toast to my 'promotion' to the role of 'Head of Strategy in Downing Street', but nobody seemed very convinced. That evening, I read some of the blogs that had been written by journalists about my demise – the likes of Ben Brogan and George Pascoe-Watson singing my praises, and offering stinging criticism of Gordon for bowing to my critics. Not for the first time, I thought: 'This is the best note to go out on; why can't I just go now?'

When I passed Peter Mandelson for the first time in the Downing Street corridor the following week, he was doubtless thinking the same thing and immediately whispered to Sue Nye: 'What is *he* still doing here?' Whenever we were in the same room, Peter wouldn't acknowledge my presence, and even when we were sitting in the same plane on Gordon's trip to South America the following March, he looked through me as if I was a ghost.

He and Gordon were sat together on the flight when I came and reported that Argentina's President Kirchner had made her usual bellicose noises about the Falkland Islands on the eve of

Gordon's visit. While I wasn't supposed to be 'briefing the press' any more, foreign trips were still regarded as my thing, so I was left to get on with it. I told Gordon and Peter cheerily that I thought it was a ready-made splash in *The Sun* and elsewhere if we issued an 'over my dead body' response from Gordon, hoping the Dark Lord would at least rate my news judgement.

Without looking at me, he said: 'Why must we play this silly game? Nothing's going to happen with the Falklands. She says this stuff for the benefit of her press. You say it for the benefit of ours. What on earth is the point? Why don't we just grow up and ignore it?'

Gordon, mouthful of biscuit, said: 'You're right, Peter', then to me: 'Play it down. Say we've heard it all before; they just want to create a row, we're not going to rise to it.' I walked away deflated and a little embarrassed, until Gordon came running after me down the plane, and whispered: 'Do a bit of the "over my dead body" stuff as well if you think we need it.' But – even if he wanted the *Sun* splash on that occasion – there was no doubt that Gordon was listening closely to Peter's advice.

One Sunday morning late in 2008, I arrived at Chequers when Gordon was due to have a large group of media couples and their kids over for lunch.

I walked into Gordon's study and listened to him chatting over the phone with Ed Balls: venturing from the media and the Labour Party to upcoming speeches and policy issues, it was the kind of easy-going meander round the houses that they used to do all the time in the Treasury. I was surprised and rather pleased that Gordon was back to talking with Ed in that way because it always put him in a better mood and helped get a lot of decisions sorted out, and he'd clearly been missing those conversations since Ed had been busy with his own department.

But as I eavesdropped, my own phone rang with Ed Balls's name popping up on the screen. I was puzzled and asked the No. 10 clerk who on earth Gordon was talking to. 'Mandelson,' he said. 'Same thing every morning.' The world was definitely changing.

48

'ROUGH SEAS MAKE GOOD SAILORS'

There were three times I felt genuinely shocked by things Gordon said. And the fact that they were all towards the end of my years working for him – when I thought I'd heard everything – made them all the more surprising.

The first was that interview with Simon Walters and Jamie Lyons in Beijing, when I was amazed he was so dismissive and that his innate professionalism had disappeared to such an extent.

The second was shortly afterwards when I was getting him to sign some letters in his No. 10 office. He closed the door and told me to sit down. This was even before the bankruptcy of Lehman Brothers.

'Do you realise how bad this is going to get? We're going to be in recession by the New Year. And there's nothing we can do. And people will make that the big issue, but that's not the worst of it. The whole bloody thing could collapse. I'm serious! The whole bloody thing.'

I genuinely didn't know at that stage what 'the whole bloody thing' meant. I was just reeling from the idea that we were going to be in recession, and how that was going to play in the press.

Much as people can say it was foolish hubris for the Brown team or Gordon himself ever to imply that we'd 'abolished the economic cycle' in Britain – periods of either unsustainably high growth or recession – that was certainly how it looked for a long while.

And those who criticise Gordon for using that rhetoric need at least to consider that it wasn't just boastfulness on his part – although there was clearly an element of that, especially in Budget speeches – but a genuine feeling that the more people believed that there would be 'no return to the old boom and bust' and acted accordingly, it would become a self-fulfilling prophecy.

Take for example, the 'housing bubble', its expansion driven by the fact that demand continued massively to out-strip supply year on year, making it ever harder to help those without property to get on the housing ladder, even with the benefit of cheap mortgages and shared equity schemes.

One of the great frustrations on the supply side was the number of wealthy individuals and house-building companies sitting on land approved for housing development but refusing to over-commit to new projects because of their historic fears that they'd do so at the wrong point in the cycle and end up with houses they couldn't sell and employees, materials and equipment they couldn't use; it was far better for them just to commit to small, quick projects that were guaranteed successes.

Following economist Kate Barker's report for the Treasury on housing supply – commissioned as a result of the euro 'Five Tests' assessment – we did consider quite radical options almost to force land-owners and construction companies not to be so timid in their investments, including the announcement of a future date from which VAT would apply to sales of new housing on green-field land, a proposal which unfortunately Gordon would never touch given his aversion to putting VAT on anything.

But in that housing context and many others, Gordon's primary concern was to convince banks, businesses, share-holders and wealthy individuals sitting on huge stocks of revenue, property and land, that – rather than short-term profit-taking and long-term asset-hoarding – they should keep expanding, take on more work and employees, and keep re-investing their income and assets for the long term, confident that it was not all going to collapse.

That was why – despite his natural caution when it came to public statements about the economy – Gordon did allow himself those hostages to fortune around boom and bust.

It's also been argued since the financial crisis, including by the two Eds, that we were 'over-reliant' on the dynamism, profits and tax revenues from the financial services sector. Factually, that's obviously true. But that implies someone should have noticed and done something at the time.

The reality was that if even the highest-paid accountants in the country – working for the most profitable banks – had no idea that those banks' balance sheets were reliant on worthless assets and debt that would be impossible to recover, how on earth was the Treasury, let alone No. 10, meant to guess that at a dozen steps removed?

Subsequent to the financial crisis, we were told privately, although it's never been confirmed publicly, that John Gieve – the old Treasury Head of Spending who became Deputy Governor of the Bank of England – had written an internal paper before the collapse of Northern Rock raising concerns about the balance sheets of a number of major banks.

If that's true, the Bank never shared the paper with Treasury ministers or – as far as I know – the Financial Services Authority, the two other members of the tripartite system responsible for financial regulation. That might add to the sense that Gieve's views, which commanded huge respect within the Treasury, weren't always so well received within the Bank of England.

The upshot of it all was that the government went into the crisis with not the slightest clue how bad things were at the banks, although typically, as soon as information started to emerge, Gordon devoured it all, ordered vast amounts more and rapidly became the country's leading authority on the nation's banking assets, closely followed by Shriti Vadera, and of course the omniscient Robert Peston.

Gordon could not contain his newfound scorn for the likes of Fred Goodwin when they spoke over the phone to discuss the position at their banks, and he ended up telling them things they didn't know themselves about the value of their assets. 'How is this possible?' he would shout incredulously afterwards. 'How do these guys not know this stuff?'

It may be one of the most frequent criticisms of Gordon that he was a micro-manager, but it made him genuinely baffled and angry to speak to people supposedly at the top of their profession who appeared to have taken no interest at all in the detail of their own banks' investments and assets.

By early October 2008, Gordon had come through the party conference with a significant bounce in the polls and delivered his successful reshuffle, including the return of Peter Mandelson. But financially, we were reaching the real crisis point.

On Monday 6 October, the London stock market suffered its biggest one-day fall since 1987 as shares crashed around the world, and no one thought that we'd reached the bottom. Since the bankruptcy of Lehman Brothers in mid-September, it was simply a question of which major multinational bank would collapse next and when, not whether it would happen.

I'd returned from my trip to Champagne with one conversation in my head: an actress with a rather affected hippy-dippy style who'd asked me to explain 'the whole problem' to her. I did my usual routine, imitating Jimmy Stewart in *It's a Wonderful Life*, explaining that barely any of the money we think we have in ISAs or current accounts actually exists in the mythical bank vaults – it's all re-invested in other people's mortgages, loans and overdrafts.

So if thousands of people tried to withdraw their savings and deposits from one particular bank at the same time, the only way that bank could cope is if other banks agreed to lend it money to help it through, and that would depend on their assessment of whether its book of mortgages, loans and overdrafts represented sound investments. 'Yeah,' the actress said, 'I've seen it. Bedford Falls. Yeah, yeah.'

'But what happens in that film,' I said, 'if people see the panic going on at George's Building and Loan and think "I'd better get my money out of Potter's bank as well", you end up with a domino effect of all the banks being under pressure, all of them having dodgy investments and not being able to turn to each other for help.' Having understood it all, she got a bit serious and said as soon as she got back to London, she'd be withdrawing all her savings.

Over a 48-hour period on that Monday and Tuesday, Gordon and Shriti worked relentlessly over the phones and in frantic meetings to agree the final details of a UK facility to underwrite the finances of every major British bank, and to drive through an internationally coordinated intervention by central banks to try and restore market confidence.

I'd hear Gordon calling up senior world leaders who were in a state of denial and panic, and telling them what the situation was and what they had to do, in terms which weren't that different from mine with the actress. I'd hear Shriti telling some 'home truths' to the heads of banks and their senior advisers: 'Do you want to be in a job by the weekend or not? Because let me tell you, if we don't get this sorted, none of us are going to be in a job for much longer.'

On the Tuesday evening, with all the announcements due the next morning, I was in Gordon's office. He looked ravaged by the intensity of the work, running on a massive overdose of caffeine, and his mind was clearly racing. There were monumental dangers in what we were about to do, and he knew it.

Firstly, by intervening in such a dramatic way in the operation of the British financial system – enabling many of the banks to part-nationalise themselves in order to survive – he was telling the British people and the stock market: 'We've got a massive problem', and trusting that their reaction wouldn't simply be to panic and start a run on every bank and its shares.

Second, it would be clear to everyone that this intervention was officially the government throwing the kitchen sink at the problem – there was nothing tentative about it. If the markets didn't buy it, and it was deemed a failure, the perception would be that nothing could actually work to stem the crisis – the only human response to which would be: 'Sell! Sell! Sell!'

Third, while there was coordinated central bank intervention planned for the morning, Gordon hadn't at this stage persuaded other world leaders that they needed simultaneously to announce their own bank rescue packages – they all wanted to see how Gordon got on first. But that itself risked panic and markets tumbling around the world if people saw the scale of the problem in Britain and realised it was probably the same in their countries.

And then there was the fourth danger, and the third thing

Gordon said that ever shocked me. He closed the door, sat on the couch and said in almost a whisper:

'We've just got to get ourselves ready in case it goes wrong tomorrow. And I mean really wrong. Even if there's a panic in another country, people will see it on the TVs, and they'll start panicking here. It's got to be given a chance to work.'

I said: 'But people will give it a chance … they'll listen to Peston and Jeff Randall and these guys in the morning, and if they say this is the solution, people will give it time, and if the Footsie's up, we should be OK.'

'You don't understand,' he said sternly. 'This is people's money. And your human instinct says: Peston may be right for everyone else, but I need to get my hands on my money. It's just like the fuel stuff all those years ago – it's totally irrational but people just panic.'

He went on: 'If the banks are shutting their doors, and the cashpoints aren't working, and people go to Tesco and their cards aren't being accepted, the whole thing will just explode. If you can't buy food or petrol or medicine for your kids, people will just start breaking the windows and helping themselves. And as soon as people see that on TV, that's the end, because everyone will think that's OK now, that's just what we all have to do. It'll be anarchy.

'That's what could happen tomorrow. I'm serious, I'm serious. And we just need to think how far we're prepared to go. We can suspend the stock exchange, but that's not going to help. We'd have to think: do we have curfews, do we put the army on the streets, how do we get order back? I'd have to resign but I couldn't go if there was just carnage out there, someone would have to be in charge.'

Shriti came in ranting about Barclays Bank, and the moment passed. Gordon concluded: 'Just be thinking about it. Think about the media side. Those guys will have to realise what a responsibility they have. They can't do what they did over the fuel stuff and stoke it all up. They've got to realise they go down as well if the whole thing collapses.'

It was extraordinary to see Gordon so totally seized by the danger of what he was about to do, but equally convinced that if decisive action wasn't taken immediately, it would get harder and harder to resolve the crisis. This was the only chance to avert his worst fears of a total meltdown in the financial system of the Western world, and the resulting collapse of social order.

That was a great leader and a great mind at work, and I would not hesitate in putting his and Shriti's actions that week up with those of President Kennedy and his advisers during the Cuban Missile Crisis. When Gordon was ridiculed a couple of months later in the House of Commons for inadvertently saying: 'We not only saved the world', I looked at Cameron and Osborne collapsing in mocking laughter, and just thought: 'You pygmies. You have no idea.'

Of course, having indeed saved the world by giving every other country a template for how to rescue their banking systems and leading the global coordination of fiscal and monetary stimulus over that period, Gordon was ultimately left frustrated at not being able to finish the job from 2010 onwards.

He had the chance when, thanks to the Dominique Strauss-Kahn scandal the following year, the position of Managing Director of the IMF became vacant. Even in normal times, that job would have been made for Gordon. It would effectively have been like a return to his heyday at the Treasury: a couple of annual set pieces, with an ongoing delivery and monitoring function in between times.

But in the circumstances of a world with an insecure recovery still facing massive economic risks, the IMF actively needed the global leadership he'd demonstrated over the 2008–10 period. That is why Presidents Obama and Sarkozy and Chancellor Merkel not only supported his candidacy, but clearly wanted him back in that leadership role.

The decision by David Cameron and George Osborne not to nominate him for the position – meaning his candidacy could not even be considered – was extraordinarily partisan, but also tremendously short-sighted.

Firstly, from a narrow political point of view, having Gordon run the IMF would have effectively neutralised the organisation's influence on the 2015 election. Any criticism in the IMF's reports on the UK economy could simply have been dismissed by Osborne with a 'What do you expect?' shrug. As it is, the IMF's verdict on his economic policies remains an important and influential one.

More importantly, from an economic standpoint, you can guarantee that if Gordon had been put in charge of the IMF in 2011, he would have spent every waking moment since trying to engineer a coordinated soft landing for China, India, Brazil and other emerging economies, along with collective action by the G7 nations to deal with the impact on their exports and bond markets.

Just as in 2008, he would be trying to stop a potential world recession turning into a global socio-political meltdown, even more so given the militarist and revolutionary leanings of many of the emerging market economies at risk. And just as in 2008, he would not be putting off that necessary action to another day and allowing the potential scale of the collapse in those emerging economies to grow ever larger.

There are few people in the world who would grasp the danger of that situation, and be able to both plan and deliver the alternative. Gordon Brown is one, and if David Cameron and George Osborne end up having to deal with the fallout for Britain from a disorderly crash in the emerging economies – as opposed to a coordinated soft landing – then their refusal to allow Gordon to take the IMF job will look foolish as well as petty.

Nevertheless, even if he would regard it as a job only half complete, Gordon can be rightly proud of the way he rose to the challenge in 2008 and 2009, and stopped a very bad economic situation becoming unimaginably worse, both in Britain and around the world. It was the biggest test he faced in his long career and he passed with flying colours.

Sometimes the recognition of that came from surprising quarters. Only a few weeks before I was sacked, I was in his office and he said excitedly: 'Have you seen this letter I've had from Duffy?'

The Welsh singer had recently won Best Pop Vocal Album at the 2009 Grammys, been nominated for two others, and had received a very personal letter of congratulations from Gordon, as had all the other British Grammy winners.

He read her hand-written response out to me, saying: 'I was completely blown away when your letter arrived and it gave me a lot of strength and encouragement.' She talked about what she'd had to give up and go through to make it in the music business, and she said: 'Your letter made me feel that my sacrifices and struggles have been worthwhile.'

He read out the last section with a faltering voice: 'As for the difficult times we face at present as a country, my grandmother used to say that "Rough Seas Make Good Sailors", so as we pull together and raise our masts, the storm will pass.'

He looked up at me with a tear in his eye, and said: 'Isn't that amazing? Isn't that lovely?'

Then with a great guffaw, he read her PS – 'Pushing my luck, but since you are the Prime Minister, Ranelagh Gardens in Fulham could really do with some recycling bins.'

WALK THROUGH THE STORM

49

THE DARKER ARTS

People tell you things. When you do the job I did, in the way that I did, you become some diabolical inversion of a priest in the confessional box; told about other people's sins precisely in the hope that you'll expose them to the world.

Labour, Conservative or Liberal Democrat; ministers, MPs or advisers; if they'd ever shared their secrets with colleagues in Westminster, the chances were I ended up being told about them by someone they'd confided in, who was not the friend they thought.

Drug use; spousal abuse; secret alcoholism; extra-marital affairs; clandestine visits to seedy saunas and brothels; a bizarre and varied range of what the newspapers would call 'unnatural sex acts'. And then dozens of instances of individuals, almost always men, deemed not safe to be left alone with junior officials late in the evening; the bullies, harassers and gropers.

The people passing on such information had myriad motives: journalists would often just want to swap gossip or find a home for a good story that they couldn't get in their papers; ambitious MPs or political advisers would want to destroy their rivals for a job in government or a seat in Parliament without getting their own hands dirty; and some individuals would just be so outraged by a colleague's behaviour, they'd want to see them get their comeuppance.

I estimate that I did nothing with 95 per cent of the stories I was told – except write them down for potential future reference, either because I wasn't sure they were true, because they couldn't be proven or, in some cases, because they related to people I knew personally and I felt what they were being accused of was totally out of character, even if true.

And occasionally, I'd be instinctively cautious about how information had been obtained, even long before we all knew about phone and email hacking.

I was once called up by a friend from my school days, who started reading me a series of eye-wateringly graphic messages which had apparently been exchanged between a very prominent Tory backbench MP and a young lover. I asked the obvious question: 'How the hell have you got these?' 'Mate of mine's a mini-cab driver. His fare fucked off without paying but left a phone in the back, so he was going to sell the phone instead, but he had a look first and this was what was on it.'

At which point, I started singing 'La la la' very loudly, shouted that there was a very bad line, I'd heard barely anything he'd said, and I was going into a meeting for the next year. I remain totally baffled how anyone in political communications or media can ever have the opposite instinct and get embroiled in anything that is obviously illegal, no matter how good the story is.

So there were some very bad stories I was told which ended up on the front pages of tabloid newspapers, there were a lot more bad stories I was told but never did anything with, and then there was a third category: stories that were nothing to do with me, but for which I was blamed because I was known to have form in this area.

Talk to Alan Milburn and he is convinced that I had a role in spreading rumours about his private life that accompanied his resignation from the Cabinet in 2003, when I was still working in VAT policy. Talk to David Miliband and – to my huge irritation – he apparently blames me for stories in October 2007 leaking his adoption of a second child from the United States and suggesting that he was infertile. Talk to Mark Clarke, former Tory candidate, and – until I persuaded him otherwise – he said he knew *for a fact* that I'd been behind some kiss-and-tell exposé from an ex-girlfriend.

And there's an uncomfortable truth here. If a journalist has ever written something embarrassing about a politician's private life, it's very difficult for the pair of them to re-establish a normal relationship because the politician is always left wondering: 'How did they find that out?', and of course the journalist is never in a position to tell them.

So much like the police asking a bang-to-rights serial burglar if he'd mind coughing to a few other unsolved cases to help clear the books, I know there were some journalists who used my sudden notoriety as an excuse to explain away the sourcing of particular stories, protecting the real source in the process: 'Well of course it was McBride, I could never say so before, but where else do you think it was from?'

And I've only myself to blame for that, given I had form for briefing scurrilous stories about sexual shenanigans. Not that I was particularly sex obsessed, but frankly – in politics – there's a lot of it about.

Politics isn't showbusiness for ugly people. They're exactly the same. Showbusiness – like politics, business and the media – is mostly full of ordinary-looking people whose position or fame gives them the ability to play way out of their league when it comes to sexual relationships, often with much more junior colleagues. At best, that's because some people find their power genuinely attractive; at worst, it's because that power makes it difficult to say no.

One way or another, it makes Westminster about as seedy and sex driven as Hollywood, and often more so, especially for those MPs who use the demands of spending their weekdays in London away from their family as an excuse to live a double life, or react to their weekends at party conference or their 'fact-finding' trips overseas like teenagers on a night out in Newcastle.

I spent one Thursday evening in 2008 in a West End bar with a large group of Labour MPs. As the dining tables at the back were cleared to make a dance floor, we were joined by a handful of young, beautiful eastern European women in tiny dresses, accompanied by one well-heeled man, who – having bought them all drinks – looked rather too happy as they then ignored him and spread out around the room, each finding an MP or two to dance alongside.

A few of the MPs knew better, made their excuses and went elsewhere. But it was left to me to wander around the rest, many of whom I hardly knew, and say: 'Watch out, I think these girls are on the clock. Anyone could be watching this and taking pictures.' After I received two invitations to go fuck myself and one paranoid demand to know whether I'd taken any pictures myself, I gave up and left them to it.

It's only fair to say that some senior women I met in politics were equally reckless and predatory when it came to sex, and I was far from a saint myself in the long period between breaking up with Penny and starting up with Balshen, but – for the most part – what I saw constantly in Westminster was men in their forties and fifties trying to co-opt junior staff in their twenties or thirties.

Indeed, when I started seeing Balshen, she felt obliged to tell me that there was one Cabinet minister who made her uncomfortable because of an incident when he entered a lift. She asked: 'Going down?', and he responded: 'Now there's a thought.' He was almost thirty years her senior.

Even in No. 10, that culture persisted. One Sunday morning, a junior member of staff called me in distress to say that a special adviser colleague had followed up a row with her on the usual Saturday night press call by sending her abusive text messages about her supposed lack of nous. After she calmed him down, his response was to send first suggestive then downright troubling text messages, culminating in one saying: 'I'm watching you through your window and I'm about to come in. What do you want me to do to you once I'm inside?'

When she told me, I wanted to tear his head off. But she begged me not to do anything about it, because – with good reason – she felt that, in those situations and in that Westminster environment, it's the junior woman who complains who usually ends up losing her job, her prospects and her friends, and the senior man who gets tapped on the wrist with one hand and patted on the back with the other. Time and again, that was true.

When I started writing this book, I was warned by an old

colleague that – whatever I did – I should not admit to 'doing in' any Labour MPs or ministers, because they said: 'Even though people know you did, you actually confirming it will make you a pariah for life.'

I decided to ignore that advice throughout this book precisely because I regret – or at least have retrospective reservations about – the vast majority of what I did and, as my old parish priest Father Cassidy used to tell me when I went to confession as a child, you can't expect forgiveness unless you speak your sins out loud.

But if there are any of those occasions I engaged in 'friendly fire' which I honestly don't regret it was where I exposed senior Labour men abusing their power and harassing junior female officials or advisers, no more than I regret exposing Tories for similar offences, or for racism, homophobia, misogyny, snobbery, hypocrisy or any other offensive behaviour.

Indeed, when I did those kinds of stories, it always irritated me afterwards when people would say: 'Were you responsible for that *News of the World* or *Mail on Sunday* splash last weekend?'

No, I'd say, the person 'responsible' was the bloke refusing to take 'no' for an answer in the House of Commons bar; or the bloke who inveigled his way back into a girl's house after she'd gone to sleep and got in bed with her naked; or the bloke who told his daughter in front of a room full of dinner guests that she looked like she'd just walked out of a council house. Actually, that last one never made it into the paper, worse luck.

If in those cases, I was making the stories up, or indeed exaggerating them, then yes, I would feel 'responsible'. But I struggled with the concept of taking the blame when those individuals were bang to rights and the only thing they had to complain about was that the misdeeds they hoped would remain secret had been made public. Well boo hoo.

Of course, people will say I have form for making stories up, including the ones in the emails that got me the sack. But that wasn't the case. Like I said, people just tell you things.

Of the six stories that I wrote down in two emails in January and

February 2009, three were told to me by very senior journalists on Tory-supporting national newspapers. They told me erroneously that the information was totally kosher, but that they couldn't get it in their papers, in one case because they were worried about losing advertising revenue, in another because their then editor had done a deal with the Tories to go easy on a story, and in the third because it was simply impossible to tell the story in a 'family newspaper' in any kind of meaningful way.

Two of the other stories were told to me by someone George Osborne (wrongly) regarded as a very close and loyal friend, to illustrate his view that the Chancellor was 'an absolute shit'. And the last one was told to me by the chief executive of one of Britain's leading household-name companies, who just enjoyed a good gossip.

At the time, I never had any reason to doubt the veracity of anything I'd been told. But they were not only unsubstantiated, they were all just sleazy, mucky stories. Even worse, one of the stories focused on a senior Tory's wife, and – even though it was seeking to attack her husband, with her as an entirely innocent party – it was still unfair to drag her anywhere near an attack on him. Beyond that, the idea that anything in those emails had a go at the wives or families of Tory politicians is a total myth.

Nevertheless, all the stories should clearly have been left to rot in the pubs where I was told them. The fact that they weren't was my major misdeed and I don't complain for one moment about the price I paid for even contemplating that they should be made public.

That's where Derek Draper comes in, Peter Mandelson's former special adviser. I like Derek a lot. He's a very funny, kind, intelligent man; he's a great dad; and he cooks a mean roast dinner. He's also a great spotter and developer of talent, one of the best 'ideas men' in the business, and superb at advising others on political strategy. The only thing he's lacked over the years – when venturing into politics himself – is a 40-foot neon arrow stationed above his head flashing the word: 'TROUBLE'. Some might say I could do with one of those myself.

I already knew Derek indirectly through his wife Kate Garraway, but we'd never met. In late 2006, as Gordon was preparing for the possible leadership contest to come, Derek submitted an unsolicited memo to Gordon about his presentational style and media profile, which – while I was determined to find it objectionable, just because of his Mandelson connections – was actually very good. It was agreed that it would be no bad thing to get Derek on board as part of the strategy at that time to reach out to Blairites and show we wanted to build a broad church.

Personally, as I got ready to step into the shoes that the likes of Draper and Alastair Campbell had once worn in No. 10, I'd begun to crave some acknowledgement and acceptance from the Blairite brigade, rather than the contempt and loathing that most of them evidently felt. I was anxious to impress Derek, and hoped that his approval would open other doors.

We became friendly and by the time he launched the website Labour List as an alternative to the Tories' Conservative Home in January 2009, we were texting and emailing each other almost every day. And one of the things he would regularly talk about was that, in parallel with Labour List, we needed a left-leaning version of the Guido Fawkes website, focusing on gossip and sleaze.

He said he'd registered the name Red Rag for it, and at one Labour List planning meeting, with the likes of Ray Collins, Labour's General Secretary, and Charlie Whelan present, Derek referred to the website with a wink as a little project he and I were working on, but said no more about it.

He subsequently asked me to write up some of the stories that were doing the rounds in Westminster in Guido style, and that's how I came to send the two emails. Much was made at the time of the fact I sent them from my Downing Street computer, but it didn't make much difference to me: I spent so much time at my computer or on my BlackBerry that whether I was at work or not at work had ceased to matter in my mind; the concept of office hours simply didn't exist.

Simultaneously in early 2009, Derek was embroiled in a

running feud with Paul Staines from the Guido website and with Iain Dale, the Tory blogger. By a strange twist, it was this feud that convinced Derek to drop the whole Red Rag idea: 'I can't simultaneously have a go at this guy Staines for gutter politics, and then get in the gutter with him, so I'm going to drop it.'

On one particular Friday, when Staines put a caption competition on his website with a photo of Gordon speaking to a group of black and Asian toddlers, his comments section rapidly filled up with the most abhorrent filth, the worst of which was simultaneously violently racist about the children and portrayed Gordon as a paedophile.

Derek and I were both outraged, and – as I concentrated on emailing the most offensive remarks to Derek – he started contacting some of the household-name retailers advertising on the Guido website to ask if they were aware this was the site they were supporting.

Staines went bananas and when the growing feud escalated into a row between them on the *Daily Politics* show at the end of March, he said Draper was a stooge for the government, and that he could produce evidence that Draper had been taking orders directly from me on what material to put on Labour List.

I was in Chile with Gordon at the time, part of his effort to whip up support for his economic plan ahead of the G20 summit, and I sat in the courtyard of the presidential palace as reports of the encounter between Derek and Staines came through, punctuated by text messages from Staines himself teasing and taunting about the information he had on me.

I determined just to enjoy the rest of the trip, most of all the journey back, when our usual party with the journalists was made even more riotous by the presence of a young BA cabin crew hitching a flight home and happy to join in the games and drinking. I sensed during that flight that it would be the last time I'd enjoy that luxury.

I met Derek as soon as I got back and asked him what he thought was going on. He said: 'I think someone's got into my emails and has leaked them to Paul at Guido Fawkes. He's making so many references to things he could only know from my emails that must be what's happened.'

'But how could anyone have got into your emails?' I asked him. 'Oh God,' he sighed, 'I've been extremely naive on my password. I've changed it now, but it was pretty obvious before.'

Then the big question.

'What's the worst anyone could have found if they've been in your emails?' 'Well, in terms of ministers I'm in contact with, who would have problems because of things they've written to me?' he asked aloud. 'Peter [Mandelson] – definitely, James Purnell – definitely and Ed Miliband – probably.'

'And then,' he said, 'there's your Red Rag emails.' My heart sank. I was hoping against hope he'd say he'd deleted them but no. The teasing and taunting from Staines made sense.

Looking back now, at least six separate email exchanges appear to have been accessed from Derek's account: an email from Peter Mandelson about Gordon's media style sent in summer 2008 – reported by the *Mail on Sunday* in June 2009; my two Red Rag emails sent in January and February 2009; another email from me to Derek in February suggesting attack lines against Iain Dale; some bawdy exchanges between Draper and the *New Statesman*'s James Macintyre in early March 2009 – featured on the Guido website the following year; and my emails about the caption competition in mid-March, referred to by Paul Staines on the *Daily Politics* at the end of that month.

What that would suggest is that, if someone did access Derek's emails, it happened in late March 2009, and they were able to retrieve material from his inbox going back at least a year.

Many people will feel I got exactly what I deserved being on the receiving end of a mysterious dark arts operation. 'Live by the smear, die by the smear,' as Paul Staines wrote himself at the time. And usually, I'd be the first to doff my cap at a job well done. But the lack of a credible explanation for how Derek's emails were obtained has always left a bad taste in the mouth.

It's hard to say 'Well done' if you think the other guy's been playing with a stacked deck.

And if somewhere sitting in a drawer, waiting to be deployed before the next election, are any damaging emails from Ed Miliband to Derek Draper, then I'd suggest this needs some attention.

50

ANATOMY OF A RESIGNATION

When your world's about to fall in, it helps to have some warning. On the evening of Wednesday 8 April 2009, I started to hear rumours that Paul Staines was trying to flog the two Red Rag emails to the newspapers, and the suggestion was that the *Sunday Times* and *News of the World* were set to print them that weekend.

That short period of grace before all hell broke loose was a fantastic kindness. I stocked up my flat in Holloway so I could hole up there if necessary and contacted some of my oldest friends so that I had some other possible places to stay; I had a tough conversation with Balshen about what was about to happen; and then, finally, an even harder conversation with my mum.

With my mum, I had to strike a balance between sounding confident and firm enough that when I told her she needed to get out of the country to her holiday apartment in France for a few days, she would just do as I asked; but not saying too much about what was happening, because then she would have refused to go. I managed it, although I broke a bit when I told her I loved her, and if she loved me too, she wouldn't look at the news for the next week.

I went into work on the Thursday as normal, but spent most of it tying up loose ends, and downloading my contact book of phone numbers and emails. I didn't want to draw suspicion by packing a bag, but I knew enough about sackings from the civil service to know that they just empty your desk drawers into a box and deliver that to you, paper clips and all, so I squirreled away a few select items from around the office into those drawers.

Two of those items brought home to me what I was about to lose in terms of my ability to make things happen within government, or at least get my ideas heard.

I'd been reading Ben Goldacre's *Bad Science* in South America, and I'd come up with an idea that we would allow pharmaceutical companies to advertise prescription medicines in the UK, in return for which they would be obliged to sign a new code on publication of their research data: good news for the advertising industry, the media, Big Pharma and patients. That idea went in the bin.

And as I packed away a signed photo of *GMTV*'s Clare Nasir from my noticeboard, I thought of the deal I'd been hatching with her boss, Martin Frizzell, where we'd allow *GMTV*, the only profit-making part of the ITV network, to take over Channel 4's morning slot, and stop them being cannibalised and swallowed up by the rest of ITV. That idea too was kaput, and so eventually was *GMTV*.

When everyone trooped off to the Westminster Arms that afternoon to mark the start of the Easter holidays, I took a longer look around No. 10 than normal and, for a change, walked out of the front door knowing that – barring miracles – it would be for the last time. At the pub, I took aside first Michael Ellam, then Michael Dugher and then Stewart Wood to tell them what was happening.

I knew that they were grown up enough to talk personally and sympathetically about what it meant for me, but then sensibly and objectively about how No. 10 should handle the story if it broke that Sunday. I still had an outside hope that the papers might decide the content of the emails was unprintable for legal reasons, and, based on what Derek had told me, there were also serious questions about how they'd been obtained.

We agreed that if I got any calls before Sunday, I'd refer them to Dugher, and he and I worked out a provisional source quote in case anyone reported the *existence* of emails proposing a planned smear campaign against the Tories, but didn't disclose their full contents. I'd still have to resign if that was the story, but at least it would be slightly less of a scandal.

The *Telegraph* called the next day – Good Friday – and said they were planning a Saturday spoiler in case the story broke on Sunday.

They weren't prepared to buy the emails but were going to turn it into a story about security concerns over how they'd been leaked. They included the quote I'd worked out with Dugher. The broadcasters picked it up overnight and by 6 a.m. on Easter Saturday, my mobile was red hot with text messages and voicemails.

Ed Balls called and asked what the full story was. I didn't know quite what to expect, but I was still taken aback by his reaction. It was the angriest I'd ever known him and, Mr Discipline that he was, he kept returning to the refrain: 'How could you be so utterly stupid? Why did you get involved in this? You of ALL people.'

He eventually stopped and asked if I'd rung Gordon, who was in Scotland for Easter. 'Not yet,' I said. 'What do you think I should say?' 'Just explain what's happened,' Ed replied, '...and tell him you think it'll be bigger than the Peston book. Use that phrase – bigger than the Peston book.' 'Isn't that just going to get him even more wound up?' I replied. 'Yeah,' said Ed, 'but it'll remind him that he's had his share of fuck-ups as well.'

Before he hung up, he said: 'I'm sorry I had a go at you, but … this is such a problem for Gordon.' 'I know,' I said and apologised again, 'but at least no one can hold him responsible for *this*.' 'That's not what I mean,' said Ed, 'that's just a short-term issue. But I've said to you before, if you're not there, he'll be totally exposed, totally vulnerable. That's the problem.'

I spent several minutes plucking up the courage to call Gordon, standing on the balcony of my flat in Holloway. I had no urge to chuck myself off, but crashing eight floors to my death certainly seemed a more attractive prospect than ringing Gordon at that point.

I finally called him, and – from his tone – I could tell immediately that he'd already spent a lot of the morning talking to other people about the story. You know you're screwed when other people are having conversations about how to handle your problem.

'What's this all about then?' he asked. I delivered the lines I'd rehearsed, including the one about the Peston book, and there was total silence at the other end. I said: 'I know I'm going to have to resign, or you'll have to sack me, whichever works best.'

There was a pause, then he asked: 'What do the emails say?' It occurred to me that – in all the conversations I'd had to date – nobody had actually asked for the gruesome details. If I was nerve-racked before calling Gordon, I was now filled with embarrassment about having to tell him; it felt like when my dad would ask me what I'd done to get sent off at football.

'Honestly, Gordon, you don't want to know.' 'What do they say?' he repeated, the only time on the call he raised his voice in real anger. I told him. He listened in silence, his only reaction when I mentioned the Tory wife – a loud sigh: 'Oh, Jesus Christ.' I finished, and there was more silence. He finally said: 'You're going to have to resign ... I'll ring you back.'

That might have been it there and then, but the discussions went on for hours. Every time I rang Dugher or Ellam or Balls, their phones were simultaneously engaged, so there were obviously conference calls going on. What became clear is that various people were worried this would be the thin end of the wedge: either other people would be shown to be involved, or other emails of mine would start to surface revealing I'd been up to even worse tricks.

Over the years, there was one mantra which guided Gordon's team in moments of scandal, such as when the row over Bernie Ecclestone's donation resurfaced in 2000, or when David Abrahams's dodgy donations were exposed in 2007. Even if journalists were battering down the doors demanding a public statement, we always took the time to establish all of the facts and look at all of the records exhaustively before saying anything, thus making sure there could be no fresh revelation to cast our statement into doubt and keep the story going.

The gut instinct of even very experienced politicians like David Blunkett or Peter Mandelson is to issue statements as quickly as possible to try and kill a story, usually based just on their selective memory of events or conversations. But that rush to comment has led to many an eventual resignation, as their stories are seen to 'unravel' or as third parties feel morally obliged to contradict what they have said.

There was another factor in this case. I was later told that some of the Labour MPs being consulted – even at that stage – were asking serious questions about how the emails had been obtained. There was no doubting I'd have to resign, but if – as some of those MPs suspected – there were some Tory black ops at work, didn't that need to be exposed and investigated at the same time? If not, what was stopping them doing the same trick again?

The word 'hacking' featured large in those conversations even then, and there was a thought that – if I was going to resign – the Labour Party or No. 10 should simultaneously call in the police to get to the bottom of how the emails had been obtained.

So I stood pacing round my flat, waiting for them to reach a conclusion, all the while broadcasters and newspapers calling and texting asking for quotes, interviews and updates. One senior journalist texted me three or four times in the course of the day with variations on: 'Do NOT say a word to any other paper. We want an exclusive deal on your story before the election: 6 figures starting with a 2.'

Eventually, Gordon rang, very formal and businesslike: 'OK, Damian, I need your word that you will tell me the truth. If the years we've worked together mean anything, I need your absolute word.' 'Yep, of course,' I said solemnly, 'I give you my word – I promise I'll tell you the truth.'

'Right, firstly, is there anyone else in No. 10 or in the government or in the Labour Party who is involved in these emails or this website? Anyone with any involvement at any level?'

'No. Absolutely, definitely not. There was one meeting with some other party people where Derek mentioned starting a website, and there were other party people copied in on the emails, but no one has said anything or done anything on this besides me and Derek. I swear to you.'

'OK, secondly, do you think that these emails might have been hacked? What's the explanation for how someone has got hold of them?'

'Right, there are only two ways these emails have got out: either someone who works with Derek and who has access to his computer has printed out several months of emails and leaked them to the Guido website, or someone else has got into his emails somehow and handed them over. He says it's definitely not the first.'

'OK, finally, what else is going to come out about you when they come for you over this? Are there other emails, or other things journalists know about you, or any scandal stuff you've been up to? And is there anything you've done where people will call for the police to be involved?'

'Look, Gordon, I honestly don't know what'll come out and it's possible some journalists will do the dirty on me about stories I did with them, but I know this is the worst thing that they could possibly get on me, so if you guys are wondering if the story is just going to get bigger and bigger, no it won't, this is as big as it can get.'

I went on: 'As for scandal stuff, any sex stuff will be old, there's no drugs, and I haven't had any dodgy freebies or money from anyone. And on the police, I never leaked any documents or got any information illegally, so there's nothing on that score. The only thing is I had a really bad fight in Cardiff last month, so if someone recognises me and gets the CCTV, that might become an issue, but I doubt they will.'

There was silence. Under normal circumstances, I think the last bit of information might have got a reaction, but Gordon was past that now. 'OK, Damian, I'll ring you back.'

The conference calls began again and, at that point, I'd had enough. I left my Holloway flat via the underground car park – just in case anyone had tracked me down – and headed up to Southgate to watch Arsenal away at Wigan on TV. The game had just kicked off when the No. 10 switchboard called and asked if they could patch me in to a conference call.

The discussion had clearly been going on a while, and – though I didn't hear anyone say anything bad – when the switchboard operator announced I was on the call, there was a sudden silence, as if everyone was wondering: 'How *long* has he been on the call?'

Gordon spoke up, and began to conduct an incredibly polite and orderly kangaroo court hearing. Jeremy Heywood was asked to advise whether there had been a breach of the special adviser code, and said that there had been; Michael Dugher was asked to give a sense of how much the Sunday papers would be reporting and how big the story was (short answers: 'Everything' and 'Massive'); and at each stage, others were asked to chip in their views.

It was a painfully drawn-out process, during which my friend Anthony Glackin came out to the beer garden and put a fresh pint of Fosters down for me. I pointed inside to the pub; he shook his head sorrowfully and made his fingers into a 0–1. He then pointed at my phone; I shook my head sorrowfully and drew a finger across my throat.

Michael Dugher finished his media summary on the call, and Gordon tried to offer some even-handed deliberations on where we were. I cut across him. I didn't want him to have to say the words.

'OK, Gordon, I think that's enough. Look, we all know I have to resign, so that's all there is to it. And I'm sorry to everyone that it's come to this and I'm sorry to you, Gordon. And I know you guys are going to have to put the boot in over the next few days trying to explain how this has happened and how I've been totally out of control for the last six months, and I'm telling you I don't mind that at all – I'm expecting it and it's absolutely what you should do in the circumstances. So don't hold back out of friendship; get your Doc Martens on, and give me a bloody good kicking.'

I said I'd write my resignation statement and send it to Dugher to issue, and that would be that.

When the call ended, Gordon rang back immediately from his mobile, not going through the switchboard. He'd clearly had the words in his head all day, saying how sorry he was, and that it was this bloody problem with email – 'you treat it like you're having a conversation in the pub, but it's not, it's there in black and white', then he started to talk about everything I'd done for him over the years, and how I'd looked out for Sarah and the boys, and how hard I'd worked, and…

I cut him off. 'I know,' I said. 'It's OK, Gordon, you don't need to say it. It's been an honour. You're a great, great man, and I'm proud to have worked for you.'

He gave the usual self-deprecating guffaw I heard whenever anyone praised him.

'No, really,' I sighed. 'It's been an honour, and I've enjoyed every minute – well, most of them – and I'm just sorry it's ended like this. But listen to me, the last piece of press advice I'll ever give you. That's it now. Don't call me again. Don't email me. The first question you'll be asked in every interview for the next fortnight is when you last spoke to me and your answer needs to be: "When I accepted his resignation".'

He said admonishingly: 'I can still speak to you!' 'No,' I said, 'you can't. And I won't answer the phone, because it's important for me as well as you that we can both tell the truth on this.'

I told him goodbye, and he still said: 'I'll talk to you later on.' A couple of days later, he called and left a voicemail saying he was checking I was OK, and sorry about all the coverage, and 'I hope your mother and Balshen are well', and telling me to ring him back. I texted Sarah and said I wasn't going to ring him back and that she needed to tell him off.

I think that did the trick, and that was the last contact we had until he left Downing Street, aside from a card and book at Christmas 2009, smuggled surreptitiously to me via Balshen.

Back in the beer garden in Southgate, I got a text message from Jeremy Heywood: 'Whatever else has happened, it is to your great credit that you helped Gordon reach the only possible decision in these circumstances.'

By this stage, after instructing No. 10 to give me a kicking, taking a hard line with Gordon on phone calls and receiving that text from Jeremy, I was feeling quite the model professional.

And then Sue called.

Sue, the real model professional, who always sat next to Gordon shaking her head as I came running down the platform at Euston just as the train pulled away; always rolled her eyes when I arrived late for a press breakfast at party conference still wearing last night's clothes; and always intervened when neces-sary and told me that – no matter how good I was at breaking bad news to Gordon – now was definitely not the time.

'Hallo you,' she said with a breaking voice, 'I just wanted to tell you that I'm really sorry, and it's been a real...' I'd never seen or heard Sue cry before, and when she broke down, I began to go myself for the first time that day. I just said: 'I know, I know. Me too. But don't start me off.'

'OK,' she said, 'but just take care. Remember you've still got Balshen, and you've got a lot of people who care about you, so don't go crazy; it'll all be alright in the end.'

I got off the phone, ignored the mounting pile of text messages in my inbox, and hammered out my resignation statement in about two minutes, something you should never do. It was a rather angry and defensive little howl of protest, which I can't bear to read now, especially as it includes a typo and the awful cliché about 'advisers becoming the story'.

I fired it off to Michael Dugher and went back inside the pub. Anthony and his brother Damien looked at me, and I said: 'There we go – all done.'

Damien replied: 'Theo's scored. Van Persie's on. And it's your round ... if you can afford one.'

51

BACK TO THE BEGINNING

After the game, Damien and I went back to his local and were joined by Balshen and her friend Yon. Balshen had clearly been crying all afternoon, but kept up a determined smile and maintained that things were going to be OK, even while tears were streaming down her face. I'd just about coped with Sue crying but I couldn't cope with Balshen, and it was the first time I cried myself.

I spent that night at Damien's and spent most of the next day going with Balshen and Yon from pub to pub, avoiding the ones with papers on the bar or Sky News on the TV. We all fell asleep in the living room in Balshen's flat in Southgate, a rare night when I didn't want to watch the paper reviews.

In the morning, Balshen called in a panic from her car after dropping Yon back home: 'There's a camera outside! I think it's ITN.' As she drove round the back of the flats, her door buzzer started ringing incessantly. I crept to the window and could see a photographer, a cameraman and a female journalist with a microphone standing outside. I got ready in a flash and made my escape via the downstairs neighbours' window and Balshen's car boot.

I ended up spending seven nights under seven different roofs, and – at a time I was being vilified for everything from my failure to return Jackie Ashley's phone calls to epitomising the 'karaoke culture' of Gordon's inner circle – I devoted every remaining shred of my professional pride to avoiding the cameras searching for me across north London.

After years of advising other people in that situation, there was no way I was going to be the guy with cameras and microphones thrust in his face by hacks seeking a quote or provoking an angry reaction; it wouldn't be me running down the street being chased by the pack.

There were crews camped outside our old family home in Finchley for a week, where my mum would have been staying if she'd not gone to France, and there were what looked like one van and two cars' worth of journalists parked round the clock in the street outside my Holloway flat, between the two entrances.

I got several calls from broadcasters and snappers telling me that, by making such a good job of evading them, I was just creating even more competition among the hacks to get the first pictures or the first doorstep or street confrontation. Some of them urged me to see sense and do one controlled interview in an environment of my choosing, after which they said the competition and pressure would dissipate.

Others were much more helpful. One good friend who worked for a broadcaster told me to call from a landline. When I did, they said: 'Keep your mobile phone off. Some of the other lot are paying contacts at the phone companies to track your signal. If you switch your phone on, do it five minutes before you get on the Underground so all your text messages come through, reply to them all on the Tube and send them all when you get above ground, then switch your phone off again. Whatever you do, don't just sit in the same place sending texts and making calls.'

They also told me the name of a particular 'friend' who was reporting anything they heard about my whereabouts to a TV producer, and they told me not to go back to a pub in Barnet whose landlord had clocked me and called in the sighting; suddenly it made sense that he'd tried to keep me behind for one on the house for good luck when I went to leave.

I could have tried to go abroad, but that kind of thing is a story in itself, and – when I wasn't indoors – I much preferred hiding in plain sight in the pubs and streets of north London, especially once I'd had the advice about my mobile phone. I had a lot to think about in terms of what I was going to do next, and I did most of that thinking in pubs along the Holloway Road: Phibbers, The George, The Hercules and The Quays all have a place in my heart for the sanctuary they provided that week.

In those first few days, I can't honestly say I was depressed or

despondent. It just felt like I was watching something happening
to someone else. The bloke on the TV or on the front of the newspapers didn't feel like me, and I hardly read or watched any of the
coverage, except when either an old colleague or a journalist would
text me and say something like: 'Have you seen that utter pile of
shit in *The Independent*? What the fuck does that idiot know?'

The trouble was that meant I only read the worst things I could
possibly read that week. Not that there were many good things
being written – although *The Observer*'s Gaby Hinsliff and the
FT's James Blitz both wrote more balanced pieces. What I mean is
I only read things that were guaranteed to wind me up: columnists who had literally never spoken to me reporting what I was
like to deal with or what kind of character I was.

And it did hurt that the vast majority of political editors and
reporters who did know me well stayed entirely silent. Some
argued that told its own tale – 'I was asked to write some devastating account of what you were like, but I refused,' one said
proudly, 'and obviously they weren't interested in me writing the
opposite.' But others were more honest; one said the atmosphere
on his paper was like the French Revolutionary Tribunals. He'd
sit there listening to colleagues who'd never met me offering their
denunciations, and he said he had to go along with it or risk
being condemned himself.

The feelings of depression and despondency only really kicked
in once the first post-scandal opinion poll was published in *The
Guardian*, showing the boost Gordon had received in their poll
conducted after the G20 summit had been wiped out. To see those
poll numbers; to see Gordon and the rest of the party having to
deal every day with the fallout from my emails; and to see Derek
forced to resign from Labour List having done nothing wrong
himself; it was only then that I started waking up every morning
with that sick feeling coming over me as reality took over.

Worst of all was to see Ed Balls dragged through the mud simply
by association with me thanks to some total garbage briefed
anonymously by one of my ex-colleagues to Isabel Oakeshott
of the *Sunday Times*. She was incredibly detailed about the

background of the whistleblower, to the extent that – if everything she'd said was accurate – I worked out there was only one person it could possibly be, someone I regarded as a close friend.

I couldn't believe it was them, or maybe just didn't want to, but I had to remind myself that what they were doing wasn't driven out of any disloyalty towards me, but out of a simple impulse to taint Ed Balls with my brush. It was another reminder that some people around Gordon had been fighting the next Labour leadership election since October 2007.

I never felt suicidal. I couldn't make things even worse for my mum or for Balshen by making them go through that as well, and – bizarrely – when I did have some drunken self-destructive thoughts while watching buses and trucks crash past on the Holloway Road, I remember the voice in my head saying: 'Yeah, but that would just keep the story going a while longer.'

I felt much better the following week when an old No. 10 colleague called to tell me that at a focus group the Labour Party had conducted the previous night most people had barely registered the scandal, and those who did thought I'd just been caught out doing what all spin-doctors did. He also said one of the polls in tomorrow's papers showed no change in Labour's ratings from after the G20.

By the time the expenses scandal had started to rear its head – doing genuine, lasting damage to Labour's poll ratings – the caravan had well and truly moved on, and when I was finally 'found' by a snapper walking to Arsenal one afternoon in May, he couldn't even sell the pictures.

And that was itself a hard thing to deal with. My decade at the heart of the Treasury and No. 10 had come to an end, as had my fortnight in the eye of the storm, and now there was just a big silent void.

I told myself what a blessing it was not to have to set my alarm for 5.59 a.m. every morning and go through the nervous torture of the pips introducing the *Today* programme, but I'd still wake up in a panic anyway and have to force myself not to switch them on.

I'd get to lunchtime, and switch my mobile phone off and on again to check it was working: how could it be that I hadn't had a single phone call or text all day? I'd call Balshen in the afternoon to make evening plans, and she'd say incredulously: 'Oh my God, are you not watching the news?', and I'd have to admit that I wasn't and had no idea why she was so busy.

None of this felt like a relief from the burdens of the job or a release from my responsibilities. I just felt totally lost and a little abandoned. In that context, I've never forgotten the Westminster people who – just like my oldest school friends and the group I went to Arsenal with – stayed constantly in touch, checking I was OK and asking if I wanted to meet up for a drink.

Colleagues like Robbie Browse, Dawn Goring, Katie Martin, Nicola Burdett, Jo Dipple, Stewart Wood, Jonathan Ashworth and Katie Myler; journalist contacts like Vincent Moss, Paddy Hennessy, Andy Porter, Kay Burley, Sumeet Desai, Gloria De Piero, Clare Nasir and Simon Walters; plus the odd, brave MP like Ian Austin and Tom Watson – in those few weeks, they went from being colleagues because of my job to being friends for life.

And despite the severe flak he'd taken over his association with me, both the reality and the myths spread by his enemies, Ed Balls would always grab the phone when I was talking to Balshen to ask how I was and what I was up to.

Obviously I wouldn't wish those weeks on anyone, but finding out who my friends really were was one of the few benefits of the experience. And they all asked the same thing: has Gordon been in touch? When I told them he was under strict orders from me not to call, they would just look hurt at the whole situation. Gloria once asked: 'Is he not worried about you?' Then after a pause: 'Actually, are you not worried about him? What's he going to do without you?'

In truth, I was now having recurring anxiety dreams about Gordon screwing up in public with me unable to stop it: one in particular where I was locked in a sound booth at party conference watching Gordon walk out to give his speech in a full set of medieval armour. When he inevitably fell over onto his front and couldn't get up, I'd wake up sweating, screaming: 'Help him, for fuck's sake, help him!'

I needed to move on, and I needed to find a new job, easier said than done when *The Times*' Danny Finkelstein had recently described me as 'the most unemployable man in Britain'.

But the very first day I picked up *The Guardian* and turned to the jobs pages, the first vacancy I saw was for a non-teaching post at my old school, Finchley Catholic High. I wrote to my former deputy headteacher, Kevin Hoare – now the head – applying for the job, but I gave him a get-out clause by writing: 'I realise that recruiting me is not something that could be done lightly at this time, and I would understand completely if it was not considered appropriate.'

Nobody told Kevin Hoare or his imminent successor – another former pupil of the school – Seamus McKenna what to do. When I went to be interviewed by them and the head of governors, Jane Inzani, they told me that they believed both in forgiveness and redemption and also in looking out for their own; and if I was prepared to work hard, they were prepared to give me a fresh start.

I started that August, working on building business links for the school, and when the teachers started to return after the summer holidays, I was pleased to recognise some faces who'd taught me when I'd joined them twenty years previously. My old physics teacher, John Shutler, gave me a giant bear-hug when he first saw me, and said: 'We'll look after you now, old boy.'

On the first full day of school, a teachers' inset day, I was due to introduce myself formally to all the staff, but as I walked into the hall, there was shouting behind me, drawing the attention of all the teachers sat there. I turned round and a swarthy man in a baseball cap, who I later discovered was Paul Staines, rushed up and handed me a lawyer's letter, 'courtesy of Nadine Dorries'.

The letter was initiating defamation proceedings about one of the stories in the Red Rag emails, and I was still absorbing the contents and thinking through the implications in a highly rattled state when I was called up to the front to introduce myself. Never a confident public speaker at the best of times, I ended up with my voice and hands shaking like a leaf, and felt humiliated in front of my new colleagues. That was a very low point in a bad year.

I talked the Dorries letter over with my lawyer brothers, and they were pretty clear that – in terms of the defamation – I didn't have a leg to stand on and could have to pay serious damages. My only argument was about the process of who or what had caused the offending email to be made public.

I hadn't got too panicked about my financial situation since leaving Downing Street, but this was different. Although it was reported I'd been on a six-figure salary in No. 10, I was actually one of the lowest-paid special advisers. I'd frozen my pay in real terms since going to the political side in 2005, and I was on the lowest rung of the senior civil service pay scale before that.

Because I'd been guilty of gross misconduct, I hadn't been entitled to any severance pay or a notice period, and beyond being paid for the work I'd done in April, the only thing the Cabinet Office were prepared to offer was some compensation for holiday that I'd not taken.

'How many days' leave have you got saved up?' I was asked by one of their HR people after I'd left. '136,' I said. She laughed. 'I'm not kidding,' I said. 'I've taken one full week off in the last eight years; aside from that it's just been the odd day here and there.' 'But you weren't allowed to carry all that leave forward,' she said soberly. 'Yeah, I know,' I replied, 'I was just saying.' In the end, they agreed to pay me for twenty days' untaken leave.

That money, plus what I had saved up in the bank and with some help from my mum and brothers, had got me through the four months I'd been unemployed. The new job at Finchley Catholic High had come at just the right time, but – on that salary – there was no way I could also afford a large libel bill.

After again consulting with my brothers, I wrote back to Dorries's lawyer, setting out the best argument I could muster in my defence – that I wasn't responsible for the emails becoming public. I offered to settle Dorries's claim, though my circumstances meant I could only offer to pay her a small amount in compensation for what had happened. Much to my relief, my offer was accepted.

With that out of the way, I settled down into the imagined anonymity of life at the school, although with several hundred students swapping gossip at the start of term, it wasn't long before word got around about who I was and what I'd done. For the most part, that just meant that when I walked down corridors during lesson changeovers, there would be the occasional shout of 'Gordon Brown!' behind me; always enough to cause a great tide of hilarity.

When I started teaching the odd citizenship class to lower school students, and a bit of politics and debating to the sixth-formers, the jokes and questioning became a bit more subtle.

When a group eventually got round to why I'd been sacked, knowing the answer full well but wanting to hear it from me, my standard response was to ask them all to think of the worst message or text they'd sent over the last thirteen days, and how they'd feel if their parents saw it. That always got a big 'Ooooh!' and a series of wincing reactions.

I'd then say: 'So imagine what it was like when people saw the worst email I'd written in thirteen years. Of course I got sacked.' Once, a smart lad at the back of the class, said: 'Yeah, sir, but not having a go, we're like fourteen. Aren't you supposed to know better than that?' All I could do was laugh, and say: 'Yep, you're absolutely right, and remember you said that when you're older.'

I loved my time back at Finchley. I became fast friends with several of the teachers, and my long days in the office with Miss McHugh and long nights in the pub with Mr Salbstein, Miss McCall and Miss McMahon, were some of the happiest of my life. I also found my quiz soulmates in the head of governors, Jane, her husband Pete and their friends the Walshes, and our team became feared all over Finchley. When I'd occasionally run outside to take a call, they'd ask amusedly whether it had been Gordon or Ed on the phone, but they didn't particularly care about the answer.

Sadly, that whole period also coincided with things coming to an end with Balshen. She'd stuck with me through everything and had always stayed bright and confident about our future, but frankly, I couldn't hack it with her still being on the inside and me now on the outside. She'd want to talk about the excitement of her day or her week working for Ed Balls or on Ken Livingstone's mayoral campaign; I wanted to hear about anything but. And if she took an interest in what I was doing at the school, I took it as condescension. In short, I was behaving like a tosser. She deserved – and now has – much better than that.

In 2011, Finchley – like every other school – was having to make savings and I was given the choice between training as a full-time teacher there or looking for a new job elsewhere. Much as I enjoyed my spells of teaching, the idea of doing what my colleagues did day-in, day-out was impossible to contemplate.

I'd never known a group of such hard-working people, all requiring such a massive range of skills, many of them deployed outside the classroom, from keeping order in a yard of 300 boys playing football in their lunchtimes to doing 'diagnostic marking' of sixty essays on the Weimar Republic in their evenings. Michael Gove wouldn't last five minutes, and I wouldn't have lasted five days.

So, I picked up *The Guardian* again and, once more, the first job I saw on the first page was as Head of Media for CAFOD, the official Catholic aid and development agency. I wrote them a letter similar to the one I'd sent Kevin Hoare, and I got a similar response through the interview process and subsequent discussions. They weren't going to exclude me based on my past because that would go against every bit of their ethos, and if I was the right person for the job, that was all that mattered.

CAFOD's a great place. It reminds me a lot of Gordon's Treasury in that every person and every team knows the big objectives we're trying to achieve, and knows specifically how they're contributing to them. There's also a real spirit of camaraderie and a genuine sense that an achievement by any bit of the organisation is an achievement by us all, similar to a Gordon Budget.

But it also has a lot of advantages over the Treasury, and over life in government generally: people's ability to get a job at CAFOD, get ahead and make an impact isn't determined by their educational background or working hours or even by their religious beliefs; it just comes down to their abilities, their values and their personality.

There's an instinctive urge at CAFOD to work in collaboration with other charities which is alien to the partisan, territorial world of Westminster. And there's a constant focus on building for the long term and tackling root problems – whether in CAFOD's anti-poverty programmes or its advocacy work – that is all too often missing from a political system which simply works one Budget, one reshuffle and one election to the next.

Just as at Finchley Catholic High, I've met people in this walk of life where – when I see how intelligent and insightful and passionate they are – I say: 'You should think about working in politics.' And, unfortunately for all of us, from the very best and most brilliant of them, the response is: 'What would be the point?' 'Well,' I say, 'you could change the way it's done. You could be the one to make a difference.' And they respond with a sympathetic smile and the mildest hint of sarcasm: 'What, like you did?'

They've got a point.

52

POLITICS, GORDON AND ME

Our political system is set up to expose human frailties, even the ones you never knew you had.

It's the cut-throat competition to be selected, elected and promoted, and the macho bear-pit of parliamentary debate; it's the booze-fuelled largesse and late nights of Westminster, and the ever-growing distance from the people that put you there; it's the worship of money, praise and favour, and the desperate kow-towing to those – including the media – who dispense them; it's the short-term motives behind most decision-making, and the partisan impulse to disagree for disagreement's sake.

At every stage, the system offers a new politician temptations to sin and shows them that their colleagues who succumb are all too often those who succeed. It encourages vanity, duplicity, greed, hypocrisy and cruelty. It rewards those whose instincts are reactionary and ruthless. It preys on those with addictive person-alities, whether it's alcohol or attention they crave.

For every MP like Stephen Timms and Vernon Coaker, who manage to experience all that and remain utterly grounded, moral and principled, there are many more who – whether straight away or worn down over time – go in the other direction.

And for someone like me, entering that world already suffering from a well-developed dark side, I was sucked in like a concu-bine at a Roman orgy and just as inevitably spat out once I'd exhausted myself.

The worst of it was that I had enough of a split personality, and an equally well-developed sense of Catholic guilt, that I could occasionally see what was happening to me, and be aware what I was doing to others, but never had the will-power to stop it.

One story illustrates that above all others. Just after the summer in 2008, Ivan Lewis – then a junior minister at the Department of Health – made an unhelpful intervention on tax policy, and I doled out the usual mild rebuke that we gave to any non-Treasury minister who spoke out about tax, telling the papers as a No. 10 source that Ivan should concentrate on his day job or he might soon find himself without one.

That would have been that, but I then received a surprising message from Ivan – via a mutual contact – telling me that he wasn't scared of my bullying and, if I tried those tactics again, I'd find that he could give just as good in return.

Hearing that, any professionalism I had, any sense of what was best for Gordon or the Labour Party or the country, any concept of right and wrong, all disappeared out of my head. As far as I was concerned, Ivan had slapped me across the cheek with a silk white glove, and he was going to get an iron fist in his face in return.

The following weekend, the *News of the World* duly splashed a story about his supposed pestering of a young civil servant who used to work in his private office. It was so obviously a hatchet job from me that many MPs and commentators immediately called it as such and it was one of the major factors that led to me being forced to step away from my press briefing role after the October reshuffle.

But at the time I didn't care. Ivan had challenged me on a personal level and, as far as I was concerned, I'd proved exactly why that was a bad idea. Even when a colleague told me Sue Nye had reflected sadly afterwards that I could sometimes be very cruel, my only reaction was to wonder why she felt any sympathy for Ivan.

A few days later though, I picked up a copy of the *News of the World* and, for the first time, looked closely at the picture they'd used of the former civil servant. She'd obviously been surprised by a snapper on her doorstep and was turning round with a slightly bewildered expression.

It dawned on me that – in among all the other unconscionable elements of my behaviour that week – at no point had I stopped to think: 'What about her?' Having been through this ordeal once, losing her job and friends as a result, she and her family had now been forced not just to see it dredged up all over again but put up in lights for everyone to gawp at. And all just so I could show Ivan I could piss higher up the wall than him.

I sat there staring at the picture and talking to myself: 'What's happened to you? What kind of person have you become?'

A few weeks later, when I was trying to engineer my exit from No. 10 after the October reshuffle, a representative from England's 2018 World Cup bid came to see me in Downing Street. They were recruiting for a Head of Communications and his opening gambit when trying to persuade me to apply for the job was: 'I'm told you're a total bastard. And we need a total bastard.'

That was my moment of clarity. I walked away from that meeting, realising that all the excuses I normally made to myself for the way I did my job had ceased to apply. Doing in Ivan Lewis and dragging that poor girl through the wringer again wasn't necessary to keep any journalists onside, or to protect Gordon, or promote his interests. The 2018 guy had called it right. It was just me being a bastard: a cruel, vindictive, thoughtless bastard.

I should have walked away that day and never come back. Or, if I'd had the gumption, I could have accepted that my new backroom role gave me a chance to go back to my policy-making roots and start actively participating in some of those Downing Street strategy meetings I used to despise.

To my eternal regret, I did neither. Instead, I did what I always did: shrugged and carried on, becoming more and more depressed and detached, and losing all sense of judgement. It had taken me thirteen years in government, six of them in a high-profile and intense role, and just two in the cauldron of No. 10, but I was finally finished; just an accident waiting to happen, which of course it duly did.

When I was feeling sorry for myself, I'd tell myself it was all the pressures of the job. I'd think that if I'd taken more holidays, if I'd had the time to get married and start a family, if I hadn't been on call twenty-four hours a day, seven days a week for six years

– and not just 'on call' but receiving calls at weddings, funerals, birthdays, Christmas lunches and Arsenal matches – maybe things would have been different.

But I knew that excuse wouldn't wash, not even in my own mind. That was because I worked for a man who faced all the temptations and pressures of politics, who worked harder than anyone else, who faced ordeals and opprobrium that most of us can't imagine, and did it all for eighteen years in the sharpest spotlight, and never once let it finish him off.

Obviously Gordon had bad days, nights and sometimes weeks, and suffered the inability to enjoy good news for more than a minute before fulminating about the bad news that would undoubtedly follow. But for all the occasional gloom and frequent glowering, he had the remarkable ability that – no matter how bad things were – he always had a plan, a big new idea, a way to bounce back.

There was something superhuman about his energy and dedication: the idea of lying in bed, slumping in front of the TV or even relaxing for a whole day with Sarah and the boys was alien to him. There was always a new book to speed-read, a new speech or article to embark on, or one of the rolodex of leaders, thinkers and artists he found fascinating to phone up and absorb ideas from.

However hard the job and however difficult Gordon could sometimes be, when I was with him I always felt as though I was in the presence of greatness and of genius, and could never feel anything less than fierce and devoted loyalty.

During the entire six years I worked directly for him, I only took one proper holiday – that is, a trip overseas for a week, where in theory I didn't have to worry about things back home. Gordon called up three times a day asking me when I was coming back and whether I could cut the holiday short. I didn't feel resentful; I actually felt guilty.

Not everyone who worked for Gordon felt the same way. Like any powerful politician, he had a fair share of disloyal shits and prima donnas around him, people hitching a ride for their own career progression, and supposed friends and acolytes who slagged him off behind his back.

But for every one of those, there were people like Sue Nye who stood by him loyally through thick and thin without a thought for their own futures; Shriti Vadera, who took almighty flak on his behalf but never complained to him about it; and Jonathan Ashworth, who continued working eighteen-hour days long after Gordon's promises to put him forward for a parliamentary seat had come to naught.

There were dozens more – civil servants and political advisers alike – who put in effort, commitment and hours in Gordon's service beyond any reasonable demands of their jobs and beyond anything that their personal ambitions or motivations could explain, most notably his diary secretary, Leeanne Johnston; his political speechwriter, Kirsty McNeill; and his broadcast adviser, Nicola Burdett, who stayed on with him after he left No. 10.

There were the assortment of polymaths who made up his policy team in No. 10, many of them veterans of the Council of Economic Advisers in the Treasury: Gavin Kelly, Matt Cavanagh, Dan Corry, Stewart Wood, Nick Pearce, Greg Beales and Michael Jacobs; each of them making Hercules look like a Hollywood diva when it came to uncomplaining labour.

And yes, there were people like Charlie Whelan and me, who – unlike most of Gordon's special advisers – worked on the political side despite having no political aspirations of our own; took daily risks with our own livelihoods; and, like Ian Austin, worked all hours of the day and night to secure him the best possible coverage.

The only thing that all of these people had in common – and several more like us – was Gordon. The only common explanation for our commitment was a shared devotion to him and his cause.

And there is an important corollary to that fact: if people assume that even half of the common media perceptions were true about how Gordon treated his staff, then that devotion, loyalty and commitment would never have existed in one person, let alone so many.

As enraged and frustrated as Gordon regularly was, he was never violent, bullying or abusive to his staff. In six years, working as closely as anyone ever did with Gordon, I never saw him throw a mobile phone or break anything; and I never saw him manhandle anyone, let alone a civil servant.

As far as I'm concerned, those were all total myths put around by over-sensitive or over-imaginative aides trying to make themselves look important to journalists and biographers; and they do a disservice to a man who was admired, respected and even loved by the vast majority of the civil servants and special advisers who worked for him.

It is notable that the same aides never tell of the frequent examples of Gordon's kindness and thoughtfulness: the lengths to which he would go to get you a personalised signed biography as a birthday or Christmas present; the genuine interest he would always take in your family; and, above all, the real tears he would shed when any of his staff lost their mothers or fathers.

When my mum rang to tell me my dad had died of cancer in November 2006, I quietly left my office, went to the empty upstairs room in the Two Chairmen pub, drank my way through several bottles of wine and pints of lager, sang the old Irish songs he'd taught me as a boy, and let the tears run down my face.

I eventually called Balshen, told her the news, and asked if she would bring over my best friends in the civil service, Robbie Browse and Dawn Goring, later on for a drink and a hug. I told her to let Sue Nye know that I couldn't face speaking to Gordon when feeling in such an emotional state, so could she make sure this was one evening he didn't call.

Sue called and told me how sorry she was, but that Gordon was insisting on speaking to me. I said I absolutely didn't want to talk to him but she said he wouldn't take no for an answer. I eventually let her transfer the call, and Gordon spoke beautifully and movingly to me about what it's like to feel proud of your sons, so he knew how proud my dad would have been of me and my brothers and all we'd achieved. It made me weep so much I couldn't even respond.

The fact was that, just like my dad, Gordon always had a far more effective weapon than a mobile phone or his big clunking fist when he was truly angry: his disapproval. Knowing that you had let him down or been the cause of one of his bad moods, and feeling the sting of his silence when you walked into the room, that was always the hardest thing, as it was the day I had to resign.

And what made that hardest to take is that – right at the last – I'd committed the two gravest sins in Gordon's book: first, I'd been undisciplined, and second, I'd been caught doing something which – because it didn't serve his interests and wasn't done with his knowledge – was the epitome of being in it for myself.

So many people I've met since April 2009 have said to me that it was wrong that I had to carry the can on my own when I was only doing Gordon's bidding, or what I was expected to do in my job. The exact opposite is true. I paid the price for losing track of what the job of working for Gordon was all about.

And the only thing I blame for that besides myself is the corrosive nature of our political system, which – over thirteen years – slowly ate away my principles, scruples and judgement to the point where someone I'd never met before could call me a bastard and one of my closest colleagues could call me cruel, and I'd almost take those things as compliments.

It was only once I got away from that life and experienced the new culture and people at Finchley Catholic High School and CAFOD that I was able to look back at those thirteen years and start to regain some sense of shame, remorse and self-aware-ness about what it had done to me, and what I'd done to others.

One day in the CAFOD office, I was sounding off loudly about someone who worked for another charity and I felt the old fire building inside me. One of my new colleagues gave me a look and said: 'Is this what you used to be like? Do you really want to go back to all that?' I felt suitably chastened, and she continued, telling me one of her husband's mottos: 'Look, the world's full of dickheads. But never let a dickhead make you act like a dickhead.'

As rules of life go, it's not a bad one. I wish I could give the same advice to my 22-year-old self walking over Blackfriars Bridge for that first day at Customs, along with a few other things: 'Never let the civil service make you act like a civil servant. Never let the Treasury make you act like a Treasury type. And whatever you do, never let politics make you act like me.'

ACKNOWLEDGEMENTS

Thanks to everyone at Biteback Publishing who made this book possible. In particular, Hollie Teague, who managed the content and editing with huge skill and infinite patience; Suzanne Sangster, who is better than I ever was at generating publicity and deciding what media to do; and marketing guru James Stephens, who I'm proud to call my fellow Gooner.

And of course to Iain Dale, my former Smeargate nemesis. He was the last person I expected to be doing this book with, but turned out to be the only publisher I considered once he'd given me his pitch. A true pro with a kind and forgiving soul. Thanks too to Biteback investor and philanthropist Lord Ashcroft, the first person to put the idea of writing a book in my mind, albeit through an intermediary, way back in 2009.

Thanks to my wonderful brothers, who were so understanding about the demands of writing this book that they never said a word about the demands they themselves were under until it was finished. And thanks to Mum, who was my one-woman focus group for key chapters, and whose nod and smile at the end of the ones she liked will always live with me.

Special thanks to my literary agent Paula for her incomparable advice and wisdom, utterly priceless when I needed validation, inspiration, or just a better phrase. And to my other old friends, who got me through 2009 and encouraged me every step over the last year, especially Big Steve, Anto, Doyley, Gaz, Damo, Paulie and Tel, and Mr & Mrs Stephen Daughton.

Finally, thanks to all the journalists, MPs, friends and former colleagues who've had to put up with me over the last few months refusing to return their phone calls or emails. When I signed the contract to write this book, I cut off all contact from key dramatis personae precisely so they could have no influence – even subconsciously – on what I wrote. I maintain that was the right thing to do, but I'm sorry if it upset anyone in the mean time.

INDEX

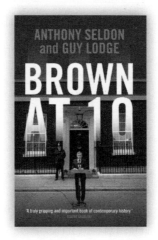

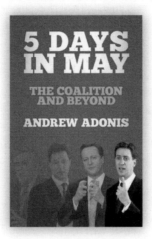